P9-DET-892

SOURCES

In the interest of relevance and readability, the editors have slightly adapted the selections for this volume. For the complete texts, please refer to the original sources.

Chapter One: Noel M. Tichy with Eli Cohen. *The Leadership Engine: How Winning Companies Build Leaders at Every Level.* New York: HarperCollins, 1997.

Chapter Two: John P. Kotter. *John P. Kotter on What Leaders Really Do.* Boston: Harvard Business School Press, 1999.

Chapter Three: Daniel Goleman, Richard Boyatzis, and Annie McKee. *Primal Leadership: Realizing the Power of Emotional Intelligence.* Boston: Harvard Business School Press, 2002.

Chapter Four: Frances Hesselbein. *Hesselbein on Leadership.* San Francisco: Jossey-Bass, 1996.

Chapter Five: Max De Pree. *Leadership Is an Art.* New York: Doubleday, 1989.

Chapter Six: James M. Kouzes and Barry Z. Posner. *The Leadership Challenge.* (3rd ed.) San Francisco: Jossey-Bass, 2002.

Chapter Seven: Lee G. Bolman and Terrence E. Deal. *Reframing Organizations: Artistry, Choice, and Leadership.* (2nd ed.) San Francisco: Jossey-Bass, 1997.

Chapter Eight: Paul Hersey and Kenneth H. Blanchard. *Management of Organizational Behavior: Utilizing Human Resources.* (5th ed.) Upper Saddle River, N.J.: Prentice Hall, 1988.

Chapter Nine: Robert K. Greenleaf. *Servant Leadership: A Journey Into the Nature of Legitimate Power and Greatness.* New York: Paulist Press, 1977.

Chapter Ten: David A. Heenan and Warren Bennis. *Co-Leaders: The Power of Great Partnerships.* Hoboken, N.J.: Wiley, 1999.

Chapter Eleven: Robert E. Quinn. *Deep Change: Discovering the Leader Within.* San Francisco: Jossey-Bass, 1996.

Chapter Twelve: Ram Charan, Stephen Drotter, and James Noel. *The Leadership Pipeline: How to Build the Leadership-Powered Company.* San Francisco: Jossey-Bass, 2001.

Chapter Thirteen: Morgan W. McCall Jr. *High Flyers: Developing the Next Generation of Leaders.* Boston: Harvard Business School Press, 1998.

Chapter Fourteen: Marcus Buckingham and Donald O. Clifton. *Now, Discover Your Strengths.* New York: Free Press, 2001.

Chapter Fifteen: Cynthia D. McCauley, Russ S. Moxley, and Ellen Van Velsor (eds.). *The Center for Creative Leadership Handbook of Leadership Development.* San Francisco: Jossey-Bass, 1998.

Chapter Sixteen: James M. Kouzes and Barry Z. Posner. *Credibility: How Leaders Gain and Lose It, Why People Demand It.* San Francisco: Jossey-Bass, 1993.

Chapter Seventeen: Joanne B. Ciulla. *The Working Life: The Promise and Betrayal of Modern Work.* New York: Times Books, 2000.

Chapter Eighteen: James O'Toole. *Leading Change: Overcoming the Ideology of Comfort and the Tyranny of Custom.* San Francisco: Jossey-Bass, 1995.

Chapter Nineteen: *Harvard Business Review on Leadership.* Boston: Harvard Business School Press, 1998.

Chapter Twenty: Lee G. Bolman and Terrence E. Deal. *Reframing Organizations: Artistry, Choice, and Leadership.* (2nd ed.) San Francisco: Jossey-Bass, 1997.

Chapter Twenty-One: Burt Nanus. *Visionary Leadership: Creating a Compelling Sense of Direction for Your Organization.* San Francisco: Jossey-Bass, 1992.

Chapter Twenty-Two: Peter F. Drucker. *The Drucker Foundation Self-Assessment Tool: Participant Workbook.* San Francisco: Jossey-Bass, 1999.

Chapter Twenty-Three: James C. Collins and Jerry I. Porras. *Built to Last: Successful Habits of Visionary Companies.* New York: HarperCollins, 1994.

Chapter Twenty-Four: Gary Hamel. *Leading the Revolution.* Boston: Harvard Business School Press, 2000.

Chapter Twenty-Five: Edgar H. Schein. *Organizational Culture and Leadership.* (2nd ed.) San Francisco: Jossey-Bass, 1992.

Chapter Twenty-Six: Gretchen M. Spreitzer and Robert E. Quinn. *A Company of Leaders: Five Disciplines for Unleashing the Power in Your Workplace.* San Francisco: Jossey-Bass, 2001.

Chapter Twenty-Seven: Larry Bossidy and Ram Charan with Charles Burck. *Execution: The Discipline of Getting Things Done.* New York: Crown Business, 2002.

Chapter Twenty-Eight: Margaret J. Wheatley. *Leadership and the New Science: Discovering Order in a Chaotic World.* San Francisco: Berrett-Koehler, 1999.

Chapter Twenty-Nine: Robert E. Quinn. *Deep Change: Discovering the Leader Within.* San Francisco: Jossey-Bass, 1996.

Chapter Thirty: Frances Hesselbein and Rob Johnston (eds.). *A Leader-to-Leader Guide on Leading Change.* San Francisco: Jossey-Bass, 2002.

Chapter Thirty-One: *Harvard Business Review,* 2001, *79*(11), 131–140.

Business Leadership

A Jossey-Bass Reader

JOSSEY-BASS BUSINESS & MANAGEMENT SERIES

JOSSEY-BASS
A Wiley Imprint
www.josseybass.com

Published by Jossey-Bass
A Wiley Imprint
989 Market Street, San Francisco, CA 94103-1741   www.josseybass.com

Page 628 is a continuation of the copyright page.

Jossey-Bass books and products are available through most bookstores. To
contact Jossey-Bass directly call our Customer Care Department within the U.S.
at 800-956-7739, outside the U.S. at 317-572-3986 or fax 317-572-4002.

Jossey-Bass also publishes its books in a variety of electronic formats. Some content
that appears in print may not be available in electronic books.

Library of Congress Cataloging-in-Publication Data

    Business Leadership: a Jossey-Bass reader. –1st ed.
        p. cm.— (The Jossey-Bass business & management series)
Includes bibliographical references and index.
    ISBN 0-7879-6441-7 (alk. paper)
    1. Leadership.   2. Management.   I. Series.
HD57.7 .B875 2003
658.4'092—dc21   2002154066

Printed in the United States of America
FIRST EDITION
PB Printing   10 9 8 7 6 5 4 3

The Jossey-Bass
Business & Management Series

Contents

(handwritten: 12 Commitment / 70)

ix

Acknowledgments

The Jossey-Bass Business and Management Team would like to give extra special thanks to Rob Brandt and Tamara Kastl, who served as coeditors of this project. Without their creativity, hard work, and leadership, this book would not have been possible.

Special thanks to Jim Kouzes for his enthusiasm, his expert advice, and his wonderful Introduction to this volume. Thanks also to Gretchen Spreitzer, Alan Shrader, Paul Cohen, Bob Quinn, Maxine Dalton, Rich Hughes, Marian Ruderman, Ellen Van Velsor, Jay Conger, Lesley Iura, and Elisa Rassen for their insightful advice and consultation. Thanks also to Sheri Gilbert and Shirley Tiangsing for their valuable contributions. And thanks, finally, to all the members of the Jossey-Bass Business and Management Team, whose joint efforts in acquiring, producing, and marketing great leadership books provided the inspiration for this reader.

Introduction

James M. Kouzes

Recently, a senior executive was relating to me that in his forty-year career, he'd been part of more than fifteen different strategic initiatives—from zero defects to management by objectives to total quality management to lean thinking to reengineering. "You name it," he said, "and we've done it." The trends have come and gone, but "I've observed one constant theme across all of them," he continued. "The theme is that leaders have to step forward and get involved with change. Although each idea on how to 'do change' is somewhat different—and they all have some good parts—without leadership, nothing works."

That could well be the theme of this volume. It's a strong statement, to be sure, but try naming one significant movement inside or outside the boundaries of business that wandered leaderless into the history books. Leadership was around long before any of the all-star team of scholars and executives in this book penned their first word, and it will be around long after they've put their final period to their final sentence. Leadership is not a fad. It's a fact. It's not here today, gone tomorrow. It's here today, here forever.

Leadership matters. And it matters more in times of uncertainty than in times of stability. We certainly have our share of uncertainty right now. We've been shaken by the horrifying acts of terrorists, disgusted by the unspeakable acts of holy men, and flimflammed by greedy scoundrels at the highest levels of business. It might seem that these egregious offenses call into question just about everything we've been telling leaders for all these years. It might seem that we should be more suspicious of the advice of any leadership scholar. Maybe. But I would submit that when you carefully read all the essays in this volume, you will come to appreciate how much business and society have strayed from the path advocated by the women and men who've spent their careers as students of the subject. More than ever, there is a need to return to the basics and to take to heart the fundamentals of leadership.

This is not to say that everyone agrees on every single trait, talent, skill, or style that characterizes leadership. There are some significant differences in the points of view contained within these pages. Thank God for the distinctive contributions. But if there weren't some continuity of content, we ought to wonder whether or not we're all observing the same phenomena.

Each piece in this ensemble work speaks for itself. Each stands on its own merits. But I've noticed some themes that weave this text together into something more than a "greatest hits" collection.

LEADERSHIP IS A SET OF SKILLS AND ABILITIES

I'd wager my 401(k) that every one of the authors and experts who have contributed to *Business Leadership* have been asked more than once, "Are leaders born or made?" I guarantee you that I get asked that question *every* time I give a speech. What's the answer?

Sure, all leaders *are* born. I've never met one who wasn't. So are all athletes, scholars, artists, accountants, salespeople, and trainers; you name it. We're *all* born. So what? It's what you do with what you have before you die that's important.

Leadership is not contained in a gene any more or any less than other pursuits. Leadership is not a place, it's not a position, and it's not a secret code that can't be deciphered by ordinary people. Leadership is an *observable set of skills and abilities.*

Of course some people are better at it than others. Again, so what? The more we attribute leadership to a set of innate character traits, the more we abdicate our own responsibility to become the best we can be. The more we wait for genetic scientists to help us select the best and the brightest, the more we avoid personal accountability for the work we now do.

It's pure myth that only a lucky few can decipher the code and that the rest of us can't. And believing in this myth creates a self-fulfilling prophecy that dooms society to having only a few good leaders. Only by assuming that leadership is a learnable set of practices can we ever discover how many good leaders there really are.

When you read Tichy, Goleman, Kotter, Hesselbein, De Pree, Kouzes and Posner, Bolman and Deal, Hersey and Blanchard, Greenleaf, and Bennis, you'll notice that not one of them reports, "Eureka, I found the gene for leadership!" They all talk about how leaders must be, what leaders do, and the impact leaders' actions have on others.

Not everyone in this volume shares the exact same point of view, but even Buckingham and Clifton—who reside more at the "leadership as talent" end of the spectrum—go to great lengths to identify the behaviors associated with it. There may not be agreement that *everyone* can become a leader, but there is agreement that leadership is a set of skills and abilities that people can master.

THE INSTRUMENT OF LEADERSHIP IS THE SELF

Humans are toolmakers. We are developers of technology and techniques that enable us to do our work more productively and live our lives more happily. Engineers, for example, have their software and computers. Golfers have their clubs and balls. Painters have their brushes and canvases. What, then, are a leader's instruments?

The leader's primary instrument is the self. That's really all we have to work with. It's not going to be the code written by some brilliant programmer, the smart chip inside the personal digital assistant, or the phrase-turning script of a clever speech-writer that will make us better leaders. It's what we do with ourselves that's going to make the difference. The extent to which leaders become masters of their craft is the extent to which they learn to play themselves. Leadership development is self-development.

The quest for becoming a better leader is first an inner quest to discover who you are. This is especially inherent in the pieces by Quinn and by Charan, Drotter, and Noel. McCall reminds us that leaders can get derailed unless they know their weaknesses as well as their strengths, and Buckingham and Clifton tell us to pay particular attention to those strengths. Van Velsor and Guthrie remind us that learning to lead is a lifelong process, not some quickie course you take on a weekend or on the Web. If you're going to prepare yourself to lead, prepare to go on a deep dive.

You cannot separate leadership from the person leading, and the person leading cannot separate himself or herself from those they lead. When leaders become celebrities and cover models—too full of themselves to worry about the welfare of others and too hip to believe that the rules we live by also apply to them—we're all in a heap of trouble.

CREDIBILITY IS THE FOUNDATION OF LEADERSHIP

Leadership is a relationship between those who aspire to lead and those who chose to follow. Sometimes the relationship is one-to-one; sometimes it's one-to-many. But regardless of whether the followers number one or one thousand, leadership is a relationship.

Barry Posner and I have been conducting research on this relationship for more than two decades. What is most striking and most evident from our research is that over time and across continents, the single most important quality people admire is *personal credibility. Credibility is the foundation of leadership.*

We want to believe in our leaders. We want to have faith and confidence in them as people. We want to believe that their word can be trusted, that they are personally excited and enthusiastic about the direction in which we are headed, and that they have the knowledge and skill to lead. If people don't believe in the messenger, they won't believe the message. Values and beliefs are at the core of personal credibility. To be credible, leaders must know who they are and what they stand for.

Our colleagues Ciulla, O'Toole, Badaracco, and Bolman and Deal share our view that ethics, morality, honesty, character, and personal discipline matter. Somewhere along the way during the irrationally exuberant, soaring-stock-market days of the 1990s, these notions came to be viewed—by some observers, at least—as quaint and unfit for the "brand me" school of leadership. No longer. Once we learned that the books had been cooked and we watched the air get sucked out of our retirement accounts, we emerged from a fantasy world to realize just how much character and courage count.

Many people around the globe, though, have been made more cynical by all the illegalities and immoralities. Many are fed up, angry, disgusted, and pessimistic about their future. Trust is so low among some groups that they'd rather keep their money under a mattress than invest it in equities. One of the most critical lessons from all this is that our entire capitalist system is really based on faith. If people don't believe in those who handle their money, their livelihoods, and their lives, they'll just refuse to participate.

We can all expect many more massive and wrenching changes in the years to come. The efficacy of any change initiative is inextricably linked to the credibility of the individuals leading the efforts. Constituents will become willingly involved to the extent that they believe in the people sponsoring the change. It is wise, therefore, for leaders to begin every significant change with a "credit check." It's not just "Do they believe that the new CRM system will improve our performance?" It's also "Do they believe in me and my ability to lead this change effort?"

LEADERS FOCUS ON THE FUTURE

Being forward-looking is what differentiates leaders from other credible people. While credibility is the foundation, the capacity to paint an uplifting and ennobling picture of the future is that special something that truly sets leaders apart. Leaders must be able to gaze across the horizon of time and imagine that greater things are ahead. They must foresee something out there, vague as it might appear from the distance, that others do not. They must imagine that extraordinary feats are possible or that the ordinary can be transformed into something noble.

The consensus among Nanus, Drucker, Collins and Porras, and Hamel is that little can happen without vision. All enterprises or projects, big and small, begin in the mind's eye. They begin with imagination and with the belief that what is merely an image can one day be made real. Without a clear view of the potential future, constituents will be as nervous as tourists driving an unfamiliar mountain road in the fog.

While the evidence is abundantly clear that constituents need and expect leaders to have a clear vision for the future, there's been a disturbing trend among some executives in the most senior ranks of large institutions. More than one could be heard uttering a phrase like "Visibility is limited" and then following it by some excuse for why they can't articulate where their organizations are headed. Well, excuse me. If you're not sure where you're headed, O Captain of the Ship, then let me the hell off. Granted, times are uncertain. Granted, you can't predict your company's stock price tomorrow. But there's absolutely no excuse for abdicating your responsibility for clearly and passionately articulating your collective destination.

Leaders must also engage their constituents in a dialogue about the future. When we can clearly see how we fit into the image of the future, we're more inclined to want to go there. It's like trying to put together a jigsaw puzzle. It's a lot easier when we can see the picture on the top of the box. Leaders must be able to paint that picture.

The Legacy You Leave Is the Life You Lead

Much as compelling words are essential to uplifting spirits, exemplary leaders know that constituents are moved by deeds. They expect leaders to show up, to pay attention, and to participate directly in the process of getting extraordinary things done. Leaders take every opportunity to show others by their own example that they are deeply committed to the aspirations they espouse. Leading by example is how leaders make visions and values tangible. It is how they provide the evidence that they are personally committed.

Bossidy and Charan remind us that you have to execute. When it comes to deciding whether a leader is believable, people first listen to the words and then watch the actions. A judgment of "credible" is handed down when the two are consonant. How you lead your life is how people judge whether they want to put their lives in your hands.

Leaders are judged by how they spend their time, how they react to critical incidents, the stories they tell, the questions they ask, the language and symbols they choose, and the measures they use. Nothing fuels the fires of cynicism more than hypocrisy, and leaders need to be constantly vigilant about aligning what they practice with what they preach. If you dream of leaving a legacy, then you'd better heed the Golden Rule of Leadership: DWYSYWD—*do what you say you will do.*

Schein and Spreitzer and Quinn remind us, also, that leadership is not a solo act. It takes collaboration to get anything significant done in organizations. There is not a single example of extraordinary achievement that occurred without the active involvement and support of many people. Long before "empowerment" came into the popular vocabulary, credible leaders knew that only when their constituents felt strong, capable, and efficacious could they ever hope to get extraordinary things done. Constituents who feel weak, incompetent, and insignificant consistently underperform, want to flee the organization, and are ripe for disenchantment, even revolution.

CHANGE IS THE WORK OF LEADERS

Ask people to make a list of exemplary leaders, people they consider leadership role models. Having done this exercise many times, I can tell you that people will recall individuals who served during times of turbulence, conflict, innovation, and change. They think of people who triumphed against overwhelming odds, who took initiative when there was inertia, who confronted the established order, who rose to the challenge of adversity, who mobilized people and institutions in the face of strong resistance. They think of people who generated momentum in society and then guided that energy toward a more fulfilling future.

This does not have to be a list of famous leaders. It can be a highly personal one. It doesn't matter. The results are the same. The study of leadership is the study of how men and women guide us through adversity, uncertainty, hardship, disruption, transformation, transition, recovery, new beginnings, and other significant challenges. It's also the study of how men and women, in times of constancy and complacency, actively seek to disturb the status quo and awaken to new possibilities.

Personal, business, and social hardships have a way of making us come face to face with who we really are and what we're capable of becoming. Only challenge produces the opportunity for greatness. And given the daunting challenges we face today, the potential for greatness is monumental.

Change is what leadership is all about. There's just leadership, and then there's something else. That's the gist of what Wheatley, Quinn, Bridges and Bridges, and Heifetz and Laurie tell us.

Stuff happens in organizations and in our lives. Sometimes we choose it; sometimes it chooses us. It's unavoidable. People who become leaders don't always seek the challenges they face. Challenges also seek leaders. Opportunities to introduce change open the door to doing one's best. Challenge is the motivating environment for excellence. Challenging opportunities often bring forth skills and abilities that people don't know they have. Given opportunity and support, ordinary men and women can get extraordinary things done in organizations. It's not so important whether you find the challenges or they find you. What *is* important are the choices you make when stuff happens.

The question is this: When opportunity knocks, are you prepared to answer the door?

Business
Leadership

What Is Leadership?

Leadership is no longer limited to a handful of executives at the top level of an organization. There are different degrees of leadership, to be sure, but in today's turbulent business world, all employees must learn how to lead if their organizations are to thrive. Our examination of leadership basics at the start of Part One begins with Noel M. Tichy's take on the importance of leadership to an organization's success. But what does leadership mean? John P. Kotter explains what a leader does and how the tasks of leadership differ from pure management. Opinions regarding the requisite qualities and attitudes of leaders are many and diverse, but some common themes emerge; we present perspectives here from Daniel Goleman,

Richard Boyatzis, and Annie McKee; Frances Hesselbein; Max De Pree; and James M. Kouzes and Barry Z. Posner.

No single style of leadership is perfect for every situation. The remaining chapters in Part One explore the notion that different contexts require different leadership styles. Lee G. Bolman and Terrence E. Deal describe four distinct types of leadership and how to practice them effectively. Paul Hersey and Kenneth H. Blanchard believe that diagnostic ability and adaptability are the keys to leading across diverse situations. Robert K. Greenleaf expounds on the concept of servant-leadership (serving first, leading second), and David A. Heenan and Warren Bennis discuss co-leadership, returning us to the idea of leadership across the workforce.

Leadership Basics

Chapter One

Why Are Leaders Important?

Noel M. Tichy with Eli Cohen

A number of management theorists don't buy the argument that leadership is the key factor in determining an organization's success. They assert that a winning culture, or efficient work processes, or any number of other ancillary attributes are the *sine qua nons* for success. I agree with them that those things are important. But leadership takes precedence over everything else.

One reason leadership takes precedence is that leaders are the people who decide what needs to be done and the ones who make things happen. Just about everyone knew long before the 1960s that many Americans were being denied basic rights and freedoms, but it took a Martin Luther King Jr. and a handful of other determined leaders to bring about the civil rights movement. In the 1960s in Detroit, poor children were starving because their parents couldn't afford to buy them food. But it took a Father Bill Cunningham and Eleanor Josaitis to start Focus: HOPE, a feeding program that they expanded into a full-scale community organization that has trained over a thousand local residents to become highly paid and highly sophisticated machinists.

It's true that one person alone can't change the world, or even a moderate-sized organization. It takes the concentrated energy, ideas, and enthusiasm of many people. But without a leader, the movement doesn't get started in the first place, or it quickly dies for lack of direction or momentum. Without leaders, good results are a matter of random chance, and therefore unsustainable.

Another reason that leadership takes precedence over the contributions of culture and management tools is that it's the leaders who create the cultures and use the tools. The management theorists who assert that corporate culture—not leadership—is the key that determines the success of an organization originally based their arguments on studies of the Japanese automakers and technology companies that took U.S. markets by storm in the 1970s and early 1980s. They bolstered their case by pointing to the strong cultures that made such U.S. companies as Hewlett-Packard, General Electric, IBM, and Xerox leaders in their fields. It's an attractive theory, in part because it holds out to non-leaders the hope that they can attain excellence if they can only get themselves into the right culture. But the lesson that they draw from the examples is not the right one. These successful cultures didn't just spring up by themselves and start shaping their members.[1]

As Professor Edgar Schein of MIT's Sloan School of Management has clearly shown, corporate culture is developed at the birth of an organization by its leaders.[2] Folksy Sam Walton, with his down-home, we're-all-in-this-together attitude, created a family of "associates"[3] (as Wal-Mart store personnel are called), all dedicated to low prices and good service. Tom Watson, with his strict dress codes and company songs, fashioned IBM into a triumphal army. Watson figured that you couldn't be the world's No. 1 company unless you thought you were, so from day one, he established an image of success.

As long as a culture fits the marketplace, it succeeds, but when the external realities change, the culture has to change as well. That's where the proponents of cultural determination go astray. They argue that good cultures will mend themselves. But that's simply not true. At certain critical stages, radical cultural shifts are needed, and without leadership, they just don't happen. IBM's buttoned-down army was a perfect vehicle to quickly establish dominance in the fledgling computer industry. But by the 1980s, it was a drag. Under John Akers and other home-grown managers, the army lumbered along, missing opportunity after opportunity and losing market share to faster, more agile competitors such as Compaq, Dell, and (until the early 1990s) Apple. Now, not only has IBM had to bring in a new CEO from outside the company, but the new CEO, Lou Gerstner, had to hire key managers from outside the company to run finance, accounting, human resources, strategy, the consumer division, and for other key posts.[4]

General Electric's culture is often cited as a paragon of successful durability, and its production of Jack Welch is held up as the proof. But the truth is that Reginald Jones selected Welch to succeed him as CEO because Welch was a radical deviant from the prevailing culture. Welch was an entrepreneurial player who spent his early formative years in GE's Plastics Division scoring successes by avoiding, thwarting, or manipulating GE's rigid corporate bureaucracy. He knew the stifling effects of the old, incremental, overly analytic, internally focused, arrogant, don't-rock-the-boat culture. So when he became CEO, he immediately set about replacing it with a new externally focused culture that prizes speed, radical change, and constructive conflict. His history as CEO is a story of selecting and developing leaders who, with him, have ripped apart the old culture and continually regenerated the company.

Another school of management theorists who disdain leaders—and who are rapidly disappearing over the horizon—are the reengineers. Reengineering came on the scene as its close cousin the total quality movement peaked. Both of these have very solid conceptual ideas and useful techniques. Unfortunately, their reputations have become tarnished because they were applied too often by the wrong people, by non-leaders.

There is a multibillion-dollar consulting industry in the world today that thrives largely on the fact that most managers don't want to lead. When non-leaders try to apply total quality management or reengineering, they call in the consultants because, first of all, they don't know what to do, and, second, they are afraid of the tough part, the execution. But this, of course, dooms the effort. If the people inside the company don't know what to do or are afraid to do it, the consultants aren't likely to come up with an appropriate and effective plan. And there's absolutely no way that even if the outsiders did, against the odds, come up with a good plan, it could be implemented without solid leadership on the inside, from the people who live there every day. I recently uncovered a $60 million expenditure in a *Fortune* 50 company to reengineer the organization, where the results were a disaster. The turf battles were worse than before, teamwork did not exist, and neither layers of management nor unproductive work had been removed. And management couldn't figure out why operations hadn't improved.

In the small number of cases, such as Motorola, AlliedSignal, Compaq, and GE, where the tools of total quality and reengineering have been wielded by real leaders, the results have been phenomenal. During Larry Bossidy's first year at AlliedSignal, all 105,000 employees were trained in total quality. Productivity, which had been growing at about 2%, grew on average 5.6% annually over the next five years.[5] But more often than not, TQM and reengineering never get anywhere near the desired finish line.

When I started to work with Ameritech in 1991, there were 100 full-time quality facilitators and 5,000 quality groups. As current CEO Dick Notebaert recalls, "We used to spend days of time going through the process, but we weren't really interested in results. We had celebrations about the process; 'You just made it to step four in a seven-step process. Let's celebrate.'"[6]

Then Bill Weiss named Notebaert and three others to form a new top leadership team. They got rid of all the full-time facilitators, sending most of them back to real jobs adding value. Then they gave the 5,000 quality groups 90 days to deliver financially measurable results or be killed. Guess what? When Ameritech looked closely, only about 10% of them could point to any financial results or any hope of financial results. The rest had gotten lost in the morass of quality tools.

In some cases, enormously painful reengineerings have set ailing companies on the road to good health by realigning work processes and eliminating unnecessary tasks. In other, all-too-frequent instances, the effort was called reengineering but involved nothing more than wholesale firings that resulted in "corporate anorexia." They destroyed people's lives and communities and only left the companies less able to compete in the marketplace and weaker than ever. A survey by the American Management Association found that only 45% of downsized companies reported any increase in operating profits.[7] In almost all the cases, whether successful or not, the radical surgery was necessary because managers in the past had failed to exercise the leadership needed to refocus the company and make smaller cuts sooner.

What Do Leaders Do?

In a broad sense, what leaders do is stage revolutions. They are constantly challenging the status quo and looking around to see if they are doing the right things, or if those things can be done better or smarter. And most importantly, when they do spot something that needs to be changed, they do something about it. In more concrete terms, they do two specific things:

- See reality—size up the current situation as it really is, not as it *used to be* or as they *would like* it to be, and
- Mobilize the appropriate responses

This is a lot harder than it sounds. Seeing reality requires that leaders remove the filters that screen out the things they might not want to see, acknowledge their own and their companies' shortcomings, and accept the need for change. When you miss a delivery, it's easy to blame a supplier for not getting the parts to you on time, or to blame the customer for having demanding specifications. It's a lot tougher to admit that your procurement system is messed up or to accept that the failure to give the customer what he wants is *your* failure and not *his* failure to be satisfied.

Facing reality is about personally accepting the case for change. This is often referred to as "acknowledging the burning platform." At Ameritech, former CEO Bill Weiss and current CEO Dick Notebaert faced reality by grasping the fact that the Chicago-based Baby Bell could not survive without entering new businesses. Merely offering phone service, even reliable, economical phone service, would no longer be enough. In a global telecommunications market, it needed to be playing in more arenas. It meant making the tough calls to stop doing some of the things it had always done, and the even gutsier calls to build new businesses.

Founders of new businesses often see realities that older competitors in the field miss. Fred Smith started Federal Express because he saw the reality that there would be an enormous demand for rapid delivery of packages in the new global marketplace and that this would make the economics of setting up such a service highly favorable. While people already in the business fretted and complained about the difficulty of modernizing older delivery systems, Smith set out to build a completely new one. In retailing, while others were battling for the pocketbooks of America's increasingly urban populace, Sam Walton saw the reality that there was a huge customer base in small towns across the country that was being ignored. His response was to create a company that revolutionized the concept of the general merchandiser. The founders of Southwest

Airlines had a different sense of reality about air travel when they began offering short-haul, low-fare, no-frills flights. That Southwest Airlines has become the most consistently profitable American airline is a testament to the reality that Herb Kelleher and his colleagues defined. While their competitors were looking inward, trying to maintain "business as usual" and doing a bit of fine-tuning around the edges, Smith, Walton, and Kelleher were looking outward to see what was actually going on with real customers, in the real marketplace, and taking the radical actions needed to please them.

In established businesses, seeing reality is often more difficult because it means letting go of ingrained ways of thinking and working. Andy Grove of Intel, in his book *Only the Paranoid Survive*, describes the shakeouts in the computer industry in the 1980s as some companies—including Intel and Microsoft—adapted to new realities, while others such as IBM, DEC, Sperry, Univac, and Wang failed to do so. As Grove explains it, around 1980, there were several successful computer companies that had proprietary designs for the chips and hardware in their computers, as well as proprietary designs for the operating systems and application software that ran them. These companies sold their large and expensive machines through their own sales and distribution networks, and they all made lots of money. Grove calls this the vertical period of the computer industry, because each company was a self-contained, vertically integrated player.

Then the invention of the microprocessor changed everything. The microprocessor carried the same power as its bigger brethren, and the same microprocessor could be put into any desktop computer. Suddenly, a dozen different companies, including Compaq, Packard Bell, Hewlett-Packard, IBM, and others, were able to start making and selling virtually the same high-powered computers.

As advances in microprocessors accelerated, Compaq was quick to adopt the latest technologies. In 1983, it introduced its fist portable computer—eighteen months before IBM's hit the market.[8] The company, founded only in 1982, reached $1 billion in sales in 1987, the shortest time ever for an American public firm to reach this milestone.[9] Michael Dell also spotted the opportunity. As a college student at the University of Texas in Austin, Dell had lots of energy and a love for computers and risk. He did not, however, have much love or patience for attending classes. So rather than go to lectures about business, he set about creating one. He would toil away in his dorm room lashing together standard parts into uniquely configured PCs that delivered just what his customers wanted. Dell saw that the new reality of interchangeable components meant a massive opportunity for his business to reach millions of buyers.[10] The company now does over $5 billion a year in sales[11] and continues to build all of its computers to order.

Among those who ignored the tide and clung to their old-line industry maps was IBM. At first it appeared that IBM was embracing the PC revolution. Its PC machines were among the hottest-selling in the market. But deep down, IBM fundamentally misunderstood the new shape of the industry. Grove, who personally witnessed the revolution as a supplier to IBM, says the company was "composed of a group of people who had won time and time again, decade after decade, in the battle among vertical computer players. The managers who ran IBM grew up in this world. When the industry changed, they attempted to use the same type of thinking regarding product development and competitiveness that had worked so well in the past."[12] As an example, Grove cites the development of OS/2. This operating system was technically outstanding. However, IBM didn't see the importance that open architecture and interchangeability had come to play in making PCs attractive to customers, so it was painfully slow in making OS/2 available for computers from other manufacturers. It took IBM almost three years to sell 600,000 copies of OS/2 (of which very few were used), while Microsoft only needed ten months to sell approximately 13 million copies of Windows 3.0.[13] When IBM finally decided to make some aggressive changes to OS/2, it was too late. Microsoft had captured people's imagination with Windows. OS/2 was a dismal failure, and a waste of money for IBM.

The same misunderstandings that plagued IBM's development of OS/2 virtually killed its efforts in PCs. Initially strong in PCs, IBM squandered its lead in the 1990s by being a "laggard with products," according to Bob Stephenson, who took over the PC business in 1995. The company was a "wholly unreliable supplier" as it clung to its vertical model for the industry and behaved antagonistically toward retailers and resellers, who actually sell a majority of the PCs in the U.S. It started to turn this around in 1993 and was losing billions as late as 1994. It took the company until 1996 to fully revamp its attitude and operations.[14]

Similarly, DEC failed to see the realities of the PC revolution. The company had burst onto the scene and broken into the mainframe-dominated market in the 1960s with its minicomputers. But faced with the next wave of technological development, the company was nearly killed in the early 1980s because it stuck with proprietary designs. In 1984, its leaders were still describing PCs as "cheap, short-lived, and not very accurate machines."[15]

DEC and IBM both almost died as the result of their leaders' failures to confront reality. As I think about their blunders, I imagine knights headed for the battlefield. Decorated with medals from past wars and flush with praises of others, they enter the battle confidently. But they enter it blindfolded and are slaughtered mercilessly. From its peak value of $106 billion in 1987, IBM had destroyed approximately $80 billion in stock market value by 1993.[16] It also went from being ranked No. 1 in *Fortune*'s 1986 list of America's most admired companies to No. 206 in 1993.[17] In 1987, DEC's sales were growing at more than 20% a year. It was the darling of Wall Street when its stock hit a peak price of $199 before the 1987 crash.[18] After demand for their once-popular mini-computers began to lag, its "matrix" management system of interlocking and overlapping committees was too slow to stop the company's downfall.[19] At the close of the 1990 fiscal year, DEC reported its first-ever loss as a public company.[20] What followed were three years of poorly executed and ineffectual turnaround plans that robbed even more value from shareholders. The company's market value, which peaked at $26 billion in 1987, had shrunk to $4.6 billion in July 1992. That's when founder Ken Olsen was ousted[21] and Robert Palmer was asked to try to save the sinking ship—a job he is still struggling to do.[22]

Facing reality is the first crucial step that leaders must take if their organizations are going to respond appropriately. But that is just the starting point. Once the leader has figured out the problem/challenge/opportunity, he or she has to:

○ Decide on a response,

○ Determine what actions need to be taken to deliver that response, and

○ Make sure those actions get implemented promptly and well

SELECTING THE RESPONSE

Finding the appropriate response to a new set of circumstances (or deciding where to place the new platform) requires both ideas and the willingness to take risks. In Ameritech's case, the response that Weiss, Notebaert, and their team came up with was to enter growth businesses that were new to the company. All of the new businesses capitalized on Ameritech's history as a communications provider, but they were definitely gambles. Signing up long-distance customers, constructing an electronic commerce network, offering enhanced cable TV services, and buying and running phone companies from Hungary to Australia all could have failed miserably. But Notebaert stuck with simple growth logic and encouraged people to get over their fear of trying something different. A real "home run," says Notebaert, has been security monitoring. "They all use telephone lines, they use the same wire and basically do the same work that we do. . . . Why should there be two trucks going out doing the same thing?" But he adds, he had to "step outside the box," and adopt a new mindset, in order to see this opportunity. Looking back to 1991, he says, "We would have growth rates of two and a half percent in telephone lines, for example, and I can remember people saying, 'Well, we're in the Rust Belt,' and then in the southeastern part of the United States, they'd have growth rates of four percent. And we'd say, 'Well, there's nothing we can do. . . . They got dealt a better hand.' In the fourth quarter of 1995, our growth rate was higher than the southern and southeastern United States. I look out my window and I see the same economy. It's called . . . getting on the ball and not being a victim."[23]

At Intel, Andy Grove has had to respond to new realities several times with equally radical changes in the company's direction.[24] In the 1970s, Intel had built a great business providing semiconductors, primarily memory chips, to the computer industry. As Grove puts it, the company's total identity was tied up in memories. "The company had a couple of beliefs that were as strong as religious dogmas. Both of them had to do with the importance of memories as the backbone of our manufacturing and sales activities."[25] It and a few other companies, including Unisem, Advanced Memory Systems, Advanced Micro Devices, and Mostek, filled nearly all the industry's memory chip needs. In Santa Clara, California, where Intel was and is headquartered, life was great. Revenues and profit were both at record levels.

Then, when Intel sat atop the PC revolution making memory chips, unsettling rumblings began to come out of the Far East. While the U.S. memory chip makers enjoyed their expanding market, competitors were approaching from Japan. Steadily they built market share on a simple formula that is by now familiar: deliver quality products at costs beneath those of their American competitors.

At Intel, finding the appropriate response involved a long process of trial and error. At first it tried to focus on value-added products. Then it tried to focus on narrow segments of the memory market where it thought it had technical advantage. Its engineers worked harder trying to accelerate development of a next generation of products. Production people innovated and wrung cost out of Intel's system. But the company was overwhelmed. The Japanese could seemingly copy an invention before Intel had even gotten it right. And their pricing was brutal. At one point Intel "got hold of a memo sent to the sales force of a large Japanese company. The key portion of the memo said 'Win with the 10% rule. . . . Find AMD [another American company] and the Intel sockets. . . . Quote 10% below their price. . . . If they requote, go 10% AGAIN. . . . Don't quit until you WIN!'"[26]

By 1984, Intel was in a crisis. The Japanese were continually strengthening when the market coincidentally slumped. Suddenly Intel, no longer the strongest kid on the block, was having to fight for its space in a shrinking, not expanding, sandbox. The memory business was slowly bleeding the company. Finally, Grove describes one day staring out the window of an office at the company's campus in Santa Clara. The only two people in the room were Grove and Gordon Moore, one of Intel's founders.[27] Grove knew that everything that they had built was on the line. He asked Moore a very tough question: "If we got kicked out and the board brought in a new CEO, what do you think he would do?" Moore responded, "He'd probably get us out of memories." Grove reflected for a moment. And then he said, "Why shouldn't you and I walk out the door, come back and do it ourselves?"[28] The solution they ultimately reached was to abandon Intel's biggest business. Memory chips had become a commodity to which they could add little value, so they decided to start out almost entirely anew, designing and building the best microprocessors in the world. It was a painful and gutsy decision that probably saved the company.[29]

Strategic Actions

Once a strategy has been selected, leaders must figure out what actions have to be taken to successfully implement it, and they must take *all* of them. Often that means walking away from old systems and setting up entirely new ones.

At Ameritech, the decision to enter new fields meant actually lobbying to give away the company's monopoly on local phone service in order to get permission to enter new fields. As a result, Weiss and Notebaert found that they had to address every aspect of the business from redefining winning (they expressly mentioned the importance of rewarding shareholders for the first time) to reorganizing the company into business units, to redefining leadership through personnel changes and leadership development. Fundamentally, they saw that they had to rebuild the company from the ground up.

At Intel, Grove and his colleagues faced a similarly daunting challenge. Once Grove had made up his mind to leave the memory chip business, he had to figure out how. What impact would this have on customers, for example? Did the company need a full product line to offer computer manufacturers? Was the technology in memories so central to Intel's other products that it had to stay a part of the company?

To answer these questions, Grove conducted discussions with Intel employees and others over lunches and at technical conferences, staff meetings, and product planning sessions. Even despite his firm conviction that the decision he and

Moore had made was correct, when Intel managers asked, "Are we getting out of the memory business?" Grove still struggled with actually saying, "Yes." He, as much as anyone, had built Intel and identified the company with its success in the memory business. It was hard for him to abandon it. He subsequently found himself taking half-steps to get out of the memory business. He would at one moment decide to do it, but then approve the R&D budget for new memory chip designs. Finally Grove started to turn the corner. He was ready to make the strategic moves necessary to implement the new plan. In what was for Grove the crossing of the Rubicon, he told the sales force to notify customers that Intel would be getting out of the memory business.

IMPLEMENTATION

Implementation of a massive organizational change is the hardest part, because it requires selling the new response—including the case for change—and weeding out the resisters and the superfluous work. Implementation of an idea requires values, emotional energy, and the edge, or guts, to see it through to the end.

Implementation is where you tackle the tough day-to-day issues. It's one thing to decide to consolidate operations and eliminate 25% of the workforce. It's another to tear down the corporate bureaucracy and streamline the processes so that 25% of the work disappears as well. This requires that leaders change their behaviors and teach others to do the same. If this doesn't happen, any boosts in the bottom line will be short-lived.

For Andy Grove at Intel, implementation meant shuttering plants and research centers and reassigning the company's best people to produce the company's products of the future—microprocessors. Moore stated at one meeting, "If we're really serious about this, half of our executive staff had better become software types in five years' time." After that meeting, Grove recalls looking around the room and wondering "who might remain, who might not." In the end, half of the members of Intel's senior leadership team were put in other jobs or left the company because they could not make the transition.[30]

Grove also made a personal commitment to change. If he was going to successfully lead a new microprocessor company, he would need to rebuild himself as well as the company. So he wrenched his calendar, his lifestyle, and his approach to leading the business. He went back to school. Rather than cling to the details of his declining business, he learned about microprocessors and software, and how microprocessors should be built to run software. He was open about his own weaknesses, going to internal people and saying, "I don't know about this, help me." He also visited software developers and asked them to teach him about their business. His calendar showed someone who was building a company rather than running an existing one.

Today, Intel is one of the most successful companies in the world. The realization that its memory chip business was unsustainable led Grove to take all the actions to cast its future with microprocessors. All of these actions, from redirecting R&D to learning about new technologies to closing some production lines and opening others, built a new company that grew to $20.8 billion in revenue and $5.2 billion in net income in 1996 from a company that had about $2 billion in revenue and about $248 million in net income in 1987. Today, Intel owns 88% of the market for microprocessors.[31] Compare that with companies such as Unisem, Mostek, and Advanced Memory Systems,[32] which saw the same things that Intel did and felt the same pain but did not take the tough actions.

Industries like microprocessors and computing are traditionally thought of as turbulent. It is in these industries that leadership, or the lack of it, is often most visible. But these days just about every industry qualifies as turbulent. Look at telecommunications, health care, retail banking, even your local travel agent. No one is safe. Times are changing, and the organizations that thrive in the future will be the ones that change with them. And in order to do this, they must have leaders who will relentlessly search for reality and demonstrate the courage to act.

How Do Leaders Bring About Change?

Just as the word implies, leaders accomplish things by leading, that is, by guiding and motivating other people. Dictators issue orders, using fear and punishment to command compliance. Leaders shape people's opinions and win their enthusiasm, using every available opportunity to send out their message and win supporters. For many of the best leaders, the full-court press is instinctive. Others take a more systematic approach, but whether consciously or instinctively, leaders always operate on three distinct levels—on the organization's technical, political, and cultural systems.

At first this may sound academic, but if you think about it for a minute, you'll see that it is true. Every group that exists for a purpose has a technical system that organizes its resources to accomplish the purpose; a political system that determines how power, influence, and rewards are used to motivate people; and

a cultural system consisting of norms and values that bind people together. All of them affect how people think and behave.
China, for example, is struggling with a technical (economic)
system that is rapidly moving toward market-driven capitalism,
while its political system is clinging to old-fashioned totalitarian
communism, and its cultural system is torn between the two. In
the U.S., on the other hand, the three systems are more aligned.
The technical system is firmly rooted in capitalism, the political
system is democratic, and the cultural environment values the
supremacy of personal freedom, as embodied in the Bill of
Rights. Sometimes it's hard to differentiate among the systems
because they are so intertwined, but all three are always at work,
and the leader who wants to make a lasting difference has to
work on all three.

At General Electric, Jack Welch tackled the technical system by designing a "GE business engine." This engine would
consist of stable, highly profitable units that generate cash, and
fast-growing businesses that would use the cash to produce even
greater returns. Welch's shorthand slogan for this was that the
company must be "No. 1 or No. 2 in every business that GE is
in, or we fix, close, or sell it." In fact, being No. 1 or No. 2 was
not enough. To remain in the GE portfolio, he declared, a business also must have well above average real returns and a distinct competitive advantage. In 1981, when Welch became
CEO, one-half of GE's $27.2 billion in revenue came from
aging slow-growth businesses. Welch decided that the company
was wasting capital by staying in businesses that weren't going
to be champions. So over his tenure, he has divested $16.2 bil-
lion of marginal businesses, including such old standbys as small
appliances and aerospace, and spent $53 billion on acquisitions
such as RCA and Borg Warner Chemicals.[33] These massive

changes shook up the old order about how GE was going to use its resources to earn profits and clearly sent the message that GE was now playing a new game.

In the political arena, Welch took on GE's massive bureaucracy. For decades, GE's "scientific management" system had been considered one of the company's greatest strengths. It allowed the company to discipline and control its far-flung and diverse businesses. But by the early 1980s, the bureaucracy had taken control, and the company was choking on its nitpicking system of formal reviews and approvals. People were judged and paid according to how well they responded to the bureaucratic rules, even though the procedures delayed decisions and often thwarted common sense. Mastering the system had become a stylized art form and a requisite for advancement. The result was that many of GE's best managers devoted far more energy to internal matters than to their customers. As GEers sometimes expressed it, the company was operating "with its face to the CEO and its ass to the customers."

Jack Welch knew this well because, as head of GE Plastics, he had spent many years hassling, and being hassled by, the enforcers at GE headquarters in Fairfield, Connecticut. He believed in risks and fast action, and grew the Plastics business rapidly by doing what he thought needed to be done and apologizing later if he got called down by the corporate staff. Welch made it to the CEO's job by outwitting the bureaucrats. He understood that they liked documentation and reports, so he became a master of the game. He became famous throughout GE for his beautifully packaged multivolume presentations that were filled with charts, graphs, timelines, and whatever other eye-catching gimmicks he could think of. The fact that he didn't get kicked off the ladder and now sits in the chairman's office is evidence that the strategy worked. But as soon as he took over, he called off the game. "One of the first things Jack eliminated when he became CEO," recalls Larry Buckley, a member of Welch's Executive Management Staff, "was fancy reports, because he knew how much money he had spent making them."[34]

Welch has replaced the bureaucracy at GE with a new political system based on "integrated diversity." The headquarters staff has been slashed to several hundred from thousands, and control over planning and much of the capital spending has been pushed out into the operating units. The headquarters in Fairfield still does allocate key resources, especially people, and teaches best practices on leadership, but the units now have the freedom, and responsibility, to play the smartest game possible in their industries.[35]

As Welch described it in a letter to shareholders: "We cleared out stifling bureaucracy, along with the strategic planning apparatus, corporate staff empires, rituals, endless studies and briefings, and all the classic machinery that makes big-company operations smooth and predictable—but often glacially slow. As the underbrush of bureaucracy was cleared away, we began to see and talk to each other more clearly and more directly. . . . Freed from bureaucratic tentacles, and charged to act independently [the businesses have done] so, with great success. Corporate management got off their backs, and instead lined up behind them with resources and support."[36]

Welch's letter paints a glowing picture of success, but his upbeat tone belies the months of anguish he experienced as he watched tradition-bound managers and workers thwart his dreams of a speedy, responsive, and cooperative GE. The problem, he finally decided, was that its corporate culture continued to value hierarchy and me-firstism. If GE was going to enjoy the benefits of the new growth engine it had so painfully built, and if its workers were going to use their new freedom from bureaucratic meddling to work faster and smarter, the corporate culture had to change as well. In the United States, you could mandate communism and start allocating power and rewards through a totalitarian government, but unless you got rid of the populace's cultural notions of personal freedom and inalienable rights, compliance wouldn't last long.

At GE, there were hundreds of thousands of workers and managers who had grown up in a business that was full of little fiefs, where control of knowledge was control of power, where nobody felt any stake in the success of other fiefs, and where very few people ever got fired. For several years, Welch worried and preached, but nothing changed. He wondered whether he wasn't being clear enough, or if people were just tuning him out. Finally, he came up with the term "boundarylessness" to describe the cultural environment that he wanted.

In a hallmark speech to several hundred GE managers in 1994, Welch explained the concept of boundarylessness using a simple analogy. "In this company, if you can picture the house, the house got taller and taller and taller. As we grew in size, we added floors. The house got wider and wider and wider. As we got more complex, we built walls functionally. The objective of all of us in this place is to blow up the internal walls—the floors vertically and the horizontal ones. That's the game we're at, that's what we are fundamentally after." He went on, changing metaphors, to explain that the "layers are insulators. They're like sweaters. When you go outside and you wear four sweaters, you don't know that it's cold out. You haven't faced reality. You're not getting the straight scoop on the temperature. You're all covered up. As you peel each sweater off, you learn more about the temperature. That's the same thing about layers."[37] The boundaryless culture Welch wanted instead was one in which information would flow freely, in which people could honestly assess reality without fear, and in which the company would capture "the speed of a small company in the body of a big one." At the core of a boundaryless company, he told them, are people who act without regard for status or functional loyalty and who look for ideas from anywhere—including from inside the company, from customers, or from suppliers.

Welch used every technique he could think of to teach this message and help people live it. He preached it over and over. He provided mechanisms for people to begin to live the new way. GE's vaunted Work-Out effort involved hundreds of thousands of GE employees, suppliers, and customers in "town hall" problem-solving meetings. Work-Out was not an elective—Welch mandated that every business conduct the sessions. And he prescribed their format—people form across functions and at different levels would come together to work on specific issues. Hierarchy and functional boundaries had to be left at the door, and everyone was asked for their ideas. The meetings were designed to produce results, and leaders were expected to implement the recommendations from workers. He followed Work-Out with other, more sophisticated tools to help people come together in teams or solve problems, such as the Change Acceleration Program and an aggressive Quality program.[38] He rewarded people for benchmarking and operating ideas from other parts of GE or other companies.

In addition to all of these programs, tools, and exhortations, he confronted those who did not believe in the cultural values. In the old days, GE may have fired a few unpleasant people who didn't meet their performance goals, but nice guys who didn't deliver and complete jerks who did deliver were welcome to stay. In the new GE, Welch declared, performance and behavior would both count. People who embraced boundarylessness but couldn't quite deliver would be helped along and given second, maybe even third chances, but stellar performers who insisted on keeping up the old walls and floors would be dismissed. And he backed up his statement by personally getting rid of some boundaryful people at the top of the company. Finally, he held others responsible for doing the same thing in their parts of the company. He once sternly told a conference of GE's several hundred managers, "People throughout this company hear us talk about boundarylessness and taking out layers, and they look at what we've done. Where we have multiple layers still left, they rightly question our integrity. . . . The only way I am going to get at this thing is to ask you to do it, to simply treat it as an integrity issue. We have no room for boundaryful people at GE, and we must become boundaryless if we are going to get the speed we need to survive."[39]

The magnitude of this GE transformation may or may not make it an extreme example of change. However, the point isn't the change, but the importance of having technical, political, and cultural systems that support and reinforce one another. Winning companies do a lot better job than losers of keeping the three working together, because their leaders are ever mindful of the need for alignment and to keep them in step with the changing demands of the marketplace.

When you look at winning organizations and compare them with the losers, the first things you notice may be good market strategies, efficient operations, and agile response times. Winning companies are exceptionally good at listening to their customers and giving them what they want. But these important qualities are really just intermediate products. From the outset, and in the end, winning is really about leadership.

Winning individuals are leaders, people with ideas and values and the energy and edge to do what needs to be done. And organizations are winners because they have good leaders, people who understand the importance of selecting the right things to do and who are able to manage the complex forces required to get them done. Because of this, winning organizations are leader-driven. They value leaders, they have cultures that expect and reward leadership, and everyone in the organization actively puts time and resources into developing leaders. Finally, winners win because of their ability to continually and consistently create more leaders at all levels of their organizations.

o   o   o

Noel M. Tichy is a professor at the University of Michigan Business School and a consultant specializing in leadership and organizational transformation.

Eli Cohen is an associate with Accel Partners. Previously he has worked with Ziff Brothers Investments and Bain & Company.

Chapter Two

What Leaders Really Do

John P. Kotter

Leadership is different from management, but not for the reasons most people think. Leadership isn't mystical and mysterious. It has nothing to do with having "charisma" or other exotic personality traits. It is not the province of a chosen few. Nor is leadership necessarily better than management or a replacement for it.

Rather, leadership and management are two distinctive and complementary systems of action. Each has its own function and characteristic activities. Both are necessary for success in an increasingly complex and volatile business environment.

Most U.S. corporations today are overmanaged and underled. They need to develop their capacity to exercise leadership. Successful corporations don't wait for leaders to come along. They actively seek out people with leadership potential and expose them to career experiences designed to develop that potential. Indeed, with careful selection, nurturing, and encouragement, dozens of people can play important leadership roles in a business organization.

But while improving their ability to lead, companies should remember that strong leadership with weak management is no better, and is sometimes actually worse, than the reverse. The real challenge is to combine strong leadership and strong management and use each to balance the other.

Of course, not everyone can be good at both leading and managing. Some people have the capacity to become excellent managers but not strong leaders. Others have great leadership potential but, for a variety of reasons, have great difficulty becoming strong managers. Smart companies value both kinds of people and work hard to make them a part of the team.

But when it comes to preparing people for executive jobs, such companies rightly ignore the recent literature that says people cannot manage *and* lead. They try to develop leader-managers. Once companies understand the fundamental difference between leadership and management, they can begin to groom their top people to provide both.

The Difference Between Management and Leadership

Management is about coping with complexity. Its practices and procedures are largely a response to one of the most significant developments of the twentieth century: the emergence of large organizations. Without good management, complex enterprises tend to become chaotic in ways that threaten their very existence. Good management brings a degree of order and consistency to key dimensions like the quality and profitability of products.

Leadership, by contrast, is about coping with change. Part of the reason it has become so important in recent years is that the business world has become more competitive and more volatile. Faster technological change, greater international competition, the deregulation of markets, overcapacity in capital-intensive industries, an unstable oil cartel, raiders with junk bonds, and the changing demographics of the work force are among the many factors that have contributed to this shift. The net result is that doing what was done yesterday, or doing it 5% better, is no longer a formula for success. Major changes are more and more necessary to survive and compete effectively in this new environment. More change always demands more leadership.

Consider a simple military analogy: a peacetime army can usually survive with good administration and management up and down the hierarchy, coupled with good leadership concentrated at the very top. A wartime army, however, needs competent leadership at all levels. No one yet has figured out how to manage people effectively into battle; they must be led.

These different functions—coping with complexity and coping with change—shape the characteristic activities of management and leadership. Each system of action involves deciding what needs to be done, creating networks of people and relationships that can accomplish an agenda, and then trying to ensure that those people actually do the job. But each accomplishes these three tasks in different ways.

Companies manage complexity first by *planning and budgeting*—setting targets or goals for the future (typically for the next month or year), establishing detailed steps for achieving those targets, and then allocating resources to accomplish those plans. By contrast, leading an organization to constructive change begins by *setting a direction*—developing a vision of the future (often the distant future) along with strategies for producing the changes needed to achieve that vision.

Management develops the capacity to achieve its plan by *organizing and staffing*—creating an organizational structure and set of jobs for accomplishing plan requirements, staffing the jobs with qualified individuals, communicating the plan to those people, delegating responsibility for carrying out the plan, and devising systems to monitor implementation. The equivalent leadership activity, however, is *aligning people*. This means communicating the new direction to those who can create coalitions that understand the vision and are committed to its achievement.

Finally, management ensures plan accomplishment by *controlling and problem solving*—monitoring results versus the plan in some detail, both formally and informally, by means of reports, meetings, and other tools; identifying deviations; and then planning and organizing to solve the problems. But for leadership, achieving a vision requires *motivating and inspiring*—keeping people moving in the right direction, despite major obstacles to change, by appealing to basic but often untapped human needs, values, and emotions.

A closer examination of each of these activities will help clarify the skills leaders need.

SETTING A DIRECTION VS. PLANNING AND BUDGETING

Since the function of leadership is to produce change, setting the direction of that change is fundamental to leadership.

Setting direction is never the same as planning or even long-term planning, although people often confuse the two.

Planning is a management process, deductive in nature and designed to produce orderly results, not change. Setting a direction is more inductive. Leaders gather a broad range of data and look for patterns, relationships, and linkages that help explain things. What's more, the direction-setting aspect of leadership does not produce plans; it creates vision and strategies. These describe a business, technology, or corporate culture in terms of what it should become over the long term and articulate a feasible way of achieving this goal.

Most discussions of vision have a tendency to degenerate into the mystical. The implication is that a vision is something mysterious that mere mortals, even talented ones, could never hope to have. But developing good business direction isn't magic. It is a tough, sometimes exhausting process of gathering and analyzing information. People who articulate such visions aren't magicians but broad-based strategic thinkers who are willing to take risks.

Nor do visions and strategies have to be brilliantly innovative; in fact, some of the best are not. Effective business visions regularly have an almost mundane quality, usually consisting of ideas that are already well known. The particular combination or patterning of the ideas may be new, but sometimes even that is not the case.

For example, when CEO Jan Carlzon articulated his vision to make Scandinavian Airline Systems (SAS) the best airline in the world for the frequent business traveler, he was not saying anything that everyone in the airline industry didn't already know. Business travelers fly more consistently than other market segments and are generally willing to pay higher fares. Thus focusing on business customers offers an airline the possibility of high margins, steady business, and considerable growth. But in an industry known more for bureaucracy than vision, no company had ever put these simple ideas together and dedicated itself to implementing them. SAS did, and it worked.

What's crucial about a vision is not its originality but how well it serves the interests of important constituencies—customers, stockholders, employees—and how easily it can be translated into a realistic competitive strategy. Bad visions tend to ignore the legitimate needs and rights of important constituencies—favoring, say, employees over customers or stockholders. Or they are strategically unsound. When a company that has never been better than a weak competitor in an industry suddenly starts talking about becoming number one, that is a pipe dream, not a vision.

One of the most frequent mistakes that overmanaged and underled corporations make is to embrace "long-term planning" as a panacea for their lack of direction and inability to adapt to an increasingly competitive and dynamic business environment. But such an approach misinterprets the nature of direction setting and can never work.

Long-term planning is always time consuming. Whenever something unexpected happens, plans have to be redone. In a dynamic business environment, the unexpected often becomes the norm, and long-term planning can become an extraordinarily burdensome activity. This is why most successful corporations limit the time frame of their planning activities. Indeed, some even consider "long-term planning" a contradiction in terms.

In a company without direction, even short-term planning can become a black hole capable of absorbing an infinite amount of time and energy. With no vision and strategy to provide constraints around the planning process or to guide it, every eventuality deserves a plan. Under these circumstances, contingency planning can go on forever, draining time and attention from far more essential activities, yet without ever providing the clear sense of direction that a company desperately needs. After awhile, managers inevitably become cynical about all this, and the planning process can degenerate into a highly politicized game.

Planning works best not as a substitute for direction setting but as a complement to it. A competent planning process serves as a useful reality check on direction-setting activities. Likewise, a competent direction-setting process provides a focus in which planning can then be realistically carried out. It helps clarify what kind of planning is essential and what kind is irrelevant.

ALIGNING PEOPLE VS. ORGANIZING AND STAFFING

A central feature of modern organizations is interdependence, where no one has complete autonomy, where most employees are tied to many others by their work, technology, management systems, and hierarchy. These linkages present a special challenge when organizations attempt to change. Unless many individuals line up and move together in the same direction, people will tend to fall all over one another. To executives who are overeducated in management and undereducated in leadership, the idea of getting people moving in the same direction appears to be an organizational problem. What executives need to do, however, is not organize people but align them.

Managers "organize" to create human systems that can implement plans as precisely and efficiently as possible. Typically, this requires a number of potentially complex decisions.

A company must choose a structure of jobs and reporting relationships, staff it with individuals suited to the jobs, provide training for those who need it, communicate plans to the work force, and decide how much authority to delegate and to whom. Economic incentives also need to be constructed to accomplish the plan, as well as systems to monitor its implementation. These organizational judgments are much like architectural decisions. It's a question of fit within a particular context.

Aligning is different. It is more of a communications challenge than a design problem. First, aligning invariably involves talking to many more individuals than organizing does. The target population can involve not only a manager's subordinates but also bosses, peers, staff in other parts of the organization, as well as suppliers, governmental officials, or even customers. Anyone who can help implement the vision and strategies or who can block implementation is relevant.

Trying to get people to comprehend a vision of an alternative future is also a communications challenge of a completely different magnitude from organizing them to fulfill a short-term plan. It's much like the difference between a football quarterback attempting to describe to his team the next two or three plays versus his trying to explain to them a totally new approach to the game to be used in the second half of the season.

Whether delivered with many words or a few carefully chosen symbols, such messages are not necessarily accepted just because they are understood. Another big challenge in leadership efforts is credibility—getting people to believe the message. Many things contribute to credibility: the track record of the person delivering the message, the content of the message itself, the communicator's reputation for integrity and trustworthiness, and the consistency between words and deeds.

Finally, aligning leads to empowerment in a way that organizing rarely does. One of the reasons some organizations have difficulty adjusting to rapid changes in markets or technology is that so many people in those companies feel relatively powerless. They have learned from experience that even if they correctly perceive important external changes and then initiate appropriate actions, they are vulnerable to someone higher up who does not like what they have done. Reprimands can take many different forms: "That's against policy" or "We can't afford it" or "Shut up and do as you're told."

Alignment helps overcome this problem by empowering people in at least two ways. First, when a clear sense of direction has been communicated throughout an organization, lower level employees can initiate actions without the same degree of vulnerability. As long as their behavior is consistent with the vision, superiors will have more difficulty reprimanding them. Second, because everyone is aiming at the same target, the probability is less that one person's initiative will be stalled when it comes into conflict with someone else's.

MOTIVATING PEOPLE VS. CONTROLLING AND PROBLEM SOLVING

Since change is the function of leadership, being able to generate highly energized behavior is important for coping with the inevitable barriers to change. Just as direction setting identifies an appropriate path for movement and just as effective alignment gets people moving down that path, successful motivation ensures that they will have the energy to overcome obstacles.

According to the logic of management, control mechanisms compare system behavior with the plan and take action when a deviation is detected. In a well-managed factory, for example, this means the planning process establishes sensible quality targets, the organizing process builds an organization that can achieve those targets, and a control process makes sure that quality lapses are spotted immediately, not in 30 or 60 days, and corrected.

For some of the same reasons that control is so central to management, highly motivated or inspired behavior is almost irrelevant. Managerial processes must be as close as possible to fail-safe and risk-free. That means they cannot be dependent on the unusual or hard to obtain. The whole purpose of systems and structures is to help normal people who behave in normal ways to complete routine jobs successfully, day after day. It's not exciting or glamorous. But that's management.

Leadership is different. Achieving grand visions always requires an occasional burst of energy. Motivation and inspiration energize people, not by pushing them in the right direction as control mechanisms do but by satisfying basic human needs for achievement, a sense of belonging, recognition, self-esteem, a feeling of control over one's life, and the ability to live up to one's ideals. Such feelings touch us deeply and elicit a powerful response.

Good leaders motivate people in a variety of ways. First, they always articulate the organization's vision in a manner that stresses the values of the audience they are addressing. This makes the work important to those individuals. Leaders also regularly involve people in deciding how to achieve the organization's vision (or the part most relevant to a particular individual). This gives people a sense of control. Another important motivational technique is to support employee efforts to realize the vision by providing coaching, feedback, and role modeling, thereby helping people grow professionally and enhancing their self-esteem. Finally, good leaders recognize and reward success, which not only gives people a sense of accomplishment but also makes them feel like they belong to an organization that cares about them. When all this is done, the work itself becomes intrinsically motivating.

The more that change characterizes the business environment, the more that leaders must motivate people to provide leadership as well. When this works, it tends to reproduce leadership across the entire organization, with people occupying multiple leadership roles throughout the hierarchy. This is highly valuable, because coping with change in any complex business demands initiatives from a multitude of people. Nothing less will work.

Of course, leadership from many sources does not necessarily converge. To the contrary, it can easily conflict. For multiple leadership roles to work together, people's actions must be carefully coordinated by mechanisms that differ from those coordinating traditional management roles.

Strong networks of informal relationships—the kind found in companies with healthy cultures—help coordinate leadership activities in much the same way that formal structure coordinates managerial activities. The key difference is that informal networks can deal with the greater demands for coordination associated with nonroutine activities and change. The multitude of communication channels and the trust among the individuals connected by those channels allow for an ongoing process of accommodation and adaptation. When conflicts rise among roles, those same relationships help resolve the conflicts. Perhaps most important, this process of dialogue and accommodation can produce visions that are linked and compatible instead of remote and competitive. All this requires a great deal more communication than is needed to coordinate managerial roles, but unlike formal structure, strong informal networks can handle it.

Of course, informal relations of some sort exist in all corporations. But too often these networks are either very weak—some people are well connected but most are not—or they are highly fragmented—a strong network exists inside the marketing group and inside R&D but not across the two departments. Such networks do not support multiple leadership initiatives well. In fact, extensive informal networks are so important that if they do not exist, creating them has to be the focus of activity early in a major leadership initiative.

CREATING A CULTURE OF LEADERSHIP

Despite the increasing importance of leadership to business success, the on-the-job experiences of most people actually seem to undermine the development of attributes needed for leadership. Nevertheless, some companies have consistently demonstrated an ability to develop people into outstanding leader-managers. Recruiting people with leadership potential is only the first step. Equally important is managing their career patterns. Individuals who are effective in large leadership roles often share a number of career experiences.

Perhaps the most typical and most important is significant challenge early in a career. Leaders almost always have had opportunities during their twenties and thirties to actually try to lead, to take a risk, and to learn from both triumphs and failures. Such learning seems essential in developing a wide range of leadership skills and perspectives. It also teaches people something about both the difficulty of leadership and its potential for producing change.

Later in their careers, something equally important happens that has to do with broadening. People who provide effective leadership in important jobs always have a chance, before they get into those jobs, to grow beyond the narrow base that characterizes most managerial careers. This is usually the result of lateral career moves or of early promotions to unusually broad job assignments. Sometimes other vehicles help, like special task-force assignments or a lengthy general management course. Whatever the case, the breadth of knowledge developed in this way seems to be helpful in all aspects of leadership. So does the network of relationships that is often acquired both inside and outside the company. When enough people get opportunities like this, the relationships that are built also help create the strong informal networks needed to support multiple leadership initiatives.

Corporations that do a better-than-average job of developing leaders put an emphasis on creating challenging opportunities for relatively young employees. In many businesses, decentralization is the key. By definition, it pushes responsibility lower in an organization and in the process creates more challenging jobs at lower levels. Johnson & Johnson, 3M, Hewlett-Packard, General Electric, and many other well-known companies have used that approach quite successfully. Some of those same companies also create as many small units as possible so there are a lot of challenging lower level general management jobs available.

Sometimes these businesses develop additional challenging opportunities by stressing growth through new products or services. Over the years, 3M has had a policy that at least 25%

of its revenue should come from products introduced within the last five years. That encourages small new ventures, which in turn offer hundreds of opportunities to test and stretch young people with leadership potential.

Such practices can, almost by themselves, prepare people for small- and medium-sized leadership jobs. But developing people for important leadership positions requires more work on the part of senior executives, often over a long period of time. That work begins with efforts to spot people with great leadership potential early in their careers and to identify what will be needed to stretch and develop them.

Again, there is nothing magic about this process. The methods successful companies use are surprisingly straightforward. They go out of their way to make young employees and people at lower levels in their organizations visible to senior management. Senior managers then judge for themselves who has potential and what the development needs of those people are. Executives also discuss their tentative conclusions among themselves to draw more accurate judgments.

Armed with a clear sense of who has considerable leadership potential and what skills they need to develop, executives in these companies then spend time planning for that development. Sometimes that is done as part of a formal succession planning or high-potential development process; often it is more informal. In either case, the key ingredient appears to be an intelligent assessment of what feasible development opportunities fit each candidate's needs.

To encourage managers to participate in these activities, well-led businesses tend to recognize and reward people who successfully develop leaders. This is rarely done as part of a formal compensation or bonus formula, simply because it is so difficult to measure such achievements with precision. But it does become a factor in decisions about promotion, especially the most senior levels, and that seems to make a big difference. When told that future promotions will depend to some degree on their ability to nurture leaders, even people who say that leadership cannot be developed somehow find ways to do it.

Such strategies help create a corporate culture where people value strong leadership and strive to create it. Just as we need more people to provide leadership; in the complex organizations that dominate our world today, we also need more people to develop the cultures that will create that leadership. Institutionalizing a leadership-centered culture is the ultimate act of leadership.

°   °   °

John P. Kotter has been a professor at Harvard Business School and is a speaker on leadership and change.

Chapter Three

Primal Leadership

Daniel Goleman
Richard Boyatzis
Annie McKee

Great leaders move us. They ignite our passion and inspire the best in us. When we try to explain why they are so effective, we speak of strategy, vision, or powerful ideas. But the reality is much more primal: Great leadership works through the emotions.

No matter what leaders set out to do—whether it's creating strategy or mobilizing teams to action—their success depends on *how* they do it. Even if they get everything else just right, if leaders fail in this primal task of driving emotions in the right direction, nothing they do will work as well as it could or should.

Consider, for example, a pivotal moment in a news division at the BBC, the British media giant. The division had been set up as an experiment, and while its 200 or so journalists and editors felt they had given their best, management had decided the division would have to close.[1]

It didn't help that the executive sent to deliver the decision to the assembled staff started off with a glowing account of how well rival operations were doing, and that he had just returned from a wonderful trip to Cannes. The news itself was bad enough, but the brusque, even contentious manner of the executive incited something beyond the expected frustration. People became enraged—not just at the management decision, but also at the bearer of the news himself. The atmosphere became so threatening, in fact, that it looked as though the executive might have to call security to usher him safely from the room.

The next day, another executive visited the same staff. He took a very different approach. He spoke from his heart about the crucial importance of journalism to the vibrancy of a society, and of the calling that had drawn them all to the field in the first place. He reminded them that no one goes into journalism to get rich—as a profession its finances have always been marginal, with job security ebbing and flowing with larger economic tides. And he invoked the passion, even the dedication, the journalists had for the service they offered. Finally, he wished them all well in getting on with their careers.

When this leader finished speaking, the staff cheered.

The difference between the leaders lay in the mood and tone with which they delivered their messages: One drove the group toward antagonism and hostility, the other toward optimism, even inspiration, in the face of difficulty. These two moments point to a hidden, but crucial, dimension in leadership—the emotional impact of what a leader says and does.

While most people recognize that a leader's mood—and how he or she impacts the mood of others—plays a significant role in any organization, emotions are often seen as too personal or unquantifiable to talk about in a meaningful way. But research in the field of emotion has yielded keen insights into not only how to measure the impact of a leader's emotions but also how the best leaders have found effective ways to understand and improve the way they handle their own and other people's emotions. Understanding the powerful role of emotions in the workplace sets the best leaders apart from the rest—not just in tangibles such as better business results and the retention of talent, but also in the all-important intangibles, such as higher morale, motivation, and commitment.

THE PRIMAL DIMENSION

This emotional task of the leader is *primal*—that is, first—in two senses: It is both the original and the most important act of leadership.

Leaders have always played a primordial emotional role. No doubt humankind's original leaders—whether tribal chieftains or shamanesses—earned their place in large part because their leadership was emotionally compelling. Throughout history and in cultures everywhere, the leader in any human group has been the one to whom others look for assurance and clarity when facing uncertainty or threat, or when there's a job to be done. The leader acts as the group's emotional guide.

In the modern organization, this primordial emotional task—though by now largely invisible—remains foremost among the many jobs of leadership: driving the collective emotions in a positive direction and clearing the smog created by toxic emotions. This task applies to leadership everywhere, from the boardroom to the shop floor.

Quite simply, in any human group the leader has maximal power to sway everyone's emotions. If people's emotions are pushed toward the range of enthusiasm, performance can soar; if people are driven toward rancor and anxiety, they will be thrown off stride. This indicates another important aspect of primal leadership: Its effects extend beyond ensuring that a job is well done. Followers also look to a leader for supportive emotional connection—for empathy. All leadership includes this primal dimension, for better or for worse. When leaders drive emotions positively, as was the case with the second executive at the BBC, they bring out everyone's best. We call this effect *resonance*. When they drive emotions negatively, as with the first executive, leaders spawn *dissonance*, undermining the emotional foundations that let people shine. Whether an organization withers or flourishes depends to a remarkable extent on the leaders' effectiveness in this primal emotional dimension.

The key, of course, to making primal leadership work to everyone's advantage lies in the leadership competencies of *emotional intelligence:* how leaders handle themselves and their relationships. Leaders who maximize the benefits of primal leadership drive the emotions of those they lead in the right direction.

How does all of this work? Recent studies of the brain reveal the neurological mechanisms of primal leadership and make clear just why emotional intelligence abilities are so crucial.

THE OPEN LOOP

The reason a leader's manner—not just what he does, but *how* he does it—matters so much lies in the design of the human brain: what scientists have begun to call the *open-loop* nature of the limbic system, our emotional centers. A closed-loop system such as the circulatory system is self-regulating; what's happening in the circulatory system of others around us does not impact our own system. An open-loop system depends largely on external sources to manage itself.

In other words, we rely on connections with other people for our own emotional stability. The open-loop limbic system was a winning design in evolution, no doubt, because it allows people to come to one another's emotional rescue—enabling, for example, a mother to soothe her crying infant, or a lookout in a primate band to signal an instant alarm when he perceives a threat.

Despite the veneer of our advanced civilization, the open-loop principle still holds. Research in intensive care units has shown that the comforting presence of another person not only lowers the patient's blood pressure, but also slows the secretion of fatty acids that block arteries.[2] More dramatically, whereas three or more incidents of intense stress within a year (say, serious financial trouble, being fired, or a divorce) triple the death rate in socially isolated middle-aged men, they have *no impact* whatsoever on the death rate of men who cultivate many close relationships.[3]

Scientists describe the open loop as "interpersonal limbic regulation," whereby one person transmits signals that can alter hormone levels, cardiovascular function, sleep rhythms, and even immune function inside the body of another.[4] That's how couples who are in love are able to trigger in one another's brains surges of oxytocin, which creates a pleasant, affectionate feeling. But in all aspects of social life, not just love relationships, our physiologies intermingle, our emotions automatically shifting into the register of the person we're with. The open-loop design of the limbic system means that other people can change our very physiology—and so our emotions.

Even though the open loop is so much a part of our lives, we usually don't notice the process itself. Scientists have captured this attunement of emotions in the laboratory by measuring the physiology—such as heart rate—of two people as they have a good conversation. As the conversation begins, their bodies each operate at different rhythms. But by the end of a simple fifteen-minute conversation, their physiological profiles look remarkably similar—a phenomenon called *mirroring*. This entrainment occurs strongly during the downward spiral of a conflict, when anger and hurt reverberate, but also goes on more subtly during pleasant interactions.[5] It happens hardly at all during an emotionally neutral discussion. Researchers have seen again and again how emotions spread irresistibly in this way whenever people are near one another, even when the contact is completely nonverbal. For example, when three strangers sit facing each other in silence for a minute or two, the one who is most emotionally expressive transmits his or her mood to the other two—without speaking a single word.[6] The same effect holds in the office, boardroom, or shop floor; people in groups at work inevitably "catch" feelings from one another, sharing everything from jealousy and envy to angst or euphoria. The more cohesive the group, the stronger the sharing of moods, emotional history, and even hot buttons.[7]

In seventy work teams across diverse industries, for instance, members who sat in meetings together ended up sharing moods—either good or bad—within two hours.[8] Nurses, and even accountants, who monitored their moods over weeks or every few hours as they worked together showed emotions that tracked together—and the group's shared moods were largely independent of the hassles they shared.[9] Studies of professional sports teams reveal similar results: Quite apart from the ups and downs of a team's standing, its players tend to synchronize their moods over a period of days and weeks.[10]

CONTAGION AND LEADERSHIP

The continual interplay of limbic open loops among members of a group creates a kind of emotional soup, with everyone adding his or her own flavor to the mix. But it is the leader who adds the strongest seasoning. Why? Because of that enduring reality of business: Everyone watches the boss. People take their emotional cues from the top. Even when the boss isn't highly visible—for example, the CEO who works behind closed doors on an upper floor—his attitude affects the moods of his direct reports, and a domino effect ripples throughout the company's emotional climate.[11]

Careful observations of working groups in action revealed several ways the leader plays such a pivotal role in determining the shared emotions.[12] Leaders typically talked more than anyone else, and what they said was listened to more carefully. Leaders were also usually the first to speak out on a subject, and when others made comments, their remarks most often referred to what the leader had said than to anyone else's comments. Because the leaders' way of seeing things has special weight, leaders "manage meaning" for a group, offering a way to interpret, and so react emotionally to, a given situation.[13]

But the impact on emotions goes beyond what a leader says. In these studies, even when leaders were not talking, they were watched more carefully than anyone else in the group. When people raised a question for the group as a whole, they would keep their eyes on the leader to see his or her response. Indeed, group members generally see the leader's emotional reaction as the most valid response, and so model their own on it—particularly in an ambiguous situation, where various members react differently. In a sense, the leader sets the emotional standard.

Leaders give praise or withhold it, criticize well or destructively, offer support or turn a blind eye to people's needs. They can frame the group's mission in ways that give more meaning to each person's contribution—or not. They can guide in ways that give people a sense of clarity and direction in their work and that encourage flexibility, setting people free to use their best sense of how to get the job done. All these acts help determine a leader's primal emotional impact.

Still, not all "official" leaders in a group are necessarily the emotional leaders. When the designated leader lacks credibility for some reason, people may turn for emotional guidance to someone else who they trust and respect. This de facto leader then becomes the one who molds others' emotional reactions. For instance, a well-known jazz group that was named for its formal leader and founder actually took its emotional cues from a different musician. The founder continued to manage bookings and logistics, but when it came time to decide what tune the group would play next or how the sound system should be adjusted, all eyes turned to the dominant member—the emotional leader.[14]

PEOPLE MAGNETS

Regardless of who the emotional leader might be, however, she's likely to have a knack for acting as a limbic "attractor," exerting a palpable force on the emotional brains of people around her. Watch a gifted actor at work, for example, and observe how easily she draws an audience into her emotional orbit. Whether she's conveying the agony of a betrayal or a joyous triumph, the audience feels those things too.

How easily we catch leaders' emotional states, then, has to do with how expressly their faces, voices, and gestures convey their feelings. The greater a leader's skill at transmitting emotions, the more forcefully the emotions will spread. Such transmission does not depend on theatrics, of course; since people pay close attention to a leader, even subtle expressions of emotion can have great impact. Even so, the more open leaders are—how well they express their own enthusiasm, for example—the more readily others will feel that same contagious passion.

Leaders with that kind of talent are emotional magnets; people naturally gravitate to them. If you think about the leaders with whom people most want to work in an organization, they probably have this ability to exude upbeat feelings. It's one reason emotionally intelligent leaders attract talented people—for the pleasure of working in their presence. Conversely, leaders who emit the negative register—who are irritable, touchy, domineering, cold—repel people. No one wants to work for a grouch. Research has proven it: Optimistic, enthusiastic leaders more easily retain their people, compared with those bosses who tend toward negative moods.[15]

Let's now take the impact of primal leadership one step further, to examine just how much emotions determine job effectiveness.

How Moods Impact Results

Emotions are highly intense, fleeting, and sometimes disruptive to work; moods tend to be less intense, longer-lasting feelings that typically don't interfere with the job at hand. And an emotional episode usually leaves a corresponding lingering mood: a low-key, continual flow of feeling throughout the group.

Although emotions and moods may seem trivial from a business point of view, they have real consequences for getting work done. A leader's mild anxiety can act as a signal that something needs more attention and careful thought. In fact, a sober mood can help immensely when considering a risky situation—and too much optimism can lead to ignoring dangers.[16] A sudden flood of anger can rivet a leader's attention on an urgent problem—such as the revelation that a senior executive has engaged in sexual harassment—redirecting the leader's energies from the normal round of concerns toward finding a solution, such as improving the organization's efforts to eliminate harassment.[17]

While mild anxiety (such as over a looming deadline) can focus attention and energy, prolonged distress can sabotage a leader's relationships and can also hamper work performance by diminishing the brain's ability to process information and respond effectively. A good laugh or an upbeat mood, on the other hand, more often enhances the neural abilities crucial for doing good work.

Both good and bad moods tend to perpetuate themselves, in part because they skew perceptions and memories: When people feel upbeat, they see the positive light in a situation and recall the good things about it, and when they feel bad, they focus on the downside.[18] Beyond this perceptual skew, the stew of stress hormones secreted when a person is upset takes hours to become reabsorbed in the body and fade away. That's why a sour relationship with a boss can leave a person a captive of that distress, with a mind preoccupied and a body unable to calm itself: *He got me so upset during that meeting I couldn't go to sleep for hours last night.* As a result, we naturally prefer being with people who are emotionally positive, in part because they make us feel good.

Emotional Hijacking

Negative emotions—especially chronic anger, anxiety, or a sense of futility—powerfully disrupt work, hijacking attention from the task at hand.[19] For instance, in a Yale study of moods and their contagion, the performance of groups making executive decisions about how best to allocate yearly bonuses was measurably boosted by positive feelings and was impaired by negative ones. Significantly, the group members themselves did not realize the influence of their own moods.[20]

For instance, of all the interactions at an international hotel chain that pitched employees into bad moods, the most frequent was talking to someone in management. Interactions with bosses led to bad feelings—frustration, disappointment, anger, sadness, disgust, or hurt—about nine out of ten times. These interactions were the cause of distress more often than customers, work pressure, company policies, or personal problems.[21] Not that leaders need to be overly "nice"; the emotional art of leadership includes pressing the reality of work demands without unduly upsetting people. One of the oldest laws in psychology holds that beyond a moderate level, increases in anxiety and worry erode mental abilities.

Distress not only erodes mental abilities, but also makes people less emotionally intelligent. People who are upset have trouble reading emotions accurately in other people—decreasing the most basic skill needed for empathy and, as a result, impairing their social skills.[22]

Another consideration is that the emotions people feel while they work, according to new findings on job satisfaction, reflect most directly the true quality of work life.[23] The percentage of time people feel positive emotions at work turns out to be one of the strongest predictors of satisfaction, and therefore, for instance, of how likely employees are to quit.[24] In this sense, leaders who spread bad moods are simply bad for business—and those who pass along good moods help drive a business's success.

Good Moods, Good Work

When people feel good, they work at their best. Feeling good lubricates mental efficiency, making people better at understanding information and using decision rules in complex judgments, as well as more flexible in their thinking.[25] Upbeat moods, research verifies, make people view others—or events—in a more positive light. That in turn helps people feel more optimistic about their ability to achieve a goal, enhances creativity and decision-making skills, and predisposes people to be helpful.[26] Insurance agents with a glass-is-half-full outlook, for instance, are far more able than their more pessimistic peers to persist despite rejections, and so they make more sales.[27] Moreover, research on humor at work reveals that a well-timed joke or playful laugher can stimulate creativity, open lines of communication, enhance a sense of connection and trust, and, of course, make work more fun.[28] Playful joking increases the likelihood of financial concessions during a negotiation. Small wonder that playfulness holds a prominent place in the tool kit of emotionally intelligent leaders.

Good moods prove especially important when it comes to teams: The ability of a leader to pitch a group into an enthusiastic, cooperative mood can determine its success. On the other hand, whenever emotional conflicts in a group bleed attention and energy from their shared tasks, a group's performance will suffer.

Consider the results of a study of sixty-two CEOs and their top management teams.[29] The CEOs represented some of the *Fortune* 500, as well as leading U.S. service companies (such as consulting and accounting firms), not-for-profit organizations, and government agencies. The CEOs and their management team members were assessed on how upbeat—energetic, enthusiastic, determined—they were. They were also asked how much conflict and tumult the top team experienced, that is, personality clashes, anger and friction in meetings, and emotional conflicts (in contrast to disagreement about ideas).

The study found that the more positive the overall moods of people in the top management team, the more cooperatively they worked together—and the better the company's business results. Put differently, the longer a company was run by a management team that did not get along, the poorer that company's market return.

The "group IQ," then—the sum total of every person's best talents contributed at full force—depends on the group's emotional intelligence, as shown in its harmony. A leader skilled in collaboration can keep cooperation high and thus ensure that the group's decisions will be worth the effort of meeting. Such leaders know how to balance the group's focus on the task at hand with its attention to the quality of members' relationships.

They naturally create a friendly but effective climate that lifts everyone's spirits.

Quantifying the "Feel" of a Company

Common wisdom, of course, holds that employees who feel upbeat will likely go the extra mile to please customers and therefore improve the bottom line. But there's actually a logarithm that predicts that relationship: For every 1 percent improvement in the service climate, there's a 2 percent increase in revenue.[30]

Benjamin Schneider, a professor at the University of Maryland, found in operations as diverse as bank branches, insurance company regional offices, credit card call centers, and hospitals that employees' ratings of service climate predicted customer satisfaction, which drove business results. Likewise, poor morale among frontline customer service reps at a given point in time predicts high turnover—and declining customer satisfaction—up to three years later. This low customer satisfaction, in turn, drives declining revenues.[31]

So what's the antidote? Besides the obvious relationships between climate and working conditions or salary, resonant leaders play a key role. In general, the more emotionally demanding the work, the more empathic and supportive the leader needs to be. Leaders drive the service climate and thus the predisposition of employees to satisfy customers. At an insurance company, for instance, Schneider found that effective leadership influenced service climate among agents to account for a 3 to 4 percent difference in insurance renewals—a seemingly small margin that made a big difference to the business.

Organizational consultants have long assumed a positive link of some kind between a business unit's human climate and its performance. But data connecting the two have been sparse—and so, in practice, leaders could more easily ignore their personal style and its effects on the people they led, focusing instead on "harder" business objectives. But now we have results from a range of industries that link leadership to climate and to business performance, making it possible to quantify the hard difference for business performance made by something as soft as the "feel" of a company.

For instance, at a global food and beverage company, positive climate readings predicted higher yearly earnings at major divisions. And in a study of nineteen insurance companies, the climate created by the CEOs among their direct reports predicted the business performance of the entire organization: In 75 percent of cases, climate alone accurately sorted companies into high versus low profits and growth.[32]

Climate in itself does not determine performance. The factors deciding which companies prove most fit in any given quarter are notoriously complex. But our analyses suggest that, overall, the climate—how people feel about working at a company—can account for 20 to 30 percent of business performance. Getting the best out of people pays off in hard results.

If climate drives business results, what drives climate? Roughly 50 to 70 percent of how employees perceive their organization's climate can be traced to the actions of one person: the leader. More than anyone else, the boss creates the conditions that directly determine people's ability to work well.[33]

In short, leaders' emotional states and actions do affect how the people they lead will feel and therefore perform. How well leaders manage their moods and affect everyone else's moods, then, becomes not just a private matter, but a factor in how well a business will do.[34]

And that gets us to how the brain drives primal leadership, for better or for worse.

o   o   o

Daniel Goleman is codirector of the Consortium for Research on Emotional Intelligence in Organizations at Rutgers University.

Richard Boyatzis is professor and chair of the Department of Organizational Behavior at the Weatherhead School of Management at Case Western Reserve University.

Annie McKee serves on the faculty of the University of Pennsylvania Graduate School of Education and is a consultant.

Chapter Four

The "How to Be" Leader

Frances Hesselbein

Chief Executive Magazine asked a number of corporate chief executives "to look over the horizon of today's headlines," "size up the future," and describe the most pressing tasks that lie beyond the millennium for chief executives. I was invited to do so as well. In my response I wrote, "The three major challenges CEOs will face have little to do with managing the enterprise's tangible assets and everything to do with monitoring the quality of: leadership, the work force, and relationships." After the magazine came out, a corporate leader wrote to me and said, "Your comments make great sense to me. I believe that the three challenges you describe are like legs on a stool. Yet I see leaders attending to just one, or perhaps two, of the legs!"

In the tenuous years that lie ahead, the familiar benchmarks, guideposts, and milestones will change as rapidly and explosively as the times, but the one constant at the center of the vortex will be the leader. The leader beyond the millennium will not be the leader who has learned the lessons of *how to do it*, with ledgers of "hows" balanced with "its" that dissolve in the crashing changes ahead. The leader for today and the future will be focused on *how to be*—how to develop quality, character, mind-set, values, principles, and courage.

The "how to be" leader knows that people are the organization's greatest asset and in word, behavior, and relationships she or he demonstrates this powerful philosophy. This leader long ago banned the hierarchy and, involving many heads and hands, built a new kind of structure. The new design took people out of the boxes of the old hierarchy and moved them into a more circular, flexible, and fluid management system that released the energy and spirit of our people.

The "how to be" leader builds dispersed and diverse leadership—distributing leadership to the outermost edges of the circle to unleash the power of shared responsibility. The leader builds a work force, board, and staff that reflect the many faces of the community and environment, so that customers and constituents find themselves when they view this richly diverse organization of the future.

This "how to be" leader holds forth the vision of the organization's future in compelling ways that ignite the spark needed to build the inclusive enterprise. The leader mobilizes people around the mission of the organization, making it a powerful force in the uncertain times ahead. Mobilizing around mission generates a force that transforms the workplace into one in which workers and teams can express themselves in their work and find significance beyond the task, as they manage for the mission. Through a consistent focus on mission, the "how to be" leader gives the dispersed and diverse leaders of the enterprise a clear sense of direction and the opportunity to find meaning in their work.

The "how to be" leader knows that listening to the customer and learning what he or she values—"digging in the field"—will be a critical component, even more so in the future than today. Global and local competition will only accelerate, and the need to focus on what the customer values will grow stronger.

Everyone will watch tomorrow's leader, as we watch today's, to see if the business practices of the organization are consistent with the principles espoused by the leader. In all interactions, from the smallest to the largest, the behavior of the "how to be" leader will demonstrate a belief in the worth and dignity of the men and women who make up the enterprise.

Key to the societal significance of tomorrow's leaders is the way they embrace the totality of leadership, not just including "my organization" but reaching beyond the walls as well. The "how to be" leader, whether he or she is working in the private, public, or social sector, recognizes the significance of the lives of the men and women who make up the enterprise, the value of a workplace that nurtures the people whose performance is essential to furthering the mission, and the necessity of a healthy community to the success of an organization. The wise leader embraces all those concerned in a circle that surrounds the corporation, the organization, the people, the leadership, and the community.

The challenges presented from outside the walls will require as much attention, commitment, and energy as the most pressing tasks within. Leaders of the future will say, "This is intolerable," as they look at the schools, at the health of children who will make up the future work force, at inadequate preparation for life and work in too many families, at people losing trust in their institutions. The new leaders will build the healthy community as energetically as they build the healthy, productive enterprise, knowing that the high-performance organization cannot exist if it fails its people in an ailing community.

Today's concerns about a lack of workers' loyalty to the corporation and a corresponding lack of corporations' loyalty to the work force are sending a clear message to the leaders of tomorrow. The pit bulls of the marketplace may find that their slash-and-crunch and hang-on-till-death philosophies are as dead as the spirits of their troops. In the end, as organizations reduce their work forces, will it be the leader of a dispirited, demoralized work force who leads the pack or will it be the new leader, guiding from vision, principle, and values, who builds trust and releases the energy and creativity of the work force?

The great observers are not forecasting good times, but in the very hazards that lie ahead for leaders, remarkable opportunities exist for those who would lead their enterprises and this country into a new kind of community—a cohesive community of healthy children, strong families, good schools, decent neighborhoods, and work that dignifies the individual. It is in this arena that leaders with new mind-sets and visions will forge new relationships, crossing all three sectors to build partnerships and community. This will take a different breed (or the old breed sloughing off the tired, go-it-alone approach), made up of leaders who dare to see life and community whole, who view work as an amazing opportunity to express everything within that gives passion and light to living, and who have the courage to lead from the front on the issues, principles, vision, and mission that become the star to steer by. Leaders of the future can only speculate on the tangibles that will define the challenges beyond the millennium. But the intangibles, the leadership qualities required, are as constant as the North Star. They are expressed in the character, the power within, and the "how to be" of leaders beyond the millennium.

o   o   o

Frances Hesselbein is chairman of the board of governors of the Peter F. Drucker Foundation. Previously, she was CEO of Girl Scouts of the USA.

Chapter Five

What Is Leadership?

Max De Pree

The first responsibility of a leader is to define reality. The last is to say thank you. In between the two, the leader must become a servant and a debtor. That sums up the progress of an artful leader.

Concepts of leadership, ideas about leadership, and leadership practices are the subject of much thought, discussion, writing, teaching, and learning. True leaders are sought after and cultivated. Leadership is not an easy subject to explain. A friend of mine characterizes leaders simply like this: "Leaders don't inflict pain; they bear pain."

The goal of thinking hard about leadership is not to produce great, or charismatic, or well-known leaders. The measure of leadership is not the quality of the head, but the tone of the body. The signs of outstanding leadership appear primarily among the followers. Are the followers reaching their potential? Are they learning? Serving? Do they achieve the required results? Do they change with grace? Manage conflict?

I would like to ask you to think about the concept of leadership in a certain way. Try to think about a leader, in the words of the gospel writer Luke, as "one who serves." Leadership is a concept of owing certain things to the institution. It is a way of thinking about institutional heirs, a way of thinking about stewardship as contrasted with ownership.

The art of leadership requires us to think about the leader-as-steward in terms of relationships: of assets and legacy, of momentum and effectiveness, of civility and values.

Leaders should leave behind them assets and a legacy. First, consider assets; certainly leaders owe assets. Leaders owe their institutions vital financial health, and the relationships and reputation that enable continuity of that financial health. Leaders must deliver to their organizations the appropriate services, products, tools, and equipment that people in the organization need in order to be accountable. In many institutions leaders are responsible for providing land and facilities.

But what else do leaders *owe?* What are artful leaders responsible for? Surely we need to include people. People are the heart and spirit of all that counts. Without people, there is no need for leaders. Leaders can decide to be primarily concerned with leaving assets to their institutional heirs or they can go beyond that and capitalize on the opportunity to leave a legacy, a legacy that takes into account the more difficult, qualitative side of life, one which provides greater meaning, more challenge, and more joy in the lives of those whom leaders enable.

Besides owing assets to their institutions, leaders owe the people in those institutions certain things. Leaders need to be concerned with the institutional value system which, after all, leads to the principles and standards that guide the practices of the people in the institution. Leaders owe a clear statement of the values of the organization. These values should be broadly understood and agreed to and should shape our corporate and individual behavior. What is this value system based on? How is it expressed? How is it audited? These are not easy questions to deal with.

Leaders are also responsible for future leadership. They need to identify, develop, and nurture future leaders.

Leaders are responsible for such things as a sense of quality in the institution, for whether or not the institution is open to influence and open to change. Effective leaders encourage contrary opinions, an important source of vitality. I am talking about how leaders can nurture the roots of an institution, about a sense of continuity, about institutional culture.

Leaders owe a covenant to the corporation or institution, which is, after all, a group of people. Leaders owe the organization a new reference point for what caring, purposeful, committed people can be in the institutional setting. Notice I did not say what people can do—what we can do is merely a consequence of what we can be. Corporations, like the people who compose them, are always in a state of becoming. Covenants bind people together and enable them to meet their corporate needs by meeting the needs of one another. We must do this in a way that is consonant with the world around us.

Leaders owe a certain maturity. Maturity as expressed in a sense of self-worth, a sense of belonging, a sense of expectancy, a sense of responsibility, a sense of accountability, and a sense of equality.

Leaders owe the corporation rationality. Rationality gives reason and mutual understanding to programs and to relationships. It gives visible order. Excellence and commitment and competence are available to us only under the rubric of rationality. A rational environment values trust and human dignity and provides the opportunity for personal development and self-fulfillment in the attainment of the organization's goals.

Business literacy, understanding the economic basic of a corporation, is essential. Only a group of people who share a body of knowledge and continually learn together can stay vital and viable.

Leaders owe people space, space in the sense of freedom. Freedom in the sense of enabling our gifts to be exercised. We need to give each other the space to grow, to be ourselves, to exercise our diversity. We need to give each other space so that we may both *give* and *receive* such beautiful things as ideas, openness, dignity, joy, healing, and inclusion. And in giving each other the gift of space, we need also to offer the gifts of grace and beauty to which each of us is entitled.

Another way to think about what leaders owe is to ask this question: What is it, without which this institution would not be what it is?

Leaders are obligated to provide and maintain momentum. Leadership comes with a lot of debts to the future. There are more immediate obligations as well. Momentum is one. Momentum in a vital company is palpable. It is not abstract or mysterious. It is the feeling among a group of people that their lives and work are intertwined and moving toward a recognizable and legitimate goal. It begins with competent leadership and a management team strongly dedicated to aggressive managerial development and opportunities. This team's job is to provide an environment that allows momentum to gather.

Momentum comes from a clear vision of what the corporation ought to be, from a well-thought-out strategy to achieve that vision, and from carefully conceived and communicated directions and plans which enable everyone to participate and be publicly accountable in achieving those plans.

Momentum depends on a pertinent but flexible research and development program led by people with outstanding gifts and unique talents. Momentum results when a corporation has an aggressive, professional, inspired group of people in its marketing and sales units. Momentum results when the operations group serves its customers in such a way that the customer sees them as their best supplier of tools, equipment, and services. Underlying these complex activities is the essential role of the financial team. They provide the financial guidelines and the necessary ratios. They are responsible for equity among the various groups who compose the corporate family.

Leaders are responsible for effectiveness. Much has been written about effectiveness—some of the best of it by Peter Drucker. He has such a great ability to simplify concepts. One of the things he tells us is that efficiency is doing the thing right, but effectiveness is doing the right thing.

Leaders can delegate efficiency, but they must deal personally with effectiveness. Of course, the natural question is "how." We could fill many pages dealing with how to be effective, but I would like to touch on just two ways.

The first is the understanding that effectiveness comes about through enabling others to reach their potential—both their personal potential and their corporate or institutional potential.

In some South Pacific cultures, a speaker holds a conch shell as a symbol of a temporary position of authority. Leaders must understand who holds the conch—that is, who should be listened to and when. This makes it possible for people to use their gifts to the fullest for the benefit of everyone.

Sometimes, to be sure, a leader must choose who is to speak. That is part of the risk of leadership. A leader must assess capability. A leader must be a judge of people. For leaders choose a person, not a position.

Another way to improve effectiveness is to encourage roving leadership. Roving leadership arises and expresses itself at varying times and in varying situations, according to the dictates of those situations. Roving leaders have the special gifts, or the special strengths, or the special temperament to lead in these special situations. They are acknowledged by others who are ready to follow them.

Leaders must take a role in developing, expressing, and defending civility and values. In a civilized institution or corporation, we see good manners, respect for persons, an understanding of "good goods," and an appreciation of the way in which we serve each other.

Civility has to do with identifying values as opposed to following fashions. Civility might be defined as an ability to distinguish between what is actually healthy and what merely appears to be living. A leader can tell the difference between living edges and dying ones.

To lose sight of the beauty of ideas and of hope and opportunity, and to frustrate the right to be needed, is to be at the dying edge.

To be a part of a throwaway mentality that discards goods and ideas, that discards principles and law, that discards persons and families, is to be at the dying edge.

To be at the leading edge of consumption, affluence, and instant gratification is to be at the dying edge.

To ignore the dignity of work and the elegance of simplicity, and the essential responsibility of serving each other, is to be at the dying edge.

Justice Oliver Wendell Holmes is reported to have said this about simplicity, "I would not give a fig for the simplicity this side of complexity, but I would give my life for the simplicity on the other side of complexity." To be at the living edge is to search out the "simplicity on the other side of complexity."

In a day when so much energy seems to be spent on maintenance and manuals, on bureaucracy and meaningless quantification, to be a leader is to enjoy the special privileges of complexity, of ambiguity, of diversity. But to be a leader means, especially, having the opportunity to make a meaningful difference in the lives of those who permit leaders to lead.

o   o   o

Max De Pree is chairman emeritus of Herman Miller, Inc., and is a member of *Fortune* magazine's Business Hall of Fame.

Chapter Six

The Five Practices of Exemplary Leadership

James M. Kouzes
Barry Z. Posner

Through our studies of personal-best leadership experiences, we've discovered that ordinary people who guide others along pioneering journeys follow rather similar paths. Though each case we looked at was unique in expression, each path was also marked by some common patterns of action. Leadership is not at all about personality; it's about practice. We've forged these common practices into a model of leadership, and we offer it here as guidance for leaders to follow as they attempt to keep their own bearings and guide others toward peak achievements.

Introducing the Five Practices

As we looked deeper into the dynamic process of leadership, through case analyses and survey questionnaires, we uncovered five practices common to personal-best leadership experiences. When getting extraordinary things done in organizations, leaders engage in these Five Practices of Exemplary Leadership:

- Model the Way.
- Inspire a Shared Vision.
- Challenge the Process.
- Enable Others to Act.
- Encourage the Heart.

These practices aren't the private property of the people we studied or of a few select shining stars. They're available to anyone, in any organization or situation, who accepts the leadership challenge. And they're not the accident of a special moment in history. They've stood the test of time, and our most recent research confirms that they're just as relevant today as they were when we first began our investigation over two decades ago—if not more so.

Model the Way

Titles are granted, but it's your behavior that wins you respect. As Gayle Hamilton, a director with Pacific Gas & Electric Company, told us, "I would never ask anyone to do anything I was unwilling to do first." This sentiment was shared across all the cases that we collected. Exemplary leaders know that if they want to gain commitment and achieve the highest standards, they must be models of the behavior they expect of others. Leaders model the way.

To effectively model the behavior they expect of others, leaders must first be clear about their guiding principles. Lindsay

Levin says, "You have to open up your heart and let people know what you really think and believe. This means talking about your values." Alan Keith adds that one of the most significant leadership lessons he would pass along is, "You must lead from what you believe." Leaders must find their own voice, and then they must clearly and distinctively give voice to their values. As the personal-best stories illustrate, leaders are supposed to stand up for their beliefs, so they'd better have some beliefs to stand up for.

Eloquent speeches about common values, however, aren't nearly enough. Leaders' deeds are far more important than their words when determining how serious they really are about what they say. Words and deeds must be consistent. Exemplary leaders go first. They go first by setting the example through daily actions that demonstrate they are deeply committed to their beliefs. Toni-Ann Lueddecke, for example, believes that there are no unimportant tasks in an organization's efforts at excellence. She demonstrates this to her associates in her eight Gymboree Play & Music centers in New Jersey by her actions. As just one example, she sometimes scrubs floors in addition to teaching classes.

The personal-best projects we heard about in our research were all distinguished by relentless effort, steadfastness, competence, and attention to detail. We were also struck by how the actions leaders took to set an example were often simple things. Sure, leaders had operational and strategic plans. But the examples they gave were not about elaborate designs. They were about the power of spending time with someone, of working side by side with colleagues, of telling stories that made values come alive, of being highly visible during times of uncertainty, and of asking questions to get people to think about values and priorities. Modeling the way is essentially about earning the right and the respect to lead through direct individual involvement and action. People first follow the person, then the plan.

Inspire a Shared Vision

When people described to us their personal-best leadership experiences, they told of times when they imagined an exciting, highly attractive future for their organization. They had visions and dreams of what could be. They had absolute and total personal belief in those dreams, and they were confident in their abilities to make extraordinary things happen. Every organization, every social movement, begins with a dream. The dream or vision is the force that invents the future.

Leaders inspire a shared vision. They gaze across the horizon of time, imagining the attractive opportunities that are in store when they and their constituents arrive at a distant destination. Leaders have a desire to make something happen, to change the way things are, to create something that no one else has ever created before. In some ways, leaders live their lives backward. They see pictures in their mind's eye of what the results will look like even before they've started their project, much as an architect draws a blueprint or an engineer builds a model. Their clear image of the future pulls them forward. Yet visions seen only by leaders are insufficient to create an organized movement or a significant change in a company. A person with no constituents is not a leader, and people will not follow until they accept a vision as their own. Leaders cannot command commitment, only inspire it.

To enlist people in a vision, leaders must know their constituents and speak their language. People must believe that leaders understand their needs and have their interests at heart.

Leadership is a dialogue, not a monologue. To enlist support, leaders must have intimate knowledge of people's dreams, hopes, aspirations, visions, and values.

Leaders breathe life into the hopes and dreams of others and enable them to see the exciting possibilities that the future holds. Leaders forge a unity of purpose by showing constituents how the dream is for the common good. Leaders ignite the flame of passion in others by expressing enthusiasm for the compelling vision of their group. Leaders communicate their passion through vivid language and an expressive style.

And leaders are in all places. When he was named captain of the soccer team as a high school junior, Dave Praklet knew he would have to do something to inspire his teammates to always give 110 percent. As he explained to us: "I had to get personal with them and tell them how good it feels to win a league championship. Or how good it feels as you step on the field for a championship game—how the adrenaline sends a tingling feeling through your entire body. Recounting these memorable moments helped me inspire the team to want to work hard. They wanted to see what it feels like and play with your heart."

Whatever the venue, and without exception, the people in our study reported that they were incredibly enthusiastic about their personal-best projects. Their own enthusiasm was catching; it spread from leader to constituents. Their belief in and enthusiasm for the vision were the sparks that ignited the flame of inspiration.

Challenge the Process

Leaders venture out. None of the individuals in our study sat idly by waiting for fate to smile upon them. "Luck" or "being in the right place at the right time" may play a role in the specific opportunities leaders embrace, but those who lead others to greatness seek and accept challenge.

Every single personal-best leadership case we collected involved some kind of challenge. The challenge might have been an innovative new product, a cutting-edge service, a groundbreaking piece of legislation, an invigorating campaign to get adolescents to join an environmental program, a revolutionary turnaround of a bureaucratic military program, or the start-up of a new plant or business. Whatever the challenge, all the cases involved a change from the status quo. Not one person claimed to have achieved a personal best by keeping things the same. All leaders challenge the process.

Leaders are pioneers—people who are willing to step out into the unknown. They search for opportunities to innovate, grow, and improve. But leaders aren't the only creators or originators of new products, services, or processes. In fact, it's more likely that they're not: innovation comes more from listening than from telling. Product and service innovations tend to come from customers, clients, vendors, people in the labs, and people on the front lines; process innovations, from the people doing the work. Sometimes a dramatic external event thrusts an organization into a radically new condition.

The leader's primary contribution is in the recognition of good ideas, the support of those ideas, and the willingness to challenge the system to get new products, processes, services, and systems adopted. It might be more accurate, then, to say that leaders are early adopters of innovation.

Leaders know well that innovation and change all involve experimentation, risk, and failure. They proceed anyway. One way of dealing with the potential risks and failures of experimentation is to approach change through incremental steps and small wins. Little victories, when piled on top of each other, build confidence that even the biggest challenges can be met. In so doing, they strengthen commitment to the long-term future. Yet not everyone is equally comfortable with risk and uncertainty. Leaders also pay attention to the capacity of their constituents to take control of challenging situations and become fully committed to change. You can't exhort people to take risks if they don't also feel safe.

It would be ridiculous to assert that those who fail over and over again eventually succeed as leaders. Success in any endeavor isn't a process of simply buying enough lottery tickets. The key that unlocks the door to opportunity is learning. In his own study of exemplary leadership practices, Warren Bennis writes that "leaders learn by leading, and they learn best by leading in the face of obstacles. As weather shapes mountains, problems shape leaders. Difficult bosses, lack of vision and virtue in the executive suite, circumstances beyond their control, and their own mistakes have been the leaders' basic curriculum."[1] In other words, leaders are learners. They learn from their failures as well as their successes.

Enable Others to Act

Grand dreams don't become significant realities through the actions of a single person. Leadership is a team effort. After reviewing thousands of personal-best cases, we developed a simple test to detect whether someone is on the road to becoming a leader. That test is the frequency of the use of the word we. In our interview with Alan Keith, for instance, he used the word "we" nearly three times more often than the word "I" in explaining his personal-best leadership experience.

Exemplary leaders enable others to act. They foster collaboration and build trust. This sense of teamwork goes far beyond a few direct reports or close confidants. They engage all those who must make the project work—and in some way, all who must live with the results. In today's "virtual" organization, cooperation can't be restricted to a small group of loyalists; it must include peers, managers, customers and clients, suppliers, citizens—all those who have a stake in the vision.

Leaders make it possible for others to do good work. They know that those who are expected to produce the results must feel a sense of personal power and ownership. Leaders understand that the command-and-control techniques of the Industrial Revolution no longer apply. Instead, leaders work to make people feel strong, capable, and committed. Leaders enable others to act not by hoarding the power they have but by giving it away. Exemplary leaders strengthen everyone's capacity to deliver on the promises they make. As a budget analyst for Catholic Healthcare West, Cindy Giordano would ask "What do you think?" and use the ensuing discussion to build up the capabilities of others (as well as educate and update her own information and perspective). She discovered that when people are trusted and have more discretion, more authority, and more information, they're much more likely to use their energies to produce extraordinary results.

In the cases we analyzed, leaders proudly discussed teamwork, trust, and empowerment as essential elements of their efforts. A leader's ability to enable others to act is essential. Constituents neither perform at their best nor stick around for very long if their leader makes them feel weak, dependent, or alienated. But when a leader makes people feel strong and capable—as if they can do more than they ever thought possible—they'll give it their all and exceed their own expectations. When leadership is a relationship founded on trust and confidence, people take risks, make changes, keep organizations and movements alive. Through that relationship, leaders turn their constituents into leaders themselves.

Encourage the Heart

The climb to the top is arduous and long. People become exhausted, frustrated, and disenchanted. They're often tempted to give up. Leaders encourage the heart of their constituents to carry on. Genuine acts of caring uplift the spirits and draw people forward. Encouragement can come from dramatic gestures or simple actions. When Cary Turner was head of Pier 1 Imports' Stores division, he once showed up in a wedding gown to promote the bridal registry. On another occasion, he promised store employees he'd parasail over Puget Sound and the Seattle waterfront if they met their sales targets. They kept their commitment; he kept his. As mayor of New York City, Rudy Giuliani wore different hats (literally) to acknowledge various groups of rescue workers as he toured ground zero after the World Trade Center towers were destroyed on September 11, 2001. But it doesn't take events or media coverage to let people know you appreciate their contributions. Terri Sarhatt, customer services manager at Applied Biosystems, looked after her employees so well that at least one reported that the time she spent with them was more valuable than the tangible rewards she was able to give out.

It's part of the leader's job to show appreciation for people's contributions and to create a culture of celebration. In the cases we collected, we saw thousands of examples of individual recognition and group celebration. We've heard and seen everything from handwritten thank-yous to marching bands and "This Is Your Life" ceremonies.

Recognition and celebration aren't about fun and games, though there is a lot of fun and there are a lot of games when people encourage the hearts of their constituents. Neither are they about pretentious ceremonies designed to create some phony sense of camaraderie. When people see a charlatan making noisy affectations, they turn away in disgust. Encouragement is curiously serious business. It's how leaders visibly and behaviorally link rewards with performance. When striving to raise quality, recover from disaster, start up a new service, or make dramatic change of any kind, leaders make sure people see the benefit of behavior that's aligned with cherished values. And leaders also know that celebrations and rituals, when done with authenticity and from the heart, build a strong sense of collective identity and community spirit that can carry a group through extraordinarily tough times.

Leadership Is a Relationship

Leadership is an identifiable set of skills and practices that are available to all of us, not just a few charismatic men and women. The "great person"—woman or man—theory of leadership is just plain wrong. Or, we should say, the theory that there are only a few great men and women who can lead us to greatness is just plain wrong. We consider the women and men in our research to be great, and so do those with whom they worked.

They are the everyday heroes of our world. It's because we have so many—not so few—leaders that we are able to get extraordinary things done on a regular basis, even in extraordinary times.

Our findings also challenge the myth that leadership is something that you find only at the highest levels of organizations and society. We found it everywhere. To us this is inspiring and should give everyone hope. Hope, because it means that no one needs to wait around to be saved by someone riding into town on a white horse. Hope, because there's a generation of leaders searching for the opportunities to make a difference. Hope, because right down the block or right down the hall there are people who will seize the opportunity to lead you to greatness. They're your neighbors, friends, and colleagues. And you are one of them, too.

There's still another crucial truth about leadership—more apparent to us this time around than it was before. It's something that we've known for a long time, but we've come to prize its value even more today. In talking to leaders and reading their cases, there was a very clear message that wove itself throughout every situation and every action: leadership is a relationship. Leadership is a relationship between those who aspire to lead and those who choose to follow.

Evidence abounds for this point of view. For instance, in examining the critical variables for success in the top three jobs in large organizations, Jodi Taylor and her colleagues at the Center for Creative Leadership found the number one success factor to be "relationships with subordinates."[2] We were intrigued to find that even in this nanosecond world of e-everything, opinion is consistent with the facts. In an on-line survey, respondents were asked to indicate, among other things, which would be more essential to business success in five years—social skills or skills in using the Internet. Seventy-two percent selected social skills; 28 percent, Internet skills.[3] Internet literati completing a poll on-line realize that it's not the web of technology that matters the most, it's the web of people.

Similar results were found in a study by Public Allies, an AmeriCorps organization dedicated to creating young leaders who can strengthen their communities. Public Allies sought the opinions of eighteen- to thirty-year-olds on the subject of leadership. Among the items was a question about the qualities that were important in a good leader. Topping the respondents' list is "Being able to see a situation from someone else's point of view." In second place, "Getting along well with other people."[4]

Success in leadership, success in business, and success in life has been, is now, and will continue to be a function of how well people work and play together. We're even more convinced of this today than we were twenty years ago. Success in leading will be wholly dependent upon the capacity to build and sustain those human relationships that enable people to get extraordinary things done on a regular basis.

The Ten Commitments of Leadership

Embedded in the Five Practices of Exemplary Leadership are behaviors that can serve as the basis for learning to lead. We call these the Ten Commitments of Leadership (see Exhibit 6.1). These ten commitments serve as the guide for our discussion of how leaders get extraordinary things done in organizations.

EXHIBIT 6.1 The Five Practices and Ten Commitments of Leadership

Practice	Commitment
Model the Way	1. Find your voice by clarifying your personal values.
	2. Set the example by aligning actions with shared values.
Inspire a Shared Vision	3. Envision the future by imagining exciting and ennobling possibilities.
	4. Enlist others in a common vision by appealing to shared aspirations.
Challenge the Process	5. Search for opportunities by seeking innovative ways to change, grow, and improve.
	6. Experiment and take risks by constantly generating small wins and learning from mistakes.
Enable Others to Act	7. Foster collaboration by promoting cooperative goals and building trust.
	8. Strengthen others by sharing power and discretion.
Encourage the Heart	9. Recognize contributions by showing appreciation for individual excellence.
	10. Celebrate the values and victories by creating a spirit of community.

o   o   o

James M. Kouzes is chairman emeritus of the Tom Peters Company, executive fellow at the Leavey School of Business, Santa Clara University, and a leadership speaker.

Barry Z. Posner is dean and professor at the Leavey School of Business, Santa Clara University. He is also a speaker and executive development program leader.

Leadership Styles

Chapter Seven

Reframing Leadership

Lee G. Bolman
Terrence E. Deal

Leadership is universally offered as a panacea for almost any social problem. Around the world, middle managers say their enterprises would thrive if only senior management provided "real leadership." A widely accepted canon holds that leadership is a very good thing that we need more of—at least, more of the right kind. "For many—perhaps for most—Americans, leadership is a word that has risen above normal workaday usage as a conveyer of meaning and has become a kind of incantation. We feel that if we repeat it often enough with sufficient ardor, we shall ease our sense of having lost our way, our sense of things unaccomplished, of duties unfulfilled" (Gardner, 1986, p. 1). Yet there is much confusion and disagreement about what leadership really means.

Sennett (1980, p. 197) writes, "Authority is not a thing; it is a search for solidity and security in the strength of others which will seem to be like a thing." The same is true of leadership. It is not a tangible thing. It exists only in relationships and in the imagination and perception of the engaged parties. Most images of leadership suggest that leaders get things done and get people to do things: leaders are powerful. Yet many examples of the exercise of power fall outside our images of leadership: armed robbers, extortionists, bullies, traffic cops. Implicitly, we expect leaders to persuade or inspire rather than to coerce or give orders. We also expect leaders to produce cooperative efforts and to pursue goals that transcend their own narrow self-interest.

Leadership is also distinct from authority, though authorities may be leaders. Weber (1947) linked authority to legitimacy. People voluntarily obey authority so long as they believe it is legitimate. Authority and leadership are both built on legitimacy and voluntary obedience. When leaders lose legitimacy, they lose the capacity to lead. Obedience to leaders is primarily voluntary rather than forced. But many examples of obeying authority fall outside the domain of leadership. As Gardner (1989, p. 7) put it, "The meter maid has authority, but not necessarily leadership."

Heifetz (1994) argues that authority is often an impediment to leadership: "Authority constrains leadership because in times of distress, people expect too much. They form inappropriate dependencies that isolate their authorities behind a mask of knowing. [The leadership role] is played badly if authorities reinforce dependency and delude themselves into thinking that they have the answers when they do not. Feeling pressured to know, they will surely come up with an answer, even if poorly tested, misleading, and wrong" (p. 180).

Leadership is also different from management, though the two are typically confused. One may be a leader without being a manager, and many managers could not "lead a squad of seven-year-olds to the ice-cream counter" (Gardner, 1989, p. 2). Bennis and Nanus (1985) offer the distinction that "managers do things right, and leaders do the right thing" (p. 21). Kotter (1988) views management as primarily being about structural nuts and bolts: planning, organizing, and controlling. He views leadership as a change-oriented process of visioning, networking, and building relationships. Gardner (1989) argues against contrasting leadership and management too sharply because leaders may "end up looking like a cross between Napoleon and the Pied Piper, and managers like unimaginative clods" (p. 3). He suggests several dimensions for distinguishing leadership from management. Leaders think longer-term, look outside as well as inside, and influence constituents beyond their immediate formal jurisdictions. They emphasize vision and renewal and have the political skills to cope with the challenging requirements of multiple constituencies.

It is hard to imagine an outstanding manager who is not also a leader. But it is misleading and elitist to imagine that leadership is provided *only* by people in high positions. Such a view causes us to ask too much of too few. Popular images of John Wayne, Bruce Lee, and Sylvester Stallone provide a distorted and romanticized view of how leaders function. We need *more* leaders as well as *better* leadership.

Leadership Context

Traditional notions of the solitary, heroic leader have led us to focus too much on the actors and too little on the stage they play their parts on. Leaders make things happen, but things also make leaders happen. Context influences both what leaders must do and what they can do. No single formula is possible or advisable for the great range of situations that potential leaders encounter.

Heroic images of leadership convey the notion of a one-way process: leaders lead and followers follow. This view blinds us to the reality of a relationship between leaders and their followers. Leaders are not independent actors. They both shape and are shaped by their constituents (Gardner, 1989; Simmel, 1950). Leaders often promote a new idea or initiative only *after* large numbers of their constituents already favor it (Cleveland, 1985). Leadership is not simply a matter of what a leader does but also of what occurs in a relationship. Leaders' actions generate responses from others that in turn affect the leaders' capacity for taking further initiatives (Murphy, 1985). As Briand (1993, p. 39) puts it, "A 'leader' who makes a decision and then attempts to 'sell' it to the public is not a wise leader and will likely not prove an effective one. The point is not that those who are already leaders should do less, but that everyone else can and should do more. Everyone must accept responsibility for the people's well-being, and everyone has a role to play in sustaining it."

It is common to equate leadership with position, but this relegates all those in the "lowerarchy" to the passive role of follower. It also reinforces the widespread tendency of senior executives to take on more responsibility than they can adequately discharge (Oshry, 1995). Administrators are leaders only to the extent that others grant them cooperation and follow their lead. Conversely, one can be a leader without a position of formal authority. Good organizations encourage leadership from many quarters (Kanter, 1983; Barnes and Kriger, 1986).

Leadership is thus a subtle process of mutual influence fusing thought, feeling, and action to produce cooperative effort in the service of purposes and values of *both* the leader and the led.

REFRAMING LEADERSHIP

Reframing offers a way to get beyond narrow and oversimplified views of leadership. Each of the frames offers a distinctive image of the leadership process. Depending on leader and circumstance, each can lead to compelling and constructive leadership, but none is right for all times and seasons. We will discuss the four images of leadership summarized in Table 7.1. For each, we examine skills and processes and provide rules of thumb for successful leadership practice.

ARCHITECTS OR TYRANTS? STRUCTURAL LEADERSHIP

Structural leadership often evokes images of petty tyrants and rigid bureaucrats who never met a rule they didn't like. In contrast to other frames, little literature exists on structural leadership. Many structural theorists have argued that leadership is neither important nor basic (Hall, 1987). But the effects of structural leadership can be powerful and enduring, if more subtle and less obviously heroic, than other forms. Collins and Porras (1994) found that the founders of many highly successful companies—such as Hewlett-Packard and Sony—had neither a clear vision for their organization nor even a particular product in mind. They were "clockbuilders"—social architects who focused on designing and building an effective organization. One of the greatest architects was Alfred P. Sloan Jr.

TABLE 7.1 **Reframing Leadership**

	Effective Leadership		Ineffective Leadership	
Frame	Leader	Leadership Process	Leader	Leadership Process
Structural	Analyst, architect	Analysis, design	Petty tyrant	Management by detail and fiat
Human resource	Catalyst, servant	Support, empowerment	Weakling, pushover	Abdication
Political	Advocate, negotiator	Advocacy, coalition building	Con artist, thug	Manipulation, fraud
Symbolic	Prophet poet	Inspiration, framing experience	Fanatic, fool	Mirage, smoke and mirrors

Sloan, who became president of General Motors in 1923, was a dominant force in the company until his 1956 retirement. The structure and strategy he established made GM the world's largest corporation. He has been described as "the George Washington of the GM culture" (Lee, 1988, p. 42), even though his "genius was not in inspirational leadership, but in organizational structures" (p. 43).

At the turn of the twentieth century, there were some thirty manufacturers of automobiles in the United States. In 1899, they produced a grand total of about six hundred cars. Most of these small carmakers stumbled shortly out of the starting gate, leaving two late entries, the Ford Motor Company (founded by Henry Ford in 1903) and GM (founded by William Durant in 1908) as front-runners in the race to dominate the American automobile industry. Henry Ford's single-minded determination to build an affordable car had Ford in a commanding lead when Sloan took over General Motors.

Under GM's founder, Billy Durant, the company's divisions operated as independent fiefdoms. Uncontrolled costs and a business slump in 1920 created a financial crisis—Chevrolet lost $5 million in 1921, and only Du Pont money and Buick's profitability kept GM afloat (Sloan, 1965). In Sloan's first year, matters got worse. GM's market share dropped from 20 percent to 17 percent, while Ford's increased to 55 percent. But things were about to change. Henry Ford had a disdain for organization and clung to his original vision of a single, low-priced, mass-market car. The Model T was cheap and reliable, and Ford stayed with the same design for almost twenty years. That worked fine in the early years when customers would buy anything with four wheels and a motor. Whereas Ford saw no great need for creature comforts in the Model T, Sloan surmised that consumers would pay more for amenities like windows to keep out rain and snow. His strategy worked, and Chevrolet soon began to gnaw off large chunks of Ford's market. By 1928, Model T sales had dropped so precipitously that Henry Ford was forced to close his River Rouge plant for a year to retool. General Motors took the lead in the great auto race for the first time in twenty years. In the next seventy years, no one ever sold more cars than General Motors.

Durant had built GM by buying everything in sight, thus forming a loose combination of previously independent firms. "GM did not have adequate knowledge or control of the individual operating divisions. It was management by crony, with the divisions operating on a horse-trading basis. The main thing to note here is that no one had the needed information or the needed control over the divisions. The divisions continued to spend lavishly, and their requests for additional funds were met" (Sloan, 1965, pp. 27–28).

Sloan recognized that GM needed a better structural form. The primary option at the time was a centralized, functional organization, but Sloan felt that such a structure would not work for GM. Instead, he created one of the world's first decentralized organizations. His strategy was simple: centralize planning and resource allocation; decentralize operating decisions. Under Sloan's model, divisions focused on making and selling cars, while top management focused on long-range strategy and the allocation of resources. The central staff made sure that top management had the information and control systems it needed to make strategic decisions.

The structure worked. By the late 1920s, Sloan headed a more versatile organization with a broader product line than Ford. With Henry Ford still dominating his highly centralized company, Ford was poorly positioned to compete with GM's multiple divisions, each producing different cars at different prices. GM pioneered a structural form that eventually set the standard for others: "Although they developed many variations and although in very recent years they have been occasionally mixed into a matrix form, only two basic organizational structures have been used for the management of large industrial enterprises. One is the centralized, functional departmentalized type perfected by General Electric and Du Pont before World War I. The other is the multidivisional, decentralized structure initially developed at General Motors and also at Du Pont in the 1920s" (Chandler, 1977, p. 463).

In the 1980s, GM found itself with another structural leader at the helm, Roger Smith. But the results were less satisfying. Like Sloan, Smith ascended to the top job at a difficult time. In 1980, his first year as GM's chief executive, all American automakers lost money. It was GM's first loss since 1921. Recognizing that the company had serious competitive problems, Smith relied on structure and technology to make it "the world's first 21st century corporation" (Lee, 1988, p. 16). He restructured vehicle operations and spent billions of dollars in a quest for paperless offices and robotized assembly plants. The changes were dramatic, but the results were not:

> *[Smith's] tenure has been a tragic era in General Motors history. No GM chairman has disrupted as many lives without commensurate rewards, has spent as much money without returns, or has alienated so many along the way. An endless string of public relations and internal relations insensitivities has confused his organization and complicated the attainment of its goals. Few employees believe that [Smith] is in the least concerned with their well-being, and even fewer below executive row anticipate any measure of respect, or reward, for their contributions. No GM chief executive's motives have ever been as universally questioned or his decisions as thoroughly mistrusted [Lee, 1988, pp. 286–287].*

Why did Sloan succeed but Smith have trouble? They were about equally uncharismatic. Sloan was a somber, quiet engineer who habitually looked as if he were sucking a lemon. Smith's leadership aura was not helped by his blotchy complexion and squeaky voice. Neither had great sensitivity to human resource or symbolic issues. Why was Sloan's structural contribution so durable and Smith's so problematic? The answer comes down to how well each implemented the right structural form. Structural leaders succeed not because of inspiration but because they have the right design for the times and are able to get their structural changes implemented. Effective structural leaders share several characteristics.

1. *Structural leaders do their homework.* Sloan was a brilliant engineer who had grown up in the auto industry. Before coming to GM, he was chief executive of an auto accessories company where he had implemented a divisional structure. When GM bought his firm in 1916, Sloan became a vice president and board member. Working under Durant, he devoted much of his energy to studying GM's structural problems. He pioneered the development of sophisticated internal information systems and better market research. He was an early convert to group decision making and created a committee structure to make major decisions. Roger Smith had spent his entire career with General Motors, but most of his jobs were in finance. Much of his vision for General Motors involved changes in production technology, an area where he had little experience or expertise.

2. *Structural leaders rethink the relationship of structure, strategy, and environment.* Sloan's new structure was intimately tied to a strategy for reaching the automotive market. He foresaw a growing market, improvements in automobiles, and more discriminating consumers. In the face of Henry Ford's stubborn attachment to the Model T, Sloan introduced the "price pyramid" (a different car for every pocketbook) and the annual model change. Automotive technology in the 1920s was evolving almost as fast as electronics in the 1990s, and the annual model change soon became the industry norm.

For a variety of reasons, GM in the 1960s began to move away from Sloan's concepts. Fearing a government effort to break up the corporation, GM reduced the independence of the car divisions and centralized design and engineering. Increasingly, divisions became marketing groups required to build and sell cars the corporation designed for them. In the early 1980s, "look-alike cars" became the standard across divisions. Many consumers became confused and angry when they found it hard to see the subtle differences between a Chevrolet and a Cadillac.

Smith's vision focused more on costs and technology than on marketing. As he saw it, GM's primary competitive problem was high costs driven by high wages. He gave little support to efforts already under way at GM to improve working conditions on the shop floor. He saw technology, not human resource management, as the wave of the future. Ironically, his two best investments—NUMMI and Saturn—succeeded precisely because of innovative approaches to managing people. "With only a fraction of the money invested in GM's heavily robotized plants, [the NUMMI plant at] Fremont is more efficient and produces better-quality cars than any plant in the GM system" (Hampton and Norman, 1987, p. 102).

3. *Structural leaders focus on implementation.* Structural leaders often miscalculate the difficulty of putting their design in place. They underestimate resistance, skimp on training, neglect the process of building a political base, and misread cultural cues. As a result, they are often thwarted by neglected human resource, political, and symbolic barriers. Sloan was no human resource specialist, but he intuitively saw the need to get understanding and acceptance of major decisions. He did that by continually asking for advice and by establishing committees and task forces to address major issues.

4. *Effective structural leaders experiment, evaluate, and adapt.* Sloan tinkered constantly with GM's structure and strategy and encouraged others to do likewise. The Great Depression produced a drop of 72 percent in sales at GM between 1929 and 1932, but the company adapted very adroitly to hard times. It increased its market share and made money every year. Sloan briefly centralized operations to survive the Great Depression but decentralized again once business began to recover. In the 1980s, Smith spent billions on his campaign to modernize the corporation and cut costs, yet GM lost market share every year and continued to be the industry's highest-cost producer. "Much of the advanced technology that GM acquired at such high cost hindered rather than improved productivity. Runaway robots started welding doors shut at the new Detroit-Hamtramck Cadillac plant. Luckily for Ford and Chrysler, poverty prevented them from indulging in the same orgy of spending on robots" ("On a Clear Day. . .," 1989, p. 77).

CATALYSTS OR WIMPS? HUMAN RESOURCE LEADERSHIP

The tiny trickle of writing about structural leadership is swamped by a torrent of human resource literature (among the best: Argyris, 1962; Bennis and Nanus, 1985; Blanchard and Johnson, 1982; Bradford and Cohen, 1984; Fiedler, 1967; Fiedler and Chemers, 1974; Hersey, 1984; Hollander, 1978; House, 1971; Levinson, 1968; Likert, 1961, 1967; Vroom and Yetton, 1973; and Waterman, 1994). Human resource theorists typically advocate openness, mutuality, listening, coaching, participation, and empowerment. They view the leader as a facilitator and catalyst who motivates and empowers subordinates.

The leader's power comes from talent, sensitivity, and service rather than position or force. Greenleaf (1973) argues that followers "will freely respond only to individuals who are chosen as leaders because they are proven and trusted as servants" (p. 4). He adds, "The servant-leader makes sure that other people's highest priority needs are being served. The best test [of leadership] is: do those served grow as persons; do they, *while being served*, become healthier, wiser, freer, more autonomous, more likely themselves to become servants?" (p. 7).

Will managers who adhere to such images be respected leaders who make a difference? Or will they be seen as naive and weak, carried along on the current of other people's energy? The leadership tightrope is real, and some managers hide behind participation and sensitivity as excuses not to walk it. There are also many human resource leaders whose skill and artistry produce extraordinary results. They apply leadership principles such as the following:

1. *Human resource leaders believe in people and communicate their belief.* Human resource leaders are passionate about "productivity through people" (Peters and Waterman, 1982). They demonstrate this faith in their words and actions and often build it into a core philosophy or credo. Fred Smith, founder and CEO of Federal Express, sees "putting people first" as the cornerstone of his company's success: "We discovered a long time ago that customer satisfaction really begins with employee satisfaction. That belief is incorporated in our corporate philosophy statement: People—Service—Profit" (Waterman, 1994, p. 89).

William Hewlett, cofounder of the electronics giant Hewlett-Packard Corporation, put it this way:

The dignity and worth of the individual is a very impor-
tant part of the HP Way. With this in mind, many years
ago we did away with time clocks, and more recently we
introduced the flexible work hours program. This is meant
to be an expression of trust and confidence in people, as well
as providing them with an opportunity to adjust their work
schedules to their personal lives. Many new HP people as
well as visitors often note and comment to us about another
HP way—that is, our informality and our being on a first-
name basis. I could cite other examples, but the problem is
that none by [itself] really catches the essence of what the
HP Way is all about. You can't describe it in numbers and
statistics. In the last analysis, it is a spirit, a point of view.
There is a feeling that everyone is part of a team, and that
team is HP. It is an idea that is based on the individual
[Peters and Waterman, 1982, p. 244].

2. *Human resource leaders are visible and accessible.* Peters and
Waterman (1982) popularized the notion of "management by
wandering around"—the idea that managers need to get out of
their offices and spend time with workers and customers. Patri-
cia Carrigan, the first woman ever to be a plant manager at
General Motors, modeled this technique in the course of turning around two different GM plants, each with a long history
of union-management conflict (Kouzes and Posner, 1987). In
both situations, she began by going onto the plant floor to
introduce herself to workers and ask how they thought the plant
could be improved. One worker commented that before Carrigan came, "I didn't know who the plant manager was. I
wouldn't have recognized him if I saw him." When she left her
first assignment after three years, the local union gave her a
plaque. It concluded, "Be it resolved that Pat M. Carrigan,
through the exhibiting of these qualities as a people person, has

played a vital role in the creation of a new way of life at the Lakewood plant. Therefore, be it resolved that the members of Local 34 will always warmly remember Pat M. Carrigan as one of us" (Kouzes and Posner, 1987, p. 36).

3. *Effective human resource leaders empower others.* Human resource leaders often like to refer to their employees as "partners," "owners," or "associates." They make it clear that employees have a stake in the organization's success and a right to be involved in making decisions. Nordstrom has its "rule number one": "Use your good judgment in all situations; there will be no other rules" (Collins and Porras, 1994, p. 117). In the 1980s, Jan Carlzon, CEO of Scandinavian Air Systems (SAS), built a turnaround effort around making the airline "the best airline in the world for business travelers" (Carlzon, 1987, p. 46). To find out what the business traveler wanted, he turned to SAS's front-line service employees to collect their ideas and suggestions. Focus groups generated hundreds of ideas and emphasized the importance of front-line autonomy to decide on the spot what passengers needed. Carlzon concluded that SAS's image to its customers was built out of a series of "moments of truth"—fifteen-second encounters between employees and customers. "If we are truly dedicated toward orienting our company to each customer's individual needs, we cannot rely on rule books and instruction from distant corporate offices. We have to place responsibility for ideas, decisions, and actions with the people who are SAS during those 15 seconds. If they have to go up the organizational chain of command for a decision on an individual problem, then those 15 golden seconds will elapse without a response and we will have lost an opportunity to earn a loyal customer" (p. 66). The

French packaging giant Carnaud enjoyed enormous growth and success after Jean-Marie Descarpentries became its chief executive in 1982. Descarpentries said his approach to management was simple: "You catalyze toward the future, you trust people, and they discover things you never would have thought of" (Aubrey and Tilliette, 1990, p. 142).

ADVOCATES OR HUSTLERS? POLITICAL LEADERSHIP

Lee Iacocca's career at Ford Motor Company was a meteoric rise through a series of sales and marketing triumphs to become the company's president. Then, on July 1, 1978, his boss, Henry Ford II, fired him, reportedly with the simple explanation, "Let's just say I don't like you" (O'Toole, 1984, p. 231). Iacocca's unemployment was brief. Chrysler Corporation, desperate for new leadership, believed that Iacocca was the answer.

Even though Iacocca had done his homework before accepting Chrysler's offer, he encountered problems worse than he anticipated. Chrysler was losing money so fast that bankruptcy seemed almost inevitable. The only way out was to persuade the U.S. government to guarantee massive loans. It was a tough sell—much of Congress, the media, and the American public were against the idea. Iacocca had to convince all of them that government intervention was in their interest as well as Chrysler's. He pulled it off with a remarkable combination of personal artistry and adroit political maneuvering. He successfully employed a set of rules for political leaders.

1. *Political leaders clarify what they want and what they can get.* Political leaders are realists above all. They avoid letting what they want cloud their judgment about what is possible.

Chrysler's problem was survival. Iacocca translated that into the realistic goal of getting enough help to make it through a couple of difficult years without going under. Iacocca was careful to ask not for money but for loan guarantees. He insisted that government guarantees would cost the taxpayers nothing because Chrysler would pay the money back.

2. *Political leaders assess the distribution of power and interests.* They map the political terrain by thinking carefully about the players, their interests, and their power. They ask: Whose support do I need? How do I go about getting it? Who are my opponents? How much power do they have? What can I do to reduce or overcome their opposition? Is this battle winnable? Iacocca needed the support of Chrysler's employees and unions, but he knew that they had little choice. The key players were Congress and the public. Congress would vote for the guarantees only if Iacocca's proposal had sufficient popular support.

3. *Political leaders build linkages to key stakeholders.* They focus their attention on building relationships and networks. They recognize the value of personal contact and face-to-face conversations. Iacocca worked hard to build linkages with Congress, the media, and the public. He spent hours meeting with members of Congress and testifying before congressional committees. After he met with thirty-one Italian-American members of Congress, all but one voted for the loan guarantees. Said Iacocca, "Some were Republicans, some were Democrats, but in this case they voted the straight Italian ticket. We were desperate, and we had to play every angle. It was democracy in action" (Iacocca and Novak, 1984, p. 221).

Iacocca gave interviews to anyone in the media who would listen. He personally signed Chrysler's advertisements in newspapers and magazines and appeared on television to make Chrysler's case. Over time, he became one of America's best-known and most respected chief executives.

4. *Political leaders persuade first, negotiate second, and use coercion only if necessary.* Wise political leaders recognize that power is essential to their effectiveness; they also know to use it judiciously. William P. Kelly, an experienced public administrator, put it well: "Power is like the old Esso ad—a tiger in your tank. But you can't let the tiger out, you just let people hear him roar. You use power terribly sparingly because it has a short half-life. You let people know you have it and hope that you don't have to use it" (Ridout and Fenn, 1974, p. 10).

The sophisticated political leader knows that influence begins with an understanding of others' concerns and interests. What is important to them? How can I help them get what they want? Iacocca knew that he had to address the widespread belief that federal guarantees would throw millions of taxpayers' dollars down a rat hole. He used advertising to respond directly to public concerns. Does Chrysler have a future? Yes, he said, we've been here fifty-four years, and we'll be here another fifty-four years. Would the loan guarantees be a dangerous precedent? No, the government already had $400 billion in other loan guarantees on the books, and in any event, Chrysler was going to pay its loans back. "You can count on it!" he said over and over. Iacocca also spoke directly to congressional concerns. Chrysler prepared computer printouts showing how many jobs would be lost in every district if Chrysler were to go under.

Iacocca got his loan guarantees. Eight years later, in 1987, Chrysler reported earnings of more than $1 billion, ranking it eleventh among all U.S. corporations. The company survived and paid back the loans early.

Prophets or Zealots? Symbolic Leadership

The symbolic frame provides a fourth turn of the leadership kaleidoscope. This frame sees organizations as both theaters and temples. In the theater, every actor plays certain roles and tries to communicate the right impressions to the right audiences. As temple, organizations are communities of faith, bonded by shared beliefs, traditions, myths, rituals, and ceremonies.

Symbolically, leaders *interpret and reinterpret experience*. What are the real lessons of history? What is really happening in the world? What will the future bring? What mission is worthy of our loyalty and investment? Data and analysis provide few adequate answers to such questions. Symbolic leaders interpret experience so as to provide meaning and purpose through phrases of beauty and passion. Franklin D. Roosevelt reassured a nation in the midst of its deepest economic depression that "the only thing we have to fear is fear itself." At almost the same time, Adolph Hitler assured Germans that their severe economic and social problems were the result of betrayal by Jews and communists. Germans, he said, were a superior people who could still fulfill their nation's destiny of world mastery. Though many saw the destructive paranoia in Hitler's message, millions of fearful citizens were swept up in Hitler's bold vision of German ascendancy.

Burns (1978) was mindful of leaders such as Franklin Roosevelt, Mohandas Gandhi, and Martin Luther King Jr. when he drew a distinction between "transforming" and "transactional" leaders. According to Burns, transactional leaders "approach their followers with an eye to trading one thing for another: jobs for votes, subsidies for campaign contributions" (p. 4). Transforming leaders are rarer. As Burns describes them, they evoke their constituents' better nature and move them toward higher and more universal needs and purposes. They are visionary leaders, and visionary leadership is inherently symbolic. Symbolic leaders follow a consistent set of practices and rules.

1. *They use symbols to capture attention.* When Diana Lam became principal of the Mackey Middle School in Boston in 1985, she faced a substantial challenge. Mackey had the usual problems of urban schools: decaying physical plant, poor discipline, racial tension, disgruntled teachers, and limited resources (Kaufer and Leader, 1987a). In such a situation, symbolic leaders will do something visible and dramatic to signal that change is coming. During the summer before assuming her duties, Lam wrote a personal letter to every teacher requesting an individual meeting. She met teachers wherever they wanted, in one case driving two hours. She asked teachers how they felt about the school and what changes they wanted. She recruited members of her family as a crew to repaint the school's front door and some of the most decrepit classrooms. "When school opened, students and staff members immediately saw that things were going to be different, if only symbolically. Perhaps even more important, staff members received a subtle challenge to make a contribution themselves" (Kaufer and Leader, 1987b, p. 3).

When Lee Iacocca first became president of Chrysler, one of his first steps was to announce that he was reducing his salary from $360,000 to $1 a year. "I did it for good, cold pragmatic reasons. I wanted our employees and our suppliers to be thinking: 'I can follow a guy who sets that kind of example,'" Iacocca explained in his autobiography (Iacocca and Novak, 1984, pp. 229–230).

2. *Symbolic leaders frame experience.* In a world of uncertainty and ambiguity, a key function of symbolic leadership is to provide plausible interpretations of experience. Jan Carlzon mobilized front-line staff at SAS around the idea that each short encounter with a customer was a "moment of truth" (Carlzon, 1987). When Martin Luther King Jr. spoke at the March on Washington in 1963 and gave his extraordinary "I Have a Dream" speech, his opening line was, "I am happy to join with you today in what will go down in history as the greatest demonstration for freedom in the history of our nation." He could have interpreted the event in a number of other ways: "We are here because progress has been slow, but we are not ready to quit yet"; "We are here because nothing else has worked"; "We are here because it's summer and it's a good day to be outside." Each of those versions is about as accurate as the next, but accuracy is not the real issue. King's assertion was bold and inspiring; it told members of the audience that they were making history by their presence at a momentous event.

3. *Symbolic leaders discover and communicate a vision.* One of the most powerful ways in which leaders can interpret experience is by distilling and disseminating a vision—a persuasive and hopeful image of the future. A vision needs to address both

the challenges of the present and the hopes and values of followers. Vision is particularly important in times of crisis and uncertainty. When people are in pain, when they are confused and uncertain, or when they feel despair and hopelessness, they desperately seek meaning and hope.

Where does such vision come from? One view is that leaders create a vision and then persuade others to accept it (Bass, 1985; Bennis and Nanus, 1985). An alternative view is that leaders discover and articulate a vision that is already there, even if in an inchoate and unexpressed form (Cleveland, 1985). Kouzes and Posner (1987) put it well: "Corporate leaders know very well that what seeds the vision are those imperfectly formed images in the marketing department about what the customers really wanted and those inarticulate mumblings from the manufacturing folks about the poor product quality, not crystal ball gazing in upper levels of the corporate stratosphere. The best leaders are the best followers. They pay attention to those weak signals and quickly respond to changes in the corporate course" (p. 114).

Early in his career, Jan Carlzon had learned this lesson the hard way when he and a group of young executives designed a set of tour packages offering Swedish senior citizens just what Carlzon thought they wanted—safe, risk-free travel to familiar places. The product bombed because the seniors really wanted variety and adventure. For Carlzon it was a memorable lesson: listen to your customers and to the front-line staff who know them (Carlzon, 1987).

Leadership is a two-way street. No amount of charisma or rhetorical skill can sell a vision that reflects only the leader's values and needs—Carlzon's team had spent a fortune on beautiful color brochures to promote the doomed tour packages.

Effective symbolic leadership is possible only for leaders who understand the deepest values and most pressing concerns of their constituents. But leaders still play a critical role. They can bring a unique, personal blend of poetry, passion, conviction, and courage to the articulation of a vision. They can play a key role in distilling and shaping the vision to be pursued. Most important, they can choose which stories to tell as a means of communicating the vision.

4. *Symbolic leaders tell stories.* Often symbolic leaders embody their vision in a story—a story about "us" and about "our" past, present, and future. "Us" could be the Sorbonne, the Chrysler Corporation, the people of Thailand, or any other audience a leader hopes to reach. The past is usually a golden one, a time of noble purposes, of great deeds, of heroes and heroines. The present is a time of trouble, challenge, or crisis: a critical moment when we have to make fateful choices. The future is the dream: a vision of hope and greatness, often linked directly to greatness in the past.

That is just the kind of story that helped Ronald Reagan, a master storyteller, become president of the United States. Reagan's golden past was the frontier, a place of rugged, sturdy, self-reliant men and women who built a great nation and took care of themselves and their neighbors without the intervention of a monstrous national government. It was an America of small towns and volunteer fire departments. America had fallen into crisis, said Reagan, because "the liberals" had created a federal government that was levying oppressive taxes and eroding freedom through regulation and bureaucracy. Reagan offered a vision: a return to American greatness by "getting government off the backs of the American people" and restoring traditional American values of freedom and self-reliance.

The success of such stories is only partly related to their historical validity or empirical support. The central question is whether they are credible and persuasive to their audiences. A story, even a flawed story, will work if it taps persuasively into the experience, values, and aspirations of listeners. Good stories are truer than true: this reflects both the power and the danger of symbolic leadership. In the hands of a Gandhi or a King, the constructive power of stories is immense. Told by a Hitler, their destructive power is almost incalculable. In the wake of World War I and the Great Depression, Germany in the 1930s was hungry for hope. Other stories might have caught the imagination of the German people, but Hitler's passion and single-mindedness brought his story to center stage and carried Europe to a catastrophe of war and holocaust.

SUMMARY

Though leadership is widely accepted as a cure for organizational ills, it is also widely misunderstood. Many views of leadership fail to recognize its relational and contextual nature and its distinction from power and position. Inadequate ideas about leadership often produce oversimplified advice to managers. We need to reframe leadership to move beyond the impasses created by oversimplified models.

Each of the frames highlights significant possibilities for leadership, but each is incomplete in capturing a holistic picture. Early in the twentieth century, implicit models of managerial leadership were narrowly rational. In the 1960s and

1970s, human resource leadership became fashionable. In recent years, symbolic leadership has moved to center stage, and the literature abounds with advice on how to become a visionary leader capable of transforming cultural patterns. Organizations need vision, but it is not their only need and not always their most important one. Ideally, managers combine multiple frames into a comprehensive approach to leadership. Still, it is unrealistic to expect everyone to be a leader for all times and seasons. Wise leaders understand their own strengths, work to expand them, and build teams that can provide leadership in all four modes—structural, political, human resource, and symbolic.

o   o   o

Lee G. Bolman is the Marion Bloch/Missouri Chair in Leadership at the University of Missouri-Kansas City and a consultant.

Terrence E. Deal is a professor at the Rossier School, University of Southern California, and a consultant.

Chapter Eight

Situational Leadership

Paul Hersey
Kenneth H. Blanchard

Situational Leadership® is based on an interplay among (1) the amount of guidance and direction (task behavior) a leader gives, (2) the amount of socioemotional support (relationship behavior) a leader provides, and (3) the readiness level that followers exhibit in performing a specific task, function or objective. This concept was developed to help people attempting leadership, regardless of their role, to be more effective in their daily interactions with others. It provides leaders with some understanding of the relationship between an effective style of leadership and the level of readiness of their followers.[1]

Thus, while all the situational variables (leader, follower(s), superior(s), associates, organization, job demands, and time) are important, the emphasis in Situational Leadership will be on the behavior of a leader in relation to followers.

Basic Concept of Situational Leadership

According to Situational Leadership, there is no one best way to influence people. Which leadership style a person should use with individuals or groups depends on the readiness level of the people the leader is attempting to influence, as illustrated in Figure 8.1.[2]

Task behavior is defined as the extent to which the leader engages in spelling out the duties and responsibilities of an individual or group. These behaviors include telling people what to do, how to do it, where to do it, and who is to do it.

An example of high amounts of task behavior might be the last time you asked someone for directions. The person was probably very precise and clear about telling you what streets to take and what turns to make. Task behavior is characterized by one-way communication from the leader to the follower.

Relationship behavior is defined as the extent to which the leader engages in two-way or multi-way communication. The behaviors include listening, facilitating, and supportive behaviors.[3]

An example of high amounts of relationship behavior might be when you reach an impasse with an assignment. You basically know how to do the assignment but need some encouragement to get you over the hump. The listening, encouraging, and facilitating a leader does in this example is an illustration of relationship behavior.

Task behavior and relationship behavior are separate and distinct dimensions. They can be placed on separate axis of a two-dimensional graph, and the four quadrants can be used to identify four basic leadership styles.[4] Figure 8.1 illustrates these styles.

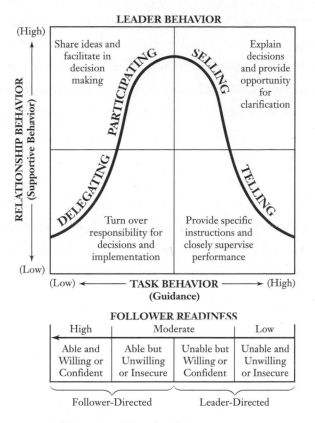

LEADER BEHAVIOR

(High)

RELATIONSHIP BEHAVIOR (Supportive Behavior)

PARTICIPATING
Share ideas and facilitate in decision making

SELLING
Explain decisions and provide opportunity for clarification

DELEGATING
Turn over responsibility for decisions and implementation

TELLING
Provide specific instructions and closely supervise performance

(Low)

(Low) ← **TASK BEHAVIOR** → (High)
(Guidance)

FOLLOWER READINESS

High	Moderate		Low
Able and Willing or Confident	Able but Unwilling or Insecure	Unable but Willing or Confident	Unable and Unwilling or Insecure

Follower-Directed   Leader-Directed

FIGURE 8.1 **Situational Leadership**

By using the four quadrants as the basis for assessing managerial success in different work settings, it became clear that it wasn't just one style that was effective. Each style was appropriate, depending on the situation.

Readiness of the Followers or Group

The more that leaders can adapt their behaviors to the situation, the more effective their attempts to influence become. The situation, in turn, is influenced by the various conditions that are present.

These variables do not operate in isolation. They are inter-active. We need to remind ourselves that the relationship between leaders and followers is the crucial variable in the leadership situation. If the followers decide not to follow, it doesn't matter what the boss or key associates think or what the job demands may be. *There is no leadership without someone following*.

In order to maximize the leader-follower relationship, the leader must first determine the task-specific outcomes the followers are to accomplish—on an individual and group basis. Without creating clarity on outcomes, objectives, subtasks, milestones, and so on, the leader has no basis for determining follower readiness or the specific behavioral style to use for that level of readiness.

Readiness Defined

Readiness in Situational Leadership is defined as the extent to which a follower demonstrates the ability and willingness to accomplish a specific task. People tend to be at different levels of readiness depending on the *task* they are being asked to do. Readiness is *not* a personal characteristic; it is not an evaluation of a person's traits, values, age, and so on. *Readiness* is *how ready a person is to perform a particular task*. All persons tend to be more or less ready in relation to a specific task, function, or objective that a leader is attempting to accomplish through their efforts. Thus, a salesperson may be very responsible in securing new sales but very casual about completing the paper work necessary to close on a sale. As a result, it is appropriate for the manager to leave the salesperson alone in terms of closing on sales but to supervise closely in terms of paper work until the salesperson can start to do well in that area too.

The two major components of readiness are *ability* and *willingness*.[5]

Ability is the knowledge, experience, and skill that an individual or group brings to a particular task or activity.

When considering the ability level of others, it is very important to be *task specific*. A person who has a Ph.D. in music and twenty years of professional experience playing the piano may be of little help in the design of a new jet engine. It is essential to focus on the specific outcome desired and to consider the ability of the followers in light of that outcome.

Willingness is the extent to which an individual or group has the confidence, commitment, and motivation to accomplish a specific task.

Willingness is only one word that describes the issue. Sometimes, it isn't so much that people are really unwilling, it's just that they've never done a specific task before. Perhaps they don't have any experience with it, so they're insecure or afraid. Generally, *if it is an issue of never having done something, the problem is insecurity.* The term "unwilling" might be most appropriate when, for one reason or another, the individuals have slipped, or lost some of their commitment and motivation. It might imply that they are regressing.

Even though the concepts of ability and willingness are different, it is important to remember that they are an *interacting influence system.* This means that *a significant change in one will affect the whole.* The extent to which followers bring willingness into a specific situation affects the use of their present ability. And it affects the extent to which they will grow and develop competence and ability. Similarly, the amount of knowledge, experience, and skill brought to a specific task will often affect competence, commitment, and motivation.

○   ○   ○

Paul Hersey is a behavioral scientist, educator, speaker, and trainer and is founder and CEO of the Center for Leadership Studies.

Kenneth H. Blanchard is a speaker and business consultant and a visiting professor at Cornell University.

Chapter Nine

The Servant as Leader

Robert K. Greenleaf

Who is the servant-leader? The servant-leader is servant first. It begins with the natural feeling that one wants to serve, to serve *first*. Then conscious choice brings one to aspire to lead. That person is sharply different from one who is *leader* first, perhaps because of the need to assuage an unusual power drive or to acquire material possessions. For such it will be a later choice to serve—after leadership is established. The leader-first and the servant-first are two extreme types. Between them there are shadings and blends that are part of the infinite variety of human nature.

The difference manifests itself in the care taken by the servant-first to make sure that other people's highest priority needs are being served. The best test, and difficult to administer, is: Do those served grow as persons? Do they, *while being served,* become healthier, wiser, freer, more autonomous, more likely themselves to become servants? *And,* what is the effect on the least privileged in society; will they benefit, or, at least, not be further deprived?

As one sets out to serve, how can one know that this will be the result? This is part of the human dilemma; one cannot know for sure. One must, after some study and experience, hypothesize—but leave the hypothesis under a shadow of doubt. Then one acts on the hypothesis and examines the result. One continues to study and learn and periodically one re-examines the hypothesis itself.

Finally, one chooses again. Perhaps one chooses the same hypothesis again and again. But it is always a fresh open choice. And it is always an hypothesis under a shadow of doubt. "Faith is the choice of the nobler hypothesis." Not the *noblest;* one never knows what that is. But the *nobler,* the best one can see when the choice is made. Since the test of results of one's actions is usually long delayed, the faith that sustains the choice of the nobler hypothesis is psychological self-insight. This is the most dependable part of the true servant.

The natural servant, the person who is *servant first,* is more likely to persevere and refine a particular hypothesis on what serves another's highest priority needs than is the person who is *leader first* and who later serves out of promptings of conscience or in conformity with normative expectations.

My hope for the future rests in part on my belief that among the legions of deprived and unsophisticated people are many true servants who will lead, and that most of them can learn to discriminate among those who presume to serve them and identify the true servants whom they will follow.

Everything Begins with the Initiative of an Individual

The forces for good and evil in the world are propelled by the thoughts, attitudes, and actions of individual beings. What happens to our values, and therefore to the quality of our civilization in the future, will be shaped by the conceptions of individuals that are born of inspiration. Perhaps only a few will receive this inspiration (insight) and the rest will learn from them. The very essence of leadership, going out ahead to show the way, derives from more than usual openness to inspiration. Why would anybody accept the leadership of another except that the other sees more clearly where it is best to go? Perhaps this is the current problem: too many who presume to lead do not see more clearly and, in defense of their inadequacy, they all the more strongly argue that the "system" must be preserved—a fatal error in this day of candor.

But the leader needs more than inspiration. A leader ventures to say: "I will go; come with me!" A leader initiates, provides the ideas and the structure, and takes the risk of failure along with the chance of success. A leader says: "I will go; follow me!" while knowing that the path is uncertain, even dangerous. One then trusts those who go with one's leadership.

Paul Goodman, speaking through a character in *Making Do*, has said, "If there is no community for you, young man, young man, make it yourself."

What Are You Trying to Do?

"What are you trying to do?" is one of the easiest to ask and most difficult to answer of questions.

A mark of leaders, an attribute that puts them in a position to show the way for others, is that they are better than most at pointing the direction. As long as one is leading, one always has a goal. It may be a goal arrived at by group consensus, or the leader, acting on inspiration, may simply have said, "Let's go this way." But the leader always knows what it is and can articulate it for any who are unsure. By clearly stating and restating the goal the leader gives certainty and purpose to others who may have difficulty in achieving it for themselves.

The word *goal* is used here in the special sense of the overarching purpose, the big dream, the visionary concept, the ultimate consummation which one approaches but never really achieves. It is something presently out of reach; it is something to strive for, to move toward, or become. It is so stated that it excites the imagination and challenges people to work for something they do not yet know how to do, something they can be proud of as they move toward it.

Every achievement starts with a goal—but not just any goal and not just anybody stating it. The one who states the goal must elicit trust, especially if it is a high risk or visionary goal, because those who follow are asked to accept the risk along with the leader. Leaders do not elicit trust unless one has confidence in their values and competence (including judgment) and unless they have a sustaining spirit (*entheos*) that will support the tenacious pursuit of a goal.

Not much happens without a dream. And for something great to happen, there must be a great dream. Behind every great achievement is a dreamer of great dreams. Much more than a dreamer is required to bring it to reality; but the dream must be there first.

Listening and Understanding

One of our very able leaders recently was made the head of a large, important, and difficult-to-administer public institution. After a short time he realized that he was not happy with the way things were going. His approach to the problem was a bit unusual. For three months he stopped reading newspapers and listening to news broadcasts; and for this period he relied wholly upon those he met in the course of his work to tell him what was going on. In three months his administrative problems were resolved. No miracles were wrought; but out of a sustained intentness of listening that was produced by this unusual decision, this able man learned and received the insights needed to set the right course. And he strengthened his team by so doing.

Why is there so little listening? What makes this example so exceptional? Part of it, I believe, with those who lead, is that the usual leader in the face of a difficulty tends to react by trying to find someone else on whom to pin the problem, rather than by automatically responding: "I have a problem. What is it? What can *I* do about *my* problem?" The sensible person who takes the latter course will probably react by listening, and somebody in the situation is likely to say what the problem is and what should be done about it. Or enough will be heard that there will be an intuitive insight that resolves it.

I have a bias about this which suggests that only a true natural servant automatically responds to any problem by listening *first*. When one is a leader, this disposition causes one to be *seen* as servant first. This suggests that a non-servant who wants to be a servant might become a *natural* servant through a long arduous discipline of learning to listen, a discipline sufficiently sustained that the automatic response to any problem is to listen first. I have seen enough remarkable transformations in people who have been trained to listen to have some confidence in this approach. It is because true listening builds strength in other people.

Most of us at one time or another, some of us a good deal of the time, would really like to communicate, really get through to a significant level of meaning in the hearer's experience. It can be terribly important. The best test of whether we are communicating at this depth is to ask ourselves first: Are we really listening? Are we listening to the one we want to communicate to? Is our basic attitude, as we approach the confrontation, one of wanting to understand? Remember that great line from the prayer of St. Francis, "Lord, grant that I may not seek so much to be understood as to understand."

One must not be afraid of a little silence. Some find silence awkward or oppressive, but a relaxed approach to dialogue will include the welcoming of some silence. It is often a devastating question to ask oneself—but it is sometimes important to ask it—"In saying what I have in mind will I really improve on the silence?"

ACCEPTANCE AND EMPATHY

These are two interesting words, acceptance and empathy. If we can take one dictionary's definition, *acceptance* is receiving what is offered, with approbation, satisfaction, or acquiescence, and *empathy* is the imaginative projection of one's own consciousness into another being. The opposite of both, the word *reject*, is to refuse to hear or receive—to throw out.

The servant always accepts and empathizes, never rejects. The servant as leader always empathizes, always accepts the person but sometimes refuses to accept some of the person's effort or performance as good enough.

A college president once said, "An educator may be rejected by students and must not object to this. But one may never, under any circumstances, regardless of what they do, reject a single student."

We have known this a long time in the family. For a family to be a family, no one can ever be rejected. Robert Frost in his poem "The Death of the Hired Man" states the problem in a conversation on the farmhouse porch between the farmer and his wife about the shiftless hired man, Silas, who has come back to their place to die. The farmer is irritated about this because Silas was lured away from his farm in the middle of the last haying season. The wife says that theirs is the only home he has. They are then drawn into a discussion of what a home is. The husband gives his view:

> *"Home is the place where, when you have to go there,*
> *They have to take you in."*

The wife sees it differently. What is a home? She says,

> *"I should have called it*
> *Something you somehow haven't to deserve."*

Because of the vagaries of human nature, the halt, the lame, half-made creatures that we all are, the great leader (whether it is the mother in her home or the head of a vast organization) would say what the wife said about home in Robert Frost's poem. The interest in and affection for one's followers which a leader has—and it is a mark of true greatness when it is gen-uine—is clearly something the followers "haven't to deserve." Great leaders, including "little" people, may have gruff, demanding, uncompromising exteriors. But deep down inside the great ones have empathy and an unqualified acceptance of the persons of those who go with their leadership.

Acceptance of the person, though, requires a tolerance of imperfection. Anybody could lead perfect people—if there were any. But there aren't any perfect people. And the parents who try to raise perfect children are certain to raise neurotics.

It is part of the enigma of human nature that the "typical" person—immature, stumbling, inept, lazy—is capable of great dedication and heroism *if* wisely led. Many otherwise able peo-ple are disqualified to lead because they cannot work with and through the half-people who are all there are. The secret of institution building is to be able to weld a team of such people by lifting them up to grow taller than they would otherwise be.

People grow taller when those who lead them empathize and when they are accepted for what they are, even though their performance may be judged critically in terms of what they are capable of doing. Leaders who empathize and who fully accept those who go with them on this basis are more likely to be trusted.

FORESIGHT:—THE CENTRAL ETHIC OF LEADERSHIP

The common assumption about the word "now" is that it is this instant moment of clock time—*now*. In usage, we qualify this a little by saying *right now*, meaning this instant, or *about now*, allowing a little leeway. Sometimes we say, "I'm going to do it now," meaning "I'm going to start soon and do it in the near future," or "I have just now done it," meaning that I did it in the recent past. The dictionary admits all of these variations of usage.

Let us liken "now" to the spread of light from a narrowly focused beam. There is a bright intense center, this moment of clock time, and a diminishing intensity, theoretically out to infinity, on either side. As viewed here, *now* includes *all* of this— all of history and all of the future. As one approaches the central focus, the light intensifies as this moment of clock time is approached. All of it is *now* but some parts are more *now* than others, and the central focus which marks this instant of clock time moves along as the clock ticks. *This is not the way it is!* It is simply an analogy to suggest a way of looking at *now* for those who wish better to see the unforeseeable—a mark of a leader.

Prescience, or foresight, is a better than average guess about *what* is going to happen *when* in the future. It begins with a state of mind about *now*, something like that suggested by the light analogy. What we note in the present moment of clock time is merely the intense focus that is connected with what has gone on in the past and what will happen in the future. The prescient man has a sort of "moving average" mentality (to borrow a statistician's term) in which past, present, and future are one, bracketed together and moving along as the clock ticks. The process is continuous.

Machiavelli, writing three hundred years ago about how to be a prince, put it this way. "Thus it happens in matters of state; for knowing afar off (which it is only given a prudent man to do) the evils that are brewing, they are easily cured. But when, for want of such knowledge, they are allowed to grow so that everyone can recognize them, there is no longer any remedy to be found."

The shape of some future events can be calculated from trend data. But, as with a practical decision mentioned earlier, there is usually an information gap that has to be bridged, and one must cultivate the conditions that favor intuition. This is what Machiavelli meant when he said "knowing afar off (which it is only given a prudent man to do)." The prudent man is one who constantly thinks of "now" as the moving concept in which past, present moment, and future are one organic unity. And this requires living by a sort of rhythm that encourages a high level of intuitive insight about the whole gamut of events from the indefinite past, through the present moment, to the indefinite future. One is at once, in every moment of time, historian, contemporary analyst, and prophet—not three separate roles. This is what the practicing leader is, every day of his life.

Living this way is partly a matter of *faith*. Stress is a condition of most of modern life, and if one is a servant-leader and carrying the burdens of other people—going out ahead to show the way, one takes the rough and tumble (and it really is rough and tumble in some leader roles)—one takes this in the belief that, if one enters a situation prepared with the necessary experience and knowledge at the conscious level, *in the situation* the intuitive insight necessary for one's optimal performance will be forthcoming. Is there any other way, in the turbulent world of affairs (including the typical home), for one to maintain serenity in the face of uncertainty? One follows the steps of the creative process which require that one stay with conscious analysis as far as it will carry one, and then withdraw, release the analytical pressure, if only for a moment, in full confidence that a resolving insight will come. The concern with the past and future is gradually attenuated as this span of concern goes forward or backward from the instant moment. The ability to do this is the essential structural dynamic of leadership.

Foresight is seen as a wholly rational process, the product of a constantly running internal computer that deals with intersecting series and random inputs and is vastly more complicated than anything technology has yet produced. Foresight means regarding the events of the instant moment and constantly comparing them with a series of projections made in the past and at the same time projecting future events—with diminishing certainty as projected time runs out into the indefinite future.

The failure (or refusal) of a leader to foresee may be viewed as an *ethical* failure, because a serious ethical compromise today (when the usual judgment on ethical inadequacy is made) is sometimes the result of a failure to make the effort at an earlier date to foresee today's events and take the right actions when there was freedom for initiative to act. The action which society labels "unethical" in the present moment is often really one of no choice. By this standard a lot of guilty people are walking around with an air of innocence that they would not have if society were able always to pin the label "unethical" on the failure to foresee and the consequent failure to act constructively when there was freedom to act.

Foresight is the "lead" that the leader has. Once leaders lose this lead and events start to force their hand, they are leaders in name only. They are not leading, but are reacting to immediate events, and they probably will not long be leaders. There are abundant current examples of loss of leadership which stem from a failure to foresee what reasonably could have been foreseen, and from failure to act on that knowledge while the leader had freedom to act.

There is a wealth of experience available on how to achieve this perspective of foresight, but only one aspect is mentioned here. Required is that one live a sort of schizoid life. One is always at two levels of consciousness. One is in the real world—concerned, responsible, effective, value oriented. One is also detached, riding above it, seeing today's events, and seeing one-self deeply involved in today's events, in the perspective of a long sweep of history and projected into the indefinite future. Such a split enables one better to foresee the unforeseeable. Also, from one level of consciousness, each of us acts resolutely from moment to moment on a set of assumptions that then govern one's life. Simultaneously, from another level, the adequacy of these assumptions is examined, in action, with the aim of future revision and improvement. Such a view gives one the perspective that makes it possible for one to live and act in the real world with a clearer conscience.

AWARENESS AND PERCEPTION

Framing all of this is awareness, opening wide the doors of perception so as to enable one to get more of what is available of sensory experience and other signals from the environment than people usually take in. Awareness has its risks, but it makes life more interesting; certainly it strengthens one's effectiveness as a leader. When one is aware, there is more than the usual alertness, more intense contact with the immediate situation, and more is stored away in the unconscious computer to produce intuitive insights in the future when needed.

William Blake has said, "If the doors of perception were cleansed, everything will appear to man as it is, infinite." Those who have gotten their doors of perception open wide enough often enough know that this statement of Blake's is not mere poetic exaggeration. Most of us move about with very narrow perception—sight, sound, smell, tactile—and we miss most of the grandeur that is in the minutest thing, the smallest experience. We also miss leadership opportunities. There is danger, however. Some people cannot take what they see when the doors of perception are open too wide, and they had better test their tolerance for awareness gradually. A qualification for leadership is that one can tolerate a sustained wide span of awareness so that one better "sees it as it is."

The opening of awareness stocks both the conscious and unconscious minds with a richness of resources for future need. But it does more than that: it is value building and value clarifying and it armors one to meet the stress of life by helping build serenity in the face of stress and uncertainty. The cultivation of awareness gives one the basis for detachment, the ability to stand aside and see oneself in perspective in the context of one's own experience, amidst the ever present dangers, threats, and alarms. Then one sees one's own peculiar assortment of obligations and responsibilities in a way that permits one to sort out the urgent from the important and perhaps deal with the important. Awareness is *not* a giver of solace—it is just the opposite. It is a disturber and an awakener. Able leaders are usually sharply awake and reasonably disturbed. They are not seekers after solace. They have their own inner serenity.

Leaders must have more of an armor of confidence in facing the unknown—more than those who accept their leadership. This is partly anticipation and preparation, but it is also a very firm belief that in the stress of real life situations one can compose oneself in a way that permits the creative process to operate.

This is told dramatically in one of the great stories of the human spirit—the story of Jesus when confronted with the woman taken in adultery. In this story Jesus is seen as a man, like all of us, with extraordinary prophetic insight of the kind we all have to some degree. He is a leader; he has a goal—to bring more compassion into the lives of people.

In this scene the woman is cast down before him by the mob that is challenging Jesus' leadership. They cry, "The *law* says she shall be stoned. What do *you* say?" Jesus must make a decision; he must give the *right* answer, *right* in the situation, and one that sustains his leadership toward his goal. The situation is deliberately stressed by his challengers. What does he do?

He sits there writing in the sand—a withdrawal device. In the pressure of the moment, having assessed the situation rationally, he assumes the attitude of withdrawal that will allow creative insight to function.

He could have taken another course; he could have regaled the mob with rational arguments about the superiority of compassion over torture. A good logical argument can be made for it. What would the result have been had he taken that course?

He did not choose to do that. He chose instead to withdraw and cut the stress—right in the event itself—in order to open his *awareness* to creative insight. And a great one came, one that has kept the story of the incident alive for two thousand years: "Let him that is without sin among you cast the first stone."

How Does One Know the Servant?

For those who follow—and this is everyone, including those who lead—the really critical question is: Who is this moral individual we would see as leader? Who is the servant? How does one tell a truly giving, enriching servant from the neutral person or the one whose net influence is to take away from or diminish other people?

Rabbi Heschel had just concluded a lecture on the Old Testament prophets in which he had spoken of true prophets and false prophets. A questioner asked him how one tells the difference between the true and the false prophets. The rabbi's answer was succinct and to the point. "There is no *way!*" he said. Then he elaborated, "If there were a *way*, if one had a gauge to slip over the head of the prophet and establish without question that he is or he isn't a true prophet, there would be no human dilemma and life would have no meaning."

So it is with the servant issue. If there were a dependable *way* that would tell us, "These people enrich by their presence, they are neutral, or they take away," life would be without challenge. Yet it is terribly important that one *know*, both about oneself and about others, whether the net effect of one's influence on others enriches, is neutral or diminishes and depletes.

Since there is no certain way to know this, one must turn to the artists for illumination. Such an illumination is in Hermann Hesse's idealized portrayal of the servant Leo whose servanthood comes through in his leadership. In stark modern terms it can also be found in the brutal reality of the mental hospital where Ken Kesey (in *One Flew Over the Cuckoo's Nest*) gives us Big Nurse—strong, able, dedicated, dominating, authority-ridden, manipulative, exploitative—the net effect of whose influence diminished other people, literally destroyed them. In the story she is pitted in a contest with tough, gutter-bred MacMurphy, a patient, the net effect of whose influence is to build up people and make both patients and the doctor in charge of the ward grow larger as persons, stronger, healthier— an effort that ultimately costs MacMurphy his life. If one will study the two characters, Leo and MacMurphy, one will get a measure of the range of possibilities in the role of servant as leader.

In Here, Not Out There

A king once asked Confucius' advice on what to do about the large number of thieves. Confucius answered, "If you, sir, were not covetous, although you should reward them to do it, they would not steal." This advice places an enormous burden on those who are favored by the rules, and it establishes how old is the notion that the servant views any problem in the world as *in here*, inside oneself, not *out there*. And if a flaw in the world is to be remedied, to the servant the process of change starts *in here*, in the servant, not *out there*. This is a difficult concept for that busybody, modern man.

So it is with joy. Joy is inward, it is generated inside. It is not found outside and brought in. It is for those who accept the world as it is, part good, part bad, and who identify with the good by adding a little island of serenity to it.

Hermann Hesse dramatized it in the powerful leadership exerted by Leo who ostensibly served only in menial ways but who, by the quality of his inner life that was manifest in his presence, lifted men up and made the journey possible. Camus, in his final testament, leaves us with "Each and every man, on the foundations of his own sufferings and joys, builds for them all."

Who Is the Enemy?

Who is the enemy? Who is holding back more rapid movement to the better society that is reasonable and possible with available resources? Who is responsible for the mediocre performance of so many of our institutions? Who is standing in the way of a larger consensus on the definition of the better society and paths to reaching it?

Not evil people. Not stupid people. Not apathetic people. Not the "system." Not the protesters, the disrupters, the revolutionaries, the reactionaries.

Granting that fewer evil, stupid, or apathetic people or a better "system" might make the job easier, their removal would not change matters, not for long. The better society will come, if it comes, with plenty of evil, stupid, apathetic people around and with an imperfect, ponderous, inertia-charged "system" as the vehicle for change. Liquidate the offending people, radically alter or destroy the system, and in less than a generation they will all be back. It is not in the nature of things that a society can be cleaned up once and for all according to an ideal plan. And even if it were possible, who would want to live in an aseptic world? Evil, stupidity, apathy, the "system" are not the enemy even though society building forces will be contending with them all the time. The healthy society, like the healthy body, is not the one that has taken the most medicine. It is the one in which the internal health building forces are in the best shape.

The real enemy is fuzzy thinking on the part of good, intelligent, vital people, and their failure to lead, and to follow servants as leaders. Too many settle for being critics and experts. There is too much intellectual wheel spinning, too much retreating into "research," too little preparation for and willingness to undertake the hard and high risk tasks of building better institutions in an imperfect world, too little disposition to see "the problem" as residing *in here* and not *out there*.

In short, the enemy is strong natural servants who have the potential to lead but do not lead, or who choose to follow a nonservant. They suffer. Society suffers. And so it may be in the future.

IMPLICATIONS

The future society may be just as mediocre as this one. It may be worse. And no amount of restructuring or changing the system or tearing it down in the hope that something better will grow will change this. There may be a better system than the one we now have. It is hard to know. But, whatever it is, if the people to lead it well are not there, a better system will not produce a better society.

Many people finding their wholeness through many and varied contributions make a good society. Here we are concerned with but one facet: *able servants with potential to lead will lead, and, where appropriate, they will follow only servant-leaders.* Not much else counts if this does not happen.

This brings us to that critical aspect of realism that confronts the servant-leader, that of *order.* There must be some order because we know for certain that the great majority of people will choose some kind of order over chaos even if it is delivered by a brutal non-servant and even if, in the process, they lose much of their freedom. Therefore the servant-leader will beware of pursuing an idealistic path regardless of its impact on order. The big question is: What kind of order? This is the great challenge to the emerging generation of leaders: Can they build better order?

Older people who grew up in a period when values were more settled and the future seemed more secure will be disturbed by much they find today. But one firm note of hope comes through—loud and clear; we are at a turn of history in which people are growing up faster and some extraordinarily able, mature, servant-disposed men and women are emerging in their early and middle twenties. The percentage may be small, and, again, it may be larger than we think. Moreover, it is not an elite; it is all sorts of exceptional people. Most of them could be ready for some large society-shaping responsibility by the time they are thirty *if* they are encouraged to prepare for leadership as soon as their potential as builders is identified, which is possible for many of them by age eighteen or twenty. Preparation to lead need not be at the complete expense of vocational or scholarly preparation, but it must be the *first priority*. And it may take some difficult bending of resources and some unusual initiatives to accomplish all that should be accomplished in these critical years *and* give leadership preparation first priority. But whatever it takes, it must be done. For a while at least, until a better led society is assured, some other important goals should take a subordinate place.

All of this rests on the assumption that the only way to change a society (or just make it go) is to produce people, enough people, who will change it (or make it go). The urgent problems of our day—the disposition to venture into immoral and senseless wars, destruction of the environment, poverty, alienation, discrimination, overpopulation—are here because of human failures, individual failures, one person at a time, one action at a time failures.

If we make it out of all of this (and this is written in the belief that we will make it), the "system" will be whatever works best. The builders will find the useful piece wherever they are, and invent new ones when needed, all without reference to ideological coloration. "How do we get the right things done?" will be the watchword of the day, every day. And the context of those who bring it off will be: all men and women who are touched by the effort grow taller, and become healthier, stronger, more autonomous, *and* more disposed to serve.

Leo the *servant*, and the exemplar of the *servant-leader*, has one further portent for us. If we may assume that Hermann

Hesse is the narrator in *Journey to the East* (not a difficult assumption to make), at the end of the story he establishes his identity. His final confrontation at the close of his initiation into the Order is with a small transparent sculpture, two figures joined together. One is Leo, the other is the narrator. The narrator notes that a movement of substance is taking place within the transparent sculpture.

> *I perceived that my image was in the process of adding to and flowing into Leo's, nourishing and strengthening it. It seemed that in time . . . only one would remain: Leo. He must grow, I must disappear.*
>
> *As I stood there and looked and tried to understand what I saw, I recalled a short conversation that I had once had with Leo during the festive days at Bremgarten. We had talked about the creations of poetry being more vivid and real than the poets themselves.*

What Hesse may be telling us here is that Leo is the symbolic personification of Hesse's aspiration to serve through his literary creations, creations that are greater than Hesse himself; and that his work, for which he was but the channel, will carry on and serve and lead in a way that he, a twisted and tormented man, could not—except as he created.

Does not Hesse dramatize, in extreme form, the dilemma of us all? Except as we venture to create, we cannot project ourselves beyond ourselves to serve and lead.

o   o   o

Robert K. Greenleaf was a consultant and lecturer in the field of servant-leadership. Previously he was in management at AT&T and taught at several universities including MIT and Harvard Business School.

Chapter Ten

The Case for Co-Leaders

David A. Heenan
Warren Bennis

If a man aspires to the highest place,
it is no dishonor to him to halt at the second.
—Cicero

An overseas visitor to our shores recently remarked: "If beings from another planet were attempting to learn about working in the United States by reading business magazines, they would have to assume that everyone in America is either a CEO or about to become one."

The point is well taken. Ours is a culture obsessed with celebrity, and so we have made superstars of Bill Gates and other fascinating leaders, just as we have made legends of favored rock stars and screen actors. Nevertheless, even as we read yet another article that implies that Microsoft *is* Bill Gates, we know better. We know that every successful organization has, at its heart, a cadre of *co-leaders*—key players who do the work, even if they receive little of the glory.

Like Microsoft's Steve Ballmer. According to insiders much of the software giant's unprecedented success is due to Ballmer, its relatively unknown second in command. Ballmer is Microsoft's president and top tactician, the person responsible for everything from getting the first Windows operating system shipped to keeping the company supplied with top-notch personnel. Although the average person hears his name and wonders "Steve who?" Ballmer has created Microsoft as surely as has his more famous boss.

"Microsoft could lose Bill Gates," former staffer Adrian King told *Forbes*, "but it could not survive without Steve's sheer will to succeed. That's what makes the company unique."

This chapter reflects our conviction that you must look beyond the Bill Gateses of the world to understand what will make organizations succeed in the new millennium. In this first comprehensive study of co-leaders and their often quiet power, we challenge the time-honored notion that all great institutions are the lengthened shadows of a Great Man or Woman. It is a fallacy that dies hard. But if you believe, as we do, that the genius of our age is truly collaborative, you must abandon the notion that the credit for any significant achievement is solely attributable to the person at the top. We have long worshiped the imperial leader at the cost of ignoring the countless other contributors to any worthwhile enterprise. In our hearts we know that the world is more complex than ever and that we need teams of talent— leaders and co-leaders working together—to get important things done. The old corporate monotheism is finally giving way to a more realistic view that acknowledges leaders not as organizational gods but as the first among many contributors.

In this new view of the organization, co-leaders finally come into their own and begin to receive the credit they so richly deserve.

Gates and Ballmer exemplify a relatively new type of alliance between a leader and his or her chief ally. In this scenario, so typical of Silicon Valley, the No. 1 and No. 2 associates seem more like buddies, or at least peers, than boss and subordinate. This new egalitarianism reflects a dramatic change in organizational life today. In Henry Ford's corporate America, the person at the top held all the power. He, and it was almost always a he, owned the company and all its assets. The workers were hired hands.

But on the cusp of the year 2000, economics is based on a very different reality. Microsoft and other high-tech companies are in the business of ideas. Good ideas belong, initially at least, to whoever has them, not to the company or the boss. Superior ideas can come from anyone in the organization, and they empower the people who have them, whether their business card says CEO or intern. If Microsoft is not a true meritocracy, it is nonetheless a company in which talent is valued and courted. Talent always has the power to walk (especially if, as in the case of Ballmer, the talent already has roughly $12 billion worth of Microsoft stock in its pocket). In such an environment, no chief executive would risk losing a key player by demanding unquestioning obedience or any of the other outdated hallmarks of the rigidly hierarchical corporation of yesterday. This new egalitarianism isn't just a matter of style. It's a question of survival. In the new climate, every leader knows that the organization's best minds will take major assets with them should they walk out the door.

Co-Leadership Defined

Co-leadership is not a fuzzy-minded buzzword designed to make non-CEOs feel better about themselves and their workplaces. Rather it is a tough-minded strategy that will unleash the hidden talent in any enterprise. Above all co-leadership is inclusive, not exclusive. It celebrates those who do the real work, not just a few charismatic leaders, often isolated, who are regally compensated for articulating the organization's vision.

Although several leading companies from Citigroup to Daimler-Chrysler have restyled themselves around coequal CEOs, co-leadership should permeate *every* organization at *every* level. There are vivid demonstrations of successful power sharing from the Halls of Montezuma to the Hills of Silicon Valley. For example, the United States Marine Corps, with its fiercely proud tradition of excellence in combat, its hallowed rituals, and its unbending code of honor, personifies co-leadership. Despite its rigid command-and-control structure, the Corps' enduring culture screams togetherness: Semper fi. Esprit de corps. The few, the proud.

Such inclusive notions of leadership are not new. The Marines have been practicing their special brand of esprit for more than 220 years. But what is new are the changed realities of the twenty-first century. In a world of increasing interdependence and ceaseless technological change, even the greatest of Great Men or Women simply can't get the job done alone. As a result, we need to rethink our most basic concepts of leadership.

The prevailing winds blow in the direction of close-knit partnerships throughout the organization. In this new organizational galaxy, power doesn't reside in a single person or corner office. Rather power and responsibility are dispersed, giving the enterprise a whole constellation of costars—co-leaders with shared values and aspirations, all of whom work together toward common goals. As we look back at what we discovered in writing this book, one realization towers above all others: *Anyone* can be a co-leader—all he or she needs is talent and an organization that values and rewards co-leadership.

We spent five years scrutinizing dozens of gifted co-leaders, analyzing how they contributed to the greatness of their organizations. We studied how they relate to the people above and below them and how they viewed the costs and rewards of being a costar. Because we believe personal stories are a lively, effective way to get important points across, we chose to make the case for co-leadership; by telling the stories of a dozen outstanding adjuncts, from General George C. Marshall to Merrill Lynch's visionary Win Smith. Other co-leaders profiled range from Anne Sullivan Macy, Helen Keller's brilliant and devoted teacher, to legendary auto executive Bob Lutz.

Co-Leaders, then, is about truly exceptional deputies—extremely talented and dedicated men and women, often more capable than their more highly acclaimed superiors. No one illustrates this better than George Catlett Marshall. As important to his country as George Washington, Marshall brought unprecedented stature to a supporting role. With World War II looming, he rebuilt the United States Army despite extraordinary initial resistance. The architect of the Marshall Plan, he was President Truman's steady right hand as secretary of state and later secretary of defense. The first soldier to win the Nobel Peace Prize in peacetime, he was also a hero to the captains of his era. Truman, Eisenhower, and Churchill all said he was the greatest man they had ever known.

Routinely called on to do the work and forgo the credit, great partners sometimes have character where more celebrated leaders have only flash. Marshall is, again, the model. In retirement he turned down million-dollar offers to write his memoirs because he felt his reminiscences might trouble some of the people in his remarkable past. Such principled restraint is hard to imagine today when no tell-all memoir seems to go unwritten.

Again and again, *Co-Leaders* illustrates how the once yawning gaps between the person at the top and the rest of the organization is closing because of rapid changes in the workplace and, indeed, the world. Although as a culture we continue to be mesmerized by celebrity and preoccupied with being No. 1, the roles of top executives are converging, the line between them increasingly blurred.

Called on to make more and more complex decisions more and more quickly, even the most da Vincian CEOs acknowledge that they can't do everything themselves. Farsighted corporations and other organizations require their leaders to do more than put effective systems in place. Future-oriented enterprises have to be able to spot the Next Big Thing and respond to it before the competition. Such organizations are like organisms, constantly adapting to shifts in the global environment. As a result, the CEO's job doesn't get easier the longer he or she is in place; it typically gets even more demanding.

In 1997 famously capable Intel chairman Andy Grove, beset by lawsuits, a bout with prostate cancer, a flaw in Intel's Pentium Pro chips, and a dip in second-quarter earnings, admitted that he was on the verge of being overwhelmed. "I don't think I've ever worked as hard," he told *Fortune*. "I've been feeling very sorry for myself the past six months. Things are running at borderline out of control inside the company and out. . . . I go home spent."

In such an environment, first-rate co-leaders are a necessity, not a luxury. In May 1998 Grove chose as his successor Craig Barrett, Intel's superbly fit chief operating officer (COO) and the person responsible for perfecting the chip maker's manufacturing processes. Grove was the first to praise Barrett for having done the operations job at Intel far better than he. And why shouldn't Grove seek a successor of Barrett's caliber? When you know you are going to be facing challenges at every turn, you want the best there is at your side.

Once a sinecure, the corner office has become a resolving door, as boards and shareholders become ever more demanding of CEOs. Increasingly, heading an important organization in America is like being one of the kings in ancient Crete who had extraordinary power and access to every perk and pleasure—but only for a time. After his year of absolute power, the king was put to death. For contemporary CEOs the pay and the perks are unbeatable while they are in office, but they can't count on being in office for long. As the tenure of the average chief executive becomes shorter and shorter, the need for depth of leadership becomes even more crucial.

The untimely death in 1997 of Coca-Cola Enterprises, Inc., CEO Roberto Goizueta reminded the world that no complex organization can afford to rely too heavily on a single leader, however gifted and charismatic. Coke never stumbled in the days following Goizueta's death, largely because he had already groomed an able successor, M. Douglas Ivester, whom Goizueta had long referred to as "my partner." The company's major divisions were already reporting to Ivester, now CEO, when the Cuban-born chief became ill. The late chairman had also nurtured a dozen more key players under Ivester, who in turn had talented protégés of his own. In famed investor Warren Buffett's view, Goizueta's "greatest legacy is the way he so carefully selected and then nurtured the future leadership of the company."

Ivester has already gone far toward instituting a co-leadership culture at Coke. *Fortune* magazine's Betsy Morris recently described the atmosphere under Ivester: "Hierarchy is out—it slows everything down; he communicates freely with people at all levels. The conventional desk job is also out. Ivester prefers that employees think of themselves as knowledge workers—their office is the information they carry around with them, supported by technology that allows them to work anywhere. . . . A CEO on a pedestal is definitely out; a CEO as platoon leader is in." Ivester knows that co-leadership is a strategy for unleashing talent throughout the organization. Much more than rhetoric about teamwork, co-leadership is a commitment to partnering at every level, to serve the constantly changing needs of the organization. Yet even someone as committed to co-leadership as Ivester may be reluctant to share *all* his or her power. Ivester works closely with a team of 14 vice presidents but has not yet been willing to name a successor.

Contrast, too, China's smooth leadership transition with the sorry state of Russia, Cuba, and Malaysia. Deng Xiaoping's death quickly surfaced two talented co-leaders: President Jiang Zemin and Premier Zhu Rongji. Yet Russia, with ailing Boris Yeltsin acting more like a tsar than the country's first democratically elected president, desperately needs a succession plan. So, too, do autocratic Cuba and Malaysia.

Increasingly, corporations, countries, and other entities are realizing that top leaders and their co-leaders are not different orders of beings but essential complements: All are needed if the enterprise is to flourish. As college basketball's North Carolina Tar Heels were reminded in 1997, success, continuity, and survival depend on having a Bill Guthridge on board as well as a Dean Smith. Like athletic teams, all organizations need the bench strength, or deep leadership, provided by great co-leaders.

Paths to Co-Leadership

In the course of studying outstanding lieutenants, we were constantly reminded that co-leadership is a *role*, not an identity and certainly not a destiny. There is no single personality type that consigns people to careers in a supporting role rather than a starring one (indeed most CEOs and other leaders have done both). True, some strong-willed individuals must run their own shows. It's hard—almost impossible actually—to imagine Donald Trump, George Steinbrenner, or Leona Helmsley finding happiness in the trenches. But they are the exceptions.

Because all leadership is situational, we are leery about categorizing co-leaders. The social world isn't nearly as orderly as the physical world. People—unlike solids, fluids, and gases—are anything but uniform and predictable. As you will see, the co-leaders described in these pages have distinguished themselves in very different fields of endeavor: Amy Tucker coaches women's basketball at Stanford, while Merrill Lynch's Win Smith helped democratize the ownership of stocks and bonds, perhaps the most important change in the U.S. economy in 50 years. And each of these great partners had or has a distinctive, often colorful personality. But in the course of our research, we found that, however they differed, each had taken one of three distinctive career paths to successful co-leadership. Each was either a fast-tracker, a back-tracker, or an on-tracker.

○ *Fast-trackers* are deputies on the way up. For presidential hopeful Al Gore and others, co-leadership is a rite of passage. Indeed being No. 2 is a time-honored way to become top dog. According to a recent survey, 86 percent of the heads of Fortune 500 companies were previous seconds in command.

Upwardly mobile lieutenants understand that the route to the corner office is paved with achievement, loyalty, and luck. Savvy deputies also appreciated firsthand the need for superior bench strength. Fast-trackers tend to be good at what psychologist Erik Erikson terms "being generative"—that is, building their own cadre of talented lieutenants. Such co-leaders often understand, in the most visceral of ways, the value of sharing power.

○ *Back-trackers* are former chiefs who have downshifted. One of history's most notable examples is Chou En-lai, who voluntarily relinquished command of the Red Army to a gifted junior officer, Mao Tse-tung. More recently, as few would have predicted, colorful cable pioneer Ted Turner seems to have found happiness as a vice chairman at Time Warner.

Some back-trackers disdain elements of the No. 1 role: deal making, strategizing, schmoozing with different interest groups, and the like. Some find the pressure and lack of privacy at the top to be major negatives. Others want to avoid the nerve-rattling revolving-door syndrome of today's executive suite. Generally speaking, these talented men and women find greater peace being the quiet power behind the throne.

° *On-trackers* are outstanding adjuncts who either didn't want the top slot or weren't promoted into it. These people find ways to prosper as supporting players. Passed over for CEO of Chrysler, Bob Lutz called his stint as second in command "absolutely the best period in my whole career." On-trackers have the ego strength to be a costar. If they are offered top billing, they will probably take it, as Harry Truman did a half century ago and as Bill Guthridge did at North Carolina in 1997. But they are also comfortable remaining part of a vibrant team of leaders.

Whatever their route to co-leadership, successful costars are consummate team players and, thus, valuable models for everyone interested in effective collaboration. Usually servant-leaders, they tend to be self-reliant, yet committed to organizational goals. Outstanding co-leaders "see themselves—except in terms of line responsibility—as the equals of the leaders they follow," says Professor Robert E. Kelley of Carnegie Mellon University. "They are more apt to disagree with leadership and are less likely to be intimidated by hierarchy and organizational structure."

We have excluded any discussion of unsuccessful partners, or off-trackers. These are people whose careers have derailed. Whereas fast-trackers are on the way up, these poor souls are on the way out.

What motivates great co-leaders? Why, in particular, are they willing to subordinate their egos, a sacrifice that seems all the more remarkable in an age that celebrates the star? We found three main reasons, which led us to classify co-leaders as follows:

1. Crusaders, like General George C. Marshall, who serve a noble cause

2. Confederates, such as Bob Lutz and Stanford assistant coach Amy Tucker, who serve an exceptional organization or enterprise

3. Consorts, like Helen Keller's teacher, Anne Sullivan Macy, and Win Smith of Merrill Lynch, who serve an extraordinary person

Of course, there is some overlap among categories. George Marshall as *crusader* was driven by the cause of freedom and world peace. Yet he was also a staunch *confederate* of the U.S. military establishment (the army, in particular) as well as a loyal *consort* to his mentor, "Black Jack" Pershing, and later to presidents Roosevelt and Truman. At different stages in Marshall's life, these loyalties enabled him to find satisfaction in a supporting role.

Critical Factors for Success

To be a successful co-leader, you need, above all, a champion who will allow you to succeed. Not every top gun is able to do that. Contrast Bob Lutz's success at Chrysler, thanks to the genuine partnership he had with CEO Robert Eaton, with Lutz's unhappiness at the auto giant when then CEO Lee Iacocca often undermined him, Great co-leaders are often born when leaders decide to do the one thing that most often distinguishes a great organization from a mediocre one—hire people who are as good or better than they are. As reserved as Lutz is flamboyant, Bob Eaton was perfectly comfortable with a partner who piloted his own jet fighter and who was a darling of the press. For Lutz's part, he long ago came to terms with being passed over for Chrysler's top job and found real happiness as Eaton's partner in everything but name. Indeed Lutz believes Eaton's willingness to share power was key to Chrysler's success. If Lutz had been made CEO in 1992, he said: "I would have had to have done it alone."

The ability to subordinate egos to attain a common goal is something both leaders and co-leaders need. Stephen Kahng built Power Computing Corp. into what *Business Week* described as the "fastest-growing computer startup of the 1990s." One of the industry's most respected technical experts, Kahng is also so nerdy and soft-spoken that his own staffers needle him about it. Knowing that he needed someone with different skills and a personality very different from his own to market the company's Apple clones and capture a greater share of the PC market, Kahng went after Joel Kocher, author of the winning marketing strategy, including direct sales, at Dell Computer Corp. Now Power Computing's president and COO, the exuberant Kocher is the antithesis of Kahng—in everything but their shared vision of market domination. Kocher is head cheerleader as well as marketing strategist, fond of such stunts as having Power Computing's staff wear camouflage fatigues every Friday on Fight Back for the Customer Day. A colleague of Kocher's at Dell told *Business Week* that he "demands, inspires, attracts, and coaches greatness"—the sort of description most people associate with CEO, not second in command. But Kahng had the wisdom and confidence to hire his complement, where a lesser leader might have been put off by Kocher's stronger charisma.

True leaders also know that the only deputies worth hiring are the ones good enough to replace them. And for their part outstanding co-leaders know that they don't have to be at the top of the organizational chart to find satisfaction—that exercising one's gifts and serving a worthy cause are far more reliable sources of satisfaction than the title on one's office door. Such people have acquired the rare ability to distinguish between celebrity and success. As that unlikely philosopher, the late Erma Bombeck, once wrote, "Don't confuse fame with success. Madonna is one, Helen Keller is the other."

Courage is one of the attributes of all great co-leaders, and one we rarely associate with that role. Deputies have to be able to speak truth to power, even when it hurts. (Real leaders demand honesty from their adjuncts, knowing that good information, even when it's unpleasant, is the basis of good decision making.) It was young George Marshall's courage in publicly correcting General Pershing that caught Pershing's eye and launched Marshall's extraordinary career. And candor like his own was one of the attributes Marshall always sought in his staffers. Yes-men may feed the boss's ego, but they serve no other useful function. Indeed they guarantee that the boss's knowledge will be limited to upbeat information and whatever he or she already knows. Good co-leaders protect their bosses when possible, but good bosses are willing to endure occasional discomfiture in order to find out what they *need* to know.

Creativity is almost as important an attribute of co-leaders as courage. Deputies have to go beyond the manual to find what best serves the organization. When George Tenet was named director of the Central Intelligence Agency in 1997, his former boss, John Deutch, told an instructive story about Tenet's ability to think on his feet and act decisively.

"George is a tremendously loyal and devoted public servant," Deutch told the *Wall Street Journal*. "The time I really realized how devoted a deputy he was was in an extremely important meeting with important foreign dignitaries. He cleared the room to tell me I needed to zip up my fly."

Every chief has the right to the loyalty of his or her deputies. Working at a leader's side, a trusted co-leader is often privy to information that could seriously compromise the boss's position if it were shared. As candid as great partners are in private, they are equally discreet in public. They can keep the boss's secrets—as long as they can continue to reconcile them with their own consciences. To some extent, all No 1s depend on an image of excellence to maintain their positions. Good co-leaders may know about personal flaws or weaknesses, but they don't feel compelled to reveal or underscore them. Especially in crises, leaders have to know that their first lieutenants will maintain the illusion of superiority, which makes leadership possible. An example of this is Vice President Al Gore's unswerving public loyalty to a bruised Clinton, despite the pressure on Gore to distance himself from the controversial president as Gore himself sought the nation's highest office.

Co-leaders need unusually healthy egos. That's a paradox really, because it would seem that they would need less ego strength than their leaders. But, especially in a society as obsessed with winning as ours, it takes extraordinary confidence to be No. 2 or No. 3. No matter how great a contribution a great co-leader makes, the majority of the credit is going to accrue to the top individual. That's the nature of the organizational beast. To some degree it may simply reflect the extent to which leaders function as symbols of their enterprises. But the fact is that even the best deputy will exist in the shadow of the boss. Bill Guthridge deserved considerable credit for Dean Smith's record-breaking 879 victories, but it was Smith whose name went into the record books, not the name of the man who spent 30 years as his assistant coach. As the self-effacing Guthridge told the press, "I knew my ego could take being life-time assistant to the best coach around."

What does the organization get from a great partnership? A great many things. Two heads really are better than one when it comes to decision making. The psychological literature indicates that groups make better choices than do individuals.

A first-rate deputy can serve as an alternative model for the rest of the organization, one that other co-leaders may relate to more easily than to the person at the top. A great second can serve as institutional insurance in that he or she can quickly get up to speed to replace the person at the top. This is, tragically, one of the roles American vice presidents have had to play when presidents have died in office, and it is the role by which most people measure the vice president. Truman, whom as vice president FDR had kept in the dark about many important issues, including the development of the atomic bomb, proved surprisingly able in the nation's top job. The very thought of Dan Quayle succeeding George Bush so frightened many voters that it became a factor in Bush's failure to win a second term in office.

But heir apparent is just one of the many roles co-leaders play. Great partners may have strengths and skills that the boss lacks. The costar can compensate or complement. William Clark had superior cartographic abilities to Meriwether Lewis, for instance, that proved invaluable to the Corps of Discovery. Co-leaders can share the burden of leadership and lighten the workload. They routinely act as facilitators for their superiors. They almost always serve as advisers as well, at best providing the kind of candid, informed counsel that every leader needs.

They are often conduits of critical information from elsewhere in the organization to the person in charge, and vice versa. They can also serve as sounding boards, counselors, confessors, and pressure valves. In bad times they may serve as lightning rods, even scapegoats. In the best of all possible organizations, they are genuine partners, though not necessarily equal ones, sharing responsibilities with the chief according to their individual skills and interests. Before Dean Smith's retirement in 1997, Bill Guthridge was responsible for the individual coaching at North Carolina, while Smith determined overall strategy—with Guthridge's quiet assistance. In the highly collaborative Clinton White House, Gore assumed major policy-shaping responsibility for several areas of national and international concern, including national security, environment, and technology.

JUST REWARDS

Although service is the paradigmatic responsibility of co-leaders, there comes a time in everyone's career when he or she asks, "What's in it for me?" Although co-leaders usually lack the name recognition and enormous salaries of CEOs and others at the very top, there are rewards in being No. 2 or No. 3.

For starters serving under someone else can be a marvelous education. As a young deputy to Pershing, Marshall attended a superb military college of one, where he was able to study a first-rate soldier in the flesh, day in and day out. Vice President Gore has been in a unique position to study President Clinton during his two terms in office. What better curriculum for a presidential hopeful than the chance to see how the incumbent handles the duties and pressures of the nation's highest office?

Clinton himself stumbled badly in his first months in office as he learned on the job. Six years later came the infamous Monica Lewinsky affair. How much better for Gore to be able to learn from someone else's mistakes—and successes—before assuming that demanding office?

Some of the greatest rewards of co-leadership grow out of the relationship with the person at the top. Some co-leaders have warm, sustaining relationships with the people they serve, as Win Smith had with Merrill Lynch cofounder Charlie Merrill. Merrill was a demanding taskmaster, but a superb mentor, and, over the decades, he and Smith became closer than many fathers and sons. Some of the letters they exchanged after illness forced Merrill into semiretirement are as tender as love letters. Accomplishing something together can forge a lasting bond. As profoundly troubled as Meriwether Lewis was, he and William Clark became close friends in the course of their epic journey and remained so afterward: Clark and his wife even moved into Lewis's house for a time.

The relationships that develop in executive offices are enormously varied. Some CEOs and COOs have healthy rivalries that energize both of them. Others have the professional equivalent of bad marriages that distract and drain them. Camaraderie grounded in shared accomplishment is one of the pleasures of any happy workplace, and it can be especially gratifying for the people who are most involved in setting the agenda and steering the enterprise.

Another frequent source of satisfaction for co-leaders is the opportunity to revel in interesting work and the pleasures of craft. CEOs often barter power and responsibility for truly engaging work. It can be hectic at the top, especially on days when one meeting follows another and even meals involve professional obligations. Many contented alter egos have talent or expertise that they are able to exercise undistracted by the top person's daunting calendar and sometimes tedious responsibilities. Amy Tucker seems to have found joy in her craft as associate head coach of the women's basketball team at Stanford, despite having tasted triumph as interim head coach. Bob Lutz was happy at Chrysler as the hands-on creator of such eye-catching vehicles as the Dodge Viper, Plymouth Prowler, and Jeep Grand Cherokee. Successful co-leaders, especially those who have decided to remain No. 2, have often concluded that what they actually do is more important than making headlines.

Some co-leaders find enormous satisfaction in serving a cause they believe in. Certainly Marshall is a superb example of someone who devoted his entire career to serving his country and indeed the world at large. For others, their work has many of the qualities of a religious vocation, and self-sacrifice is a price they are willing to pay. Born into island royalty, Bernice Pauahi Bishop believed that education could save her beloved fellow Hawaiians and devoted much of her life to creating the Kamehameha Schools. Eschewing the Hawaiian crown, she found another way to improve the condition of her people. As one observer said: "Refusing to rule her people, she did what was better, she served them."

Sometimes redefining power reflects a decision that there are more important things in life than other trappings of success. Princess Pauahi refused the crown because she believed accepting it would destroy her happy marriage to Charles Reed Bishop, who favored Hawaii's annexation by the United States. Amy Tucker is regularly offered head coaching jobs, especially now that women's basketball is booming, but she doesn't want to leave Stanford, a vibrant intellectual community in scenic Northern California.

As the happy buzz at visionary companies such as Steve Jobs's Pixar Animation Studios makes clear, the most exciting work being done today is collaborative, accomplished by teams of people working toward a common goal. Often there is still a Numero Uno, at least on the organizational chart. But in the growing number of global enterprises that trade in innovation, the real power is in the hands of the men and women who have the best ideas and the most valuable skills, whatever their job titles. In the workplaces of the new millennium, one of the leader's most important roles is to retain the necessary talent and unleash it. The rise of co-leadership reflects the fact that, despite the exalted terms in which we talk about No. 1s, they can actually accomplish things only when effectively teamed with other people.

Leadership Redefined

If we still treat some CEOs like celebrities, we are increasingly beginning to see them more as stewards than kings. No one has been more articulate on this change in our traditional view of leadership than management sage Peter Drucker, who said in praise of such nonimperial leaders as Harry Truman and GE's Jack Welch: "They both understood executives are not their own masters. They are servants of the organization—whether elected or appointed, whether the organization is a government, a government agency, a business, a hospital, a diocese. It's their duty to subordinate their likes, wishes, preferences to the welfare of the institution."

To some degree this more egalitarian understanding of leadership reflects a backlash against CEOs who earn far more than they deliver. The surge in executive compensation in recent years has dismayed and infuriated the vast majority of people who work hard for modest pay. Thirty years ago the average chief executive in the United States earned 44 times as much as the average factory worker. According to the AFL-CIO, the ratio is now more than 300 to 1. Consequently, corporate boards as well as workers are beginning to question whether anyone deserves to make more than the budgets of some nations. Indeed Bob Eaton's $16 million annual compensation as CEO of Chrysler horrified German shareholder activists contemplating the 1998 merger of the Detroit automaker and Daimler-Benz AG. Eaton's German counterpart, Jürgen Schrempp, receives just $2 million a year.

Even *Business Week*, hardly a journal to foment revolution, huffed about the hubris of the chieftains of American business. "They are team leaders, not celebrities or one-man bands," the magazine editorialized. Yes, some extraordinary CEOs may deserve extraordinary compensation. "But usually, a chief executive works with a team of people who manage thousands of employees, each contributing to the success or failure of the company. A team leader requires respect to function. Making 200 times the average paycheck, simply because the market has a good year, doesn't generate respect."

That the American workplace needs to be rethought is increasingly obvious. The mounting anger over executive pay is only one piece of evidence. It is not a happy sign when the business best-seller list is topped by volumes devoted to Dilbert, the cartoon Everyworker, and the Orwellian hell in which he labors. This is organizational humor at its darkest, and one of its loudest messages is that it is time for sweeping change.

Although increasing numbers of firms are naming co-CEOs and showing other signs of embracing co-leadership, sharing power has its pitfalls. It will be interesting to see if Bob Eaton can work as comfortably with co-CEO Schrempp as Eaton once teamed with Lutz. The corner suite that houses incompatible executive peers can be an unhappy, unproductive place indeed. Boards can help keep the peace, but executive egos often make real partnerships impossible. You need only look at the vice presidency of the United States to see how hard it is for some No. 1s to share power. Even leaders who were abused as veeps had trouble treating their own vice presidents decently after becoming president. Truman, for example, was no better to Vice President Alben Barkley than FDR had been to him. Power is only shared by those who first choose to share it. In light of this first law of co-leadership, more and more organizations—and their governing boards—are realizing that willingness to share power is one of the criteria by which leaders must be judged.

As someone who knows both the executive experience and the subordinate one, the co-leader is a good model for a new, more egalitarian hybrid better adapted to the needs of the new millennium—people who can both command and follow, as the situation requires.

In American society the urge to be a star and the urge to achieve common goals as part of a community have always tugged us in different directions. As celebrity becomes less and less associated with genuine achievement, we need to think more clearly about what is best for our organizations and for ourselves. Great co-leaders remind us that we don't need to be captain to play on the team, that doing something we want to do and doing it well can be its own reward. That said, learning the secrets and skills of great No. 2s remains the surest path to becoming No. 1.

○　　○　　○

David A. Heenan is a trustee of the estate of James Campbell, one of the nation's largest landowners. He has taught at the Wharton School and the Columbia Graduate School of Business.

Warren Bennis is distinguished professor of the Marshall School of Business and founding chairman of the Leadership Institute at the University of Southern California.

Becoming a Leader

Where do leaders come from? Wherever one falls in the nature-versus-nurture debate, there are steps one can take to expand one's leadership abilities. The chapters in Part Two show how individuals who aspire to leadership positions can improve their chances and highlight some of the challenges they will face along the way. According to Robert E. Quinn, those that would grow and better themselves must continually step beyond their comfort zones, like the mythical hero who ventures where others fear to go and faces unknown trials. There are a number of important boundaries that a leader must cross during his or her development. Ram Charan, Stephen Drotter, and James Noel illustrate the major passages, both functional and philosophical, that a typical leader must traverse, while Morgan W. McCall Jr. reveals how promising leaders can stray off course. Along with the courage to take on the unknown and an understanding of the challenges ahead, a leader needs skills and knowledge to succeed. Some of this we are born with: Marcus Buckingham and Donald O. Clifton explain that yearnings and instinctive reactions help expose and clarify one's natural talents. Some development comes from outside sources: Ellen Van Velsor and Victoria A. Guthrie propose that continuous learning is essential to a leader's success and provide suggestions for lifelong learning.

Chapter Eleven

The Heroic Journey

Robert E. Quinn

Energy is neither created nor destroyed. At any given moment, it flows toward some points in the universe and away from others. The amount of energy we feel has much to do with the alignment between ourself and our surrounding environment. We can be aligned with our environment in such a way that we feel either strong and empowered or weak and powerless.

When we feel the strongest and at the "top of our game," we radiate large amounts of energy. When this energy and drive are directed toward some important task, good things tend to happen. As we experience success, we learn and grow. We gain a new perspective. As we apply this new understanding, we tend to become even more energized. During these periods, the self and the surrounding environment are more in alignment.

A key insight about dynamic alignment can be derived from an observation made by Fred Kofman and Peter Senge (1993). They point out that the self is a form of energy, and its state is entirely dependent on its relationship with the surrounding environment. They state:

> *Newtonian physicists were startled to discover that at the core of the atom, at the center of matter there is . nothing, no thing, pure energy. When they reached into the most fundamental building block of nature, they found a pregnant void—stable patterns of probability striving to connect with other patterns of probability. This discovery revolutionized the physical sciences, initiating the quantum era.*
>
> *By the same token, we are startled to discover that at the core of the person, at the center of selfhood there is . nothing, pure energy. When we reach into the most fundamental basis of our being we find a pregnant void, a web of relationships. When somebody asks us to talk about ourselves, we talk about family, work, academic background, sports affiliations, etc. In all this talk, where is our "self"? The answer is nowhere, because the self is not a thing, but as Jerome Brunner says, "a point of view that unifies the flow of experience into a coherent narrative"—a narrative striving to connect with other narratives and become richer [p. 14].*

What does this mean? These statements imply that the self is not a thing but an unfolding process. We are energized when we are learning and progressing, and we begin psychologically to die when we allow ourselves to stagnate. That is where we encounter the process of slow death.

Relationships often play a key role. We have our greatest sense of joy and meaning when we connect with others in mutually enhancing ways. When we are disempowered, when we choose "peace and pay," we do not create or attract mutually enhancing relationships. We are left to ourselves, depleted, tired, and disempowered.

If decay begins when we choose to stop growing, why do we ever stop? The answer is that there are times when we cannot "unify the flow of experience into a coherent narrative." These are the times when we lose our sense of self and our inaction causes us to stagnate. Like the resistant boy on the playground, we are tightly gripping our swing and cannot let go. Our internal voice tells us to do something, to move on, to engage the unknown, but our courage fails. We remind ourselves how much we value the pleasure we derive from the swing, and we tighten our grip.

The swing might represent any pattern of old and comfortable behavior—a job, a habit, a relationship, or any other pattern. The present self is very tied to this established pattern. We sense that without the pattern, the self would no longer exist.

This view exacerbates our problem. The longer we stay on the swing, the less courage we have to change. We get caught in a vicious cycle and can see no way out. At such times, the notion of realignment seems utopian at best. We come to believe that we are powerless, reflecting that all human beings are determined by their environments—that there is no such thing as individuality, freedom, choice, or impact. We are so into this sense of defeated and frustrated self that we do not recognize that our best self is not the old self but a new self that is slowly emerging.

A Framework for Personal Change:
The Hero's Journey

In today's changing global economy, uncertainty and constant change are an ongoing concern and an ever-present reality. Under these conditions, we often feel insecure, and we grasp for any source of stability and predictability.

In the workplace, we particularly yearn for a sense of direction. Working with large organizations, I often encounter middle managers who express a need to know the "vision"—the general framework of future direction that will guide and unite their efforts, a unifying vision that will allow them to make informed decisions within their own zone of discretion. They yearn for a leader who can align the internal and external realities and make the organization successful. They want someone who can guide them through the uncharted, threatening world of the unfamiliar. They long to feel confident that their organization, of which they are an integral part, will strive to be a vital and healthy concern.

Most of us have very high expectations of our leaders, and we are easily and quickly disillusioned by their failure to meet our expectations. We seldom, however, hold the same expectations for ourselves. We feel little responsibility to be the person who empowers self and, in so doing, empowers the surrounding community. Contemplating this tendency of ours, I am reminded of the work of Joseph Campbell, the well-known mythologist. He provides some interesting insights into the process of energizing self and community.

Common usage defines the word *myth* to mean something untrue. There is another use for the word, however. A myth is also a story that provides meaning and insight. It helps us make sense of our world and our existence in it. It may be a fictional story, like the tale of Cinderella, or a true story, like that of George Washington crossing the Delaware River. In either case, the myth or story provides a psychological framework, a schema or paradigm that can guide decisions.

Some myths, in their underlying message, are common across many cultures. Such myths are believed to reflect some basic needs in the human psyche. Campbell (1949) has identified a common myth that occurs in every culture. He calls it the hero's journey. The myth is about personal enlightenment and collective renewal. Campbell describes the hero's journey as follows:

> *The mythological hero, setting forth from his common day hut or castle, is lured, carried away, or else voluntarily proceeds to the threshold of adventure. There he encounters a shadow presence that guards the passage. The hero may defeat or conciliate this power and go alive into the kingdom of the dark (brother-battle, dragon-battle, offering, charm), or be slain by the opponent and descend in death (dismemberment, crucifixion). Beyond the threshold, then, the hero journeys through a world of unfamiliar yet strangely intimate forces, some of which severely threaten him (test), some of which give magical aid (helpers). When he arrives at the nadir of the mythological round, he undergoes a supreme ordeal and gains his reward. The triumph may be represented as the hero's sexual union with the goddess-mother of the world (sacred marriage), his recognition by the father-creator (father atonement), his own divinization (apotheosis), or again—if the powers have remained unfriendly to him—his theft of the boon he came to gain (bride-theft, fire-theft); intrinsically it is an expansion of consciousness and therewith of being (illumination,*

*transfiguration, freedom). The final work is that of the
return. If the powers have blessed the hero, he now sets
forth under their protection (emissary); if not, he flees and
is pursued (transformation flight, obstacle flight). At the
return threshold the transcendental powers must remain
behind; the hero reemerges from the kingdom of dread
(return, resurrection). The boon that he brings restores the
world (elixir) [p. 245].*

The hero's journey is a story of individual transformation, a change of identity. In embarking on the journey, we must leave the world of certainty. We must courageously journey to a strange place where there are a lot of risks and much is at stake, a place where there are new problems that require us to think in new ways.

Because there is much at stake, we must engage and resolve the problems before us. To do this successfully, we must surrender our present self—we must step outside our old paradigms. This venture outside of our current self will cause us to think differently. To continue our journey is to reinvent the self. It is then that our paradigms change and we experience an "expansion of consciousness." We begin to realign ourself with our surrounding environment. Not only do we view the world differently, but we view it more effectively.

Our new way of viewing the world also causes us to see ourselves differently. There is a change in our state of being, a change in self. As a result of this realignment of self, we can more effectively impact our environment. Success begins to breed success, and we are filled with drive and energy. In this way, we can empower others, and we become an asset to ourselves, our organizations, and our community.

Basically, the hero's journey is a theory of change. In some form, it exists in every culture. It is a theory of change that we all, at some level, understand. Yet the word *hero* can be problematic. There are many famous heroes. These people tend to appear almost larger than life. In taking the hero's journey, they do the seemingly impossible. Surviving their amazing feats, they gain our respect, and we confer on them near-deity status.

I like to think about the hero's journey in other terms. I like to think about a little boy who is being encouraged to leave a safe, known, and desirable place to journey to a place that he has only been told about. I like to think of the blue-collar laborer who, after an agonizing deliberation, decides to risk the job rather than follow an unethical directive. I like to think about the hero's journey in terms of you and me and our continual search for meaning and direction in our lives.

In our search for meaning and direction, we have a problem. Traditionally, our paradigms, myths, or scripts have told us what to do. They have helped organize our lives. Whenever we follow them, we feel safe. But today, our environment keeps changing. Because environments are dynamic and our myths are based in the past, our strategies often fail, and we feel a sense of alienation. Increasingly, it is becoming necessary for us to re-create our paradigms, myths, scripts, or frameworks.

New paradigms are created by engaging a new action path, one in which we must separate from the status quo and courageously face and tackle uncertainty. When successful, this process alters our original frameworks and our original self. We become highly aligned, successful, empowered, and able to help and inspire others. Only when this realignment is successful are we able to become leaders and change agents.

The problem is that the new alignment lies on the other side of uncertainty.

○   ○   ○

Robert E. Quinn is a professor at the University of Michigan Business School and a consultant and speaker.

Chapter Twelve

Six Leadership Passages

Ram Charan
Stephen Drotter
James Noel

The six turns in the pipeline that we'll discuss here are major events in the life of a leader. They represent significant passages that can't be mastered in a day or by taking a course. Our goal here is to help you become familiar with the skills, time applications, and work values demanded by each passage, as well as this particular leadership gestalt. Once you grasp what these passages entail and the challenges involved in making each leadership transition, you'll be in a better position to use this information to unclog your organization's leadership pipeline and facilitate your own growth as a leader. Going through these passages helps leaders build emotional strength as they take on tasks of increasing complexity and scope. The following six chapters will provide you with ideas and tools to achieve full performance at all leadership levels in your organization.

As you read about each passage, you'll naturally apply it to your own organization and may question how we've defined and divided each turn in the pipeline. The odds are that you'll immediately think of at least one (and probably more) leadership transitions that apply to your own company that we have not addressed in the Leadership Pipeline model. While there certainly are other transitions, they are too small or incomplete to qualify as a major passage. For instance, many global companies have business general managers at the country level and regional executives with responsibility for several countries. These regional executives report to a person with a title such as global consumer products head. Although this global consumer products head manages group managers (the regional executives in this case), she isn't an enterprise manager because she reports to a CEO or president and has little accountability for corporate profit and loss matters. For our purposes here, we would categorize her as a group manager, even though she may have responsibility for other group managers.

Similarly, you may wonder why the transition from team member to team leader isn't worthy of its own passage. First, this is usually a subset of Passage One (managing self to managing others). Second, team leaders frequently lack the decision-making authority on selection and rewards that first-line managers receive. Third, team leaders usually focus on technical or professional matters (getting a project or program completed) and aren't tested in more general management areas.

Each organization is unique, and each probably has at least one leadership passage with distinctive aspects. It's likely, however, that you can fit that distinctive passage into one of our six passages. As you become more attuned to each of them, we believe you'll see how they apply to your own situation and organization. If there is a passage in your business that doesn't fit our model, create your own definition of the transition and tell us about it.

Passage One:
From Managing Self to Managing Others

New, young employees usually spend their first few years with an organization as individual contributors. Whether they're in sales, accounting, engineering, or marketing, their skill requirements are primarily technical or professional. They contribute by doing the assigned work within given time frames and in ways that meet objectives. By sharpening and broadening their individual skills, they make increased contributions and are then considered "promotable" by organizations. From a time application standpoint, the learning involves planning (so that work is completed on time), punctuality, content, quality, and reliability. The work values to be developed include acceptance of the company culture and adopting professional standards. When people become skilled individual contributors who produce good results—especially when they demonstrate an ability to collaborate with others—they usually receive additional responsibilities. When they demonstrate an ability to handle these responsibilities and adhere to the company's values, they are often promoted to first-line manager.

When this happens, they are at Passage One. Though this might seem like an easy, natural leadership passage, it's often one where people trip. The highest-performing people, especially, are reluctant to change; they want to keep doing the activities that made them successful. As a result, people make the job transition from individual contributor to manager without making a behavioral or value-based transition. In effect, they become managers without accepting the requirements. Many consultants, for instance, have skipped this turn, moving from transitory team leadership to business leader without absorbing much of the learning in between. The result, when business leaders miss this passage, is frequently disaster.

The skills people should learn at this first leadership passage include planning work, filling jobs, assigning work, motivating, coaching, and measuring the work of others. First-time managers need to learn how to reallocate their time so that they not only complete their assigned work but also help others perform effectively. They cannot allocate all of their time to putting out fires, seizing opportunities, and handling tasks themselves. They must shift from "doing" work to getting work done through others.

Reallocating time is an especially difficult transitional requirement for first-time managers. Part of the problem is that many neophyte managers still prefer to spend time on their "old" work, even as they take charge of a group. Yet the pressure to spend less time on individual work and more time on managing will increase at each passage, and if people don't start making changes in how they allocate their time from the beginning, they're bound to become liabilities as they move up. It's a major reason why pipelines clog and leaders fail.

The most difficult change for managers to make at Passage One, however, involves values. Specifically, they need to learn to value managerial work rather than just tolerate it. They must believe that making time for others, planning, coaching, and the like are necessary tasks and are their responsibility. More than that, they must view this other-directed work as mission-critical to their success. For instance, first-line knowledge managers in the financial services industry find this transition extremely difficult. They value being producers, and they must learn to value making others productive. Given that these values had nothing to do with their success as individual contributors, it's difficult for them to make this dramatic shift in what they view as meaningful. While changes in skills and time applications can be seen and measured, changes in values are more difficult to assess. Someone may appear as though he's making the changes demanded by this leadership turn but in fact be adhering to individual-contributor values. Value changes will only take place if upper management reinforces the need to shift beliefs and if people find they're successful at their new jobs after a value shift.

Passage Two: From Managing Others to Managing Managers

This leadership passage is frequently ignored, especially relative to the previous passage (where the transition to new responsibilities is more obvious). Few companies address this passage directly in their training, even though this is the level where a company's management foundation is constructed; level-two managers select and develop the people who will eventually become the company's leaders.

Perhaps the biggest difference from the previous passage is that here, managers must be pure management. Before, individual contributions were still part of their job description. Now, they need to divest themselves of individual tasks. The key skills that must be mastered during this transition include selecting people to turn Passage One, assigning managerial and leadership work to them, measuring their progress as managers, and coaching them. This is also the point where managers must begin to think beyond their function and concern themselves with strategic issues that support the overall business.

All this is difficult to do if a given manager at this passage still values individual contributions and functional work to the exclusion of everything else. Too often people who have been promoted to manager-of-manager positions have skipped Passage One; they were promoted to first-line managers but didn't change skills, time applications or work values. As a result, they clog the leadership pipeline because they hold first-line managers accountable for technical work rather than managerial work. Because they themselves skipped the first passage and still value individual contributions above managerial ones, they poison the managerial well. They help maintain and even instill the wrong values in those individuals who report to them. They choose high technical achievers for first-line managerial spots rather than true potential leaders; they are unable to differentiate between those who can do and those who can lead.

Managers at Passage Two need to be able to identify value-based resistance to managerial work, a common reaction among first-line managers. They need to recognize that the software designer who would rather design software than manage others cannot be allowed to move up to leadership work. No matter how brilliant he might be at software design, he will become an obstacle in the leadership pipeline if he derives no job satisfaction from managing and leading people. In fact, one of the tough responsibilities of managers of managers is to return people to individual-contributor roles if first-line managers don't shift their behaviors and values.

Coaching is also essential at this level because first-line managers frequently don't receive formal training in how to be a manager; they're dependent on their bosses to instruct them on the job. Coaching requires time—they need to go through the instruction-performance-feedback cycle with their people repeatedly before lessons sink in—and some managers aren't willing to reallocate their time in this way. In many organizations, coaching ability isn't rewarded (and the lack of it isn't penalized). It's no wonder that relatively few managers view coaching as mission-critical.

PASSAGE THREE: FROM MANAGING MANAGERS TO FUNCTIONAL MANAGER

This transition is tougher than it seems. While on the surface the difference between managing managers and functional management might appear negligible, a number of significant challenges lurk below the surface. Communication with the individual-contributor level now requires penetrating at least two layers of management, thus mandating development of new communication skills. What is just as significant, functional heads must manage some areas that are outside their own experiences. This means they must not only endeavor to understand this "foreign" work but also learn to value it.

At the same time, functional managers report to multifunctional general managers and therefore have to become skilled at taking other functional concerns and needs into consideration. Team play with other functional managers and competition for resources based on business needs are two major transitional skills. At the same time, managers at this turn should become proficient strategists, not only for their function but blending their functional strategy with the overall business strategy. From a time-application standpoint, this means participating in business team meetings and working with other functional managers. All this takes away from time spent on purely functional responsibilities, thus making it essential that functional managers delegate responsibility for overseeing many functional tasks to direct reports.

This leadership passage requires an increase in managerial maturity. In one sense, maturity means thinking and acting like a functional leader rather than a functional member. But it also means that managers need to adopt a broad, long-term perspective. Long-term strategy, such as state-of-the-art, futuristic thinking for their function, is usually what gives most managers trouble here. At this level, their leadership entails creating functional strategy that enables them to do something better than the competition. Whether it's coming up with a method to design more innovative products or reach new customer groups, these managers must push the functional envelope. They must also push it into the future, looking at sustainable competitive advantage rather than just an immediate but temporary edge.

> Tom's experiences illustrate the challenges new functional managers face. Six months ago, Tom was named the director of plant operations. In this capacity he has five direct reports: four run large factories and one who runs purchasing of raw materials. Although Tom's experiences have made him appreciative of sales, financial, and other functional areas, Tom has trouble planning beyond immediate functional requirements and keeping in touch with line workers where the action is. Not only is it difficult for Tom to define the steps necessary for the plants to become a more integrated manufacturing facility, but he's also finding that he's lost touch

with many of the workers he used to communicate with on a regular basis. At many organizations, a guy like Tom would just muddle through, and his strengths would compensate for his weaknesses, at least on the surface. But upon closer inspection, Tom would not be a full performer in his leadership position. For instance, it's important that Tom develop the skill of skip-level communication; he needs to know, without diminishing the authority of the plant managers and the first-line manager, what individual contributors are working on and how well they're being managed. If Tom doesn't develop this skill, he may alienate the plant manager and the first-line managers by usurping their authority or he may be out of touch with how well his direct reports are supervising their people.

Luckily, Tom's organization has an assessment program in place that has identified his struggle with Passage Three and is providing him with coaching and the chance to attend a first-rate executive development program that will help him build the skills required at this leadership level.

Passage Four: From Functional Manager to Business Manager

This leadership passage is often the most satisfying as well as the most challenging of a manager's career, and it's mission-critical in organizations. Business mangers usually receive significant autonomy, which people with leadership instincts find liberating. They also are able to see a clear link between their efforts and marketplace results. At the same time, this is a sharp turn; it requires a major shift in skills, time applications, and work values. It's not simply a matter of people becoming more strategic and cross-functional in their thinking (though it's important to continue developing the abilities rooted in the previous level). Now they are in charge of integrating functions whereas before they simply had to understand and work with other functions. But the biggest shift is from looking at plans and proposals functionally (Can we do it technically, professionally, or physically?) to a profit perspective (Will we make any money if we do this?) and to a long-term view (Is the profitability result sustainable?). New business managers must change the way they think in order to be successful.

There are probably more new and unfamiliar responsibilities here than at other levels. For people who have only been in one function their entire careers, a business manager position represents unexplored territory; they must suddenly become responsible for many unfamiliar functions and outcomes. Not only do they have to learn to manage different functions, but they also need to become skilled at working with a wider variety of people than ever before; they need to become more sensitive to functional diversity issues and communicating clearly and effectively. Even more difficult is the balancing act between future goals and present needs and making trade-offs between the two. Business managers must meet quarterly profit, market share, product, and people targets, and at the same time plan for goals three to five years into the future. The paradox of balancing short-term and long-term thinking is one that bedevils many managers at this turn—and why one of the requirements here is for thinking time. At this level, managers need to stop doing every second of the day and reserve time for reflection and analysis.

When business managers don't make this turn fully, the leadership pipeline quickly becomes clogged. For example, a common failure at this level is not valuing (or effectively using) staff functions. Directing and energizing finance, human resources, legal, and other support groups are crucial business manager responsibilities. When managers don't understand or appreciate the contribution of support staff, these staff people don't deliver full performance. When the leader of the business demeans or diminishes their roles, staff people deliver half-hearted efforts; they can easily become energy-drainers. Business managers must learn to trust, accept advice, and receive feedback from all functional managers, even though they may never have experienced these functions personally.

Passage Five: From Business Manager to Group Manager

This is another leadership passage that at first glance doesn't seem overly arduous. The assumption is that if you can run one business successfully, you can do the same with two or more businesses. The flaw in this reasoning begins with what is valued at each leadership level. A business manager values the success of his own business. A group manager values the success of other people's businesses. This is a critical distinction because some people only derive satisfaction when they're the ones receiving the lion's share of the credit. As you might imagine, a group manager who doesn't value the success of others will fail to inspire and support the performance of the business managers who report to him. Or his actions might be dictated by his frustration; he's convinced he could operate the various businesses better than any of his managers and wishes he could be doing so. In either instance, the leadership pipeline becomes clogged with business managers who aren't operating at peak capacity because they're not being properly supported or their authority is being usurped.

This level also requires a critical shift in four skill sets. First, group managers must become proficient at evaluating strategy for capital allocation and deployment purposes. This is a sophisticated business skill that involves learning to ask the right questions, analyze the right data, and apply the right corporate perspective to understand which strategy has the greatest probability of success and therefore should be funded.

The second skill cluster involves development of business managers. As part of this development, group managers need to know who among the function managers is ready to become business managers. Coaching new business managers is also an important role for this level.

The third skill set has to do with portfolio strategy. This is quite different from business strategy and demands a perceptual shift. This is the first time managers have to ask these questions: Do I have the right collection of businesses? What businesses should be added, subtracted, or changed to position us properly and assure current and future earnings?

Fourth, group managers must become astute about assessing whether they have the right core capabilities to win. This means avoiding wishful thinking and taking a hard, objective look at their range of resources and making a judgment based on analysis and experience.

Leadership becomes more holistic at this level. People may master the required skills but they won't perform at full leadership capacity if they don't begin to see themselves as a broad-gauged executive. By broad-gauged, we mean that managers need to factor in the complexities of running multiple businesses, thinking in terms of community, industry, government, and ceremonial activities. They must also prepare themselves for the bigger decisions, greater risks and uncertainties, and longer time spans that are inherent to this leadership level. They must always be cognizant of what Wall Street wants them to achieve in terms of the financial scorecard. Group managers can't take a specialist mentality into a realm that mandates holistic thinking. They need to evolve their perspective to the point that they see issues in the broadest possible terms.

We should also point out that some smaller companies don't have a group manager passage. In these companies, CEOs usually undertake a group manager's responsibilities.

Passage Six: From Group Manager to Enterprise Manager

When the leadership pipeline becomes clogged at the top, it negatively impacts all leadership levels. A CEO who has skipped one or more passages can diminish the performance of managers who not only report directly to him but individuals all the way down the line. They not only fail to develop other managers effectively, they also don't fulfill the responsibilities that come with this position.

The transition during the sixth passage is much more focused on values than skills. To an even greater extent than at the previous level, people must reinvent their self-concept as an enterprise manager. As leaders of an institution, they must be long-term, visionary thinkers. At the same time, they must develop operating mechanisms to know and drive quarter-by-quarter performance that is in tune with longer-term strategy. The trade-offs involved can be mind-bending, and enterprise leaders learn to value these trade-offs. In addition, this new leadership role often requires well-developed external sensitivity, an ability to manage external constituencies, sense significant external shifts, and do something about them proactively (rather than reactively). Again, CEOs value this outward-looking perspective.

Enterprise leaders need to come to terms with the fact that their performance as a CEO will be based on three or four high-leverage decisions annually; they must set these three or four mission-critical priorities and focus on them. There's a subtle but fundamental shift in responsibility from strategic to visionary thinking and from an operations to a global perspective. There's also a "letting go" process that should take place during this passage if it hasn't taken place previously. Enterprise leaders must let go of the pieces—that is, the individual products and customers—and focus on the whole (How well do we conceive, develop, produce, and market all products to all customers?).

Finally, at this level a CEO must assemble a team of high-achieving and ambitious direct reports, knowing that some of them want his job and picking them for the team despite this knowledge. This is also the only leadership position in the organization where inspiring the entire employee population through a variety of communication tools is essential.

Leadership pipeline problems occur at this level for two common reasons:

- CEOs are often unaware that this is a significant passage that requires changes in values.
- It's difficult to develop a CEO for this particular leadership transition.

In terms of the latter, preparation for the chief executive position is the result of a series of diverse experiences over a long time. The best developmental approach provides carefully selected job assignments that stretch people over time and allow them to learn and practice necessary skills. Though coaching might be helpful as an adjunct to this development process, people usually need time, experience, and the right assignments to develop into effective CEOs.

The former point is a matter of will and conscious effort. We've seen too many CEOs fail because they didn't view this leadership turn as a necessary one to make—or to make fully. They sustain the same skills, time applications, and work values that served them well as group managers and never adjust their self-concept to fit their new leadership role. They behave as though they are running a portfolio of businesses, not one entity.

Passages Through the Pipeline

Knowledge about each passage helps reveal "hidden" leadership problems at every organizational layer; this knowledge also provides a way to solve these problems. Too often, organizations don't realize that their leaders aren't performing at full capacity because they aren't holding them accountable for the right things. Companies focus only on the economic requirements of a given job rather than the skills, time applications, and values of a specific leadership level. As a result, a business manager is allowed to spend most of his time acquiring new customers rather than developing an effective business strategy. Or the business manager's boss, the Group Manager, never questions or explores what the business manager values about his work and whether those values are appropriate for the leadership the company requires from him. But when this manager's strategy is flawed and important goals aren't achieved, he isn't held accountable (or he isn't held accountable for the right thing).

If, however, the organization was acutely aware of these leadership passages, the problem could be quickly diagnosed and the manager developed accordingly. The organization would be aware that this business manager is still doing his job as though he's at Passage One, that he values face-to-face selling above all else, and that he has never acquired basic strategic skills crucial to his current leadership level. A development program could be created targeting these deficiencies. Concurrently, this business manager's boss, the Group Manager, would be held accountable for developing the business manager and coaching him about the importance of strategic planning and how he should be allocating his time.

By establishing appropriate requirements for the six leadership levels, companies could greatly facilitate the succession planning, development, and selection processes in their organizations. Individual managers could clearly see the gap between their current level of performance and the desired level; they could also see gaps in their training and experience and where they may have skipped a passage (or parts of a passage) and how that's hurting their performance. The clarity of leadership requirements would also help the human resources function, in that HR could make development decisions based on where people fall short in skills, time applications, and values rather than relying on generalized training and development programs. In addition, an individual's readiness for a move to the next leadership level could be clearly identified rather than inaccurately tied to how well they performed in their previous position. These leadership passages provide companies with a way to "objectify" selection. Rather than selecting based on past performance, personal connections, and personal preferences, managers can be held to a higher, more effective standard. Organizations can select someone to make a leadership turn when he's clearly working at the level to which he is assigned and demonstrating some of the skills required at the next level. And of course, the Pipeline model provides organizations with a diagnostic tool that helps them identity mismatches between individual capabilities and leadership level and remove the mismatched person if necessary.

You should also be aware of three other benefits to the pipeline. First, having a leadership pipeline in place can reduce emotional stress for individual employees. When someone skips leadership passages and is placed in a position for which he lacks the skills, time applications, and work values it takes a large emotional toll. The Pipeline model makes skipping passages unlikely. Second, this model helps people move through leadership passages at the right speed. People who ticket-punch their way through jobs don't absorb the necessary values and skills; people who get stuck in a passage never "go" places where they can acquire new skills and evolve their leadership capacity. The Pipeline model provides a measurement system identifying when someone is ready to move to the next leadership level. Third, the Pipeline model reduces the typical time frame needed to prepare an individual for the top leadership position in a large corporation. Because the Pipeline model clearly defines what is needed to move from one level to the next, there's little or no wasted time on jobs that merely duplicate skills.

From a pure talent perspective, however, the most significant benefit of the Pipeline methodology is that you don't need to bring in stars to prime the leadership pump and unclog the pipeline. You can create your own stars up and down the line, beginning at the first level when people make the transition from managing themselves to managing others.

○   ○   ○

Ram Charan is an adviser to CEOs and senior executives in companies ranging from start-ups to the Fortune 500.

Stephen Drotter heads an executive succession planning company and has worked in human resource management with General Electric, CIGNA, and Chase Manhattan Corporation.

James Noel is a consultant and executive coach and has worked in management at Citibank, General Electric, and Philip Morris.

Chapter Thirteen

The Derailment Conspiracy

Morgan W. McCall Jr.

The world is too complex for a simple report card of strengths or weaknesses to explain what we observe about human behavior, talent, and the development of abilities. Overly simplistic models have created a shaky foundation upon which most executive development systems have been constructed. The dynamics underlying the derailment of talent (summarized in Exhibit 13.1) suggest starting with a different set of assumptions: every strength can be a weakness; blind spots matter eventually; success after success can lead to arrogance; and "bad luck" happens, but often what a person does when things go wrong is the determining factor.

EVERY STRENGTH CAN BE A WEAKNESS

Every strength, even those that have led to success, can be or become a weakness. For the brilliant, there are the potential downsides of dismissing others' ideas, not listening, or letting

EXHIBIT 13.1 **The Dynamics of Derailment**

Strengths become weaknesses	Remarkable strengths that made a person successful can become liabilities in situations where other strengths are more important.
Blind spots matter	Weaknesses and flaws that didn't matter before or were forgiven in light of strengths or results become central in a new situation.
Success leads to arrogance	Success goes to a person's head, leading to the mistaken belief that he or she is infallible and needs no one else. This often occurs at precisely the time when these assumptions are least viable.
Bad luck occurs	Sometimes derailment results from a run-in with fate that is not an accurate reflection of the person's talent. Sometimes, however, bad luck is exacerbated by one of the other dynamics, suggesting that fate does not always act alone.

Source: Adapted from Morgan W. McCall Jr. and Michael M. Lombardo, *Off the Track: Why and How Successful Executives Get Derailed* (Greensboro, N.C.: Center for Creative Leadership, 1983), pp. 2–3.

arrogance take root. Admirably adhering to principle can evolve into fanaticism or imposing one's beliefs on others. An extraordinary ability to build high-performing teams can seduce a person into ignoring other relationships that aren't going as well. How often is a leader who, at one point, is described as decisive and setting high standards, later seen as imperial, autocratic, or dictatorial?[1] How far is it to go from acting in a self-assured, self-confident manner to acting arrogant and cocky? From being broadly strategic and carefully analytical to being unfocused and indecisive?

The corporate version of the right stuff is built on the assumptions that there is a finite list of virtues that defines effective executive leadership, and that these virtues distinguish exceptional from average executives. If every strength is also a potential weakness, however, neither assumption holds. The list of virtues in Exhibit 13.2 was adapted from an actual list of competencies developed by a large international organization—it is quite typical. In the right-hand column are potential dark sides for each strength. Take, as an example, the competency "customer-focused." How could anyone question the value of focusing on the customer's needs? *Fortune* did, in an article entitled "Ignore Your Customer," which described how Chrysler, Compaq, Fox Broadcasting, Motorola, and Steelcase have done just that to great success.[2] These companies believe that customer input can be confusing or wrong (remember New Coke?), and that breakthroughs may require faith in the product more than they require listening to the customer.

Among the front pagers, there are many examples of notable strengths becoming notable weaknesses. When Edward Lucente assumed second-in-command at Digital Equipment, he was said to have the toughness and discipline needed to change the culture. But he was later described as abrasive and autocratic. Same story for Michael Gartner, who was brought in from the outside by General Electric presumably because he was tough enough to do whatever was deemed necessary to turn around the NBC news division. Later, after acting toughly, he was described as out of touch, prickly, an outsider.[3] In both

EXHIBIT 13.2 **Competencies and Their Dark Sides**

Competency	Potential Dark Side
Is a team player	Not a risk taker, indecisive, lacks independent judgment
Is customer-focused	Can't create breakthroughs, can't control costs, unrealistic, too conservative
Is biased toward action	Reckless, dictatorial
Is an analytical thinker	Prone to analysis paralysis, afraid to act, inclined to create large staffs
Has integrity	Holier-than-thou, rigid, imposes personal standards on others, zealot
Is innovative	Unrealistic, impractical, wastes time and money
Has global vision	Misses local markets, over-extended, unfocused
Is good with people	Soft, can't make tough decisions, too easy on people

cases, one has to suspect that the very attributes for which they were chosen became a part of their undoing.

Robbie Ftorek illustrates a different angle on strengths becoming weaknesses. A coach of the Los Angeles Kings, he was described as good technically and a good teacher—strengths perfectly suited to the Kings when they were a struggling team with a lot of young, inexperienced players. As the team matured and acquired veteran players, including superstar Wayne Gretzky, Ftorek's teaching style was no longer so well received. The more he attempted to tell the veterans how to play, the deeper his former strengths got him into trouble.

The problem with strengths that have led to success is a result of the success itself. It is difficult to abandon what has worked, even when circumstances change, and it may be nearly impossible to give up old patterns if no new skills have been developed to replace the old ones.

Being a tactical genius is hardly a flaw in a situation that calls for tactical skill. But a tactical orientation that results in a preoccupation with details or mires a person in technical problems can prevent an executive from grasping the big picture.

Learning tactical proficiency at the expense of strategic perspective is especially common in organizations and in jobs where performance is assessed by short-term (quarterly or even daily) results. Of the collection of front pagers, William Fife was hit the hardest by this particular malady. Described as a hard-working, down-to-earth, shirt-sleeve kind of guy—the positive side of tactical skill—Fife's "too-aggressive emphasis on short-term results" eventually led him into questionable financial deals in pursuit of short-term profits.[4] In this case, the flaw played out in two spheres: the short-term results were attained at the expense of long-term strategy, and immersion in short-term thinking blinded him to the larger consequences of his actions.

Technical expertise is another strength that is effective in some leadership situations, especially at lower management levels. When, however, a manager's superior expertise leads to overmanaging—telling people how to do their jobs rather than letting them do their jobs—it becomes a liability. This tendency is especially self-destructive when the people being overmanaged know more about what they are doing than their boss does—and sooner or later, a successful executive will end up managing people and functions outside of his or her expertise. Among other things, overmanagers can be guilty of meddling in things they don't understand, alienating people whose help they need, making a lot of mistakes because they don't listen to experts or because the experts don't care to help them, or getting mired in details and not thinking broadly. Some micromanagers get so busy doing everyone else's job that they don't do their own.

The point is that the value of a given attribute in an executive's repertoire is relative—to the immediate situation, to the organization's strategic direction, to the executive's other strengths and weaknesses, and to the observer's relationship to the executive. All too often, it seems that certain attitudes and behaviors are viewed positively (demanding, decisive, persevering, tough-minded) until things go wrong; then they miraculously turn into weaknesses (dictatorial, arbitrary, stubborn, bullying). In reality, people are complex tapestries of values, attitudes, beliefs, and abilities. It is misleading to believe that these ten or those ten virtues apply to all successful executives in all situations, even within the same company. How that tapestry is woven, not its individual threads, determines how it looks. The room it is hung in and the surrounding decor—not individual threads—determine whether the colors and patterns of the tapestry are a good fit.

Because there is no list of ultimate strengths, the perfect executive is a myth. Executive development and selection practices built on the assumption that the myth is true can never be completely successful. Development systems need to be built on some other foundation that incorporates the intriguing variety among talented people.

Blind Spots Matter Eventually

The world is not always fair, nor does justice always triumph in the end. Nonetheless, the stories of the front pagers suggest that flaws that have been overlooked or have lain dormant for long periods can and often do become a manager's nemesis. Weaknesses do catch up. Especially with derailed senior executives, it seems unlikely that the flaws that eventually did them in appeared suddenly. In most cases, the flaws that later were fatal had existed for a long time, if not in their pure form, then certainly as recognizable precursors.

Insensitivity was the most commonly reported flaw among derailed executives in our research and was one of the sharpest differentiators between derailed and successful executives. It was also a dominant theme among the front-pager derailments.[5] Horst Schroeder was described as imperious, demanding, abrasive, unwilling to listen, abrupt, and intolerant of dissent, yet he had a sixteen-year track record of success.[6] It wasn't until he stumbled as president and needed the support of his subordinates that the consequences of his alleged treatment of others emerged.

Richard Snyder supposedly ruled Simon and Schuster by "intimidation and fear," becoming something of a legend within the firm. According to the *Wall Street Journal*, "Scores of former employees tell of meetings where he would threaten to lop off someone's hands or private parts, or tear out their throat for some failure to perform."[7]

Humiliating managers in front of peers or subordinates, cutting people off, demeaning others' ideas—everyone who has ever worked for an insensitive boss (and most of us have) knows the story and the incredible visceral response such treatment generates. Power and intimidation can produce compliance, but insensitivity can lead to lack of support at crucial junctures, failure of subordinates to pass on important information, active sabotage, loss of ideas from below, and a host of counterproductive activities. Organizations seem quite willing to overlook the flaw of insensitivity as long as someone gets results, but at the higher levels of management, alienating others in most cases assures that good results will not be sustained over time. It can't be very useful to have large numbers of people eager to see one fail.

The reason that formerly benign flaws become lethal usually involves a change in context. Talented people—people who get results, people who have visible achievements—tend to change situations often. They get promoted, are offered developmental assignments, find themselves assigned to important projects, are given increased responsibility, or otherwise move into new and often more visible settings. These opportunities typically bring with them a new boss, new job demands, or perhaps a new organizational culture (if the change involves a move to a different part of the organization or to headquarters), and these in turn call into question the continued success of a person's particular pattern of strengths and weaknesses. Finding themselves in situations that no longer play to their strengths, they are left with only their weaknesses to draw on.

Of course, successful people have many changes in jobs and bosses during their careers, and most of these transitions go smoothly. The deciding factor turns out to be the magnitude of the difference between what went before and what the new territory demands. Traditionally, boundary jumps have held the biggest threat: changing functional areas, for instance, moving from marketing to finance; moving from one division or business to another, such as going from a defense-related business to a consumer business; or switching from line to staff. More recently, however, organizations have been undergoing internal transformations that have led to derailments without a literal cross-boundary shift. The trend toward moving authority down and eliminating layers of hierarchy, for example, has shifted effective leadership from autocratic to empowering, with the resulting requirement that people successful with one style must shift to a new one. One might say that the territory changed underneath them.

Similarly, globalization, deregulation, consolidation, acquisition, and divestiture all create new territory that changes the relevance of existing patterns of strengths and weaknesses. Once again, the operative element is the degree of difference between what was and what is now. International assignments vary considerably in the degree of "difference" confronted—variations in climate, disease, political conditions, religion, language, and a host of other possibilities add to the normative and stylistic differences across cultures. The demands they impose are not inherently derailing, unless something in the new situation calls for strengths where a person happens to be weak.

Several implications may be drawn from the relative nature of weaknesses. First, two dynamic processes leading to derailment—strengths becoming weaknesses and weaknesses becoming important—strongly suggest that fixed-template models of executive effectiveness are inadequate. To reflect reality, they must incorporate context, time, and the interactions among strengths and weaknesses.

Second, defining effectiveness solely in terms of results masks significant developmental needs from both organizations and the managers. Understandably eager to achieve business results, organizations may be inclined to overlook how results are achieved—especially since judgments about differences in style are often subjective, and as we have seen, similar actions can be viewed as positive or negative depending on the context and outcome. An individual rewarded for results alone might reasonably conclude that the means for achieving those results were acceptable or admirable, even if they weren't. Unfortunately, ignoring or rewarding weaknesses sets the stage for future derailments, and ironically, the individual and the organization are co-conspirators in writing the script.

Given the obvious danger that weaknesses present in a changing world, why don't people—especially talented people—correct their weaknesses before they cause havoc? There are perhaps several reasons, but the bottom line is that they haven't yet been hurt by them. Because of the confidence built by success and the presence of demonstrated strengths, it is possible to dismiss potential weaknesses as unimportant or as nonexistent. John Steinbeck observed a biological parallel during his exploration of the Sea of Cortez. He wrote, "If an animal is good to eat or poisonous or dangerous the natives of the place will know about it and know where it lives. But if it have none of these qualities, no matter how highly colored or beautiful, he may never in his life have seen it."[8] So it may be with weaknesses, so easy to overlook unless they bite. What is even more dangerous developmentally, weaknesses may be seen as strengths, as "good to eat," because indeed they are in some situations.

This observation suggests a third and less obvious implication involving the situational nature of weaknesses. Because changing context can make weaknesses matter, well-intended promotions or developmental moves can turn into lethal situations. Many executive leadership skills are learned through exposure to challenging new situations, so a major challenge to any executive development system is managing these crucial moves effectively. The goal, after all, is to enhance and preserve talented people, not to destroy them. Putting talented people in situations that expose their weaknesses can be developmental or fatal, depending on how both the person and the organization handle the situation.

Success After Success Leads to Arrogance

William Hazlitt aptly described the dangers of arrogance: "Do not imagine that you will make people friends by showing your superiority over them; it is what they will neither admit nor forgive."[9] Most of the front pagers were said to have been arrogant at least to some degree, sometimes to an extraordinary degree, and arrogance often figured prominently in their derailments. Self-confidence, so important to success, sometimes grew bloated by the success that fed it. Blinded by the bright light of their own achievements, immensely talented people can fly too close to the sun, like Icarus. Forced out of the top spot at Ford Motor Company, Don Petersen was described by his detractors as believing his own press clippings.[10] According to *Fortune* magazine, a competitor said of the Mars brothers, "Their own hubris was their downfall. They are arrogant, and when your arrogance exceeds your intellect you've got trouble."[11] *Business Week* even devoted a cover story to the phenomenon as it relates to chief executives, dubbing their (mis)perception that they can do no wrong as "CEO disease."[12] The article implied that the pampering and power of high office is the culprit, and certainly that is part of the story. But in studies of derailment, aloofness and arrogance among successful people is not restricted to those who make it to the very top. Each successive success, whether a technical accomplishment or a business result, adds to the opportunity to believe one's own press clippings or to admire the trophy case. Whether they were military aviators, physician managers, or executives, none were above interpreting accomplishments as further proof that there was something special about them (as indeed there was). For some, that specialness translated into egotism, resulting in behavior that served to alienate those on whom they depended.

In a complex environment characterized by interdependence, arrogance has the unfortunate outcome of depriving a leader of the loyalty needed to operate effectively. People usually aren't eager to go the extra mile to help such a person succeed, as Robert Schoellhorn, removed by the Abbott Laboratories board, found out. Even though he led a major comeback of the company, presided over steady and uninterrupted increases in revenue, earnings, and profits, and basked in external admiration, such achievements did not save him after he reportedly lost the respect of his executives. Described as "the grandiose man who ruled over his company as if it were a private fiefdom," Schoellhorn went from being one business magazine's 1986 Executive of the Year to becoming a case study of egotism in the 1991 *Business Week* cover story.[13] The reason? He became a victim of his own success.

Arrogance has some special qualities that merit separate treatment. One is that arrogance grows over time with success. Unlike preexisting strengths that become weaknesses in a different situation or preexisting weaknesses that become important later on, arrogance develops over time and causes people to lose their bearings. In effect, it sets up the other derailment dynamics by creating a feeling of invincibility and a blindness to one's impact and its potential consequences. The derailment cases were filled with people who were unaware of important information, failed to see the significance of crucial events, couldn't understand why their behavior had negative consequences, or ignored the obvious disrepair in critical relationships.

In some cases where total "blindness" was not possible, the importance of what was seen was diminished. It appeared that NBC's Michael Gartner accepted that his behavior was arrogant and aloof—he had been told repeatedly that it was—but he dismissed it with a shrug, saying "I don't try to be, but I am who I am."[14] At the extreme, arrogance feeds a belief that a person is immune to any consequences, as William Manchester's account of Douglas MacArthur's defiant confrontation with President Truman suggested.[15] Disagreeing with Truman's decision to settle for an armistice in the Korean conflict, MacArthur criticized and embarrassed his commander-in-chief publicly, forcing the showdown in which Truman removed him from command.

The net effect of arrogance as it grows over time is that once-effective people become increasingly out of touch and less effective. This may be the result of one or both of two dynamics. The first is that arrogance is associated with attributes that contribute to success (and therefore is at least partially justified); the second is the tendency to believe that exceptional attributes exempt their possessor from "normal" constraints.

It has been observed that "great egoists are almost always optimists."[16] In the case of MacArthur (and some of the physician managers we studied),[17] this dynamic played out as a misplaced belief that expertise in one area made him an expert in others. As one historian noted, "MacArthur's qualities are so indisputably great in his own field that it comes as something of a shock to explore the record and find that in others he can be narrow, gullible, and curiously naïve."[18] Nonetheless, it is confidence—even if misplaced—that allows a person to be daring and to take on challenges that others avoid. The difference between boldness and foolish bravado may be determined by the outcome rather than the circumstances, so successful people may well come to believe that arrogance (pronounced "optimism" or "willingness to take risks") is actually a reason for their success.

The second way that arrogance erodes effectiveness is by creating the perception that the normal rules do not apply. Pursuit of results sometimes raised the specter of Faustian temptation—how far are you willing to go, what are you willing to sacrifice, to achieve success? Power and a long track record of success conspired to blind some executives to their dependence on others, sometimes to the extent of believing that their actions were above scrutiny. Like the pilot heroes of *The Right Stuff*, they may have been treated as if they were expected to bend the rules, eventually coming to see themselves as living by a different set of standards.

This blindness is seen in the corporate world as well. According to Mitchell Engel, executive vice-president of Foote, Cone and Belding Advertising, who sued Paul Kazarian for breach of contract, "Kazarian revels in being a renegade. He's a . . . self-perceived boy wonder. Rules have never been important to him."[19]

The psychologist Harry Levinson, who has spent many years observing executives as they ascend to power, reports that it is not uncommon to see a grandiose self-image develop.

Levinson described the phenomenon for *Business Week:* "They think they have the right to be condescending and contemptuous to people who serve them. They think they are entitled to privilege and the royal treatment."[20]

In summary, the development of arrogance is one of the most insidious of the derailment dynamics. It is a negative that grows from a positive, deriving as it does from actual talent and success. It not only has an immediate and direct negative impact through the overt behaviors it spawns, but it also blinds people to the impact of other behaviors as well. It shapes the expectations of the egotist and of those supervising him or her in ways that further separate behavior from direct consequences, especially through bending rules and special treatment. The erosion of talent, as well as its development, is embedded deeply in the day-to-day context of work. Any process aimed at the development of executive talent must recognize the potential downside of success, build in reassessment over time, and provide mechanisms for dealing with talented people who lose their perspective.

Bad Luck and Reactions to It

The fourth dynamic of derailment involves what appears to be bad luck. Sometimes talented people are just unlucky. Through no fault of their own, they lose a run-in with fate. There are victims of capricious circumstances, risk takers in corporate cultures that don't tolerate mistakes, scapegoats for others' errors, and innocent targets of "personal chemistry." Talented people can be swept out in large-scale corporate housecleanings, outplaced by generic agreements resulting from mergers to acquisitions, tainted by association with a regime that loses favor, sabotaged by jealous rivals, or dragged down despite personal achievement by uncontrollable market forces or others' mistakes.

Many factors that affect performance are out of the actor's control, and poor performance is surely a major derailing factor at the senior levels. For example, when the ousted General Motors chief Robert Stempel took the helm, he not only inherited the poor decisions of his predecessor but was also greeted by a recession that sent the economy into a nosedive.[21] Ironically, it may not matter whether the trouble is the result of forces outside of the person's control or a product of the person's errors or actions. In the case of Horst Schroeder, for example, eroding market share caused by a shift in consumer preferences to oats, when Kellogg's products were based on corn and wheat, could hardly be blamed on Schroeder. Nonetheless, the expectation was that market share would increase during Schroeder's watch; when it didn't, his boss wanted to know why and began to look more closely into what was going on. It was then that Schroeder's own mistakes and counterproductive behavior got serious attention.

But to say that bad luck is one dynamic of derailment is at once to acknowledge the obvious while obscuring the significant. The people who most believe bad luck is the cause of derailment are the derailers themselves. This "it wasn't my fault" interpretation of history sometimes masks an individual's contribution to the resulting ill fortune. Accepting responsibility for one's actions, even when external circumstances play heavily, is a prerequisite for learning.

Another way of looking at "bad luck" is to consider it broadly as a change in circumstances. Successful executives sometimes attribute their success to good luck. Beneath this superficial explanation, however, effective executives are pre-pared to take advantage of changes of fortune when they appear.[22] Those who derail represent the other side of the coin, lacking an ability to respond effectively when circumstances turn against them and then blaming the outcome on the cir-cumstances.

As career success translates into increased responsibility, the potential ramifications of mistakes or poor business perform-ance, whether internally or externally caused, increase as well. The final scenario of many derailments begins with some kind of performance problems (which may be unusual, given the prior success of the manager), and that "trouble" launches events that can take several different courses. Trouble can be a lone assassin, especially in organizations that are unforgiving, when the executive is in a highly visible position and has to take responsibility, or in cases where ethics or the law may be vio-lated. But more often, trouble is only a backdrop against which something is revealed about a person's temperament or charac-ter by the way the situation is handled; attention is drawn to the person, with flaws surfacing that had not been considered as such before; long-standing weaknesses become central to resolving the situation; or pent-up anger finds release (people are ready to get revenge by pushing the perpetrator out of the revolving door).

For some, "bad luck" in the form of a setback revealed a sheer lack of experience with failure—many talented and suc-cessful people have not had many flops and therefore have not had an opportunity to learn how to deal with them. When a setback is major and highly visible, the inadequacies of talented people may be seen in the harsh and revealing light of adver-sity. By failing to admit the problem, covering it up, or trying to blame it on others, some managers display an inability or a refusal to take responsibility for their actions. Others under duress may let their frustration exaggerate their existing flaws and end up lashing out at other people, withdrawing, or otherwise behaving in unproductive ways. The reaction to trouble, not the reason for it, becomes a defining factor through what it reveals about the person on the spot.

Another way bad luck in the form of trouble plays out is in its effect on attention. Successful, talented people have track records composed of many more successes than failures. Whereas success after success can lull the successful person into overconfidence and an inflated self-image, it also affects the behavior of outside observers vis-à-vis the star performer. Just as squeaky wheels may get the grease, smoothly running machines may be ignored. For example, the boss of a successful performer quite naturally might spend more time and energy on other matters rather than on monitoring where there is no problem. As noted earlier, this was clearly the case with LaMothe at Kellogg—he fully expected Horst Schroeder to continue his excellent performance, so he spent his time dealing with other matters. It appears that only when the situation began to deteriorate did he begin to pay close attention to his subordinate's actions. So it was in many of the derailment cases. Because things were expected to be right, it was sometimes quite a while before problems were detected. But when they were noticed, problems were highlighted starkly against the backdrop of prior success. Whatever gain there may be in the freedom from scrutiny bought with success is more than offset by the possible overreaction to the appearance of failure.

Sometimes bad luck is a change in situation that brings a weakness to the forefront, not just through increased attention but because the skill deficit prevents solving the problem or makes it worse. One weakness frequently exposed when "luck" changes the situation is the inability to build and maintain effective working relationships with key players. Someone unable to deal with a boss with a different style might, by bad luck, get a boss with a different style and find that building the relationship is the most important task.

One account of Richard Snyder's story offers a detailed look at a relationship with a new boss that unraveled rather quickly after Viacom bought Paramount. Snyder had managed to maintain a workable relationship with a difficult boss for years before the acquisition brought him Frank Biondi, a boss with a different set of values and style. Perhaps lulled by relief at the change, it may have been Snyder's weaknesses in conjunction with the new boss's expectations that eventually did him in.

As chairman of Simon and Schuster (a Paramount subsidiary), Snyder for ten years reported to Paramount chairman Martin Davis, in what could only be described as a very demanding relationship to manage.[23] Davis, according to the *Wall Street Journal* report, disliked Snyder intensely and showed it by countermanding decisions, constantly looking over his shoulder, at times publicly humiliating him, and eventually choosing his own executives for key roles in Snyder's operation.

The contrast in styles when Viacom took over had a dramatic effect. Where Davis had micromanaged, Viacom preferred to stand back and let Snyder run the operation. Apparently he did so with gusto, intensifying his own predilections to overmanage and intimidate, at the same time neglecting the relationship with his new bosses, particularly his immediate superior, Frank Biondi (who, ironically was himself ousted as CEO of HBO because of a disagreement with his boss, according to *Fortune*).[24] The quid pro quo for autonomy was keeping headquarters informed, and particularly not surprising top executives with bad news. It appears that Snyder enjoyed his autonomy too much to spend a lot of time making sure the brass stayed informed and they began to feel that information was hard to come by, superficial, and even misleading. They were hit several times by unanticipated decisions and events, sometimes finding out about them from the newspaper instead of from their own executive. As word of Snyder's heavy-handed and dictatorial leadership style filtered up, there were rumblings of mass resignations. Finally, the tumult was too much for Biondi, who fired him.[25] In retrospect, it might be said that Snyder was unlucky in getting Biondi for a boss. The reality was both more complex and more interesting.

In still other cases, bad luck simply provided the opening through which accumulated animosity could be released. "Friends come and go, but enemies accumulate," and many derailments result when successful executives find themselves confronted with their past.[26] It goes without saying that we tend to remember—vividly—people who achieve their success at our expense. So it was with some of the derailed executives, whose "bad luck" appeared when someone they had mistreated reappeared at a later date as their boss, a member of their board, a major customer, the union leader, the technical person on whom a project depended, or the head of a competing company.

It is almost impossible to live life without making some enemies, and leadership requires making decisions that sometimes leave resentment. But some people behaved in needlessly callous ways, and even though they got away with it for a long time, they ended up paying a stiff price. Believing they didn't need anyone else and treating people that way, they set themselves up for a fall. When the chips were down, no one stepped forward to bail them out. On the other hand, when they stumbled, there were many eager hands to help them out the door.

To summarize, when things go wrong for people who have a track record of success, trouble causes other people to look more closely. Even when the decline in performance is not directly their fault, the scrutiny often calls attention to various flaws that may have been there all along. In looking for an explanation for why things are going wrong, these flaws may assume greater importance than they have in the past or sometimes more than they actually merit.

When performance decline is caused by someone's own mistakes and not by external forces, derailment still is not automatic. Although there are unforgiving environments where one mistake is too many, most of the derailments resulting from trouble were less the result of the mistake than of the way people handled the mistakes they made. Often people's flaws caused them to make ineffective responses to the trouble they faced, so it was the interaction of trouble and weaknesses that got them derailed. Someone who was seen as untrustworthy might respond to a mistake by blaming others or trying to cover it up. Someone who was insensitive to others might strike out at people trying to help or make matters worse by further alienating those affected by the mistake.

Trouble, then, is often the context in which successful people's flaws assume an importance they never had while things were going smoothly.

The most obvious implication of the four dynamics of derailment is that there is no standing still. No one is immune to the dynamic forces that threaten career success—a current strength in danger of being overplayed, a weakness lying in wait, achievement inflating the ego, or fate lurking around the next corner. The relevance of these findings is not just that jeopardy is a way of life for the talented but rather that the painful lessons of derailment offer clues for development, certainly for individuals who aspire to careers in leadership but also for organizations that hope to create a context in which talent is preserved and enhanced.

THE UNINDICTED CO-CONSPIRATORS

Whether failing to listen to advice and feedback, refusing to change when change was needed, behaving in ways that alienated other people, or some other act of self-destruction, individuals who derailed *always* played a significant role in their own demise. Even when the organization, bad luck, or other external forces were heavily involved, which made placing blame difficult, individuals still contributed wittingly or unwittingly to the sequence of events. Because those who derailed were often unaware of their own role or actively denied it, they could be described as conspirators in their own misfortune.

But knowing that individuals always played a part in their derailments tells only part of the story. Their organizations also were responsible to varying degrees, as appeared to be the case for Horst Schroeder's misadventure at Kellogg. Organizational practices and reactions—from failing to provide clear feedback to rewarding counterproductive behavior—set the stage for what was to come. If one accepts the premise that talented people who later derail represent a loss to the organization and that the loss is at least in part the result of the organization's actions, then the organization has a great deal to gain by improving the context it creates. What makes it difficult is that the ways in which organizations undermine development and contribute to derailments are often subtle and hard to detect. Often, in fact, the most deleterious actions are the best intended, resulting in an "unconscious conspiracy" between an organization and an individual who together, in pursuit of effectiveness, produce a derailment.[27] (See Figure 13.1.)

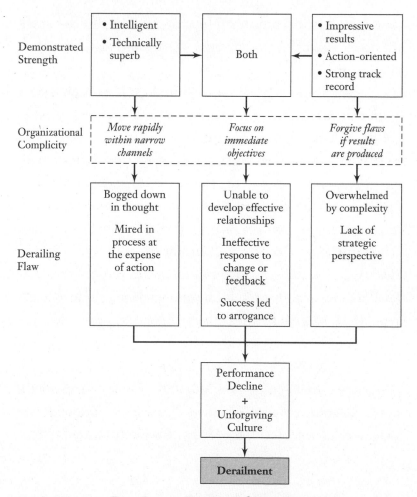

FIGURE 13.1 **Derailment Patterns of High Potentials**

The organization creates a climate that can make learning and change harder or easier, depending on prevalent assumptions about development; on what is valued, measured, and rewarded; on how the inevitable mistakes of learning are treated; on how developmental opportunities are distributed; and on what is done to assist people in their development efforts. In short, the way an organization is designed and run creates the soil in which the seeds of both development and derailment are sown. Although it cannot directly determine how any given individual will turn out, it does directly affect the developmental environment in which individuals make their choices.

Even well-managed and successful organizations may have a difficult time balancing the drive for results and the need to develop talent. The "organizational complicity" that may lead to the derailment of talented people is not the result of maliciousness or opposition to the idea of development; it would be easier to confront if it were. Instead, organizations *acting rationally* create the very forces that eventually lead to derailments. This rationality, of course, is defensible from the point of view that executive ability is something one has or does not. The kind of rationality that results in wasted talent is ultimately not rational, although it may make sense in one frame of reference.

∘   ∘   ∘

Morgan W. McCall Jr. is a professor at the University of Southern California's Marshall School of Business and former Senior Behavioral Scientist with the Center for Creative Leadership.

Chapter Fourteen

The Traces of Talent

Marcus Buckingham
Donald O. Clifton

"How can you identify your own talents?"

First, if you want to reveal your talents, monitor your *spontaneous, top-of-mind reactions* to the situations you encounter. These top-of-mind reactions provide the best trace of your talents. They reveal the location of strong mental connections.

Kathie P., a senior manager for a computer software company, gave us a dramatic example. She was bound for her company's annual sales meeting in the Dominican Republic. Squeezing into her tiny seat she glanced around her to see who was sharing the puddle jumper. Spread out in the back row was Brad, the aggressive, opinionated, and impatient CEO. In front of him was Amy, a genius at the details of software design, the best in the company. Across from her was Martin, a gregarious, charming Brit who through his network of contacts had singlehandedly turned around their flagging European operations.

And then there was Gerry, the insipid head of marketing who as usual had angled his way into the seat next to Brad.

"The problems began right after takeoff," Kathie recalled. "We had just cleared the clouds when the alarm went off. I didn't even know planes had alarms, but suddenly it started braying like a donkey—*eee-aww, eee-aww*—filling the cabin with this terrible sound. The main lights went out, and the emergency lights started flashing red. As I felt the plane drop what seemed like a thousand feet in a second or two, I looked through the open cabin door and saw both pilots, necks flushed and stiff, turn to each other. I sensed immediately that neither of them had any idea what was going on.

"There was a moment of silence in the cabin—shock, I imagine—and then suddenly everyone started talking at once. Amy craned over and said, 'Kathie, can you see the dials? Can you see the dials?' Martin pulled out a tiny bottle of Smirnoff from his bag and jokingly cried out, 'At least give me one last drink!' Gerry started rocking back and forth, moaning, 'We are all going to die. We are all going to die.' Brad was immediately at the cockpit door. I still don't know how he squeezed out of those backseats, but there he was, screaming at the top of his lungs, 'What the hell do you think you guys are doing up here?'

"Me? What was I doing?" Kathie said. "Watching, I suppose, as always. The funny thing was, nothing was wrong with the plane at all. A faulty system had triggered the alarm, and then the pilots had just panicked and pushed the plane into a sharp descent."

Each of these reactions under extreme stress revealed dominant talents and to some extent helped explain each person's performance on the job. Kathie's keen observations of human nature undoubtedly contributed to her success as a manager. Amy's instinctive need for precision was the foundation for her genius at software design. Martin's ability to find the humor in every situation had presumably endeared him to his growing network of European clients. Brad's compulsion to take charge was the foundation for his leadership. Even Gerry's wailing was confirmation of his suspect backbone (this one is not a true talent since it is hard to see where and how it could be applied productively).

While this is a dramatic example of how people reveal themselves under stress, daily life offers thousands of less intense situations that also provoke revealing reactions.

Think of a recent party where you didn't know most of the guests. Who did you spend the majority of your time with, those you knew or those you didn't? If you were drawn to the strangers, you may be a natural extrovert, and your behavior may well reflect the theme "Woo," defined later as an innate need to *win others over*. Conversely, if you actively sought out your closest friends and hung out with them all evening, resenting the intrusions of strangers, this is a good sign that Relator— a natural desire to deepen existing relationships—is one of your leading themes.

Recall the last time that one of your employees told you he could not come to work because his child was sick. What was your first thought? If you immediately focused on the ill child, asking what was wrong and who was going to take care of her, this may be a clue that Empathy is one of your strongest themes of talent. But if your mind instinctively jumped to the question of who would fill in for the missing employee, the theme Arranger—the ability to juggle many variables at once—is probably a dominant talent.

Or how about the last time you had to make a decision when you did not have all the facts? If you relished the uncertainty, sure in your belief that any movement, even in the wrong direction, would lead to a clearer perspective, you are probably blessed with the theme Activator, defined as a bias for action in the face of ambiguity. If you stopped short, delaying action until more facts became available, a strong Analytical theme may well be the explanation. Each of these top-of-mind reactions implies distinct patterns of behavior and therefore offers clues to your talents.

While your spontaneous reactions provide the clearest trace of your talents, here are three more clues to keep in mind: yearnings, rapid learning, and satisfactions.

Yearnings reveal the presence of a talent, particularly when they are felt early n life. At ten years of age the actors Matt Damon and Ben Affleck, already close friends, would find a quiet spot in the school cafeteria and hold meetings to discuss their latest acting "projects." At thirteen Picasso was already enrolled in adult art school. At five the architect Frank Gehry made intricate models on the living room floor with wood scraps from his father's hardware store. And Mozart had written his first symphony by the time he turned twelve.

These are the eye-catching examples, but the same holds true for each of us. Perhaps because of your genes, or your early experiences, as a child you found yourself drawn to some activities and repelled by others. While your brother was chasing his friends around the backyard, you settled down to tinker with the sprinkler head, pulling it apart so that you could figure out how it worked. Your analytical mind was already making its presence known.

When your mother, as a surprise on your seventh birthday, took you to McDonald's instead of having a party at home as you had planned together, you burst into tears. Even at this tender age your disciplined mind resented surprises in your routine.

These childhood passions are caused by the various synaptic connections in your brain. The weaker connections manage little pull, and when well-intentioned mothers (or other terrible circumstances) force you down a particular path, it feels strange and makes you cry. By contrast, your strongest connections are irresistible. They exert a magnetic influence, drawing you back time and again. You feel their pull, and so you yearn.

Needless to say, social or financial pressures sometimes drown out these yearnings and prevent you from acting on them. The Booker Prize–winning novelist Penelope Fitzgerald, burdened by the demands of providing for her family without the help of her alcoholic husband, wasn't able to honor her urge to write until well into her fifties. Once released by their permanent separation, this urge proved as irresistible as a teenager's. Over the last twenty years of her life she published twelve novels, and before her recent death at eighty, she was widely considered at the top of her game, "the best of all British novelists," according to one of her peers.

Anna Mary Robertson Moses probably holds the record for stymieing a powerful talent. Born on a farm in upstate New York, she began sketching as a young child and was so intent on incorporating every nuance of her surroundings that she mixed the juice of berries and grapes to bring color to her drawings. But her ardent sketching was soon pushed aside by the demands of the farming life, and for sixty years she didn't paint at all. Finally, at the age of seventy-eight, she retired from farming, allowed herself the luxury of letting her talent loose, and, like Penelope Fitzgerald, was quickly borne aloft by its pent-up energy. By the time of her death twenty-three years later she had painted thousands of scenes remembered from her childhood, exhibited her pictures in fifteen one-woman shows, and became known around the world as the artist Grandma Moses.

Your yearnings may not prove quite as inexorable as those of Grandma Moses, but they will exert a consistent pull. They have to. Your yearnings reflect the physical reality that some of your mental connections are simply stronger than others. So no matter how repressive the external influences prove to be, these stronger connections will keep calling out to you, demanding to be heard. If you want to discover your talents, you should pay them heed.

Of course, you can occasionally be derailed by what one might call a "misyearning," such as yearning to be in public relations because of the imagined glamour of cocktail parties and receptions or aspiring to be a manager because of a need to control. (Obviously, the best way to diagnose a misyearning is to interview an incumbent in the role and learn what the day-to-day realities of the role are really like once the blush has left the rose.) These false signals aside, your yearnings are worth following as you strive to build your strengths.

Rapid learning offers another trace of talent. Sometimes a talent doesn't signal itself through yearning. For a myriad of reasons, although the talent exists within you, you don't hear its call. Instead, comparatively late in life, something sparks the talent, and it is the speed at which you learn a new skill that provides the telltale clue to the talent's presence and power.

Unlike Picasso, his precocious contemporary, Henri Matisse didn't feel any yearning toward painting. In fact, by the time he was twenty-one he had never even picked up a brush. He was a lawyer's clerk, and most of the time a sick and depressed lawyer's clerk. One afternoon while he was recuperating in bed after another bout of flu, his mother, in search of something—anything—to lighten his spirit, put a box of paints in his hands. Almost instantly both the direction and the trajectory of his life changed. He felt a surge of energy as though released from a dark prison and seeing the light for the first time. Feverishly studying a "how-to-paint" manual, Matisse filled his days with painting and drawing. Four years later, with no schooling but his own, he was accepted into the most prestigious art school in Paris and was studying under the master Gustave Moreau.

Frederick Law Olmsted needed a similar situation to spark his talent, but as with Matisse, once revealed, his talent launched him to levels of excellence in his field at an unprecedented pace. Olmsted, a restless man with little to show for his thirty years, discovered his life's calling (what today we call landscape architecture) when he visited England in 1850. There he was struck by, in his words, the "hedges, the English hedges, hawthorn hedges, all in blossom and the mild sun beaming through the watery atmosphere." A few years later, after returning to the United States and refining his ideas, he won the most extensive landscape design competition ever held: New York's Central Park. It was his first commission.

You may have had a similar experience. You start to learn a new skill—in the context of a new job, a new challenge, or a new environment—and immediately your brain seems to light up as if a whole bank of switches were suddenly flicked to "on." The steps of this skill fly down the newly opened connections at such speed that very soon the steps disappear. Your movements lose the distinctive jerkiness of the novice and instead assume the grace of the virtuoso. You leave your classmates behind. You read ahead and try things out before the curriculum says you should.

You even become unpopular with the trainer as you challenge him with new questions and insights. But you don't really care because this new skill has come to you so naturally that you can't wait to put it into practice.

Of course, not everyone has experienced eureka moments that determined the direction of their lifelong career, but whether the skill is selling, presenting, architectural drafting, giving developmental feedback to an employee, preparing legal briefs, writing business plans, cleaning hotel rooms, editing newspaper articles, or booking guests on a morning TV show, if you learned it rapidly, you should look deeper. You will be able to identify the talent or talents that made it possible.

Satisfactions provide the last clue to talent. Your strongest synaptic connections are designed so that when you use them, it feels good. Thus, obviously, if it feels good when you perform an activity, chances are that you are using a talent.

This seems almost too simple, much like the advice that "if it feels good, do it." Clearly, it is *not* as simple as this. For various reasons—most of them having to do with our psychological history—nature has conspired to encourage a few of our more antisocial impulses. For example, have you ever caught yourself feeling good when someone else stumbles? Have you ever felt an impulse to put someone else down in public or even to shirk responsibility and blame someone else for your failings? Many people do, no matter how ignoble it seems. Each of these behaviors involves building one's good feelings on the back of someone else's bad feelings. These are not productive behaviors and should be avoided. As we said earlier, those who are tempted to use their talents to delight in other people's failure should perhaps reexamine their values.

You are better served by tuning your antenna toward identifying those *positive* activities that seem to bring you psychological strength and satisfaction. When we interviewed the excellent performers in our study, what was most striking was the sheer range of activities or outcomes that made people happy. Initially, when we asked people what aspect of their work they enjoyed the most, we heard a common refrain: Almost all of them liked their job when they met a challenge and then overcame it. However, when we probed a little deeper, the diversity—what they actually meant by "challenge"—emerged.

Some people derived satisfaction from seeing another person achieve the kind of infinitesimal improvement most of us would miss. Some people loved bringing order to chaos. Some people reveled in playing the host at a major event. Some people delighted in cleanliness, smiling to themselves as they vacuumed themselves out of a room. Some people were idea lovers. Some people mistrusted ideas and instead thrilled to the analytical challenge of finding the "truth." Some people needed to match their own standards. Some people, whether or not they had met their own standards, felt empty if they hadn't also outperformed their peers. For some people only learning was genuinely meaningful. For some people only helping others provided meaning. Some people even got a kick out of rejection—apparently because it offered them the chance to show just how persuasive they could be.

This list could legitimately become as long as the roll call of the entire human race. We are all woven so uniquely that each of us experiences slightly different satisfactions. What we are suggesting here is that you pay close attention to the situations that seem to bring you satisfaction. If you can identify them, you are well on your way to pinpointing your talents.

How can you identify your sources of satisfaction? Well, we need to tread carefully here. Telling someone how to know if she is genuinely enjoying something can be as vacuous as telling her how to know if she is in love. On some level the only sage advice is "You either feel it or you don't."

We will take a risk however, and offer you this tip: When you are performing a particular activity, try to isolate the tense you are thinking in. If all you are thinking about is the present—"When will this be over?"—more than likely you are not using a talent. But if you find yourself thinking in the future, if you find yourself actually anticipating the activity—"When can I do this again?"—it is a pretty good sign that you are enjoying it and that one of your talents is in play.

Spontaneous reactions, yearnings, rapid learning, and satisfactions will all help you detect the traces of your talents. As you rush through your busy life, try to step back, quiet the wind whipping past your ears, and listen for these clues. They will help you zero in on your talents.

o   o   o

Marcus Buckingham is Global Practice Leader for the Gallup Organization's Strength Management Practice.

Donald O. Clifton is the past chairman of the Gallup Organization and current chair of the Gallup International Research and Education Center.

Chapter Fifteen

Enhancing the Ability to Learn from Experience

Ellen Van Velsor
Victoria A. Guthrie

As quickly as the world is changing, the capacities needed by its leaders also change. To maintain their effectiveness, people in positions of leadership must be able to learn, actively and continuously.

According to research by the Center for Creative Leadership (Bunker and Webb, 1992), most managers are *not* active and continuous learners. Most people learn easily within their comfort zone but find it much more difficult to learn when operating under new challenges. Most people prefer to stay with the behaviors that have made them successful in the past, even if the conditions of the past no longer apply. A type of inertia develops. We have come to call the experience of overcoming this inertia "going against the grain." To go against their grain, leaders must let go of proven strengths and comfortable ways of learning long enough to acquire new ones. They must be strong and secure enough to make themselves vulnerable to the stresses and setbacks in the learning process.

Some people are naturally active learners. By virtue of their personalities or early life experiences, they have the personal resources and skills to learn easily. But they are the exceptions. Most people require considerable support for their learning.

We believe that people can learn to become better learners. This chapter focuses on helping managers and the human resource professionals who work with them improve their ability to learn from potentially developmental experiences. It begins with a discussion of what it means to learn from experience, as well as the factors that appear to be operating for people who learn easily. We then turn to what can be done to enhance the ability to learn from experience (for oneself or in working with others).

The Ability to Learn from Experience

What is the ability to learn from experience, and why does it feel so hard? In our view, the ability to learn from experience involves being able to

- Recognize when new behaviors, skills, or attitudes are called for, which involves being able to see when current approaches are not working
- Engage in a variety of development experiences to learn new skills or test skills that are previously untested, and to try new approaches or reframe points of view (as opposed to avoiding the situation or denying the need)

○ Develop and use a variety of learning tactics to acquire the new skills, approaches, or attitudes

Each of these activities or capacities plays an important role in the ability to learn from experience. We believe these skills can be developed and that the ability to learn from experience can thereby be enhanced. Yet for many people, these skills do not come easily or naturally.

Learning from experience can be difficult because it is a different way of thinking about learning. Most people think of learning in the mode of classroom activities, like reading and listening to lectures. They do not consider current experience as being the best teacher. It does not occur to them to spend time reflecting on their experiences and extracting from them the lessons contained within. They do not consider how they could do better at learning from experience.

Learning from experience is also difficult because of the sense of inertia referred to earlier. Inertia holds people back. Doing things how they've always done them, using skills they already have, and continuing to see the world as they've always seen it is a comfortable way of being. People like to use their strengths and get positive feedback on their achievements. This inertia gets worse the older people get—and the higher they go in organizations. If they have been successful, it is harder than ever to let go of what has worked for them. It is usually not until they face demands seriously out of line with their skills and perspectives that they begin to admit that the old ways may not be working.

Learning from experience can feel risky, too. Recognizing the need for new learning is stressful because it requires that people admit to themselves (and possibly to others) that what they are now doing is not working or that their current skills are inadequate. For most people, such an admission provokes some level of anxiety. It often seems easier to respond by shutting down, giving up, or denying the need for new ideas or behaviors.

To make matters worse, there is an active tension in most organizations between producing bottom-line results and developing people. Rather than give employees a developmental assignment where failure is a possibility alongside learning, most organizations prefer to put proven performers in key roles, doing what they already know how to do well. This only reinforces the tendency to stay with what is known and comfortable because it is safer.

Finally, learning from experience is difficult because it requires a level of support that many people do not have in their organizations. Support for the risk of learning (and failure) is one kind of support, but support also includes processes and relationships that help people receive and hear the information they need to hear, understand the meaning of that information, create development plans, persist in their efforts to learn and grow new skills, and have the courage to change outmoded behaviors and attitudes.

Individual Differences in the Ability to Learn

Our model of leadership development argues that people are more likely to learn from an experience if three elements are present: assessment, challenge, and support. However, the model incorporates a fourth element in the leadership development process: the ability to learn. Assessment, challenge, and support are elements of the development event itself; the ability to learn is a characteristic of the person involved in the event. Some people do not learn from a potentially developmental experience even if each of the first three elements is in place in just the right proportion. Others gain tremendous benefit from even the most minimal experience. The explanation lies in their varying abilities to learn. What accounts for these differences, and is there any way to bring about change?

Over the years, an extensive body of research has accumulated on personality, much of which relates to learning. Although it is not the purpose of this chapter to provide comprehensive coverage of that literature, we touch briefly on several factors that seem relevant to working with people who want to improve their ability to learn. It is also worth mentioning that, although many might consider some of these characteristics as hardwired aspects of personality, we believe that most of them can indeed be developed or enhanced through development experiences that are rich and balanced in assessment, challenge, and support.

THE ROLE OF INTELLIGENCE

We address intelligence first not because it is the most important quality but because it is the one that, for most people, comes to mind first in connection with learning. We believe that intelligence, as traditionally defined, plays a relatively small role in a person's ability to learn from experience in adulthood.

Although many people think of only one kind of potential when they hear the word *intelligence*, experts in the fields of psychology and education are now presenting the case for multiple forms of intelligence, each in itself complex, and each important in certain areas of life.

Howard Gardner (1993) defines seven intelligences: linguistic, musical, logical-mathematical, spatial, bodily-kinesthetic, interpersonal, and intrapersonal. What most North Americans mean by *intelligence* is the combination of linguistic, logical-mathematical, and spatial intelligences as defined by Gardner. Because of its long history in U.S. school systems, this combination is probably the first thing most people think of as learning. Yet it is doubtful that superior power in these three areas is a prerequisite for the kind of learning from experience that is important for long-term leadership effectiveness (Argyris, 1991). Very "smart" managers often derail because they are unable to recognize the need for personal change or new behaviors.

On the other hand, the two types of "personal" intelligence seem likely to affect and be affected by leadership development experiences. Gardner describes interpersonal intelligence as the ability to understand other people, and intrapersonal intelligence as the ability to form an accurate model of oneself and to be able to use that model to operate effectively in everyday life.

Obviously, interpersonal intelligence is critical to effective leadership. It is also an important capacity in leadership development because learning from developmental experience often means learning from other people, sometimes directly (as in a developmental relationship) and sometimes indirectly (through interacting with others in a training program or in an assignment). Intrapersonal intelligence is closely aligned with the concept of self-awareness. Many formal leadership development experiences have as a key goal enhancement of self-awareness;

that is, they work toward enabling people to form and then use a more accurate or comprehensive view of self.

SELF-ESTEEM AND SELF-EFFICACY

Self-esteem can be defined in two ways, one global (feelings about self as a good person in general), and one specific (feelings of worth in relation to a specific task or category of tasks). Specific self-esteem is sometimes referred to as self-efficacy. Although self-efficacy may be most relevant to specific learning situations, global self-esteem also plays a significant role in the ability to learn. For example, although my feelings about how good a manager I am may have much impact on my reaction to feedback about my strategic skills, how I feel about myself in general is still a factor in learning the new skills. Generally, if I believe I'm a reasonably good manager and an intelligent and acceptable person overall, those beliefs enable me to seek and face critical feedback on strategic skills with the motivation to learn those skills. If, on the other hand, I feel that I'm a good person but a poor manager (or if I feel I am not a very worthwhile or capable person overall), I will probably have greater difficulty being motivated to learn these new managerial skills.

Self-esteem is a well-researched aspect of personality, yet much of the research has focused on self-esteem in relation to task performance rather than learning. We know that people with high self-esteem are less likely to be affected by various kinds of stress and more apt to work harder in response to negative feedback than people with low self-esteem. It seems reasonable to believe that self-esteem has a similar relationship to learning—that having a strong sense of self-worth and a good measure of confidence in their abilities helps people face the possibility that their familiar skills are no longer adequate to the new challenges they face. For people with relatively high self-esteem, engaging in a new and challenging opportunity seems like less of a risk. Research has shown that high-self-esteem individuals seek more feedback because they feel they have less to fear in it (Ashford, 1986).

Yet research has also shown that people with very high self-esteem (overconfidence) may be less susceptible to influence by others or to cues from their environment (Brockner, 1988) and may therefore have difficulty noticing that new skills are needed. Overconfidence can be a serious stumbling block to learning, especially if a person has been rewarded over time for many successes and strengths. We believe openness to feedback is a first gateway to development; people with very high self-esteem may tend not to open that door wide enough, on their own.

People with relatively low self-esteem have different issues—they tend to be highly affected by feedback. They are more likely to be actively looking for information as to "what I may be doing wrong" and less able to do anything constructive with negative feedback when they do receive it. If people with low self-esteem receive negative feedback on task performance, they tend to focus on themselves (what's wrong with me), rather than on the task (what would be a better way). Performance may continue to decline as a result. Although in leadership development work a critical task is to understand self (that is, awareness of strengths and development needs), the individual receiving developmental feedback needs to be able to turn the focus on self outward to the task of setting development goals.

So, although people whose self-esteem is low may be well aware that new skills and behaviors are needed, they need more help and encouragement to engage in opportunities to learn.

With regard to learning and feedback, research has shown that the *stability* of self-esteem may be even more important than its level (Kernis and others, 1993). Compared to people with stable self-esteem, those with unstable self-esteem are more likely to perceive that their self-worth is on the line in any situation related to performance or personal feedback and therefore may be more likely to avoid or react defensively in feedback situations. Unstable self-esteem may make it very difficult for people to admit that new skills or behaviors are called for.

OPENNESS TO EXPERIENCE

In the past ten years, researchers have come to agree that one of several stable factors in personality is "openness to experience" (McCrae and Costa, 1985, 1987). People who are open to experience tend to see life as a series of ongoing learning experiences and seek out the new and relish the opportunities it brings (rather than the problems). They appear to have a sense of adventure, to enjoy trying out new ideas, having novel experiences, or meeting new people.

Openness to experience has been found to be correlated with training proficiency (Barrick and Mount, 1991). A key component of success in training is the attitude of the individual going into the event, and people who score high on openness tend to have positive attitudes toward unfamiliar (learning) experiences in general and a greater willingness to engage in them.

Conscientiousness or Need for Achievement

Research (Young and Dixon, 1996) has also shown that openness to experience is not all a manager needs to get the most out of training, or other potentially developmental experiences. In other words, openness to experience appears to be a necessary factor in learning or change, but not a sufficient one.

In addition to openness to new experience or information, a learner needs to be willing to take responsibility for using the new information to modify perspectives or behaviors, and for the persistence to work through difficult issues to accomplish the desired changes. This responsible persistence is related to another stable personality characteristic, called conscientiousness, and to one's need for achievement.

These two characteristics are important because they tell us something about how likely a person is to seek out and accept responsibility for learning, work hard to learn as a result of feedback, and persist in pursuit of difficult learning goals.

Beliefs About Learning and Orientations to Change

Beliefs can be hard to change. The manager who firmly believes that you can't teach an old dog new tricks is not as likely to learn from a development experience as one who sees learning as a lifelong activity and a string of interesting opportunities. Similarly, the person who believes that outcomes are a result of luck, fate, or other factors is less likely to take initiative in leadership or in leadership development.

The term *locus of control* has been used to describe a person's view of self as responsible for and able to effect outcomes.

Locus of control can be internal (people believe that outcomes are a direct result of their own efforts) or external (people see outcomes as resulting more from luck, fate, or other factors not under their control). Locus of control might influence people's reaction to assessment feedback, what they believe about the relation between effort and mastery, and how they feel about the rewards they can expect from a learning effort. Trainees with internal locus of control are more likely to act on feedback and remain committed to difficult goals longer because they see themselves as in control of their own development and are likely to believe that their efforts will bring improvement.

For people who are internally focused (as are most U.S. managers), locus of control may not be an issue in their development. But for those whose locus of control seems to be external, who believe that whatever happens is a result of factors outside of their control, what we would call development experiences may be less likely to bring about individual change. External locus of control may be more likely in managers from areas of the world other than the United States, among people who do not so readily subscribe to the view that adult development is a worthwhile end toward which to strive.

UNDERSTANDING FEELINGS AND MANAGING ANXIETY

For most people, recognizing that they do not know how to do something and then responding to the challenge in a learning mode produces considerable anxiety. Managing this anxiety is, therefore, critical to learning from experience. Although it is an ability that comes naturally to some people, it is also a skill that can be developed. We explore this skill in the following section.

Developing Learning Skills and Strategies

People approach learning in different ways. The approach that someone takes to learning is partly a matter of personal style, influenced by acquired skills and reinforced by habit. Some people prefer to learn from direct experience, where action-oriented experimentation strategies can be employed; others are more comfortable learning from reflection, reading, conversations with other people, or classroom training.

In our research and practice, we have made some effort to categorize the variety of ways in which people learn. Our expectation is that if people have reference to a behavioral taxonomy, they are able to expand their own repertoire of learning tactics and thus eventually master a greater variety of learning challenges. Implicit in this statement is the belief that particular challenges are best approached in certain ways and that people who use the greatest variety of tactics are the best learners.

We have categorized learning tactics in four major groupings:

1. Thinking tactics are solitary, internal cognitive activities. This includes recalling the past to search for similar or contrasting events; imagining the future through such activities as visualization; or accessing knowledge, facts, and wisdom through sources such as the library or the Internet.

2. Taking action comprises all the behaviors that have to do with direct, hands-on experimentation, jumping in with little hesitation to learn, in the moment, by doing.

3. Accessing others involves activities such as seeking advice and support, identifying role models and coaches, and seeking their help.

4. Feeling tactics are those activities and strategies that allow people to manage the anxiety associated with trying something new so that they can take advantage of an opportunity to learn. Rather than being paralyzed by fear of failure, an individual might talk through his fear with a trusted peer (or write about it in a journal) before moving to a new and challenging assignment.

We believe that in approaching an unfamiliar task—an opportunity for learning—people not only use a preferred approach to learning but also tend to move in a pattern, beginning with their most preferred tactic and moving to another tactic only if the first doesn't work. For example, if I am likely to confront a new situation with a preferred tactic of taking action, I will do this even in those situations where it would be better to read the directions (the thinking tactic) or ask for help from others. Once I become sufficiently frustrated, I might stop and use my feelings to deal with that frustration and then look for someone who might provide help or advice. But I will probably go through this preferred sequence (action, then feeling, then accessing others) regardless of whether it makes the most sense to do so or not. It is all too easy to become stuck using one tactic, or one sequence of tactics, over and over, even if it is not working. In fact, "blocked" learners (Bunker and Webb, 1992) do just that, trying harder and harder without changing their approach.

The problem is, of course, that the preferred approach isn't always the most effective approach. It may be the one that people are most skilled in applying because they have used it the longest, but it may not be what is needed at the moment. In our view, maximizing the ability to learn from a variety of experiences means learning to expand the variety of learning skills or tactics people are most comfortable with, or at least learning to work (for short periods) outside the personal comfort zone. New skills and behaviors are often learned only by using different approaches to learning.

To illustrate, consider the case of Fred, who started his career during the early days of the do-more-with-less wave that followed downsizing and reengineering. He has learned to be quick, opportunistic, and action-oriented. He can think and act on the fly. However, he has received feedback that sometimes he is perceived as sloppy and slapdash, presenting uninformed and ill-conceived plans, and favoring the tactical over the strategic. To develop as a leader, he needs to learn to be more thoughtful, reflective, solitary, and integrative. Yet his action-oriented style (of working and learning) does not lend itself to learning these skills. The "just do it" approach won't make Fred more reflective. Being more reflective probably doesn't appeal to him. It has not been important to his success in the past, and in truth he may have been frustrated in the past with reflective people since he sees them as slow to make decisions. The first thing Fred has to do is deal with his feelings about what is being asked of him; then he needs to find a very different way of learning this skill.

In general, our research suggests that effective learners are facile in their use of all tactics. Consider next the example of Sarah, who graduated with a high GPA from an excellent school. She joined an organization where she established a record as an extraordinary achiever (as an individual contributor). She was thoughtful, reflective, thorough, and assertive. Unfortunately, in leadership roles she was not good at spanning boundaries and working with others to accomplish a task. Having received consistent feedback to the effect that she was perceived as an abrasive loner—albeit a smart one—she set a personal goal of becoming better able to accomplish tasks with others in a group setting.

The "thinking" approach to learning felt natural to Sarah: reading and reflecting. So she set forth energetically on her goal by getting the best new books on leadership and teamwork. Once she felt she had read and thought about the problem enough, she took action, trying to apply what she'd learned to her everyday interactions with people. Things did not go well. She soon realized that her old style of learning (reading and reflecting) would not be sufficient; she would have to learn from others how to best work with others. That is, she would also have to use the "accessing others" tactic to complete her learning goal. She would have to share her goal with peers, find role models, and seek feedback on her attempts to change. She realized that this would be a new and uncomfortable learning style; the mere thought of talking to others about her issues generated considerable anxiety. To be successful, she would also need to employ a "feeling" tactic to manage the anxiety.

The development of feeling tactics may be the most important step one can take in becoming a better learner, because facing new challenges—adopting new learning tactics to develop new skills—often creates significant psychological discomfort. Dealing successfully with this discomfort is a critical first step in being able to go against the grain and learn from experiences.

FINDING THE COURAGE AND DEVELOPING THE SKILLS

People are faced with new challenges whenever the context in which they work and live changes: globalization of markets, promotion, move to a new function or business, marriage or divorce, the birth of a child, and so on. It takes a certain amount of courage to recognize the need for new skills, behaviors, or attitudes and then use what are uncomfortable learning tactics to learn those skills.

People sometimes do not find that courage, staying instead with what is known and comfortable. Yet the results of failing to learn are serious. Over time, people feel caught in a rut, doing the same thing with the same results over and over. Or, as change overtakes them, their performance suffers. Derailment from the career they intend or desire is usually the result when a person's skills and perspectives do not fit what the job is demanding of the person. Someone who is at first well suited for a position or role can, over time, become ill suited, as the job or the organization's demands outpace the person's ability to develop requisite skills. Sometimes, derailment happens because managers continue to use or overuse their strengths, when new skills are required.

How can people find the courage and develop the skills to learn? From our model of leadership development, two of the three elements seem most important: (1) assessment and feedback, and (2) support. (As may be obvious, challenge is built into the process of learning new skills.) Another factor involves using a variety of development experiences to help people learn. Finally, we have found through our research that the timing of a development experience in relation to other career or life events is relevant to the ability to learn from experience.

Assessment and Feedback

To know whether their current skills fit well or poorly with the challenges they face, people need good information: about themselves (current strengths and development needs) and about the challenges. They need various kinds of information, delivered to them in various forms, and not just once but continuously over time.

Information about self comes from assessment and feedback. For development to occur, people need to get feedback, either formally or informally, on current skills and perspectives, to take stock of where they are and what they need to learn. In this sense, assessment has two related purposes: to be a vehicle for delivering information on current strengths and weaknesses, and to help people recognize that the need for new skills exists.

Assessment takes various forms. A feedback-intensive program usually provides a variety of opportunities for assessment and feedback, including personality inventories (to enhance understanding of self), experiential exercises or simulations, and 360-degree leadership surveys (to improve understanding of how others see your strengths and weaknesses and to compare your self-ratings of skills and perspectives to ratings made by others). The 360-degree instruments can also be used outside of a program, as an efficient and cost-effective way of helping people monitor their performance and stay in touch with their development needs over time and through different work situations.

A key benefit of both a feedback-intensive program and 360-degree feedback is that they improve the accuracy or comprehensiveness of people's views of themselves. Being presented with the views of significant others (bosses, peers, direct reports, fellow participants in a program) to encounter shades of contrast and similarity to one's own self-view, is a powerful experience and can be a step toward understanding behavior from other points of view.

Both the feedback-intensive program and 360-degree feed-back can work to unfreeze people, giving them the opportunity to take a look at themselves and decide that development is nec-essary or desired. Part of what happens in an unfreezing process is that a person's self-efficacy is enhanced by affirmation of strengths. We know from our work in evaluating feedback-intensive programs that a key benefit is enhanced confidence and self-esteem (Van Velsor, Ruderman, and Phillips, 1989; Young and Dixon, 1996). Therefore, it is often true that peo-ple who, by virtue of personality or motivation, may not seem ready for a development experience can benefit from feedback on a 360-degree instrument or a feedback-intensive program; the experience provides just enough support to motivate the person to dig deeper, set goals for improvement, and build interest in further development.

Sources and Importance of Support for Learning

With all its inherent difficulties—the need to go against the grain, the risk of exposing weaknesses, the fear of failure—learning is hard. Most people need support during the process.

Support can take a variety of forms. For example, if the development experience is a new assignment, the learner-man-ager can be put in touch with a network of others currently doing similar work in such assignments, or benefit from a sup-portive relationship with a senior manager who is a veteran of that type of work. If the developmental experience is feedback on a 360-degree instrument, the support comes in the form of a well-designed process for administering and delivering the feedback (Tornow and London, 1998), competent specialists to interpret the results, and good development planning materials (Leslie and Fleenor, 1998).

People often think of support in the form of one-on-one relationships, and this kind of support is usually essential for learning. Even though people with low self-esteem may have some difficulty in learning from challenging experiences, our research shows that a supportive boss moderates the effects of low self-esteem on learning (Ruderman, Ohlott, and McCauley, 1996).

Using a Variety of Development Experiences

People learn from a variety of development experiences, and development experiences enhance their ability to learn. For example, an individual can learn important leadership lessons from a developmental relationship, and the experience of being effectively coached can contribute to development of the learning tactic we've called accessing others. There is often a reciprocal relationship between a development experience and the learning tactics, whereby each reinforces the other.

The best approach in helping managers develop the wide range of leadership skills and learning tactics they need is one that combines multiple kinds of experience over the course of their career. For example, if a manager is facing a challenge (perhaps in an assignment) that she has never faced before (as was the case with Sarah, in our earlier example), she may need to adopt learning tactics that are unfamiliar and uncomfortable for her. In that case, what she learns in the assignment itself (which is one development experience) is enhanced by other development experiences occurring at the same time, say, a coaching relationship with a seasoned manager who is good at the learning tactics she needs, participation in a skills-based training program focused on learning tactics, a teamwork or working-with-others workshop, or a supportive relationship with someone who models the teamwork behaviors and skills she is trying to learn.

Timing of Development Experiences

In a recent research project, we interviewed a group of senior executives about successful and derailed managers in their organizations. This comment came out of one of those interviews: "I was coaching her. We had many sessions together where the problems were identified and we tried to come up with an action plan. Some problems she owned, others she didn't. She really didn't change. She would change for a week or two, then return to baseline."

This executive was describing a person whose career in their organization was soon to be cut short. Is she permanently unable to change? We don't know, from this one description, but we suspect not. All people can make changes if they feel motivated, and all people can widen the scope of the tactics they use for learning. However, there are times, for everyone, when facing new challenges and learning in them is easier or more difficult than usual (Van Velsor and Musselwhite, 1986). Timing, in other words, is a critical piece of the puzzle.

When things are going well, many people tend not to seek out input from others on how they are doing, and they may not even be open to it. Regardless of whether they are avid or resistant learners in general, most people are readier for information or feedback when things are not going well for them, when they see that they may be in danger of failing. If people have reason to question their present ways of understanding, their perspectives or approaches, or their own competence, they usually want to know why things aren't working and are open to hearing that change of some kind is in order.

In particular, managers' need for new knowledge or skills tends to be higher during periods of transition, and so they are more open to learning from development experiences during these times. For example, when starting a new assignment, many people are keenly aware of how much they do not know and are eager to build the strengths that will help them succeed. They are very receptive to such experiences as a good coaching relationship. Once they have had some time to get their feet wet in the new assignment, they usually benefit from a comprehensive assessment experience (Conger, 1992).

On the other hand, there do seem to be times when people cannot and probably should not take on new developmental challenges—periods of high work overload or intense personal trauma, for instance. If they are emotionally overloaded, most people are unable to process new information about self or performance, even with additional support.

In summary, the timing of a development experience can have a significant effect on ability to learn. People all but lose their ability to learn (temporarily) in response to life events that significantly affect motivation. So, despite the stable influence of personality and the acquisition of various learning tactics, people's ability to learn can be higher at one point and lower in another, based on the need they perceive for new learning and based on the stress of other significant life events.

We close this discussion with the following example, taken from *Lessons of Experience* (McCall, Lombardo, and Morrison,

1989). It illustrates how powerful learning can be when people are ready, when new learning tactics are acquired, and when the timing is right.

> When I first became a supervisor of a group of development engineers, I looked at management like an engineer would. I read all about performance reviews, and boy, was I ready to give performance reviews! I told them in detail all the things they did wrong, and all the things they did right. No one had ever given them that kind of feedback before. But I just about killed those engineers, and nearly crushed the morale of that organization. I was clearly not a skilled coacher of people. So I went out and got some help. I finally learned that just as you had to know the laws of physics to be a good engineer, you had to know the laws of psychology to be a good manager. This was a tremendous lesson for me: that you can't just translate the skills of one profession into another. When you're going into a new profession, you'd better learn as much as you can about it before you jump. Take as much time as you can learning the differences so that you don't use your own experience when it really doesn't apply [p. 28].

Learning from Small Events

For the most part, we have focused in this chapter on the larger, more dramatic events and strategies that stimulate learning and development. We have not paid much attention to the smaller, day-to-day experiences that affect people both at home and in the workplace. Yet a very practical way to accomplish personal development is seeing the small and midsized events and challenges that everyone regularly faces as opportunities to practice new ways of learning (Lombardo and Eichinger, 1989). Common challenges such as having an annual performance-appraisal conversation, supporting a coworker through a family crisis, or negotiating with a spouse over child rearing or household planning provide a means to develop a comfort level with new learning tactics and competence with change (Lee, Guthrie, and Young, 1995). These more or less ordinary events can build self-esteem while simultaneously letting people try on new behaviors.

GUIDELINES FOR THE PRACTITIONER

To enhance your ability to learn from experience and to increase the quantity and quality of that learning, we recommend the following:

1. Focus on how you learn, as much as where and what you learn. Do you tend to begin a learning process by reading and reflecting, moving into action only after an extended period of time spent thinking? Do you jump right into action, trying this and that on your own without ever seeking information from others who may have more expertise or experience? How do you feel about using other tactics, and how might you use current skills to manage the anxiety you feel when trying new behaviors?

2. Expand your repertoire of learning tactics. Coaching can help managers who do not naturally tend to access others; it also helps prod the reflective learner into action. The use of a journal can help the action-oriented learner get more from the development experience (although it may require coaching to get this kind of learner to journal).

3. Self-esteem enhances people's ability to learn from experience because it builds their ability to see new perspectives

without threatening their current perspectives. It also increases the motivation to learn by decreasing people's anxiety about their weaknesses (it is OK to need to learn) and by building on the belief that people can learn and improve. Self-esteem is a cornerstone to learning from experience. A feedback-intensive program is a good way to boost self-confidence and build self-awareness, both of which motivate people to want to develop new learning skills.

4. Review development systems and programs currently in place, as well as assignments that are or could be used for individual development. Do they reflect a balance of assessment, variety of challenging experiences, and mechanisms for support? A good assessment enhances ability to learn in people who are already motivated, by showing them where to start. It also helps motivate people who do not appear ready for a development experience. Challenge enhances ability to learn by creating the demand for and opportunity to develop new skills and new ways of learning. Finally, ability and willingness to learn are nourished by coaches, mentors, and work partners who provide encouragement and support in the form of honest feedback, knowledge, and experience.

5. Find ways to get more regular and more informal feedback, including feedback on the ability to learn, from coworkers and others. It is very difficult, in the press of everyday business, for managers to keep in touch with the need to develop a new skill or use a different approach. For the same reasons, their opportunities for formal feedback and assessment (performance appraisals or structured developmental feedback using personality or 360-degree leadership instruments) are relatively infrequent. Informal feedback in the context of even small-scale

development events can provide the bulk of your opportunities for development.

o   o   o

Ellen Van Velsor is a research scientist at the Center for Creative Leadership.

Victoria A. Guthrie is the director of innovative program initiatives at the Center for Creative Leadership.

Part Three

Developing Character

What values are essential to leadership? To inspire others to follow your lead, you need to model the values and characteristics that will make you most effective and will instill confidence in your employees. James M. Kouzes and Barry Z. Posner explain that the foundation of leadership is credibility. To be credible, you need to possess the key characteristic of admired leaders, honesty. Joanne B. Ciulla maintains that a healthy workplace needs to be honest to create an environment based on trust and commitment. James O'Toole shows that trust derives from the respect a leader displays for followers.

While striving to maintain their credibility, leaders will encounter many defining moments in their careers. Joseph L.

Badaracco Jr. says a defining moment forces you to make a choice between two rights. The correct response may not be clear or may not even exist. Over many years, the actions resulting from defining moments form an individual's character. Finally, Lee G. Bolman and Terrence E. Deal demonstrate that being committed to doing the right thing isn't just a moral obligation; there are financial rewards for leading a company that has soul.

Chapter Sixteen

Leadership Is a Relationship

James M. Kouzes
Barry Z. Posner

The results of our surveys over the last decade have been strikingly consistent. Time and again, people sent a clear message about the qualities leaders must demonstrate if they want others to enlist voluntarily in a common cause and to commit themselves to action freely. What are these crucial attributes?

KEY CHARACTERISTICS OF ADMIRED LEADERS

According to our research, the majority of us look for and admire leaders who are honest, forward-looking, inspiring, and competent. Take a moment to examine the data from our surveys. The results from our most current sample are displayed in Table 16.1, in the column for 1993.

TABLE 16.1 **Characteristics of Admired Leaders**

Characteristic	Percentage of U.S. Respondents Selecting, 1993	Percentage of U.S. Respondents Selecting, 1987
Honest	87	83
Forward-looking	71	62
Inspiring	68	58
Competent	58	67
Fair-minded	49	40
Supportive	46	32
Broad-minded	41	37
Intelligent	38	43
Straightforward	34	34
Courageous	33	27
Dependable	32	32
Cooperative	30	25
Imaginative	28	34
Caring	27	26
Mature	14	23
Determined	13	20
Ambitious	10	21
Loyal	10	11
Self-controlled	5	13
Independent	5	10

As you can see, these four characteristics—being *honest, forward-looking, inspiring,* and *competent*—rank well above the rest. If the qualities alone were running for office, these are the ones that would achieve consensus and victory. Let's examine each of them.

Honest

In virtually every survey we conducted, honesty was selected more often than any other leadership characteristic. Honesty is absolutely essential to leadership. If people are going to follow someone willingly, whether it be into battle or into the boardroom, they first want to assure themselves that the person is worthy of their trust. They want to know that the would-be leader is truthful and ethical. No matter where we have conducted our studies—regardless of country, geographical region, or type of organization—the most important leadership attribute since we began our research in 1981 has always been honesty.

This finding is reinforced by a study done jointly by Korn/Ferry International, the highly respected and successful search firm, and the Columbia University Graduate School of Business. Surveying over 1,500 top executives in twenty countries (from the United States, Japan, Western Europe, and Latin America), the study looked into external threats, strategies for growth, areas of expertise, and personal characteristics of the CEO and the importance of these related topics now and in the year 2000.

The joint survey reports that "ethics are rated most highly among the personal characteristics needed by the ideal CEO in the year 2000. Respondents expect their chief executive to be above reproach."[1] In 1988, 88 percent of executives believed ethics to be essential. The exact figures did vary somewhat by country and region, but the importance of being ethical was consistently ranked highly.[2] Similarly, office workers value honesty highly. In the most recent *Worldwide Office Environment*

Index, sponsored by Steelcase and conducted by Louis Harris and Associates, significant numbers of office workers (for example, 85 percent in the United States) said it was very important for their management to be honest, upright, and ethical.[3]

No matter the country, the benefits of honesty cannot be overstated. Employees must know where they stand—as they only can with someone who is honest with them. Irene Prazak, vice president of Norstar Bank of Upstate New York, addressed this point in emphasizing her manager's honesty and explaining its importance to her: "You know exactly where you stand, and I have known exactly where I have stood, from day one. Now that's important to someone like me, because then I become a good follower."[4]

Forward-Looking

Janice Lindsay, director of internal communications and editorial services for the Norton Company, defines her ideal leader as "somebody who sets and defines the vision and encourages you to follow that vision, and then is there when you need them."[5] We expect our leaders to have a sense of direction and a concern for the future of the organization. Leaders must know where they are going. They must have a destination in mind when asking us to join them on a journey into the unknown.

In the joint Korn/Ferry–Columbia University study, 75 percent of respondents ranked "conveys a strong vision of the future" as a very important quality for CEOs to have now; it was so ranked by an almost unanimous 98 percent for the year 2000.[6] The desirability of this management style did not vary by more than three percentage points across the regions studied. This finding suggests that, especially for senior executives, being forward-looking is the most essential of the leadership attributes.

Our study indicates that being forward-looking is also very important for front-line supervisors and middle managers. If leaders are to be admired and respected, they must have the ability to see across the horizon of time and imagine what might be. We are not inclined to follow those who are directionless. Honest or not, leaders who don't know where they are going are likely to be joined by the rest of us for only as far as we ourselves can see.

Constituents ask that a leader have a well-defined orientation toward the future. We want to know what the organization will look like, feel like, be like when it arrives at its goal in six months or six years. We want to have it described to us in rich detail so that we will know when we have arrived and so that we can select the proper route for getting there.

Inspiring

We admire and respect leaders who are dynamic, uplifting, enthusiastic, positive, and optimistic. We expect them to be inspiring. Yet it is not enough for leaders to have dreams of the future. They must be able to communicate these in ways that encourage us to sign on for the duration and to work hard toward the objective.

Once again, confirmation comes from around the globe for the need to be inspiring. Of executives surveyed, 91 percent said that by the year 2000 it will be very important that CEOs be inspiring. This quality is rated as more important than "analytic," "organized," and "tough."[7] If you're planning to be leading in the year 2000, you'd better start looking on the bright side.

Joseph Gagliardi, vice president of marketing for Hertz Equipment Rental Corporation, testifies to the importance of uplifting people's spirits: "I think you've got to come to the work station day to day feeling that you can make a difference and just getting that enthusiasm throughout your department, because no one does it alone. I think enthusiasm becomes contagious, and the task becomes almost a fun pursuit."[8]

Competent

The fourth most admired leadership attribute is competence. If we are to enlist in another's cause, we must see the person as capable and effective. The universal expectation is that the person be able to get things done for the business unit. In this sense, having a winning track record is the surest way to be considered competent.

The type of competence that constituents look for seems to vary with the leader's role. For example, those who hold officer positions are expected to demonstrate abilities in strategic planning and policy making. If a new technology challenges the organization, a person more knowledgeable about that technology may be perceived to be a more appropriate leader. A leader on the line or at the point of customer contact will typically have to be more technically competent than someone more removed. Yet it is not necessary that the leader have the same level of technical competence as constituents do. Much more significant is that he or she takes the time to learn the business, to know the current operation before making changes and decisions that affect everyone in the organization.

We are, however, noticing a trend toward requiring more technical competence of leaders. The age of the generalist manager may be coming to a close. This situation is especially true in the knowledge industries. Although an effective leader in a high-technology company may not need to be a master programmer, he or she must understand the business implications of electronic data interchange and networking. A good leader in a professional services firm may have little direct client responsibility but must have towering competence as a consultant.

Expertise in leadership skills per se is another dimension of competence. The abilities to challenge, inspire, enable, act as a model, and encourage—the practices identified in our prior study of leadership bests and published in our book, *The Leadership Challenge*—must be demonstrated if leaders are to be seen as capable.[9]

Consistency and Change over Time

Honest, forward-looking, inspiring, competent: these characteristics have, over the last decade, been consistently selected by all respondent groups as the four most admired leadership characteristics. Ten-year follow-up surveys of American Management Association and Federal Executive Institute Alumni Association members confirm the continuity in what we want from our leaders.[10]

Yet though these leadership attributes have remained remarkably stable, we have observed some recent changes in emphasis. In the years since we published *The Leadership Challenge*, both the quality of being forward-looking and that of being inspiring have increased in their importance. More people want their leaders to provide future direction and show enthusiasm than in years past. These times of transition require leaders with the vision and the energy to sustain hope.

Competence remains one of the four most admired characteristics, but it has been assigned less value than in the past. Some constituents appear to be looking for more vision and direction, more inspiration and excitement in these times of turmoil, than for a track record of getting things done. This shift causes us great concern because it runs counter to the need for greater expertise among leaders—and all organizational members for that matter. Given the increasing complexity of organizations and their environments, it is doubtful that any leader could navigate the white waters of today's organization without clear competence. We must acknowledge that, relative to our original study, fewer people have elected to choose competence, but we should all pause to consider the implications of being led by forward-looking and inspirational individuals who lack the capacity to implement their visions of the future.

The quality that has changed most in relation to the others is supportiveness. When we first reported our findings in 1987, supportiveness ranked eleventh, having been selected by 32 percent of the respondents. It now ranks sixth overall, with 46 percent of respondents identifying being supportive as an admired leadership characteristic.

Perhaps because of wrenching global economic and political changes, people require more understanding and help from their leaders. Perhaps the increase in diversity in the workplace has created a need for more affirmation and assistance. Perhaps the reason is the empowerment movement, which is enabling more and more to realize their potential in self-managing teams and self-directed work environments. Whatever the cause, more people today expect leaders to be supportive than just a few years ago.

Another significant change is in the value of being ambitious. In 1987, 21 percent selected it as an admired leadership quality; in our most recent study, only 10 percent did. Maybe the message is finally getting through that a self-serving style is no longer so beneficial to success in organizations as once thought.

These modest changes in preference suggest that our expectations of leaders can be somewhat dynamic. The external environment may influence what we look for and admire in a leader at any given moment in time. However, the shifting winds still do not steer us away from seeking leaders who are at their core honest, forward-looking, inspiring, and competent. This collection of four qualities has endured over time and across organizations; they are required fundamentals of leadership.

Global and Local Expectations

Honest, forward-looking, inspiring, and competent: these remain the prerequisites to developing ourselves globally as leaders. Yet to be leaders, we must also learn to adapt to and shape our local surroundings. Expectations can vary from organization to organization, function to function, group to group, and level to level.

In one organization we studied, being supportive was selected as a most admired characteristic by significantly more people (56 percent of the overall organization) than in any other group we have studied. In this organization being understanding and helpful were considered dramatically more important by all—whether exempt or nonexempt, male or female, young or old—than in other companies. Thus, to be successful there, one would have to develop the skills to be supportive along with the skills to demonstrate the other four attributes.

In comparison, another organization we surveyed selected the quality of courage significantly more often than the international norm. As you might imagine, the differences between the organization valuing supportiveness and that favoring courageousness were great. The organizations were as different as night and day, even though each was among the best in its respective industry.

These findings lend support to the concept of corporate culture. Organizations seek to differentiate themselves not just in terms of products, but also in the desired qualities of their leadership. In so doing, they send messages about what people should develop in themselves to become successful. In fact, if organizations do not develop a unique culture, they will have a difficult time persuading high-quality people to join and remain. Who wants to work in an organization that is just like any other?

People may also see the world a bit differently based on their roles. Managers consistently look for a leader who is forward-looking; often fewer than 50 percent of nonmanagers do. More than 60 percent of exempt employees generally look for supportiveness; fewer than 40 percent of senior managers do. Professionals in the human resources function are more likely to value supportiveness than professionals in other areas. More women than men tend to appreciate supportive leaders. People in finance tend to value the quality of being inspiring less than those in sales. Quite understandably, ethnic minorities often look for more broad-minded leaders than do people from the majority population group. Understanding these local differences is important.

And if we are to be able to move about as leaders, serving one constituent group today and another tomorrow, it is critical to keep a global perspective. Much as specific attributes may vary from country to country, organization to organization, and function to function, some things remain constant and universal. We have come to refer to these as transportable leadership characteristics. As leaders, we are expected to carry at least four of these qualities with us wherever we go, from one organization to the next, one situation to the next, one constituency to the next.

Taken singularly, the characteristics of being honest, forward-looking, inspiring, and competent provide a consistently useful guide for leadership selection, action, and development. Taken together, they communicate a powerful message, one that offers a deeper understanding of the fundamentals of leadership. But they mean much more.

DISCOVERING CREDIBILITY AS THE FOUNDATION

The qualities of being honest, inspiring, and competent compose what communications researchers refer to as source credibility.[11] In assessing the believability of a source of information—whether it is the president of the company, the president of the country, a sales person, or a TV newscaster—researchers typically use the three criteria of trustworthiness, expertise, and dynamism. Those who rate highly in these areas are considered to be credible sources of information.

These three dimensions of source credibility are strikingly similar to three of the four most frequently selected items in our survey: honesty, competence, and inspiration. What we found quite unexpectedly in our initial research and have reaffirmed ever since is that, above all else, people want leaders who are credible. We want to believe in our leaders. We want to have faith and confidence in them as people. We want to believe that their word can be trusted, that they have the knowledge and skill to lead, and that they are personally excited and enthusiastic about the direction in which we are headed. Credibility is the foundation of leadership.

Given the significance of our discovery, we expected to find numerous references to credibility in the research on management and leadership during the last ten years. To our amazement and dismay, the shelves were bare. We were able to locate studies of credibility and cooperation, credibility and reception of feedback, and credibility and persuasiveness; but credibility and leadership was a topic largely ignored. Why the dearth of research on this subject? Isn't it important for executives to know that credibility is what makes their messages believable to others?

In the late 1970s and in the 1980s, self-help and management books boomed. But in large measure this was a triumph of image over character, style over substance. In the 1990s, there is growing recognition that gaining credibility is far more important than being dressed for success. Credibility is the foundation on which leaders and constituents will build the grand dreams of the future. Without credibility, visions will fade and relationships will wither.

Building Equity

Max De Pree, chairman of Herman Miller, one of America's most admired companies, has written, "The first responsibility of a leader is to define reality. The last is to say thank you. In between the two, the leader must become a servant and a debtor. That sums up the progress of an artful leader."[12]

Leaders typically do not conceive of themselves as servants and debtors, but De Pree's observation provides a very useful analogy to use when thinking about the importance of credibility in enlisting others in a common vision. Just think about a time when you might need to borrow money, when you might have to become indebted. Imagine that you are trying to get a mortgage to build the house of your dreams. You sit down across the desk from the loan officer at your local financial services company. After you've completed all the paperwork, the first thing that the loan officer is likely to do is check your credit.

Credit and credibility share the same root origin, *credo*, meaning "I trust or believe." A loan officer checking your credit is literally checking on your store of believability, searching to know whether you can make good on your word. The officer wants to know whether to believe you when you say that you will pay the loan back on time and with interest.

When it comes to leaders, in many respects constituents act like loan officers. When a leader makes promises (like signing a promissory note) about what he or she will do to guide the organization on a journey to an uplifting new future, people instinctively do a credit check. They ask themselves, "The last time this person made such a promise, was he being honest about it?" "Did she tell the truth, or was that just some campaign pledge to get our support?"

People also ask themselves, "Does he have the enthusiasm to keep people excited along the difficult road to the future?" "Does she inspire others to make the sacrifices necessary to make it to the end?" And they wonder, "Does she have the competence to get us from where we are now to where we'd like to be?" "Does he have a track record of accomplishment that would give us confidence in his abilities?"

If the answers to these essential questions are yes, then people are likely to willingly give their time, talent, and toil. If the answers are no, people are not likely to volunteer. When leaders ask others to follow their new strategic directions, their visions of exciting possibilities of a better tomorrow, people first decide, most often intuitively, whether those leaders are to be believed.

Fostering Trust

Of all the attributes of credibility, however, there is one that is unquestionably of greatest importance. The dimension of honesty accounts for more of the variance in believability than all of the other factors combined. Being seen as someone who can be trusted, who has high integrity, and who is honest and truthful is essential. You may know someone is clearly competent, dynamic, and inspirational. But if you have a sense that that person is not being honest, you will not accept the message, and you will not willingly follow. So the credibility check can reliably be simplified to just one question: "Do I trust this person?"

If your response is yes, then follow. Even if your endeavor is unsuccessful, you will still respect yourself. If your response is "I don't know," get more information, and fast. But if your answer is no, find another job or find another leader. Even if you are successful, you will not respect yourself. Every time we follow someone we do not trust, we erode our self-esteem. We are diminished in our own and in others' eyes, and we become less valuable to ourselves and to others.

We recently offered these recommendations to a group of managers. A young woman raised her hand. She said she was in no position to fire her leader or to get another job at the moment. Thus, for her, there had to be a third alternative. What did she advise? "Revolt!"

Revolt sounded to us like a much more radical solution than getting another job or getting another leader, but in the 1990s it has to be added to the list of alternatives. It was noteworthy to us that about a week after revolt was added to the list, the cover of *Business Week* boldly displayed the headline "GM: The Board Revolt."[13] It's not exactly what we'd expect on the cover of a conservative business publication, but it supports the manager's observation. From the boardroom to the factory floor, from Wall Street to Main Street, from south central Los Angeles to Eastern Europe, from voting booths in the United States to the squares of the former Soviet Union, revolt is in the air. Peaceful or bloody, discontent with leadership is extraordinarily high, and leaders had better take note.

EARNING CREDIBILITY

A credibility check is rooted in the past. It has to do with reputation. Reputation is human collateral, the security we pledge against the performance of our obligations as leaders, friends, colleagues, and constituents. It is what supports the natural human instinct to want to trust. Reputation is to be cherished and cared for. A damaged one lowers people's estimation of a leader's worth and their motivation to follow.

Credibility, like reputation, is something that is earned over time. It does not come automatically with the job or the title. It begins early in our lives and careers. People tend to assume initially that someone who has risen to a certain status in life, acquired degrees, or achieved significant goals is deserving of their confidence. But complete trust is granted (or not) only after people have had the chance to get to know more about the person. The credibility foundation is built brick by brick. And as each new fragment is secured, the basis on which we can erect the hopes of the future is gradually built.

We know from our research that being forward-looking is the quality that distinguishes leaders from other credible people. We also know that without a solid foundation of personal credibility, leaders can have no hope of enlisting others in a common vision. In this book, we will be talking about the sound base on which visions stand and are supported; we will not be talking much about the dreams themselves. Instead, we focus on the leader's foundation of credibility, knowing that only when it is strong can the dreams of the future be supported.

We recognize that the taller and more expansive a leader's dream, the deeper the foundation must be. The less stable the ground underneath, the more solid it must be. Especially in uncertain times, when boldness may be required, leadership credibility is essential in generating confidence among constituents. Without that, nothing can be built—at least nothing that can survive the test of time.

But does building the foundation warrant the effort? Does credibility really matter? Don't we hear almost daily of business, political, labor, and religious leaders who have become successful yet lack credibility? Besides, isn't business about getting results, and if people without credibility still get good results, then what difference does it make anyway?

It matters a great deal. Despite the evidence that some people can succeed, for a time, in ways that are devious and dishonest, credibility has a significantly positive outcome on individual and organizational performance.

○   ○   ○

James M. Kouzes is chairman emeritus of the Tom Peters Company, executive fellow at the Leavey School of Business, Santa Clara University, and a leadership speaker.

Barry Z. Posner is dean and professor at the Leavey School of Business, Santa Clara University. He is also a speaker and executive development program leader.

Chapter Seventeen

Honest Work

Joanne B. Ciulla

Neither famine nor disaster ever haunt men
who do true justice; but lightheartedly they tend
the fields which are all their care.
—Hesiod

Hesiod had no illusions about work—lightheartedly or not, tending the fields was still the backbreaking work of tending the fields. However, work seemed better when honest workers received a just reward for their labor. Justice, Hesiod argued, is at the heart of a good life, and when life is good, work is better. Today we often assume the reverse; if work is good, then life will be better. Whether life makes work better or work makes life better depends in part on which is more important. For some, work is simply the means of making a living; for others, it is that and an end in itself.

Twentieth-century management theories shaped the meaning of work and the expectations about it. History has shown that there was no golden age of work. Besides providing the necessities of life, work can also provide great misery or great joy. The misery of work is frequently caused by others, whereas the joy we usually find on our own. That is why, when people dream of their ideal jobs, they often dream of working for themselves.

Critical analysis of the history of work helps us reflect on the following questions: First, has work gotten better? More important, what does "better" mean? Clearly wage labor is better than slavery. For most people, work is less physical, dirty, and dangerous than it was for the slave, the peasant, the indentured laborer, and the early industrial worker. But "better" should also include the moral relationship between employers and employees. Is there more fairness in the workplace? Are individuals treated better? Has worked improved our lives? Again this depends on what "better" means. While work may improve the material conditions of life, does it improve the quality of our lives? Do our jobs make us better persons?

I have criticized modern management for focusing more on trying to make one *feel* good than on creating a just workplace. One result of the psychological approach to management and the innovations of welfare capitalism in the twentieth century was the eventual decline of unions, which were supposed to ensure justice at work. Another result of modern management techniques was that they reshaped the social significance of work so that work slowly took over a larger slice of our lives. Lastly, while employees were busy having their "hot buttons" pushed, hanging from ropes in Outward Bound programs, and building teams and task forces, wages remained stagnant, while behind boardroom doors corporate executives patted themselves on the back with bonuses, stock options, and platinum parachutes. In the past thirty years the incomes of the rich have gone up, while middle-income wages barely kept pace with inflation and the real wages of low-income workers fell.[1] One look at the wage gap between executives (successful and otherwise) and the average worker, and work doesn't seem very fair.

Today employers know they can't promise much to employees, especially when they must promise so much to stockholders. They know they can't get trust and commitment with smoke and mirrors. Nonetheless, most still try. Their inflated rhetoric sometimes creates cynicism or feelings of betrayal in employees. In some organizations, employees are "empowered," but no one seems to be in control. When an economic downturn occurs, business leaders, like stealth bomber pilots, drop their load of pink slips—and watch the value of their stock options soar. Then they put their hands in their pockets and whistle at the sky. "Redundancies," they insist, are the result of stiff competition, the market, Wall Street, foreign labor markets, or the workers themselves. This stance allows management to shun responsibility and maintain power over employees without accountability to them. Workers, however, are held accountable not only for their own mistakes but for the mistakes and "bad luck" of management or the economy. Empowered, so-called, on the job, they are powerless over their employment itself. They may work long hours, produce high-quality products, and still lose their jobs. When workers get laid off, they shake their fists at the same sky as if some primitive god of fate governs them. Or worse, they take it personally and blame themselves.

We may lament the passing of the paternalistic corporation that once provided some community, security, and material well-being, but today's economic environment allows for no going back. And some elements of the former era are not worth revisiting. The downsizings of the 1990s were a wake-up call. The social compact—You do your job well and you stay employed—is dead, at least for the time being. Jobs were lost and lives were ruined, but one message came through loud and clear: Employment insecurity is the new way of life, even during times of low unemployment. Many workers have begun to rethink their commitment to employers, because their employers have changed their commitment to them. The extra sacrifices of missed family birthdays because of long hours at the office no longer make sense, and maybe never did. As the old saying goes, people on their deathbeds rarely wish that they had spent more time at the office.

So what can work promise and what *can* it deliver? From the perspective of business, the first step toward honest work is to abandon management practices that amount to psychological manipulation or empty propaganda. Neither is efficacious anymore (if they ever really were), especially with young people who have been brought up on *Dilbert*, talk-show psychology, leftover 1960s rebellion, contemporary politics, and advertising. Managers often fret that young workers lack commitment and view employment as short-term. This short view is not because workers in their twenties, say, are lazy or morally decadent. It is because they are realists. They have watched as the middle-aged men in suits lost their jobs. They know the economy is, while seemingly robust, always precarious. A "get it while you can" attitude makes perfect sense in this environment. Twenty-somethings often tell us they want to work for ten or fifteen years, make their fortunes, and quit. Unlike their middle-aged elders who look at them oddly or dub them "slackers," they are not mourning some lost age of work; they are simply trying to construct a strategy for leading a good life. Whether this strategy is feasible for most people is questionable.

If businesses believe they reap greater benefits from a lean, mean, and easily disposable workforce, they also have to understand the costs. There are no quick fixes for the loss of trust and goodwill. Hiring, firing, and training people are expensive propositions. We also don't know what a nomadic workforce will do to communities and families that are already fragile. Some workers find the variety and challenge of job-hopping exciting; others hate the uncertainty. The irony is that if job security is really rare, smart employers will have to start offering security provisions as a means of luring top talent into their organizations. A few already have.

Corporations say they try to help employees balance work and family by providing perks ranging from on-site day care to personal shoppers during the holidays.[2] Such programs work on the assumption that if you make people's lives easier, they will work better. While the programs are well-meaning, employees run the risk of working in "Pullman Towns." Similarly, prayer meetings belong in the community, not in the workplace, even if employees say they want them. In an environment where employment is precarious, it is important for people to be connected to activities and organizations unrelated to work. In this way they build more stability into their lives. If they lose or change their jobs, they'll have other friends, communities, and interests to support them. Even employee benefits like health insurance are good things but can have unintended consequences. Some people find themselves chained to jobs they hate because they can't afford to lose coverage. Or if they lose their jobs, they are unable to pay for life-saving medicines or medical treatments. They depend on their jobs not only to subsist, but to keep themselves or a loved one *alive*. Corporate day care may be a good deal for parents, but when the parents lose their jobs, the children's lives are disrupted as well. This is why, in a world where job security is increasingly fragile, we need to move away from entrusting important elements of our welfare and social life to employers. The problem with a Pullman Town is that it can be attractive, convenient, paternalistic, and well-ordered. But we end up living with greater dependency on the fate of our employers. In today's volatile work world this doesn't make sense. Moreover, when other aspects of our lives become circumscribed in the workplace, we lose our perspective on both work *and* life.

Honest work rests on the assumption that the best way to keep promises is to make promises you can keep. One bogus promise that some employers make is that although they can't promise job security, they can promise training for "employability." While it is true that experience in one job can help one get another, it is misleading to think that an employer knows how to train a person for all the skills that will be needed in the future. Much of what students learn in business and technical schools is already obsolete by the time they enter the workforce.

If the old social compact is dead, what might a new one look like? If an organization can't promise job security, it can at least promise to share information. Here most managers would balk—"We can't tell employees about layoffs in advance, it would ruin morale." Yet if you ask anyone who has worked in a company that is downsizing, he or she will tell you that the rumor mill carries stories of layoffs long before they are announced. In the information age it is increasingly difficult to keep secrets. While management can't share all information, they should share as much as possible information that affects the lives of employees. Management can give employees some information so that the employees can plan their future. Honest work means telling painful truths and preparing others for them. Basically, it's "treating workers like adults."

The old social compact was either paternalistic, therapeutic, or a little of both. Under this unwritten, unspoken contract the company's primary moral commitment was to care—"You do your job well and we'll take care of you." If the company cared for employees, employees usually cared for the company. Sociologist Richard Sennett asserts that the corrosion of character is inevitable in the current unstable employment environment. He writes that the scarcity of long-term commitment disorients and loosens bonds of trust, and divorces will from behavior.[3] But he assumes that long-term relationships are the only avenues to commitment and that long-term employment with one firm is the key to character development. However, while work itself is important for character, there is no reason to believe that changing employers frequently will harm one's character. Serial employment does not necessarily have the same impact as chronic unemployment. People can still gain a sense of self-efficacy, discipline, integrity, and pride from the work they do and from the fact of employment itself.

Mutual respect may be one way to forge short-term bonds of commitment. One of the most tangible ways to show respect for others and to earn their respect is by telling them the truth.[4] We don't always enjoy hearing the truth or like the bearer of truth, but we grow to trust those who tell it to us. Keeping employees informed offers a minimal level of moral decency and is perhaps the best avenue to building trust. If both employers and workers are subject to the whims of the market, shared information help to level the playing field and allows both to look after their own interests.

Respect, trust, and honesty work two ways. Employees also have to deliver on their promises. But workers sometimes engage in their own untruths. There have always been people who are lazy and think employers owe them a living. Others deceive themselves with inflated ideas about the value of their talents and contributions. These lies are often fed by managers who are too lazy or self-interested to give them honest assessments of their work performance. The most common lies told in the workplace (and for that matter in the classroom) are about performance. It's easier and less time-consuming to tell people that they are above average than to tell them they are below it and why. When you respect someone, you not only feel that you owe the person the truth, but that he or she is capable of handling the truth. The truth will help the person to become better. Obviously most employees and students are not above-average, but they have a better chance of really becoming above-average if you tell them how they can improve.

We need to examine the traditional work ethic and see how it fares. Under this ethic, integrity is contingent on how a person works, not where he or she works or for how long. In the past, people tended to chart their career paths through one organization, and a strong work ethic often got them ahead. (Sure, sometimes they got ahead because of office politics.) Today they may have to chart their own careers through many organizations. Those who are most successful will still be the ones who work well and hard. The old work ethic has been around for a long time and is not likely to die off completely in the future. One's personal integrity will still depend on how one works, even if work takes on new forms, in new locations, and for multiple employers.

Lastly, management theorists and employers have to discard the idea that employees must devote their lives to work to do a good job. No, TQM does not have to be "a way of life." If anything, those who lead good, full lives outside of work are just as likely or more likely to do a good job. But jobs should be designed so that they are not overly tedious or demeaning. And what we do at work shouldn't inhibit our ability to pursue a good life outside of it. Technology that allows one to work away from the office is a positive step toward integrating work with life, as long as it doesn't result in a person's always being on call or at work. Some innovations, such as flexible work hours, telecommuting, and job sharing, are positive.

One reason why I have been critical of modern work goes beyond injustice in the workplace, management manipulation, or economic insecurity. When I look at the historical big picture, I am perplexed at the domination of life by paid employment at a time when life itself should be getting easier. We live in extraordinary times, in which a majority of people in postindustrial societies have an unprecedented array of choices about how they live, where they live and work, and what they buy. Machines *are* our slaves, and the basic necessities of life are, for the majority of people, relatively easy to obtain. This is an era when life should be filled with all sorts of rewarding activities. Yet many find themselves caught up not only in long hours of work but in debt, and suffering from stress, loneliness, and crumbling families. Why? In part because we always want more, in part because we don't realize that we have choices.

We now face the problem of rising expectations, rising frustrations, and numerous choices and rewards. We think we are entitled to have everything, or, in the phrase that some feminists have recently abandoned, to having it all—a great job, a large income, plenty of leisure, and security.[5] With so many desires and so many choices, some can't or don't choose how they want to live. Instead they let advertisers, employers, or the opinions of others choose for them. Yet if we are willing to make some trade-offs between an interesting or prestigious job, consumption, leisure, and security, we can gain control and possibly improve the quality of our lives. Of all these trade-offs, containing our desire to consume may be the most difficult, but also the most liberating. The seductive array of things that we can buy ties us to our jobs and often deprives us of our time.

Maybe work dominates many lives today because we have not fully developed a talent for making so many decisions. As Aristotle suggests, we have not learned how to use our freedom. Perhaps now, more than ever, young people need to take Aristotle's advice and study the liberal arts so that they can learn how to make life choices. We have let work dominate us because it organizes our lives and it has obvious built-in rewards. But one can only marvel at the possibilities for work and life once those who "long for something more" figure out what that "something" is and choose to pursue it.

The broader question is, Do we know what kind of life we want and are we willing to give up something for it? Or, to put it another way, Is the life we have now worth what we are giving up for it? Meaningful work is rare, but is out there to be found either in a paid job or in our free time, if we really want it. Not everyone wants it, finds it, or considers the same things meaningful. A work-dominated life is fine if it is a conscious choice and makes one happy. But if it doesn't, then we should start thinking of how to fit work into our lives instead of fitting our lives into our work.

o   o   o

Joanne B. Ciulla is a consultant and professor at the University of Richmond's Jepson School of Leadership Studies.

Chapter Eighteen

Why Amoral Leadership Doesn't Work

James O'Toole

Few leaders have been as successful at the art of change as South Africa's Nelson Mandela. On the eve of his ultimate electoral victory, May 1, 1994, the *New York Times*'s Bill Keller recapped Mandela's lengthy career, attempting to elucidate the essence of the Nobel Prize winner's leadership. The reporter concluded that, all things considered, Mandela was a pragmatist, a realist, a man willing to do whatever the situation required in order to succeed:

- Try as admirers will to sentimentalize Mr. Mandela, the president-in-waiting of a reborn South Africa is at heart the most practical of men.

- He is not unfeeling, but passion—even anger at what he has endured—does not drive him or distract him. He enjoys debate, but he is not a great philosopher or intellectual. He has principles, but he will bend them if they stand in the way of his objective—which, for the last half century, has been ending white domination.

In this view, President Mandela personifies contingency leadership, the Realism advocated by so many political theorists since the time of Machiavelli. Indeed, most students of leadership today subscribe to contingency theory—the most thoughtful of whom include Henry Kissinger and Gary Wills. Moreover, most corporate executives who say that how they lead change "depends on the situation" are also Realists; among the most successful of these are Goodyear's Stanley Gault, American Airlines's Robert Crandall, and, the subject of this chapter, General Electric's Jack Welch. They are wrong.

The moral and logical error inherent in contingency theory is *relativism*, the belief that there are no universal truths or objective knowledge save scientific proofs. In the relativist's belief system, there are no rights and wrongs—or if there are, these are purely personal concerns and as such are irrelevant to the practical arenas of statecraft and corporate leadership. We see evidence that relativism is erroneous when we read the career of Nelson Mandela not in Realist but rather in Rushmorean terms.[1] Like Lincoln and Jefferson, Mandela was pragmatically willing to compromise wherever necessary on tactics, policies, strategies, alliances, and the like. But ipso facto, this ability to play the game of politics does not, as Keller implies, make one a Realist with no guiding principles. Keller himself notes that Mandela never compromised on "his objective": the goal of freedom and political equality for his people. Had Keller built his story around this point, he might have concluded that Mandela created followers precisely because they knew he would not compromise that goal, which was *their* goal. They trusted Mandela to act, at all times, in their interest.

The central fact about Mandela's leadership is that the people of South Africa trusted him. Mandela offered a clue why this was so in his response to a question posed by another American reporter on that same historic day. When asked what he had learned from his years of struggle, Mandela said the lesson was that "people respond to how you treat them. If you treat them with respect, and ignore the negatives, you get a positive reaction." You will recognize this as a restatement of the fundamental Rushmorean principle that trust derives from the respect a leader displays for followers. Respect for followers is made manifest by listening to them, faithfully representing them, pursuing their noblest aspirations, keeping promises made to them, and never doing harm to them or to their cause. Significantly, throughout his long career, Mandela was known as the quintessential listener. Though far from an eloquent phrasemaker, when he spoke at his party's victory rally, he addressed the party faithful not as his followers but as fellow leaders from whom he had learned by listening: "I am your servant. I don't come to you as a leader, as one above others. We are a great team. Leaders come and go, but the organization and the collective leadership that has looked after the fortunes and reversals of this organization will always be there. And the ideas I express are not ideas invented in my own mind."

Trustworthiness, respect, promise-keeping, service, faithfulness—these are moral principles. The subtle difference between Realist and Rushmorean leadership is that whereas the former is relativistic, the latter is founded on a few clear, inviolable moral principles. Hence the point of this chapter: lacking a moral compass, leaders in the Realist-relativist-contingency school are prone, when pressed by the inevitable exigencies of public life, to behave in ways that destroy the trust of followers. Because people will not follow the lead of those they mistrust, contingency leaders will often encounter insurmountable obstacles on the road to leading change.

This distinction is simple and basic, but it is not obvious. For example, the confusion between Realism and Rushmorean leadership surfaces when General Electric's Jack Welch is advanced as the model leader of change that young executives should emulate. Because the failure to distinguish between a pragmatic philosophy like Welch's, on the one hand, and a values-based philosophy like Mandela's, on the other, is at the heart of why leaders fail to bring about change, it is essential that we clarify this subtle difference. To do so, we must first take an important philosophical detour to understand the moral error at the root of Welch's contingency leadership.

CONTINGENCY IN PRACTICE

We may seem to have strayed far from the contingency philosophy of leadership, but in fact we are now better able to see its inherent flaws. The moral error inherent in "it all depends" is that there is no limit to it. The practical error, in the words of contemporary philosopher Mario Bunge, is that "when anything goes, nothing goes well."[2] We can see that what is wrong with contingency theory is that it stands on the quicksand of relativism: It says to the leader, in effect, sometimes it is OK to be tough, even abusive—*it all depends*. As long as "it all depends," Realists will believe that they must be abusive to be effective. That is because *in the eyes of the Realist, there is always a crisis*. The essence of the crisis is the evil and anarchic nature of humans, which must be controlled by a firm commander. In this way, contingency theory, like moral relativism, lends itself to abuse. Once one admits that tyranny is at any time permissible, existing conditions henceforth will be defined as the permissible exception. The Rushmoreans therefore draw a firm line and insist that it is never permissible to behave like Singapore's Lee Kwan Yew or Sunbeam-Oster's Kazarian. People must always be treated with respect; no crisis justifies abusive behavior. Simply put, it does *not* all depend.

Hence contingency theory should be rejected on the grounds that it is always immoral to treat people paternalistically or disrespectfully. Contingency theory also fails basic tests of moral philosophy. For example, by turning its tenets into prescriptions or guidelines for action, we can test its validity. Thus we might ask: When is it appropriate to abuse and disrespect people? When should we not include people in decisions that directly affect them? When is it right for leaders to break faith with followers and betray their trust? When should a leader behave immorally toward followers? In answering such questions, situationalists can only justify their line of reasoning with reference to a world totally devoid of civilized behavior— the world of Machiavelli—in which leadership is no more than an exercise in power.

Still, it might be objected that this is not the intent of contingincy thinking. It is *not* a moral philosophy but instead an empirical observation about pragmatic behavior. As such, one goes too far afield to cite the morality of slavery and the like in what is simply a discussion of practical business matters. After all, business leadership is solely about effectiveness. The proof is that stockholders judge CEOs on how effectively they meet the challenges of change, not on if they obey the Golden Rule or respect natural rights. Thus have we not introduced extraneous questions and confused a straightforward issue of effectiveness?

Over the past several years, a small library has sprouted up on the topic of leadership, and with only a few notable exceptions, the distinction we are drawing here is blurred or contradicted therein. At the core of these texts one is almost certain to find statements along the following lines:

1. A prime task of leadership is to bring about constructive change.
2. How the leader acts to effect change will depend on the situation.
3. Few leaders succeed at achieving constructive change.

Because the first and third of these assertions are based on verifiable observation, we can accept them as true enough for practical purposes. The second assertion, a restatement of contingency theory, is of a different order. To verify a theory requires one or more intervening steps between observation and assertion, steps associated with logical reasoning. This higher barrier to validation notwithstanding, almost all social scientists—and the vast majority of civilians—accept it as true. Whether they are familiar with the jargon of contingency or not, nearly everyone finds it self-evident that there are no universal truths about leadership.

To most observers, it is as clear as the Saharan sky that no basic, immutable principles constitute a single "best way" to lead. Even Gary Wills, whose adherence to contingency theory is weak, nonetheless cites sixteen different types of leadership, the differences among them being situational.[3] One need only consider famous personages as Wills does in *Certain Trumpets* to conclude that each leader must do different things to bring about change. Reviewing the familiar careers of leaders from Pericles to Ross Perot, we might also conclude that leaders must each act with different styles, behave in different ways, and pursue different methods of power and persuasion in light of the exigencies of their particular times, places, challenges, and constituencies.

Hence we may quickly confirm by casual observation that leadership is situational, that "it all depends," and that leaders must do whatever it takes to overcome the resistance to change. Moreover, this commonplace observation is strategically buttressed by prevailing conventions in the social sciences and, as noted, by the ascendant academic values of cultural and moral relativism. Thus a powerful troika of casual observation, science, and ideology all conspire to reinforce the theory of contingency. So powerful and persuasive is this triumvirate of scholarly virtues that contingency advocates ignore countervailing sources of knowledge—in particular, those derived from logic, history, and moral reasoning. For example, advocates of contingency fail to note possible links among the three assertions listed earlier. They do not consider the possibility that so few leaders succeed at leading change (assertion 3) *because* so many are adherents, consciously or unconsciously, of situational leadership (assertion 2).

Moreover, if assertion 2 were valid, there would be no rigorous way to think about leadership. A logical consequence of "it all depends" is that there is no body of knowledge about leadership and hence no "thing" to be learned. If there are no generalizable truths about leadership, it follows that what does not exist cannot be taught. Like the theory of contingency itself, there is more than partial truth here. Obviously, some things about leadership cannot be taught; for example, no cookie-cutter approach to organizational transformation can be applied across the board at IBM, GM, and wherever else leaders seek to bring about change (if there were such a magic formula, all companies would succeed and none would fail).

In fact, only a very few things about leadership can be said to be universally true. Fortunately, these are the most important things; unfortunately, these things are lost on leaders who believe in contingency because they do not know where to look, what to look for, or how to look—because they do not believe that such things are even there to be discovered. Indeed, leadership can be learned only if we change our lenses of perception from the dominant trio of casual observation, social science, and ideology to the more useful triad of logic, history, and morality. Having changed focus, one begins to see that leaders fail to bring about constructive change because they fail to apply the lessons of moral experience. Leading change may be the most difficult of social endeavors, but certain leaders have done it nevertheless. Analysis undistorted by the warped lenses of contingency will reveal that successful leaders share certain core values that allow them to overcome ever-present resistance.

Jack Welch: Contingency Leader Par Excellence

That is not to say that all leaders who bring about effective change are Rushmoreans. To clarify what values-based leadership is, we must understand what it is not. Let me illustrate by reference to General Electric's CEO, Jack Welch, who is today's most admired, most studied, and most quoted corporate leader.[4] In late 1993, *Fortune* said of Welch that he "is widely acknowledged as the leading master of corporate change in our time." The general approbation that accompanies the mention of Welch's name stems from two sources. First, during his tenure, GE's financial performance has been second to none among the largest U.S. corporations. Between 1981 and 1993, the company eliminated more than two hundred thousand jobs while increasing its market value by some $68 billion and tripling its net annual income. Second, he stands out among corporate executives in his ability to articulate the era's dominant leadership philosophy. American executives and scholars are therefore comfortable with Welch not only because he makes a great deal of money for his shareholders, but also because he says the right things about leadership (and says them with remarkable consistency). One thing he invariably says is, "It all depends."

A 1984 *Fortune* story had also featured Welch. His picture on the cover was the captioned "America's Toughest Boss." What *Fortune* meant by "tough" most people would call "abusive." The distinction is essential. Neither Welch's many defenders nor his few detractors argue that he did not have tough choices to make in the 1980s—the toughest of which involved closing factories, selling businesses, and laying off workers. Facing the demise or survival of a firm, a CEO may have little choice but to make such tough calls. Therefore the toughness controversy was not about workforce reductions; it was about Welch's day-to-day treatment of the people who reported to him.

In the early 1980s, journalists started to use the now-famous sobriquet "Neutron Jack" in describing Welch's relationship with subordinates (at the time, the media were obsessed with the neutron bomb, a test weapon storied for its ability to wipe out entire populations while leaving buildings unscathed). In terms meant to be flattering to Welch, *Fortune* said that employees who brought Welch news of unsatisfactory performance were berated, insulted, scolded, and ridiculed—often in front of their peers: "According to former employees, Welch conducts meetings so aggressively that people tremble. He attacks almost physically with his intellect—criticizing, demeaning, ridiculing, humiliating."

At GE, Welch was said to set the standards and the rules; if his underlings didn't meet the former or follow the latter, they were punished. (Such behavior is still prevalent—and still admired by the editors of *Fortune*. In a 1993 feature article, the magazine used the following phrases to characterize a group of America's "toughest" CEOs who were held out as masters of the art of change: "doesn't listen," "impatient," "unreasonable," "micromanages," "humiliates employees," "slams doors and kicks over chairs," "advises to 'fire 'em so they'll understand you are serious.'")

Welch brooked no nonsense from his troops, whom he treated as wayward children when they strayed from the path he had set for the firm. He argued that he alone knew best what was needed to change GE, and it was irrelevant if the people who worked for him didn't like it. He was in a competitive war, and he had no choice but to act as any general would under those circumstances. "Empowerment and transformation are California talk," he said—and he left no doubt that they were inappropriate for the conditions GE was facing in the early 1980s. Anyhow, the proof was in the pudding: he was succeeding in turning GE around and making money.

Then, in the mid 1980s, something unexpected happened: like Saul on the road to Damascus, Welch became a sudden convert to a different—some would say opposing—school of leadership from the one he had so recently espoused. He went from being a general to being almost a good shepherd. Seemingly overnight, there was a "new" Jack Welch, a CEO who now spoke as passionately in favor of a humanistic style of management as he had recently done in defense of command and control. In books, articles, and videos, he was seen treating Americans to the thoughts of the new Welch, especially the necessity that leadership be built on integrity and trust. He spoke eloquently about the need for employee voice, involvement, participation, inclusion, and, yes, even a dollop of the California-style empowerment he had so recently ridiculed.

The leader's job, he informed the world, was not to command but instead to articulate a set of principles that would energize all members of the firm, gaining their voluntary adoption of the firm's values. The CEO's "vision" would allow all employees to understand their roles in the enterprise and thereby motivate them to perform at the peak of their abilities and contribute ideas that were essential for the company to increase productivity. No more did GE want macho leaders bent on dictating; the company now sought out, in Warren Bennis's words, maestros who would engage in coaching. Welch's most quoted observation was that GE was no longer hiring tyrants like the old Jack Welch!

By the early 1990s, Welch had become the nation's most authoritative spokesman for a style of leadership that he had forcefully opposed for most of his managerial career—the "new management" philosophy that had been advocated for forty years by such theorists and consultants as Douglas McGregor, Peter Drucker, J. Edwards Deming, and Bennis himself, and practiced for as long—longer in some instances—by the corporate executives we have begun to call the Rushmoreans,

Robert Owen, James Lincoln, Robert Townsend, Thornton Bradshaw, Robert Galvin, Jan Carlzon, and Max De Pree. There is more than a touch of irony in this. Welch came to be known as dedicated to overcoming unreasonable resistance to change among his followers. But equally interesting is why Welch himself had resisted necessary change for so many decades!

Welch was unlike his predecessors in one important way: *he couched his arguments and actions in terms of contingency.* In his many interviews, he has always been careful to say that Neutron Jack did no wrong in the 1980s. Instead, he goes out of his way to say—even now when he acts in the opposite fashion— that he was right to do what he did *then*. Understand that Welch is no hypocrite; he is completely consistent in word and deed, and there is no evidence that he prevaricates to curry favor with the press, stockholders, or anyone else. We must take him at his word.

What is refreshing about Jack Welch is that he never engages in mea culpas about his former behavior. He shows no sign of regret for having been abusive, for having treated employees with disrespect, for having approached people as means and not as ends. Quite the opposite; in the tradition of General George Patton, he proudly claims to have been right to act that way at that time. Consistent with his philosophy of contingency, he argues that the circumstances of the time necessitated his actions and behavior. He merely did what he had to do to succeed. He had to be tough because GE was starting to lose its competitive edge: the company had gotten fat, dumb, and unproductive; its workforce was unmotivated and complacent; and nearly everyone in the company was resistant to the changes that were necessary to ensure its survival in the long run. In the early 1980s, he saw that GE was about to enter a competitive war, and to win it he would have to whip the troops into battle-ready shape. Here relativists warn that no one has standing to condemn Welch for having abused his employees. He had no choice: *they were resisting change.* And doesn't history now offer support that he was right to have acted as he did? Simply compare GE's record to that of the other denizens of *Fortune*'s top ten in the 1980s—GM, IBM, U.S. Steel, et al. They didn't change, and look what happened to them.

Hence his insistence that he was correct to have acted as he did then. And today? "Our current values are the only ones that will work in this decade," he asserts. The contingency theorists argue that he has again been proved right, as demonstrated by GE's impressive economic performance so far in the 1990s. He was right to be a tough, take-charge authoritarian in the 1980s, and he is right in the 1990s to be a listener concerned with drawing out the ideas of all employees. Contingency theory— the philosophical basis for his leadership—is again validated by observation.

But what about the future? Welch remains consistent: he says it all depends. Maybe he will have to be tough, maybe soft—who can predict? He consequently refuses to rule out the option that some future situation may require the reinvention of Neutron Jack. And why not? Remember, there was nothing wrong with that style; leadership is a matter of expediency, he tells us, not a question of right or wrong. In an instructive video discussion with Warren Bennis, Welch deftly fielded a question about the appropriateness of the leadership styles of such tough-guy college basketball coaches as Indiana's Bobby Knight and the University of California's Lou Campanelli (who, we recall, lost his job over the issue of abusive treatment of his players): "They are dealing with young minds for two or three years, then [the players graduate] and go on. The coaches can brutalize them, kick them, yell at them, motivate them to a high standard for a short time. [That's because] the coaches don't have to deal with them for a lifetime. College coaches grab a kid by the shirt and shake him, but you can't do that for twenty years to the same person."

Welch—always philosophically consistent—thus refused to criticize abusive coaches on moral grounds. To him, the issue is not whether it is ever right to abuse people but rather whether it is expedient to do so in a corporate setting. He concluded only that it is inexpedient in the long run. In contingency terms, he left open the possibility that it might be pragmatic to be abusive "for two or three years," especially when the leader has sufficient turnover that he doesn't have to deal continually with the abused parties. Again note Welch's total absence of hypocrisy: his argument in defense of the coaches is exactly the one he uses to explain his own tough behavior toward GE employees in the 1980s (many of whom he no longer has to deal with because they were among the two hundred thousand whose positions were subsequently eliminated): a leader must do whatever it takes to achieve the objectives. To his credit, Jack Welch practices the contingency leadership he preaches.

WELCH AND DE PREE

Most businesspeople seem to agree with him that leaders must be tough in times of crisis. In discussing Jack Welch with corporate executives, I have seldom heard negative comments about his leadership style or philosophy. Indeed, for as long as

GE was making money, Welch was commonly portrayed as unflawed by his many admirers. This is in sharp contrast to similar discussions that I have had concerning the leadership of Max De Pree, the recently retired CEO of Herman Miller. I have seldom gotten through a seminar on leadership when De Pree's philosophy was not attacked, dismissed, or rejected, often virulently. On one memorable occasion, a theretofore phlegmatic and unemotional executive confessed to a roomful of seminar participants: "I don't like Max De Pree." This was surprising—particularly in light of the fact that De Pree is a patient, gentle, avuncular man completely devoid of arrogance, while Welch is a feisty, ex–hockey player with little tolerance of others, be they fools or geniuses.

For the longest time I puzzled over why corporate audiences who viewed videos of the two leaders so often warmed to Welch and turned cold to De Pree. The root cause could not be financial success: during De Pree's long tenure at the helm of Herman Miller, the company was among the most profitable of the entire *Fortune* 500. It could not be hypocrisy: throughout his career, De Pree practiced what the new Welch only began to preach in the late 1980s. It could not be differences in their current messages or practices: when asked, few executives were able to identify more than minor differences between the recent statements of Welch and what De Pree had always said. After many sessions of listening carefully to the reactions of businesspeople, I finally came to understand that they were not reacting to what Welch or De Pree said or did; rather, their acceptance or rejection of each was based on philosophical grounds.

The philosophical difference is this: Welch now advocates the necessity for employee voice, participation, and inclusion on the pragmatic grounds that such practices *work*, while De Pree argues in favor of such principles on the grounds that they are *right*. Put another way, Welch's starting point is that leadership is *a pragmatic exercise* in getting the leader's will enacted through the efforts of followers; to De Pree leadership is, at base, *a moral activity*. In my experience, businesspeople are more comfortable with a philosophy of leadership rooted in expediency than with one rooted in morality. That they are so is understandable because if they were to abandon contingency theory, they would surrender a broad range of options relating to their exercise of power.

De Pree's philosophy is, in the eyes of many executives, not only impractical but also moralistic. By this I do not imply that De Pree's open admission of Christianity is offensive to them; in fact, unlike many Christians today who seek to impose their values on others, De Pree's faith is personal, and he is refreshingly tolerant of those sinners (like myself) who are patently not of the Christian persuasion. Yet one can see why executives view the fundamental premise of his leadership philosophy in such a harsh light. To follow his basic moral premise that all men and women are created in the image of the same Maker—which is at the root of humanistic natural law as well as Christian ethics—would greatly restrict the options of a leader. For example, from this starting point De Pree concludes that all employees have certain inalienable rights; in particular, that all are entitled to be treated with respect and all are entitled to be treated as ends and not means. At the highest level of abstraction, as we have seen, these rights are absolute. For example, there are *no* circumstances in which it is permissible for a leader to treat followers with disrespect; there is *never* a valid reason for leaders to abuse followers. In essence, then, he says, it does *not* "all depend."

In sharp contrast, contingency theory rejects the notion of any "higher law." As Welch so clearly articulates it, in the final reckoning, the call belongs to the leader, who is free to do whatever is necessary to get followers to perform. In effect, the leader reserves the right to act however he or she sees fit. Under contingency theory, it is always right for the leader to do whatever is necessary, given only one limitation: that the action works to advance his or her ends. Pragmatically, "whatever is necessary" includes anything that the leader decides is required by circumstances to achieve the goal being pursued. For example, if the situation requires disrespect of followers—in other words, abuse—so be it. Of course, contingency theorists seldom discuss their beliefs in these terms. In the hard-nosed, practical world of observation, science, and ideology, there is little room for soft questions of morality.

Efficiency is the ultimate defense of contingency leadership, and, as discussed, the example invariably given is the necessity of efficacious action in an emergency, with war offered as the extreme of such situations. As we have seen, contingency theorists are on their strongest ground when they claim that "leaders must do whatever has to be done in a crisis." After all, the opposite is unthinkable—who would advocate indecisive leadership when lives are at stake? "Do you want the troops to take a vote in the middle of a battle?" they ask.

Welch himself makes this case. In the early 1980s, he saw the need to downsize quickly. This requisite for bold, decisive action necessitated running roughshod over certain niceties of participation (niceties that he now calls, in perfect contingency thinking, necessities for the 1990s). Today he argues that his only regret is not having been tough enough in the midst of the 1980s crisis: "My biggest mistake was agonizing too long over difficult decisions. I should have done it faster. But we're all human. We don't like to face up to some of these unpleasant things. And I didn't want to break this company. In hindsight, I was generally erring on the side of being afraid of breaking it. GE would be better off if I had acted faster."

Let us try generalizing this contingency argument beyond the confines of GE. A company finds itself in a crisis and needs a decisive leader to take firm, bold, quick action. Because contingencies demand such speedy, authoritative steps, the participation of managers in the decisions that affect them would be both inefficient and inappropriate. To save the sinking ship, the leader has no choice but to bark firm directions—and to worry about hurt feelings later. If the leader doesn't act quickly and decisively, there will not be a later to worry about. And if one requires a moral justification for this unfettered exercise of power, it is this: without a strong hand at the helm in a time of chaos, the vessel will not survive.

Consider an alternative scenario: the leader must act quickly to save the company. She calls in the people normally involved in the decision-making process, as well as those who will be directly affected. She quickly and candidly explains the nature of the contingency to these individuals. What is likely to happen next in this scenario? I suggest the following as the most probable dénouement: if the leader has built the trust of those around her in the past, it is a good bet that they will say to her in this moment of clear crisis, "It's your call. We trust your judgment. Let us know how we can be of help." Then, even if the leader makes a bad call, there is some basis for rebuilding trust after the crisis has passed. Admittedly, this scenario will be viewed as hopelessly naive and optimistic by the cynical standards of the situationalist. But even in purely expedient terms, doesn't a leader have more power if it is granted than if it is unilaterally usurped?

NASA's series of experiments in the 1970s add further evidence that the contingency of a crisis demands more than speed and "taking charge" on the part of a single strong leader. Furthermore, the issue isn't the theoretical one posed by Realists: no one advocates "taking a vote in the middle of a battle." The mundane issue is what happens *after* a crisis when a leader has arbitrarily excluded from the decision-making process the people who were affected and who were accustomed to participating. In almost all instances, the people excluded will sense a betrayal of trust. Whatever credits for trustworthiness the leader may have accumulated in the past will thus be expended in one furious round of decisive command. Such credit is not easily reclaimed; in many organizations, trust once lost is never regained. I stress this issue of trust because it is the factor that Welch himself says is most required for his new style of leadership.

If in fact crisis situations demand the infringement of basic morality, contingency theory is valid on practical grounds. But if a crisis can be handled without suspension of moral principles—for example, if one can fight a war without suspending democracy—the philosophy is invalid in practice. Bear in mind that Welch, ever consistent with contingency thinking, does not claim that the leader's only path to success is along the authoritarian route; he merely says that *sometimes* the leader must be a tyrant. In particular, he says that the contingency of a crisis demands an authoritarian response. In sum, we question his conclusions on moral, logical, and historical grounds:

○ Morally, is it ever right for a leader to be a tyrant? We have seen that there is an absolute moral prohibition against the infringement of basic human rights.

○ Logically, is it a fact that only tyrants are effective in emergencies? The NASA experiment and the careers of the Rushmoreans offer evidence that the contingency of a crisis may be handled effectively without resorting to tyranny.

○ Historically, has it proved necessary to suspend basic rights during crises? During the Civil War, didn't Lincoln keep Congress in session—and didn't he himself stand for reelection in the darkest days of the conflict? During World War II, didn't Churchill maintain parliamentary democracy even during the Battle of Britain?

Here, no doubt, the contingency theorist will object: Welch isn't talking about the high value of democracy; he is concerned only with the low value of productivity. He is wrong. In all cases, we are discussing the process of effective and moral leadership, be it of a nation or of a corporation. In this context, it is irrelevant if the goal is Mandela's freedom or Welch's productivity. What concerns us is how followers are included in the process of defining and achieving goals.

Even if we were to accept Welch's singular and circumscribed measure of leadership effectiveness, questions may still be raised about his performance: Would productivity have been higher over the long term at GE had Welch behaved with moral consistency throughout his tenure? Doubtless he succeeded in the past while being abusive, but would he have been even more successful had he treated people with the same respect during the crisis of the 1980s as he says he does now? And would he be even more successful now if GE employees knew that they could trust him never to revert to being Neutron Jack? No one knows the answers to such questions, but is it more logical to accept the assertion of no than to consider the possibility of yes?

Welch and Patton: Must a Leader Be Tough to Be Demanding?

Finally, Realists will argue that the proof is in the pudding: Jack Welch's tough style brought out the highest performance among his troops. In essence, the argument goes, a leader must be tough to elicit the best from followers. I would argue that GE might have been more productive had Welch understood the moral nuances among the words *demanding, tough,* and *abusive*. All great leaders are demanding in that they inspire the best in their followers—and such leaders are willing to accept nothing less than the highest performance from them. On this score, Max De Pree was a thoroughly demanding leader, unwilling to accept from Herman Miller employees anything but the highest levels of product design and quality, customer satisfaction, and overall financial performance. Yet in the many years I studied Herman Miller, I never heard of De Pree having abused anyone.

Perhaps the most demanding CEO in America is Walt Disney's Michael Eisner, himself a friend and admirer of Welch's. Indeed, like Welch, Eisner pushes all of his people hard and incessantly to improve their performance. Eisner never seems satisfied with the results; he always believes that his people can do better. Because he never lets up, some employees have told him to his face that he can be an irritating perfectionist. Yet I have never heard a Disney employee say that Eisner has ever treated anyone with less than perfect respect. He is obviously flawed as a leader, but his flaws are related to his ego rather than to his morality. Eisner may not have handled his parting of the ways with Jeffery Katzenberg with aplomb, but the severance was downright humane compared with Neutron Jack's old style. Indeed, one Disney manager told me, "I don't think Michael knows how to be abusive."

It is important to recognize that Welch does not argue that abuse is moral; he doubtless sees abuse as an evil necessity. Like General George Patton, he believes that it is sometimes necessary to treat people with less than respect to motivate them to perform. We must ask if this is true—particularly now that Welch is being advanced as a role model for young leaders. If Welch's philosophy is flawed—if, for example, it is possible to be demanding without being abusive—then it is incumbent on us to find a more appropriate philosophy and a better role model. Let me suggest one test of Welch's effectiveness as a leader: the behavior of his followers. To test Welch's leadership, one might ask the following questions of, and about, his managers around the world:

- Is there consistency between what Welch preaches and the actual practices of GE?

- Is the organization in fact encouraging the free expression of ideas at all levels in the firm? Is this translating into change and innovation?

- Do the people who report to Jack Welch, and the people who in turn report to them, behave toward their followers like the new Welch or like the old Neutron Jack?

- Is GE's culture both moral and effective? Do the names of GE's divisions appear in the news in connection with legal, ethical, and regulatory violations?

On such judgments, the jury is still out. But evidence continues to mount that Welch's leadership of GE is seriously flawed on the dimension of morality, if not on the dimension of effectiveness:

- In 1989, the company paid $3.5 million to GE employees who claimed their division had defrauded the government. One allegation by the GE whistleblowers was that the company had faked test results on defense contracts.
- In 1990, GE paid $30 million in penalties for defense contracting overcharges.
- In 1993, the company's NBC subsidiary apologized and paid court costs to GM when it was revealed that the network had rigged a test crash of a GMC pickup.
- In 1994, it was revealed that a trader at GE's Kidder Peabody subsidiary faked $350 million in sales.

Perhaps more than any other large American corporation, GE is faced with an imposing backlog of lawsuits relating to environmental transgressions and fraud in defense contracting. Moreover, its ham-fisted handling of its Hungarian acquisition, Tungsram, has soured relations between U.S. business and the growing economies of Eastern Europe. Welch himself pooh-poohs all of the above, pointing to the profits he has earned for GE's shareholders. Indeed, as he has moved the company away from domestic manufacturing and into the more ethically free-wheeling world of financial services, there is no gainsaying that GE's billions of dollars worth of divestitures and acquisitions have proved profitable in the main. Be that as it may, the issue is that Welch clearly is not practicing values-based leadership. To what transcendent, higher-order values has he dedicated himself and his company?

There is no question that Welch has been a success. Much like General Patton—who was recognized by admirers and critics alike as a military genius—Welch achieves his objectives at least as well as his competitors and definitely faster. On this point, my former colleague Morgan McCall calls attention to the perhaps unconscious parallels between the following epigrams:[5]

"War is a very simple thing, and the determining characteristics are self-confidence, speed, and audacity."
—General George Patton, 1947

"[Leadership requires] speed, simplicity, and self-confidence."
—Jack Welch, 1993

Indeed, the question we should ask about Welch is the same question that Generals Eisenhower and Bradley raised about Patton: Is there a better way? Can one have the same level of success without incurring high human costs? Indeed, would Welch have been even more successful had he taken the higher road? What might have happened at GE had the old Jack Welch been like the new one all along? What would have happened to GE's bottom line if there had been no necessity for Welch to change styles? In light of the answers to those questions, one might revisit the basic issue: Is contingency theory merely a rationalization for certain kinds of otherwise indefensible behavior? In short, does "it all depend"?

When introduced, contingency theory was an improvement over the competing theories advanced by such great minds as Plato, Confucius, Machiavelli, Carlyle, Emerson, Tolstoy, and

Weber. Their theories—each intriguing and partly valid—were found to be too confining to serve as guides to effective leadership. The challenge remains to identify a moral alternative to contingency theory that does not founder on that failing of oversimplicity.

Justice Oliver Wendell Holmes once said, "I wouldn't give a fig for the simplicity this side of complexity, but would give my life for the simplicity the other side of complexity." What Holmes meant is that we should not be seduced by facile theories—for example, leadership theories based on such concepts as charisma, chance, natural hierarchies, or testosterone levels. Such ideas foster the most dangerous exercise of simplicity: unidimensional thinking in a multidimensional world.

An advantage of contingency theory is that it acknowledges leadership's many levels of complexity. That would make it a marvelous step forward were it not for the unfortunate fact that so many leaders get lost in the maze. Leaders who see only the complexity of situations become confused and indecisive and consequently allow their organizations to drift into deadlock, gridlock, paralysis. More often, as we have seen, contingency theory is used as an excuse for expedient behavior, encouraging leaders to cut through complexity with the confidence that "this is one of those times when I have to be tough." The epigrams cited attest to the attraction of such simplicity to Patton and Welch.

Indeed, almost all advocates of contingency theory are tempted to interpret the ever-present complexity of life—the confusion and chaos endemic to modern society—as a crisis demanding toughness. This is perhaps better than getting mired in complexity, but neither option seems ideal.

Leaders must act, and to act requires an element of simplicity. Leaders must ultimately reduce complexity to a manageable size, reformulate it, and clarify it in terms simple enough for followers to understand. But leaders cannot succeed at this task unless they themselves understand that the complexity of the modern world derives from an absence of certainty—that is, from disagreement fueled by the differing values of followers. To cut through this complexity requires the creation of transcendent values, a collective view that followers recognize as morally superior to their own narrower interests even while encompassing them. As Nelson Mandela understood, people will follow only leaders who take them where they want to go. Leaders thus beget followers, and they do so by allowing the followers to take the leader's dream as their own. This can occur only when leaders acknowledge the legitimacy of followers' competing beliefs and diverse values. Hence the overall conclusion of our inquiry: for leadership to be effective, it must be moral, and the sine qua non of morality is respect for people. Significantly, this concept of leadership that we are calling Rushmorean is not new. It has coexisted and competed with Realism for centuries. It was first expressed by the Chinese philosopher Lao-tzu some six hundred years before the birth of Christ:

A leader is best
When people barely know that he exists,
Not so good when people obey and acclaim him,
Worst when they despise him.
"Fail to honor people,
They fail to honor you;"
But of a good leader, who talks little,

When his work is done, his aim fulfilled,
They will all say, "We did this ourselves."[6]

The cynic might argue that what Lao-tzu advocated is no different from the philosophy of Jack Welch because at base it is manipulative. But in fact there is a great difference in that the leadership called for by Lao-tzu is constrained by the moral principle of respect for people. As Jefferson told Du Pont, moral leadership requires the full inclusion of followers. That is why Jefferson trusted the American people to be the best judges of their own interests in the long run. He trusted the citizenry because in the final analysis, he respected them. In contrast, it was said of Richard Nixon that he trusted no one, and the American people returned the sentiment. Moral and effective leadership always comes down to that basic attitude about people. Gandhi observed that ultimately, immoral leaders always fail because their followers feel disrespected. Amoral contingency leaders fail for the same reason.

We do not know what, along his private road to Damascus, changed in Jack Welch. Was it his attitude toward trusting others? If he now truly respects the value of others, he may go down as a great leader. But the jury is still out. As Sophocles cautioned, "Count no man fortunate until you know his end." If Jack Welch ultimately stumbles and falls, it is likely to be because he does not believe in the Taoist principle "Fail to honor people, and they fail to honor you"—a principle shared, as we must again note, by all major religions and humanistic philosophies. It is not too late, of course, for Welch to renounce contingency leadership and go into history in better company than George Patton! But to embrace the Rushmorean approach, he will first have to overcome the Pattonesque belief that such leadership is "soft" and unacceptably "feminine."

o   o   o

James O'Toole is research professor at the Center for Effective Organizations, University of Southern California, and chairman of the board of academic advisers to Booz Allen Hamilton's Strategic Leadership Center.

Chapter Nineteen

The Discipline of Building Character

Joseph L. Badaracco Jr.

We have all experienced, at one time or another, situations in which our professional responsibilities unexpectedly come into conflict with our deepest values. A budget crisis forces us to dismiss a loyal, hardworking employee. Our daughter has a piano recital on the same afternoon that our biggest client is scheduled to visit our office. At these times, we are caught in a conflict between right and right. And no matter which option we choose, we feel like we've come up short.

Managers respond to these situations in a variety of ways: some impulsively "go with their gut"; others talk it over with their friends, colleagues, or families; still others think back to what a mentor would do in similar circumstances. In every case, regardless of what path is chosen, these decisions taken cumulatively over many years form the very basis of an individual's character. For that reason, I call them *defining moments*.

What is the difference between a tough ethical decision and a defining moment? An ethical decision typically involves choosing between two options: one we know to be right and another we know to be wrong. A defining moment, however, challenges us in a deeper way by asking us to choose between two or more ideals in which we deeply believe. Such challenges rarely have a "correct" response. Rather, they are situations created by circumstance that ask us to step forward and, in the words of the American philosopher John Dewey, "form, reveal, and test" ourselves. We form our character in defining moments because we commit to irreversible courses of action that shape our personal and professional identities. We reveal something new about us to ourselves and others because defining moments uncover something that had been hidden or crystallize something that had been only partially known. And we test ourselves because we discover whether we will live up to our personal ideals or only pay them lip service.

As I have interviewed and studied business leaders, I have found that the ones who are most satisfied with the way they resolve their defining moments possess skills that are left off most job descriptions. Specifically, they are able to take time out from the chain of managerial tasks that consumes their time and undertake a process of probing self-inquiry—a process that is more often carried out on the run rather than in quiet seclusion. They are able to dig below the busy surface of their daily lives and refocus on their core values and principles. Once uncovered, those values and principles renew their sense of purpose at work and act as a springboard for shrewd, pragmatic, politically astute action. By repeating this process again and again throughout their work lives, these executives are able to craft an authentic and strong identity based on their own, rather than on someone else's, understanding of what is right. And in this way, they begin to make the transition from being a manager to becoming a leader.

But how can an executive trained in the practical, extroverted art of management learn to engage in such an intuitive, personal process of introspection? In this chapter, I will describe a series of down-to-earth questions that will help managers take time out from the hustle and bustle of the workplace. These practical, thought-provoking questions are designed to transform values and beliefs into calculated action. They have been drawn from well-known classic and contemporary philosophers but remain profound and flexible enough to embrace a wide range of contemporary right-versus-right decisions. By taking time out to engage in this process of self-inquiry, managers will by no means be conducting a fruitless exercise in escapism; rather, they will be getting a better handle on their most elusive, challenging, and essential business problems.

In today's workplace, three kinds of defining moments are particularly common. The first type is largely an issue of personal identity. It raises the question, Who am I? The second type is organizational as well as personal: both the character of groups within an organization and the character of an individual manager are at stake. It raises the question, Who are we? The third type of defining moment is the most complex and involves defining a company's role in society. It raises the question, Who is the company? By learning to identify each of these three defining moments, managers will learn to navigate right-versus-right decisions with grace and strength. (See Exhibit 19.1.)

EXHIBIT 19.1 A Guide to Defining Moments

For Individuals: Who Am I?

1. What feelings and intuitions are coming into conflict in this situation?

2. Which of the values that are in conflict are most deeply rooted in my life?

3. What combination of expediency and shrewdness, coupled with imagination and boldness, will help me implement my personal understanding of what is right?

For Managers of Work Groups: Who Are We?

1. What are the other strong, persuasive interpretations of the ethics of this situation?

2. What point of view is most likely to win a contest of interpretations inside my organization and influence the thinking of other people?

3. Have I orchestrated a process that can make manifest the values I care about in my organization?

For Company Executives: Who Is the Company?

1. Have I done all I can to secure my position and the strength of my organization?

2. Have I thought creatively and boldly about my organization's role in society and its relationship to stockholders?

3. What combination of shrewdness, creativity, and tenacity will help me transform my vision into a reality?

Who Am I?
Defining Moments for Individuals

The most basic type of defining moment demands that managers resolve an urgent issue of personal identity that has serious implications for their careers. Two "rights" present themselves, each one representing a plausible and usually attractive life choice. And therein lies the problem: there is no one right answer; right is set against right.

Conflicting Feelings

When caught in this bind, managers can begin by taking a step back and looking at the conflict not as a problem but as a natural tension between two valid perspectives. To flesh out this tension, we can ask, *What feelings and intuitions are coming into conflict in this situation?* As Aristotle discussed in his classic work *Ethics*, people's feelings can actually help them make sense of an issue, understand its basic dimensions, and indicate what the stakes really are. In other words, our feelings and intuitions are both a form of intelligence and a source of insight.

Consider, for example, the case of a young analyst—we will call him Steve Lewis—who worked for a well-known investment bank in Manhattan.[1] Early one morning, Lewis, an African-American, found a message on his desk asking if he could fly to St. Louis in two days to help with a presentation to an important prospective client. The message came as a surprise to him. Lewis's company had a clear policy against including analysts in presentations or client meetings. Lewis, in fact, knew little about the subject of the St. Louis meeting, which concerned a specialized area of municipal finance. He was especially surprised to learn that he had been selected over more senior people in the public finance group.

Lewis immediately walked down the hall into the office of his friend and mentor, also an African-American, and asked him if he knew about the situation. His friend, a partner at the company, replied, "Let me tell you what's happening, Steve. Look at you and me. What do we have in common? Did you know that the new state treasurer of Missouri is also black? I hate for you to be introduced to this side of the business so soon, but the state treasurer wants to see at least one black professional at the meeting or else the company has no chance of being named a manager for this deal."

What if at this point Lewis were to step back and reframe the situation in terms of his feelings and intuitions? On the one hand, Lewis believed firmly that in order to maintain his self-respect, he had to earn his advancement at the company—and elsewhere in life. He was not satisfied to move up the ladder of success based on affirmative action programs or being a "token" member of the company. For that reason, he had always wanted to demonstrate through his work that he deserved his position. On the other hand, as a former athlete, Lewis had always prided himself on being a team player and did not believe in letting his teammates down. By examining his feelings and intuitions about the situation, Lewis learned that the issue at hand was more complex than whether or not to go to the presentation. It involved a conflict between two of his most deeply held beliefs.

Deeply Rooted Values

By framing defining moments in terms of our feelings and intuitions, we can remove the conflict from its business context and bring it to a more personal, and manageable, level. Then we can consider a second question to help resolve the conflict: *Which of the responsibilities and values that are in conflict are most deeply rooted in my life and in the communities I care about?* Tracing the roots of our values means understanding their origins and evolution over time. It involves an effort to understand which values and commitments really mean the most to us.

Let's apply that approach to the case of Steve Lewis. On the one hand, he had no doubt that he wanted to become a partner at a major investment bank and that he wanted to earn that position based on merit. Since his sophomore year of college, Lewis had been drawn to the idea of a career on Wall Street, and he had worked hard and purposefully to make that idea a reality. When he accepted his current job, he had finally set foot on the path he had dreamed of, and neither the long hours nor the detailed "grunt" work that was the lot of first-year analysts gave him misgivings about his choice. He believed he was pursuing his own values by seeking a successful career at a Wall Street investment bank. It was the kind of life he wanted to live and the kind of work he enjoyed doing.

On the other hand, when Lewis considered his African-American background, he thought about what his parents had taught him. One episode from the early 1960s stood out in particular. His parents made a reservation at a restaurant that reputedly did not serve blacks. When they arrived, the hostess told them there had been a mistake. The reservation was lost, and they could not be seated. The restaurant was half empty. Lewis's parents turned around and left. When they got home, his mother made a new reservation under her maiden name. (His father had been a popular local athlete, whose name was widely recognized.) The restaurant suspected nothing. When they returned an hour later, the hostess, though hardly over-joyed, proceeded to seat them.

Lewis was still moved by the memory of what his parents had done, even as he sat in his office on Wall Street many years later. With his parents' example in mind, Lewis could begin to sense what seemed to be the best answer to his present dilemma. He would look at the situation as his parents' son. He would view it as an African-American, not as just another young investment banker. Lewis decided that he could not go to the meeting as the "token black." To do so would repudiate his parents' example. He decided, in effect, that his race was a vital part of his moral identity, one with a deeper and stronger relation to his core self than the professional role he had recently assumed.

Shrewdness and Expediency

Introspection of the kind Steve Lewis engaged in can easily become divorced from real-world demands. We have all seen managers who unthinkingly throw themselves into a deeply felt personal cause and suffer serious personal and career setbacks. As the Renaissance philosopher Niccolò Machiavelli and other ethical pragmatists remind us, idealism untempered by realism often does little to improve the world. Hence, the next critical question becomes, *What combination of shrewdness and expediency, coupled with imagination and boldness, will help me implement my personal understanding of what is right?* This is, of course, a different question altogether from What should I do? It acknowledges that the business world is a bottom-line, rough-and-tumble arena where introspection alone won't get the job done. The process of looking inward must culminate in concrete action characterized by tenacity, persuasiveness, shrewd-ness, and self-confidence.

How did Lewis combine idealism with realism? He decided that he would join the presentation team, but he also gambled that he could do so on terms that were at least acceptable to him. He told the partner in charge, Bruce Anderson, that he felt honored to be asked to participate but added that he wanted to play a role in the presentation. He said he was willing to spend every minute of the next 30 hours in preparation. When Anderson asked why, Lewis said only that he wanted to earn his place on the team. Anderson reluctantly agreed. There was, it turned out, a minor element of the presentation that required the application of some basic analytical techniques with which Lewis was familiar. Lewis worked hard on the presentation, but when he stood up during the meeting for the 12 minutes allot-ted him, he had a terrible headache and wished he had refused Anderson's offer. His single day of cramming was no substitute for the weeks his colleagues had invested in the project. Nev-ertheless, his portion of the presentation went well, and he received praise from his colleagues for the work he had done.

On balance, Lewis had soundly defined the dilemma he faced and had taken an active role in solving it—he did not attend the meeting as a showpiece. At the same time, he may have strengthened his career prospects. He felt he had passed a minor test, a rite of passage at his company, and had demon-strated not only that he was willing to do what it took to get the job done but also that he would not be treated as a token mem-ber of the group. The white analysts and associates who were passed over probably grumbled a bit; but Lewis suspected that, if they had been dealt his hand, they would have played their cards as he did.

Who Are We?
Defining Moments for Work Groups

As managers move up in an organization, defining moments become more difficult to resolve. In addition to looking at the situation as a conflict between two personal beliefs, managers must add another dimension: the values of their work group and their responsibilities to the people they manage. How, for example, should a manager respond to an employee who repeatedly shows up for work with the smell of alcohol on his breath? How should a manager respond to one employee who has made sexually suggestive remarks to another? In this type of defining moment, the problem and its resolution unfold not only as a personal drama within one's self but also as a drama among a group of people who work together. The issue becomes public and is important enough to define a group's future and shape its values.

Points of View

Many managers suffer from a kind of ethical myopia, believing that their entire group views a situation through the same lens that they do. This way of thinking rarely succeeds in bringing people together to accomplish common goals. Differences in upbringing, religion, ethnicity, and education make it difficult for any two people to view a situation similarly—let alone an entire group of people. The ethical challenge for a manager is not to impose his or her understanding of what is right on the group but to understand how other members view the dilemma. The manager must ask, *What are the other strong, persuasive interpretations of the ethics of this situation?*

A classic example of this kind of problem involved a 35-year-old manager, Peter Adario. Adario headed the marketing department of Sayer Microworld, a distributor of computer products. He was married and had three children. He had spent most of his career as a successful salesman and branch manager, and he eagerly accepted his present position because of its varied challenges. Three senior managers reporting to Adario supervised the other 50 employees in the marketing department, and Adario in turn reported to one of four vice presidents at corporate headquarters.

Adario had recently hired an account manager, Kathryn McNeil, who was a single mother. Although she was highly qualified and competent, McNeil was having a hard time keeping up with her work because of the time she needed to spend with her son. The pace at work was demanding: the company was in the middle of finishing a merger, and 60-hour work weeks had become the norm. McNeil was also having difficulty getting along with her supervisor, Lisa Walters, a midlevel manager in the department who reported to Adario. Walters was an ambitious, hard-driving woman who was excelling in Sayer Microworld's fast-paced environment. She was irritated by McNeil's chronic lateness and unpredictable work schedule. Adario had not paid much attention to Walters' concerns until the morning he found a handwritten note from her on top of his pile of unfinished paperwork. It was her second note to him in as many weeks. Both notes complained about McNeil's hours and requested that she be fired.

For Adario, who was himself a father and sympathetic to McNeil's plight, the situation was clearly a defining moment, pitting his belief that his employees needed time with their families against his duty to the department's bottom line. Adario decided to set up a meeting. He was confident that if he sat down with the two women the issue could somehow be resolved. Shortly before the meeting was to begin, however, Adario was stunned to learn that Walters had gone over his head and discussed the issue with one of the company's senior executives. The two then had gone to McNeil's office and had fired her. A colleague later told him that McNeil had been given four hours to pack her things and leave the premises.

Where Adario saw right versus right, Walters saw right versus wrong. She believed that the basic ethical issue was McNeil's irresponsibility in not pulling her weight and Adario's lack of action on the issue. McNeil's customer account was crucial, and it was falling behind schedule during a period of near-crisis at the company. Walters also believed that it was unfair for one member of the badly overburdened team to receive special treatment. In retrospect, Adario could see that he and Walters looked at the same facts about McNeil and reached very different conclusions. Had he recognized earlier that his view was just one interpretation among many, he might have realized that he was engaged in a difficult contest of interpretations.

Influencing Behavior

Identifying competing interpretations, of course, is only part of the battle. Managers also need to take a hard look at the organization in which they work and make a realistic assessment of whose interpretation will win out in the end. A number of factors can determine which interpretation will prevail: company culture, group norms, corporate goals and company policy, and the inevitable political jockeying and battling inside organizations. In the words of the American philosopher William James, "The final victorious way of looking at things will be the most completely impressive to the normal run of minds." Therefore, managers need to ask themselves, *What point of view is most likely to win the contest of interpretations and influence the thinking and behavior of other people?*

Peter Adario would have benefited from mulling over this question. If he had done so, he might have seen the issue in terms of a larger work-family issue within the company. For Adario and McNeil, the demands of work and family meant constant fatigue, a sense of being pulled in a thousand directions, and the frustration of never catching up on all they had to do. To the other employees at Sayer Microworld, most of whom were young and not yet parents, the work-family conflict meant that they sometimes had to work longer hours because other employees had families to attend to. Given the heavy workloads they were carrying, these single employees had little sympathy for Adario's family-oriented values.

Truth as Process

Planning ahead is at the heart of managerial work. One needs to learn to spot problems before they blow up into crises. The same is true for defining moments in groups. They should be seen as part of a larger process that, like any other, needs to be managed. Effective managers put into place the conditions for the successful resolution of defining moments long before those moments actually present themselves. For in the words of William James, "The truth of an idea is not a stagnant property inherent in it. Truth happens to an idea. It becomes true, is made true by events. Its verity is in fact an event, a process." Managers can start creating the conditions for a particular interpretation to prevail by asking, *Have I orchestrated a process that can make my interpretation win in my group?*

Adario missed subtle signals that a process opposed to his own had been under way for some time. Recall that Walters had sent Adario two notes, each suggesting that McNeil be replaced. What were those notes actually about? Were they tentative announcements of Walters's plans or tests of Adario's authority? And what did Walters make of Adario's failure to respond? She apparently interpreted his reaction—or lack thereof—as an indication that he would not stand in the way of firing McNeil. Walters may even have thought that Adario wanted McNeil fired but was unwilling to do it himself. In short, Adario's defining moment had gone badly because Walters presented a compelling story to the company's top management; she thereby preempted Adario and filled the vacuum that he had created through his inaction.

Instead of waiting for the issue of work versus family to arise and take the group by surprise, Adario could have anticipated the problem and taken a proactive approach to defining a work culture that valued both family and work. Adario had ample opportunity to prevent the final turn of events from occurring. He could have promoted McNeil to others inside the company. In particular, he needed to emphasize the skills and experience, especially in account management, that she brought to the company. He also could have created opportunities for people to get to know McNeil personally, even to meet her son, so that they would understand and appreciate what she was accomplishing.

Playing to Win

One of the hallmarks of a defining moment is that there is a lot at stake for all the players in the drama. More often than not, the players will put their own interests first. In this type of business setting, neither the most well-meaning intentions nor the best-designed process will get the job done. Managers must be ready to roll up their sleeves and dive into the organizational fray, putting to use appropriate and effective tactics that will make their vision a reality. They need to reflect on the question, *Am I just playing along or am I playing to win?*

At Sayer Microworld, the contest of interpretations between Walters and Adario was clearly part of a larger power struggle. If Walters didn't have her eye on Adario's job before McNeil was fired, she probably did afterward: top management seemed to like her take-charge style. Whereas Adario was lobbing underhand softball pitches, Walters was playing hardball. At Sayer Microworld, do-the-right-thing idealism without organizational savvy was the sure path to obscurity. Adario's heart was in the right place when he hired McNeil. He believed she could do the job, he admired her courage, and he wanted to create a workplace in which she could flourish. But his praiseworthy intentions needed to be backed by a knack for maneuvering, shrewdness, and political savvy. Instead, Walters seized the moment. She timed her moves carefully and found a powerful ally in the senior manager who helped her carry out her plan.

Although Adario stumbled, it is worth noting that this defining moment taught him a great deal. In following up on McNeil's firing, Adario learned through the grapevine that many other employees shared his view of the work-family dilemma, and he began acting with more confidence than he had before. He told his boss that he disagreed with the decision to fire McNeil and objected strongly to the way the decision had been made. He then told Walters that her behavior would be noted in the next performance review he put in her file. Neither Walters nor the vice president said very much in response, and the issue never came up again. Adario had staked his claim, albeit belatedly. He had learned, in the words of Machiavelli, that "a man who has no position in society cannot even get a dog to bark at him."

Who Is the Company?
Defining Moments for Executives

Redefining the direction of one's own life and the direction of one's work group requires a thoughtful blend of personal introspection and calculated action. But the men and women charged with running entire companies sometimes face an even more complex type of defining moment. They are asked to make manifest their understanding of what is right on a large stage—one that can include labor unions, the media, shareholders, and many other company stakeholders. Consider the complexity of the dilemma faced by a CEO who has just received a report of package tampering in one of the company's over-the-counter medications. Or consider the position of an executive who needs to formulate a response to reports in the media that women and children are being treated unfairly in the company's foreign plant. These types of decisions force top-level managers to commit not just themselves or their work groups but their entire company to an irreversible course of action.

Personal and Organizational Strength

In the face of such overwhelming decisions, executives typically call meetings, start negotiations, and hire consultants and lawyers. Although these steps can be helpful, they can prove disappointing unless executives have taken the time, and the necessary steps, to carve out a powerful position for themselves in the debate. From a position of strength, leaders can bring forth their vision of what is right in a situation; from a position of weakness, leaders' actions are hollow and desperate. Also, before CEOs can step forth onto society's broad stage with a personal vision, they must make sure that their actions will not jeopardize the well-being of their companies, the jobs of employees, and the net income of shareholders. That means asking, *Have I done all I can to secure my position and the strength and stability of my organization?*

In 1988, Edouard Sakiz, CEO of Roussel Uclaf, a French pharmaceutical company, faced a defining moment of this magnitude. Sakiz had to decide whether to market the new drug RU-486, which later came to be known as the French abortion pill. Early tests had shown that the drug was 90% to 95% effective in inducing miscarriages during the first five weeks of a woman's pregnancy. As he considered whether to introduce the drug, Sakiz found himself embroiled in a major international controversy. Antiabortion groups were outraged that the drug was even under consideration. Pro-choice groups believed the drug represented a major step forward in the battle to secure a woman's right to an abortion. Shareholders of Roussel Uclaf's parent company, Hoechst, were for the most part opposed to RU-486's introduction because there had been serious threats of a major boycott against Hoechst if the drug were introduced. To the French government, also a part owner of Roussel Uclaf, RU-486 meant a step forward in its attempts to cut back on back-alley abortions.

There is little doubt that at one level, the decision Sakiz faced was a personal defining moment. He was a physician with a long-standing commitment to RU-486. Earlier in his career while working as a medical researcher, Sakiz had helped develop the chemical compound that the drug was based on. He believed strongly that the drug could help thousands of women, particularly those in poor countries, avoid injury or death from botched abortions. Because he doubted that the drug would make it to market if he were not running the company, Sakiz knew he would have to secure his own position.

At another level, Sakiz had a responsibility to protect the jobs and security of his employees. He understood this to mean taking whatever steps he could to avoid painful boycotts and the risk of violence against the company. His decision was complicated by the fact that some employees were passionately committed to RU-486, whereas others opposed the drug on ethical grounds or feared that the protests and boycotts would harm Roussel Uclaf and its other products.

How could Sakiz protect his own interests and those of his employees and still introduce the drug? Whatever path he chose, he could see that he would have to assume a low public profile. It would be foolish to play the courageous lion and charge forth pronouncing the moral necessity of RU-486. There were simply too many opponents for that approach to work. It could cost him his job and drag the company through a lengthy, painful process of dangerous turmoil.

The Role of the Organization in Society

What makes this third type of defining moment so difficult is that executives are asked to form, reveal, and test not only themselves and their work groups but also their entire company and its role in society. That requires forging a plan of action that functions at three levels: the individual, the work group, and society at large. In which areas do we want to lead? In which areas do we want to follow? How should we interact with the government? With shareholders? Leaders must ask themselves, *Have I thought creatively, boldly, and imaginatively about my organization's role in society and its relationship to its stakeholders?*

What role did Sakiz want Roussel Uclaf to play? He certainly did not want to take the easy way out. Sakiz could have pleased his boss in Germany and avoided years of controversy and boycotts by withdrawing entirely from the market for contraceptives and other reproductive drugs. (Nearly all U.S. drug companies have adopted that approach.) Sakiz could have defined Roussel Uclaf's social role in standard terms—as the property of its shareholders—and argued that RU-486 had to be shelved because boycotts against Roussel Uclaf and Hoechst were likely to cost far more than the drug would earn.

Instead, Sakiz wanted to define Roussel Uclaf's role in a daring way: women seeking nonsurgical abortions and their physicians would be among the company's core stakeholders, and the company would support this constituency through astute political activism. That approach resonated with Sakiz's own core values and with what he thought the majority of employees and other stakeholders wanted. It was clear to him that he needed to find a way to introduce the drug onto the market. The only question was how.

From Vision to Reality

To make their ethical visions a reality, top-level executives must assess their opponents and allies very carefully. What allies do I have inside and outside my company? Which parties will resist or fight my efforts? Have I underestimated their power and tactical skill or overestimated their ethical commitment? Whom will I alienate with my decision? Which parties will retaliate and how? These tactical concerns can be summed up in the question, *What combination of shrewdness, creativity, and tenacity will make my vision a reality?* Machiavelli put it more succinctly: "Should I play the lion or the fox?"

Although we may never know exactly what went through Sakiz's mind, we can infer from his actions that he had no interest in playing the lion. On October 21, 1988, a month after the French government approved RU-486, Sakiz and the executive committee of Roussel Uclaf made their decision. The *New York Times* described the events in this way: "At an October 21 meeting, Sakiz surprised members of the management committee by calling for a discussion of RU-486. There, in Roussel Uclaf's ultra-modern boardroom, the pill's long-standing opponents repeated their objections: RU-486 could spark a painful boycott, it was hurting employee morale, management was devoting too much of its time to this controversy. Finally, it would never be hugely profitable because much would be sold on a cost basis to the Third World. After two hours, Sakiz again stunned the committee by calling for a vote. When he raised his own hand in favor of suspending distribution of RU-486, it was clear that the pill was doomed."

The company informed its employees of the decision on October 25. The next day, Roussel Uclaf announced publicly that it was suspending distribution of the drug because of pressure from antiabortion groups. A Roussel Uclaf official explained the decision: "The pressure groups in the United States are very powerful, maybe even more so than in France."

The company's decision and Sakiz's role in it sparked astonishment and anger. The company and its leadership, critics charged, had doomed a promising public-health tool and had set an example of cowardice. Sakiz's colleague and friend, Etienne-Emile Baulieu, whose research had been crucial to developing RU-486, called the decision "morally scandalous" and accused Sakiz of caving in to pressure. Women's groups, family-planning advocates, and physicians in the United States and Europe came down hard on Sakiz's decision. Other critics suggested sarcastically that the company's decision was no surprise because Roussel Uclaf had decided not to produce contraceptive pills in the face of controversy during the 1960s.

Three days after Roussel Uclaf announced that it would suspend distribution, the French minister of health summoned the company's vice chairman to his office and said that if the company did not resume distribution, the government would transfer the patent to another company that would. After the meeting with the minister of health, Roussel Uclaf again stunned the public: it announced the reversal of its initial decision. The company would distribute RU-486 after all.

Sakiz had achieved his goals but in a foxlike manner. He had called out to his allies and rallied them to his side, but had done so in an indirect and shrewd way. He had used the predictable responses of the many stakeholders to orchestrate a series of events that helped achieve his ends, without looking like he was leading the way. In fact, it appeared as if he were giving in to outside pressure.

Sakiz had put into place the three principal components of the third type of defining moment. First, he had secured his own future at the company. The French health ministry, which supported Sakiz, might well have been aggravated if Hoechst had appointed another CEO in Sakiz's place; it could then have retaliated against the German company in a number of ways. In addition, by having the French government participate in the decision, Sakiz was able to deflect some of the controversy about introducing the drug away from the company, protecting employees and the bottom line. Finally, Sakiz had put Roussel Uclaf in a role of technological and social leadership within French, and even international, circles.

A Bow with Great Tension

As we have moved from Steve Lewis to Peter Adario to Edouard Sakiz, we have progressed through increasingly complex, but similar, challenges. These managers engaged in difficult acts of self-inquiry that led them to take calculated action based on their personal understanding of what was right in the given situation.

But the three met with varying degrees of success. Steve Lewis was able to balance his personal values and the realities of the business world. The result was ethically informed action that advanced his career. Peter Adario had a sound understanding of his personal values but failed to adapt them to the realities he faced in the competitive work environment at Sayer

Microworld. As a result, he failed to prevent McNeil's firing and put his own career in peril. Edouard Sakiz not only stayed closely connected to his personal values and those of his organization but also predicted what his opponents and allies outside the company would do. The result was the introduction of a drug that shook the world.

The nineteenth-century German philosopher Friedrich Nietzsche once wrote, "I believe it is precisely through the presence of opposites and the feelings they occasion that the great man—the bow with great tension—develops." Defining moments bring those "opposites" and "feelings" together into vivid focus. They force us to find a balance between our hearts in all their idealism and our jobs in all their messy reality. Defining moments then are not merely intellectual exercises; they are opportunities for inspired action and personal growth.

o   o   o

Joseph L. Badaracco Jr. is professor of business ethics at Harvard Business School and faculty chair of the Nomura School of Advanced Management in Tokyo.

Chapter Twenty

Reframing Ethics and Spirit

Lee G. Bolman
Terrence E. Deal

You can't energize people or earn their support unless the organization they are committing to has soul.
—Robert Haas, CEO, Levi Strauss

Soul? In a company that makes denim pants? Not long ago, Haas might have been laughed at for linking spirituality with business. Not anymore. Haas is among a growing number of business leaders who believe that a company with soul is more likely to do the right things and to become successful over the long term.

What does Haas mean when he talks about soul? Dictionaries define it in terms like "immaterial essence" or "essential nature." For organizations, groups, or families, soul is a bedrock sense of who we are, what we care about, and what we believe in.

Who cares? Why should a company, a school, or a public agency be concerned about soul? Many organizations and most management writers ignore the topic. For example, Treacy and Wiersema's strategy best-seller, *The Discipline of Market Leaders* (1995), mentions Southwest Airlines thirteen times, always in glowing terms, to make the case that Southwest attained its market leadership by being a "low total cost" provider. Hamel and Prahalad's influential book *Competing for the Future* (1994) mentions Southwest four times, crediting the carrier's success to its creative departure from the airline industry's hub-and-spoke strategy. Southwest's results were certainly impressive: in the decade from 1985 to 1995, it was the most profitable airline in the U.S. airline industry by a wide margin, and its chief executive, Herb Kelleher, was touted as America's best CEO by *Fortune* magazine in 1994 (Labich, 1994). Was strategy at the heart of the company's success?

Not in Kelleher's mind. He claimed that the airline industry was tactical, not strategic, because things change so fast. He offered a very different explanation for what makes Southwest work—one that talked about people, humor, love, and soul. Simply put, Kelleher "cherishes and respects" his eighteen thousand employees, and his "love" is returned in what he calls "a spontaneous, voluntary overflowing of emotion" (Farkas and De Backer, 1996, p. 87).

Kelleher's style is undoubtedly distinctive: "Kelleher has been known to sing 'Tea for Two' while wearing bloomers and a bonnet at a company picnic (featuring a chili cook-off) in front of 4,000 employees. He regularly helps flight attendants serve drinks and peanuts when he flies. One Easter, he walked a plane's aisle clad in an Easter bunny outfit, and one St. Patrick's Day he dressed as a leprechaun. When Southwest started a new route to Sacramento, Kelleher sang a rap song at a press conference with two people in Teenage Mutant Ninja costumes and two others dressed as tomatoes" (Levering and Moskowitz, 1993, p. 413).

Kelleher claimed that the most important group in the company was the Culture Committee, a seventy-person cross section of employees established to perpetuate the company's values and spirit. His charge to the committee: "It's very important that this be continued. And we want you to be a missionary and an ambassador. We want you to carry the spiritual message of Southwest Airlines" (Farkas and De Backer, 1996, p. 93).

Spiritual message? Love? From a CEO who is notorious for his preference for cigarettes and bourbon? Is there any reason to treat this as more than an outlying fluke? There are plenty of skeptics. A competing airline executive grumbled, "Southwest runs on Herb's bullshit" (Petzinger, 1995, p. 284). But there are many other successful leaders who embrace a philosophy much like Kelleher's. Ben Cohen, cofounder of the ice-cream company Ben and Jerry's Homemade, observes: "Businesses tend to exploit communities and their workers, and that wasn't the way I thought the game should be played. I thought it should be the opposite—that because the business is allowed to be there in the first place, the business ought to support the community. What we're finding is that when you support the community, the community supports you back. When you give love, you receive love. I maintain that there is a spiritual dimension to business just as there is to the lives of individuals" (Levering and Moskowitz, 1993, p. 47).

Herb Kelleher and Ben Cohen are colorful, to put it mildly. Organizational success may not require the CEO to dress as the

Easter bunny or as an Eastern mystic. (Cohen occasionally appeared at company celebrations in the person of Habeeni Ben Coheeni, whose stomach was the "mound of round" on which partner Jerry Greenfield broke cinder blocks with a sledgehammer.) An understated counterpoint to such hijinks is Aaron Feuerstein, president of the textile manufacturer Malden Mills. The day after a fire destroyed most of his plant in December 1995, Feuerstein announced that all three thousand of his workers would remain on the payroll for the following month. In January, he announced he would pay them for another month, and he extended the offer again in February. "The second time was a shock. It was the third time that brought tears to everyone's eyes" (Ryan, 1996, p. 4). By March, most of his employees were back on the job. Feuerstein's generosity went against the advice of members of his board and cost him several million dollars. But he felt a responsibility to both workers and community. He quoted Hillel, a first-century Talmudic scholar: "Not all who increase their wealth are wise." Said Feuerstein, "If you think the only function of a CEO is to increase the wealth of shareholders, then any time he spends on Scripture or Shakespeare or the arts is wasteful. But if you think the CEO must balance responsibilities, then he should be involved with ideas that connect him with the past, the present and the future" (Ryan, 1996, p. 5).

Despite unusually bad winter weather, Malden Mills was back in production faster than anyone expected. "Our people became very creative," said Feuerstein. "They were willing to work 25 hours a day."

Growing evidence suggests that tapping a deeper level of human energy pays off. Collins and Porras (1994) and De Geus (1995) both found that a central characteristic of corporations that achieved outstanding, long-term success was a core ideology emphasizing "more than profits" (Collins and Porras, 1994, p. 48) and providing "guidance and inspiration to people inside the company" (p. 88). "They need profits in the same way as any living being needs oxygen. It is a necessity to stay alive, but it is not the purpose of life" (De Geus, 1995, p. 29). Merck & Company, America's most successful pharmaceutical firm, states its core purpose as preserving and improving human life. Is this kind of statement more than words? Are such noble sentiments evident in key decisions and everyday behavior? Merck can point to a number of instances in which it sold a drug at a loss, or gave it away, to fulfill the core value of putting patients first. In one famous example, Merck had to decide whether to develop and distribute a drug for river blindness, an affliction of the poor in many Third World countries. Cost-benefit analysis was clear—the drug had little chance of making money. For companies with eyes fixed on the bottom line, such a decision would be a no-brainer. Merck developed the drug anyway and then gave it away free. A stunning outcome from Collins and Porras's research is that companies that emphasize values beyond the bottom line were more profitable in the long run than companies who stated their goals in purely financial terms.

Recent decades have regularly produced scandals in which major corporations were found to have engaged in unethical, if not illegal, conduct. The 1980s in particular were frequently characterized as a decade of remarkable greed, corruption, and dishonesty in business. A movement to do something about the apparently abysmal state of ethics in management has been building momentum. One strand of those efforts has spotlighted ethics as a curriculum topic in professional training programs. A second strand has emphasized corporate ethics statements. A third strand has pushed for stronger legal requirements, such as the Foreign Corrupt Practices Act, which forbids U.S. corporations from bribing foreign officials to get or retain business.

These are important initiatives, but they do not go deep enough. Solomon (1993) calls for an "Aristotelian ethic":

> *There is too little sense of business as itself enjoyable (the main virtue of the "game" metaphor), that business is not a matter of vulgar self-interest but of vital community interest, that the virtues on which one prides oneself in personal life are essentially the same as those essential to good business—honesty, dependability, courage, loyalty, integrity. Aristotle's central ethical concept, accordingly, is a unified, all-embracing notion of "happiness" (or, more accurately,* eudaimonia, *perhaps better translated as "flourishing" or "doing well"). The point is to view one's life as a whole and not separate the personal and the public or professional, or duty and pleasure [p. 105].*

Solomon chose the term *Aristotelian* in part "because it makes no pretensions of presenting something very new, the latest 'cutting-edge' theory or technique of management, but rather reminds us of something very old, a perspective and a debate going all the way back to ancient times. The idea is not to infuse corporate life with one more excuse for brutal changes, a new wave of experts and seminars and yet another downsizing bloodbath. It is to emphasize the importance of continuity and stability, clearness of vision and constancy of purpose, corporate loyalty and individual integrity" (p. 104).

Solomon reminds us that ethics and soul are central to both the good life and the good organization. The world's philosophical and spiritual traditions offer much wisdom to guide us in our search for better ways to live life and conduct business. To this point, we have primarily emphasized the frames as lenses for understanding and tools for influencing organizations. The heads and hands of leaders are vitally important. But so are their hearts and souls. In this chapter, we examine the implications of the frames for organizations as ethical communities and for the moral responsibilities of leadership. Table 20.1 summarizes our view.

The Factory: Excellence and Authorship

Our oldest image of organization is as factories engaged in a production process. Raw materials (steel or peanuts or five-year-olds) come in the front end, and finished products (refrigerators or peanut butter or educated citizens) leave at the back. The ethical imperative of the factory is excellence: to ensure that work is done as well and as efficiently as possible to produce outputs of the highest quality. Since the publication of Peters and Waterman's famous book *In Search of Excellence* (1982), almost everyone has claimed to be searching for excellence, though there are more than enough flawed products and mediocre services to make it clear that not everyone's quest has been successful.

One cause of disappointment is overlooking that organizational excellence requires much more than sermons from top management: it requires commitment and autonomy at all levels of the organization. How do leaders foster such commitment? Bolman and Deal (1995, p. 102) maintain that "leading is giving. Leadership is an ethic, a gift of oneself." Crucial for creating and maintaining excellence is the gift of authorship:

TABLE 20.1 **Reframing Ethics**

Metaphor	Organizational Ethic	Leadership Contribution
Factory	Excellence	Authorship
Extended family	Caring	Love
Jungle	Justice	Power
Temple	Faith	Significance

Giving authorship provides space within boundaries. In an orchestra, musicians each develop individual parts within the parameters of a particular musical score and the interpretative challenges posed by the conductor. Authorship turns the pyramid on its side. Leaders increase their influence and build more productive organizations. Workers experience the satisfactions of creativity, craftsmanship, and a job well done. Gone is the traditional adversarial relationship in which superiors try to increase their control while subordinates resist them at every turn. Trusting people to solve problems generates higher levels of motivation and better solutions. The leader's responsibility is to create conditions that promote authorship. Individuals need to see their work as meaningful and worthwhile, to feel personally accountable for the consequences of their efforts, and to get feedback that lets them know the results [p. 106].

Stung by a comment from a company officer—"Our quality stinks!"—Motorola embarked on one of the world's most ambitious and successful quality improvement efforts. The initiative added some $3.2 billion to Motorola's bottom line between 1987 and 1992 (Waterman, 1994, p. 229). Central to the effort was extensive training and empowerment of front-line workers. One of those workers was Hossain Rasoli, a technician, who worked on power transformers. Before the quality program, he wondered how the product was doing in the field but never knew. As part of the new initiative, he was given a level of responsibility he'd never had before: the charge to improve product quality. "I call it my baby," he says, pointing to the power amplifier. "I take pride in this product. If it fails in the field, I feel hurt, or I get depressed" (Waterman, 1994, p. 245). Rasoli used his training in problem solving and statistical-process control to determine the power amplifier's weakest components. He then went to the development engineers and asked them to redesign the parts. The result was a 400 percent improvement in reliability. One manager said of Rasoli, "He is now recognized as Mr. PA [power amplifier]. He knows more about this product than any designer, any vendor, any manager, anyone else" (p. 246).

Southwest Airlines offers another unique image of authorship—its associates are encouraged to be themselves, have fun, and, above all, use their sense of humor. Only on Southwest are you likely to hear required FAA safety briefings sung to the music of a popular song or delivered as a stand-up comedy routine ("Those of you who wish to smoke will please file out to our lounge on the wing, where you can enjoy our feature film, *Gone with the Wind*"). Too frivolous for something as weighty as safety announcements? Just the opposite—it's a way to get passengers to pay attention to announcements they usually ignore. And it is just as surely a way for flight attendants to have fun and feel authorship.

One of the Saturn Company's greatest accomplishments has been giving autoworkers the special feeling that comes from putting their personal signature, as well as a fender or windshield wiper, on a new car. Saturn employees frequently telephone customers to ask how they enjoy their car. If they see a Saturn stopped along a road, they volunteer assistance. Said one Saturn worker in a recent testimonial, "When given a chance, everyone would prefer to build a superior automobile. At Saturn, they give us that chance."

The Family: Caring and Love

Caring—one person's compassion and concern for another—is both the purpose and the ethical glue that hold a family together. Parents care for children and, eventually, children care for parents. A caring family, or community, requires servant-leaders who serve the best interests of the family and its stakeholders. This implies a profound and challenging responsibility for leaders to understand the needs and concerns of family members so as to serve the best interests of individuals and the family as a whole. The gift of servant-leaders is love.

> *Love is largely absent in the modern corporation. Most managers would never use the word in any context more profound than their feelings about food, films or games. They shy away from love's deeper meanings, fearing both its power and its risks. Caring begins with knowing—it requires listening, understanding and accepting. It progresses through a deepening sense of appreciation, respect and, ultimately, love. Love is a willingness to reach out and open one's heart. An open heart is vulnerable. Confronting vulnerability allows us to drop our masks, meet heart to heart and be present for one another. We experience a sense of unity and delight in those voluntary, human exchanges that mold "the soul of community" [Whitmyer, 1993, p. 81].*

They talk openly about love at Southwest Airlines: they fly out of Love Field in Dallas, their symbol on the New York Stock Exchange is LUV, the employee newsletter is called *Luv Lines*, and their twentieth anniversary slogan was "20 Years of Loving You" (Levering and Moskowitz, 1993). They hold an annual Heroes of the Heart ceremony to honor family members who have gone above and beyond even Southwest's high standards of duty. There are, of course, ups and downs in any family, and the airline industry certainly brings both good days and bad. Through life's peaks and valleys, love holds people together in a caring community. A Southwest employee said, "Herb loves us. We love Herb. We love one another. We love the company. One of the primary beneficiaries of our collective caring is our passengers."

For Levi Strauss, the issue of caring came to a head in trying to apply the company's ethical principles (honesty, fairness, respect for others, compassion, promise-keeping, and integrity) to the thorny dilemmas of working with foreign subcontractors. How should the company balance concerns for domestic employees and overseas workers? Even if pay and working conditions at foreign subcontractors are below those in the United States, are inferior jobs better than no jobs? A task force was set to work to collect data and formulate guidelines for ethical practice. Ultimately, the company wound up making some tough decisions. It pulled out of China because of human rights abuses, despite that nation's enormous long-term market potential. In a factory in Bangladesh employing underage children, Levi's made an arrangement for the children to go back to school while the contractor continued to pay their salaries (Waterman, 1994).

The Jungle: Justice and Power

Let us turn now to a third image of the organization: as a jungle. Woody Allen captured the competitive, predator-prey imagery succinctly with the observation that "the lion shall lie down with the lamb, but the lamb won't get much sleep." As the image implies, the jungle is a politically charged world of conflict and the underregulated pursuit of self-interest. Politics and politicians are routinely viewed as objects of scorn. Is there any ethical obligation associated with the political frame? We believe that there is: the duty of justice. In a world of competing interests and scarce resources, we are continually compelled to make trade-offs. We cannot give all parties everything they want, but we can honor a value of fairness in making such decisions. Solomon (1993) views justice as the ultimate virtue in corporations because fairness—the perception that employees, customers, and investors are all "getting their due"—is the glue that holds things together.

In a world of people and groups with very different interests and worldviews, justice is never easy to define, and disagreement about criteria is inevitable. The key gift that leaders can offer is power. People with a voice in key decisions are far more likely to feel a sense of justice than those with no seat at the table, whose interests are easily ignored.

Hoarding power produces a powerless organization. People stripped of power look for ways to fight back: sabotage, passive resistance, withdrawal, or angry militancy. Giving power liberates energy for more productive use. When people have a sense of efficacy and an ability to influence their world, they seek to be productive. They direct their energy and intelligence toward making a contribution rather than obstructing progress.

The gift of power enrolls people in working toward a common cause. It also creates difficult choice points. If leaders clutch power too tightly, they activate old patterns of antagonism. If they cave in and say yes to anything, they put the organizational mission at risk (Bolman and Deal, 1995).

Authorship and power are related—autonomy, space, and freedom are at issue in both. Yet there is an important difference. Artists, authors, and craftspeople can experience authorship even working alone. Power, by contrast, is meaningful only in relationship to others: it is the capacity to influence others and get things to happen on a broader scale. Authorship without power is isolating and splintering. Power without authorship can be dysfunctional and oppressive.

The gift of power is important at multiple levels—the individual, the group, and the organization. At the individual level, people want power to influence their immediate work environment and the factors that impinge on them. Many traditional workplaces still suffocate their employees with time clocks, rigid rules, and authoritarian bosses. Consider again Hossain Rasoli, Motorola's "Mr. Power Amplifier." Putting his own signature on the product gave him a sense of authorship. His ability to persuade others in the organization gave him power as well. In one case, Rasoli was so distressed that he went to a vice president to complain because the purchasing department planned to bring in a new vendor for a particular component. Rasoli was very firm: "You're not going to put this in my product." He won (Waterman, 1994, p. 246).

At Saturn, workers' power is symbolized by "the rope"—a rope with a handle, hanging at regular intervals along the assembly line. Anyone who sees the smallest deviation from Saturn's high standards is authorized to pull the rope and stop the line. One Saturn worker remembered with pride the day he pulled the rope: "It wasn't a major thing. Just a broken retainer clip. In the old [General Motors] world it had to be a life or death issue. At Saturn, they've given us the rope to do the job right, to build a car we can all be proud of."

At the group level, a challenge in organizations and societies around the world is responding to ethnic, racial, and gender diversity. Gallos and Ramsey (1996) get to the heart of the complexity: "Institutional, structural and systemic issues are very difficult for members of dominant groups to understand. Systems are most often designed by dominant group members to meet their own needs. It is then difficult to see the ways in which our institutions and structures systematically exclude others who are not 'like us.' It is hard to see and question what we have always taken for granted and painful to confront personal complicity in maintaining the status quo. Privilege enables us to remain unaware of institutional and social forces and their impact" (p. 215).

Thus justice requires that leaders systematically enhance the power of subdominant groups—ensuring access to decision making, creating internal advocacy groups, building diversity into organizational information and incentive systems, and strengthening career opportunities (Cox, 1994; Gallos and Ramsey, 1996; Morrison, 1992). All this will only happen if there is a rock-solid commitment from top management, the one condition that Morrison found to be universal in organizations that were leaders in responding to diversity.

Another version of the justice as power issue can be seen in Southwest Airlines's relationships with its unions. Labor unions' central purpose is to give employees power—a voice in decisions affecting them—but this process is regularly distorted by unproductive labor-management conflict. Herb Kelleher starts from the premise that the purpose of bargaining is to give the workers not as little as possible but rather as much as possible while still enabling the company to prosper over the long term. After all, he says, they help make it work; they should share in the profits.

THE TEMPLE: FAITH AND SIGNIFICANCE

A organization, like a temple, can be seen as a sacred place—an expression of human aspirations, a monument to faith in human possibility. A temple is a gathering place for a community of people with shared traditions, values, and beliefs. Members of a community may be diverse in many ways—age, background, economic status, and personal interests. But they are held together by shared faith and a spiritual commitment to one another. In a work organization, faith is strengthened when individuals feel that the organization is characterized by excellence, caring, and justice. But above all, they must feel that it is doing something worth doing—that the work is a calling that adds something of value to the world.

Significance is partly about work itself but even more about how the work is understood. That point is made by an old story about three stonemasons' accounts of their work. The first said he was "cutting stone." The second reported that he was "building a cathedral." And the third said simply that he was "serving God."

Temples need spiritual leaders. *Spiritual* here means not a specific religion or a particular theology but rather a genuine concern for the human spirit. Dictionary definitions of *spirit* include "the intelligent or immaterial part of man," "the animating or vital principle in living things," and "the moral nature of humanity." Spiritual leaders help people find meaning and faith in work and answers to fundamental questions that have confronted humans of every time and place: Who am I as an individual? Who are we as a people? What is the purpose in my life and in our collective life? What ethical principles should we follow? What legacy will we leave?

Spiritual leaders offer the gift of significance, rooted in confidence that the work is worthy of one's efforts, and the institution deserves one's commitment and loyalty. Work is exhilarating and joyful at its best, arduous, frustrating, and exhausting in less happy moments. Many adults embark on their careers with enthusiasm, confidence, and a desire to make a contribution. Some never lose that spark, or calling, but many do. They become frustrated with working conditions and discouraged by how hard it is to make a difference or even to know if they have. Tracy Kidder (1989) put it well in writing about teachers: "Good teachers put snags in the river of children passing by, and over time, they redirect hundreds of lives. There is an innocence that conspires to hold humanity together, and it is made up of people who can never fully know the good they have done" (p. 313). The gift of significance helps people sustain their faith rather than burn out and retire on the job.

Significance is built through the use of many expressive and symbolic forms: rituals, ceremonies, icons, music, and stories. Organizations without a rich symbolic life become empty and sterile. The magic of special occasions is vital in building significance into collective life. Moments of ecstasy are exclamation points that mark life's major passages. Without ritual and ceremony, transitions remain incomplete, a clutter of comings and goings. "Life becomes an endless set of Wednesdays" (Campbell, 1983).

When ritual and ceremony are authentic and attuned, they fire the imagination, evoke insight, and touch the heart. Ceremony weaves past, present, and future into life's ongoing tapestry. Ritual helps us face and comprehend life's everyday shocks, triumphs, and mysteries. Both help us experience the unseen webs of significance that tie a community together. When inauthentic, such occasions become meaningless, repetitious, and alienating. They waste our time, disconnect us from work, and splinter us from one another. "Community must become more than just gathering the troops, telling the stories, and remembering things past. Community must also be rooted in values that do not fail, values that go beyond the self-aggrandizement of human leaders" (Griffin, 1993, p. 178).

Stories give flesh to shared values and sacred beliefs. Everyday life in organizations brings many heartwarming moments and dramatic encounters. Turned into stories, these events fill an organization's treasure chest with lore and legend. Told and retold, they draw people together and connect them with the significance of their work.

Music captures and expresses life's deeper meaning. When people sing or dance together, they bond to one another and experience emotional connections that are otherwise hard to express. Harry Quadrocchi, chief executive officer of Quadgraphics, convenes employees once a year for an annual company gathering. A management chorus sings the year's themes. Quadrocchi himself voices the company philosophy in a solo serenade.

Max De Pree, famed as both a business leader and an author of elegant books on leadership, is clear about the role of faith in business: "Being faithful is more important than being successful. Corporations can and should have a redemptive purpose. We need to weigh the pragmatic in the clarifying light of the moral. We must understand that reaching our potential is more important than reaching our goals" (1989, p. 69). Spiritual leaders have the responsibility of sustaining and encouraging faith in themselves and in recalling others to the faith when they have lost it.

SUMMARY

Organizational ethics must ultimately be rooted in soul—an organization's understanding of its deeply held identity, beliefs, and values. Each frame offers a perspective on the ethical responsibilities of organizations and the roles of leaders. Every organization needs to evolve for itself a sense of its own ethical and spiritual core. The frames offer guidelines for that process.

Signs are everywhere that institutions in many developed nations are at a critical juncture because of a crisis of meaning and moral authority. Rapid change, high mobility, globalization, and racial and ethnic conflict tear at the fabric of community. The most important responsibility of managers is not to answer every question or always to make the right decision. They cannot escape their responsibilities to track budgets, motivate people, respond to political pressures, and attend to symbols. As leaders, they serve a deeper, more powerful, and more durable function when they are models and catalysts for such values as excellence, caring, justice, and faith.

o   o   o

Lee G. Bolman is the Marion Bloch/Missouri Chair in Leadership at the University of Missouri-Kansas City and a consultant.

Terrence E. Deal is a professor at the Rossier School, University of Southern California, and a consultant.

Forming the Vision

Forming the organization's vision is one of the most important responsibilities of a leader. Visions inspire and motivate people. They give employees a common purpose to work toward. But how do you form the vision? The chapters in Part Four guide you through the questions you should ask about your organization in order to discover what the vision should be and how to frame it.

Burt Nanus begins by illuminating what a vision is and what it is not. Peter F. Drucker guides you to think about how to create a short and sharply focused vision, one that will be most effective at rallying people together to work toward the common goal. Although this piece is directed to nonprofit organizations, the message is equally important for businesses.

Next we look at what it takes to be a visionary company and a revolutionary leader. James C. Collins and Jerry I. Porras explain that visionary companies have organizational vision that allows them to stay at the top for generations. A lack of creativity and curiosity has doomed many companies. To create a vision, the leader needs to learn how to see things differently. Gary Hamel teaches leaders how to become revolutionaries by rekindling the imagination.

Chapter Twenty-One

Where Tomorrow Begins: Finding the Right Vision

Burt Nanus

Do not worry about holding high position;
worry rather about playing your proper role.
—Confucius

Some years ago, when I was serving as director of the University of Southern California's Center for Futures Research, I was visited by a senior executive of a fast-growing food manufacturing company. He said he was concerned about the future of his company. "Are your sales or profits declining?" I asked. "On the contrary," he replied, "they've never been better." "Do you have a problem with marketing or product obsolescence?" I suggested. "No, our product position just seems to be getting stronger each year." "Well, then, are you worried about keeping your technological edge or finding good workers or meeting a challenge from foreign competition?" I wondered. "Not at all," he said, "we're the best in our industry."

"Look here," I finally said with some exasperation, "just what is it that's bothering you?" "Well," he explained, "that's just it. Everything is going so well that I'm getting uneasy. Maybe we've just been lucky until now. Maybe I'm missing something. Or maybe there's something just over the horizon that will clobber us. Besides, when things were tough, I was so busy managing crises that I never had time to think about the future. I used to believe that if everything's going well, leave it alone, or as the old adage says, 'If it ain't broke, don't fix it.' Now I know that's wrong. The best time to try something new, to take risks, to move off in a different direction is in good times, not bad. Isn't that what leadership is all about—fixing things that aren't broken?"

Of course, he was right on the mark. The cause of my visitor's concern soon became clear. As a leader, he sensed he might have to provide a new sense of direction for his organization. The old vision, the one originally provided by the founder of the company, had been spectacularly correct and had brought the firm to its current high level of success. But the world was changing, and my visitor wondered whether the original vision would still provide the right direction over the next decade. He was concerned, properly so, with the question "what's next, and why?" He was starting the search for a new vision.

His concern was anything but frivolous. Progress in organizations, like all human progress, is driven by the idealism and optimism captured in a persuasive and appealing vision of the future. In fact, Margaret Mead, the great anthropologist, found this to be a universal human trait, as true for primitive tribes, nomads, and subsistence farmers as for the most industrialized communities in the world. In her own eloquent words: "From comparative materials, it seems quite clear that the utopias men live by are of vital importance in such mundane matters as whether they will struggle to preserve the identity of their society, their class, their religion, or their vocation; whether they will plant trees which take two lifetimes to mature; whether they will take thought to stop the forests from being depleted, the good soil from being washed into the sea, or the gene pool from becoming exposed to too much radiation" (Mead, 1971, p. 44).

But not just any vision will do. Strong leaders want to find that special vision that will shift their organizations into overdrive, that will speed things up in the right direction while conserving energy and power. To be effective, to truly inspire and motivate excellence and achievement in organizations, leaders must find the right vision from among the many good and bad possibilities always available. The purpose of this chapter is to provide some guidance in making that choice.

PROPERTIES OF A GOOD VISION

If your childhood was like mine, you dreaded the inevitable question from well-meaning friends and relatives: "and what do you want to be when you grow up?" How in the world were we supposed to know? When I was small, I didn't even know what the possibilities were. Once I saw a firefighter on a big red truck and immediately that was what I wanted to be. The next week I'd want to be the cowboy I'd seen in a movie or a favorite teacher or a shortstop for the New York Yankees. As I grew older, the images proliferated. I thought about being a lawyer like my Uncle Leon, an astronaut, an architect, the governor of a state, a mathematician, or maybe president of a big company. The trouble was, I hadn't the slightest idea what people really did in those jobs, and I knew there were many other careers I hadn't even heard of.

Images are like that. They explode inside your head and can dazzle and overwhelm you with a collage of apparently limitless possibilities. But of course, most of us never seriously take any steps to become an astronaut or a professional athlete. Most of the images that appear in our brains are recognized as unrealistic, unattainable, uninformed, or undesirable. They soon lose their power to feed our fantasies or motivate our behaviors. They are not the right visions, the ones that we expect to make a difference in our lives.

So what are we looking for in a vision? To start with, we need to acknowledge that a vision is a mental model of a future state of a process, a group, or an organization. As such, it deals with a world that exists only in the imagination, a world built upon plausible speculations, fabricated from what we hope are reasonable assumptions about the future, and heavily influenced by our own judgments of what is possible and worthwhile. A vision portrays a fictitious world that cannot be observed or verified in advance and that, in fact, may never become reality. It is a world whose very existence requires an act of faith.

Does this seem too flimsy a fabric upon which to weave our tapestry of intentions? Would you, like many leaders, rather make decisions solely on the basis of history? Consider, then, that history itself is much like a vision—only facing backward. In its own way, history is also a mental model of questionable accuracy and frequent reformulation. After all, the events and people described by the historian no longer exist, and some, like King Arthur and Robin Hood, may never have existed. The mental construct we call history is nearly always based on secondary sources that are woefully fragmented and incomplete.

The historian examines a mass of incomplete raw material, selects from among the supposed "facts" those that fit a particular interpretation of events, adds a healthy dose of speculation about all the things that may have happened for which no evidence exists, and tries to weave together a story that purports to tell not just what happened but also why it happened and what resulted.

If you still want to think of history as "reality" you have only to think of any recent public event now fading into history—say, the Kennedy assassination, the Watergate break-in, or the Iran-Contra affair. Despite the minute scrutiny of thousands of distinguished scholars, journalists, and jurists and hundreds of thousands of pages of testimony and interpretation, there are still large domains of uncertainty about exactly what happened in these events, why they occurred, and what their long-range consequences may be. And these were sensational, widely covered, intensely scrutinized events! What about the many developments that are not even noticed today, much less recorded, that will become part of the "factual" record only in retrospect, perhaps a hundred years from now, when historians try to reconstruct what happened in the late twentieth century as we have tried to understand the fall of Rome?

So it is clear that history, like vision, is also a mental model. For all its pretensions to reality, history is heavily conjectural, full of judgments and values, and frequently reflects the historian's desire to influence today's policies. And, as we've just discussed, even our knowledge of the present is necessarily incomplete.

Thus, we may well wonder whether these mental constructs—"history" and "current events"—are really that much more substantial bases on which to act than a plausible vision of the future. From the perspective of leadership, they are not, for compared with history or current events, a vision is a mental construct that we have within our power to transform into reality. In fact, a vision is the only form of mental model that people and organizations can bring into being through their commitment and actions, and therein lies its usefulness and its power.

A second property of all visions is that they are idealistic, what Margaret Mead called utopian. A vision has no power to inspire or energize people and no ability to set a new standard or attract commitment unless it offers a view of the future that is clearly and demonstrably better for the organization, for the people in the organization, and/or for the society within which the organization operates. Often the vision is something entirely new—not a variation on existing activities, not a copy of what some other organization is doing—but something genuinely new, an innovative departure that clearly represents progress and is a step forward. The vision, in short, must be manifestly desirable, a bold and worthy challenge for those who accept it.

So any vision is a mental model of a desirable or idealistic future for the organization. But beyond that, what about the better visions, those that have the ability to renew or transform an organization? Consider Toyota's dream of producing a vehicle—later called the Lexus—engineered to go beyond the existing standards of high-performance luxury automobiles. Or consider Walt Disney's vision, as he described it, for a new kind of amusement park:

> *The idea of Disneyland is a simple one. It will be a place for people to find happiness and knowledge. It will be a place*

for parents and children to spend pleasant times in one another's company: a place for teachers and pupils to discover greater ways of understanding and education. Here the older generation can recapture the nostalgia of days gone by, and the younger generation can savor the challenge of the future. Here will be the wonders of Nature and Man for all to see and understand. Disneyland will be based upon and dedicated to the ideals, the dreams and hard facts that have created America. And it will be uniquely equipped to dramatize these dreams and facts and send them forth as a source of courage and inspiration to all the world.

Disneyland will be something of a fair, an exhibition, a playground, a community center, a museum of living acts, and a showplace of beauty and magic. It will be filled with the accomplishments, the joys and hopes of the world we live in. And it will remind us and show us how to make those wonders part of our own lives [Thomas, 1976, pp. 246–247].

Powerful and transforming visions like these tend to have special properties:

∘ They are appropriate for the organization and for the times. They fit in terms of the organization's history, culture, and values, are consistent with the organization's present situation, and provide a realistic and informed assessment of what is attainable in the future. This is not to suggest that the organization will not be changed by the vision. It almost certainly will be, perhaps quite radically. But if the vision is not appropriate for the organization, the time, cost, and pain of transformation may be so great as to make implementation of the vision all but impossible. In this case, a totally new organization might be a better choice, as IBM found when it decided to enter the personal computer business.

○ They set standards of excellence and reflect high ideals. They depict the organization as a responsible community with a sense of integrity that strengthens and uplifts everyone in it.

○ They clarify purpose and direction. They are persuasive and credible in defining what the organization wants to make happen and, therefore, what are legitimate aspirations for people in the organization. They provide agendas that create focus and hold out hope and promise of a better tomorrow.

○ They inspire enthusiasm and encourage commitment. They widen the leader's support base by reflecting the needs and aspirations of many stakeholders, transcending differences in race, age, gender, and other demographic characteristics, and drawing stakeholders into a community of concerns about the future of the organization.

○ They are well articulated and easily understood. They are unambiguous enough to serve as a guide to strategy and action and to be internalized by those whose efforts are needed to turn the vision into reality.

○ They reflect the uniqueness of the organization, its distinctive competence, what it stands for, and what it is able to achieve.

○ They are ambitious. They represent undisputed progress and expand the organization's horizons. Often, they call for sacrifice and emotional investment by followers, which are forthcoming because of the inherent attractiveness of the vision.

Visions that have these properties challenge and inspire people in the organization and help align their energies in a common direction. They prevent people being overwhelmed by immediate problems because they help distinguish what is truly important from what is merely interesting. In a sense, these visions program the mind to selectively pay attention to the things that really matter.

Such visions also play a key role in designing the future by serving as the front end of a strategy formulation process. When Toyota articulated its Lexus vision—that is, to produce a new line of cars that exceeded the then-existing standards of high-performance luxury automobiles—it still needed a strategy for attaining the vision. The vision provided the direction, but the strategy provided the framework for getting there. Among other things, the strategy undoubtedly included objectives relating to the intended technical quality and performance of the car, some marketing and production goals, a reformulation of supplier and distribution arrangements, and carefully drawn financial projections.

A good strategy may be indispensable in coordinating management decisions and preparing for contingencies, but a strategy has cohesion and legitimacy only in the context of a clearly articulated and widely shared vision of the future. A strategy is only as good as the vision that guides it, which is why purpose and intentions tend to be more powerful than plans in directing organizational behavior. As Yogi Berra is reported to have said, "If you don't know where you're going, you might end up someplace else."

What Vision Is Not

You might conclude from the preceding section that a vision is some sort of magic elixir that cures all organizational ills. This is unfortunately not the case. For every Lexus, there may be a score of Edsels. No matter how well formulated, a vision can fail if it is inappropriate or if it is poorly communicated or implemented. Sometimes visions fail because they were overly ambitious or unrealistic from the start. Sometimes they are overtaken by events and become obsolete before they can be realized.

For a balanced view of what vision can and cannot accomplish, we must be clear on what vision is not:

○ While a vision is about the future, it is not a prophecy (although after the fact it may seem so). If I say my vision is to become a great writer, I certainly am not predicting that I will become one, no matter how much my vision may shape my style of writing or my approach to a subject. Although there have been visions so powerful that those who first offered them seem in retrospect to be prophets—for example, Mahatma Gandhi's vision of an independent India or Henry Ford's vision of a car in every garage—these visions had power not because they were prophecies but because of the way they captured the imagination of others, mobilized resources, and reshaped the reality of their times.

○ A vision is not a mission. To state that an organization has a mission is to state its purpose, not its direction. For example, the mission of a farmer hasn't changed in thousands of years: it is to grow food and bring it to market at a price that pays for all the costs of production and provides an acceptable standard of living (or profit) for the farmer. However, one particular farmer might have a vision of passing on to his children a farm with twice the acreage he currently has, while another may dream about opening a canning operation on her property, and a third may aim to be a pioneer in growing organic vegetables.

○ A vision is not factual. It doesn't exist and may never be realized as originally imagined. It deals not with reality but with possible and desirable futures. It is full of speculation, assumptions, and value judgments. In organizations that depend heavily on the decision-making model of fact gathering, performance measurement, and verification, vision may seem to be an anachronism. But the absence of a factual basis for vision does not necessarily imply a lack of information or substance. Visions should be the well-informed results of systematic processes that ensure some degree of comprehensiveness and confidence.

○ A vision cannot be true or false. It can be evaluated only relative to other possible directions for the organization. That is, it can be seen as better or worse, more or less rational, safer or riskier, more or less appropriate, or even just good enough.

○ A vision is not—or at least should not be—static, enunciated once for all time. The unraveling of the Soviet Union is eloquent testimony to the dangers of staying with a vision—in this case, the Marxist-Leninist ideal—long after it has proven wrong and counterproductive. Rather, vision formulation should be seen as a dynamic process, an integral part of the ongoing task of visionary leadership. Part of the genius of the American system is an electoral process that forces the testing and redevelopment of a vision for the future of the nation every four years.

○ A vision is not a constraint on actions, except for those inconsistent with the vision. Instead, it is designed to unleash and then orient the energies of the organization in a common direction, to open up opportunities rather than to restrict them, and to serve as a catalyst for the changes needed to ensure the long-term success of the venture.

Thus far, we have been discussing what vision is, what it is not, and how to tell the difference between good and bad visions. But where does a vision come from? Is it simply a dream born mysteriously in the mind of a leader, a rare stroke of genius, or can it be the result of a considered and systematic process?

WHERE DOES VISION COME FROM?

My wife and I like to travel. Every so often, we'll come to a building or a town square that quite literally stops us in our tracks. It might be a cathedral, an unusual house, or maybe a particularly beautiful park or public monument. As we gaze at the arresting sight, I always wonder, "How in the world did the architect or artist think of that?" After all, where there is now what seems such a perfectly natural and obvious part of the landscape was at one time just an empty lot full of weeds.

Every remarkable artistic achievement starts as nothing more than a dream, usually of one individual, and not infrequently contested and ridiculed by friends and colleagues. Such a dream is a vision not much different from one a leader develops for an organization, for leadership itself is also an art form. Visionary leaders, like artists, are astute and perhaps idiosyncratic observers and interpreters of the real world. Leaders, like artists, try to rearrange the materials at their disposal—that is, the people, processes, and structures of an organization—to create a new and more powerful order that will succeed and endure over time. And the best visionary leaders, like the best artists, are always seeking to communicate directly and viscerally a vision of the world that will resonate with the deepest meanings of people and cause them to embrace it as worthwhile and elevating.

Denise Shekerjian, in an excellent study of forty winners of the Macarthur Award, concluded that the great ideas of these artists, scientists, and social movers and shakers were born of a combination of instinct and judgment. She says: "What intuition provides is an inkling, an itch, a yearning, a mist of possibilities. What judgment provides is structure, assessment, form, purpose. Blend them together—and in the example of Robert Coles [Pulitzer Prize–winning author and child psychiatrist], season this marriage with a strong dose of moral imagination—and you will begin to recognize the tiny, pert buds of opportunity that, if pursued, may well lead to a dramatic flowering of the most creative work of your career" (1990, p. 170).

So where does a leader's vision come from? Vision is composed of one part foresight, one part insight, plenty of imagination and judgment, and often, a healthy dose of chutzpah. It occurs to a well-informed open mind, a mind prepared by a lifetime of learning and experience, one sharply attuned to emerging trends and developments in the world outside of the organization. Creativity certainly plays an important part, but it is a creativity deeply rooted in the reality of the organization and its possibilities.

We mustn't pretend that vision is always the result of an orderly process. It often entails a messy, introspective process difficult to explain even by the person who conceives the vision. Vision formation is not a task for those who shun complexity or who are uncomfortable with ambiguity. Still, there are some basic elements that are part of all attempts to formulate vision, and they are what this book is about. Specifically, they are information, values, frameworks, and insight.

While vision is in a very real sense a dream, it is a special kind of dream built upon information and knowledge. The art of developing an effective vision starts with asking the right questions—and asking lots of them.

Values are the principles or standards that help people decide what is worthwhile or desirable. They are abstract ideas that embody notions of what truly matters, or should matter, in the performance of an organization and in the ways an organization satisfies its responsibilities to its constituencies—workers, customers, investors, and the rest of society.

Your values as a leader guide your selection of a vision in a variety of ways. Values influence the questions you ask about possible directions. They guide the choice of information you seek to answer the questions and how the information is evaluated. They determine which possible visions you consider, what criteria you use to select among them, and what measures of success you use to judge whether your organization is moving toward its vision.

Information and values are the raw materials within a structure or framework that allows you to see the big picture. One important part of that framework is your mental model of how your organization and its industry or peer group operates. Another part is a set of scenarios that captures your understanding of how the outside world may change in the future and what implications those changes may have for your organization.

It all comes together as a result of synthesis or insight. Sometimes a powerful intuition and drive in the hands of a strong leader are all that is needed. For example, the growth and shape of Southern California is often attributed to Harry Chandler and the Chandler family, who controlled the Los Angeles Times and were major landowners in the area. Chandler sensed what would work, decided what would be the best developmental path for Los Angeles and the region, and then simply made it happen. As Halberstam describes it: "They are Chandlers; their bustling prosperous region exists to an uncommon degree because they envisioned it that way. They did not so much foster the growth of Southern California as, more simply, invent it. . . . The city is horizontal instead of vertical because they were rich in land, and horizontal was good for them, good for real estate. There is a port because they dreamed of a port. . . .[Harry Chandler] was a dreamer, and he was always dreaming of the future of Los Angeles, of growth and profit; the commercial future of Los Angeles, tied as it was to the commercial future of Harry Chandler" (1979, p. 136).

Even here, however, one detects a considerable amount of calculation at work, the fruit of analysis and contemplation (if not blatant self-interest) rather than intuition or insight all alone. Intuition is a creative process still somewhat mysterious and poorly understood. However, intuition rarely stands alone and can be assisted by several structured methods.

Finally, the vision must be successfully implemented. As Warren Bennis and I said in an earlier work: "In the end, the leader may be the one who articulates the vision and gives it legitimacy, who expresses the vision in captivating rhetoric that fires the imagination and emotions of followers, who—through the vision—empowers others to make the decisions that get things done. But if the organization is to be successful, the image must grow out of the needs of the entire organization and must be 'claimed' or 'owned' by all the important actors" (1985, p. 109).

There are few things sadder for an organization than an exciting vision that is poorly implemented. Remington Rand, for example, entered the computer business more than forty years ago because it saw the revolutionary potential for such devices. For a short time, it virtually owned the world computer market, but it was a classic case of a great vision poorly implemented. Many years passed before Remington Rand's executives fully accepted the new machine and committed the company to the technical support, marketing, service, and other functions necessary to make computers truly useful for customers. And by the time they did, IBM, which saw the vision much later than Remington Rand but implemented it much better, had obtained an unassailable market advantage.

GETTING STARTED

Let's assume you are setting out to develop a new vision for your organization. Where do you start?

○ Learn everything you can about your organization, similar organizations, and your industry. There is no substitute for being well informed on the strengths and vulnerabilities of your own group and on the challenges and opportunities in its environment.

○ Bring your major constituencies (for example, customers, investors, the local community, the board of directors, unions, suppliers, and so on) into the visioning process, at first simply through informal conversations and later by soliciting formal suggestions. At a minimum, make sure you completely understand their expectations and needs and the dependence of your organization on their support.

○ Keep a playful open mind as you explore the options for a new vision. The correct sense of direction for your organization may be obvious, but don't bet on it! After all, everybody in the industry may be moving in a certain direction, but that doesn't mean it is right for your organization. Indeed, that in itself may be sufficient reason to set off down another path.

○ There is no need—and certainly no expectation—that your final choice of vision be your own original idea. Often some of the best ideas for new directions float up from the depths of the organization, but only if they are sought and welcomed when they arrive. Encourage inputs from all your colleagues and subordinates, involve them in the visioning process, and let them know how much you appreciate them all the way through.

○ If you are new to the organization, don't disparage the previous leadership or its vision. Everyone knows that you'll be doing some things differently, and they will expect some changes in direction. Instead, show that you understand and appreciate the existing vision, praise your predecessors for bringing the organization to its current stage, and promise to move on, retaining the best of the past but taking full benefit of expected opportunities in the future.

Ultimately, no matter how much help you receive, no matter if the vision was first developed by others and merely adopted and embraced by you, your success as a visionary leader will be measured by the effectiveness of your vision in moving the organization forward. That is what leaders are paid for and, more important, why they are respected and followed.

o   o   o

Burt Nanus is professor emeritus of management at the University of Southern California's Marshall School of Business and a leadership consultant.

Chapter Twenty-Two

What Is Our Mission?

Peter F. Drucker

Each social sector institution exists to make a distinctive difference in the lives of individuals and in society. Making this difference is the mission—the organization's purpose and very reason for being. Each of more than one million nonprofit organizations in the United States may have a very different mission, but changing lives is always the starting point and ending point. A mission cannot be impersonal; it has to have deep meaning, be something you believe in—something you know is right. A fundamental responsibility of leadership is to make sure that everybody knows the mission, understands it, lives it.

Many years ago, I sat down with the administrators of a major hospital to think through the mission of the emergency room. As do most hospital administrators, they began by saying, "Our mission is health care." And that's the wrong definition. The hospital does not take care of heath; the hospital takes care of illness. It took us a long time to come up with the very simple and (most people thought) too-obvious statement that the emergency room was there *to give assurance to the afflicted.* To do that well, you had to know what really went on. And, to the surprise of the physicians and nurses, the function of a good emergency room in their community was to tell eight out of ten people there was nothing wrong that a good night's sleep wouldn't fix. "You've been shaken up. Or the baby has the flu. All right, it's got convulsions, but there is nothing seriously wrong with the child." The doctors and nurses gave assurance.

We worked it out, but it sounded awfully obvious. Yet translating the mission into action meant that everybody who came in was seen by a qualified person in less than a minute. The first objective was to see everybody, almost immediately—because that is the only way to give assurance.

It Should Fit on a T-Shirt

The effective mission statement is short and sharply focused. It should fit on a T-shirt. The mission says *why* you do what you do, not the means by which you do it. The mission is broad, even eternal, yet directs you to do the right things now and into the future so that everyone in the organization can say, "What I am doing contributes to the goal." So it must be clear, and it must inspire. Every board member, volunteer, and staff person should be able to see the mission and say, "Yes. This is something I want to be remembered for."

To have an effective mission, you have to work out an exacting match of your opportunities, competence, and commitment. Every good mission statement reflects all three. You look first at the outside environment. The organization that starts from the inside and then tries to find places to put its resources is going to fritter itself away. Above all, it will focus on yesterday. Demographics change. Needs change. You must search out the accomplished facts—things that have already happened— that present challenges and opportunities for the organization. Leadership has no choice but to anticipate the future and attempt to mold it, bearing in mind that whoever is content to rise with the tide will also fall with it. It is not given to mortals to do any of these things well, but, lacking divine guidance, you must still assess where your opportunity lies.

Look at the state of the art, at changing conditions, at competition, the funding environment, at gaps to be filled. The hospital isn't going to sell shoes, and it's not going into education on a big scale. It's going to take care of the sick. But the specific aim may change. Things that are of primary importance now may become secondary or totally irrelevant very soon. With the limited resources you have—and I don't just mean people and money but also competence—where can you dig in and make a difference? Where can you set a new standard of performance? What really inspires your commitment?

WHY DOES THE ORGANIZATION EXIST?

Defining the nonprofit mission is difficult, painful, and risky. But it alone enables you to set goals and objectives and go to work. Unless the mission is explicitly expressed, clearly understood, and supported by every member of the organization, the enterprise is at the mercy of events. Decision makers throughout will decide and act on the basis of different, incompatible, and conflicting ideas. They will pull in opposing directions without even being aware of their divergence, and your performance is what suffers. Common vision, understanding, and unity of direction and effort of the entire organization depend on defining the mission and what the mission *should* be.

Make Principled Decisions

One cautionary note: *Never subordinate the mission in order to get money.* If there are opportunities that threaten the integrity of the organization, you must say no. Otherwise, you sell your soul. I sat in on a discussion at a museum that had been offered a donation of important art on conditions that no self-respecting museum could possibly accept. Yet a few board members said, "Let's take the donation. We can change the conditions down the road." "No, that's unconscionable!" others responded, and the board fought over the issue. They finally agreed they would lose too much by compromising basic principles to please a donor. The board forfeited some very nice pieces of sculpture, but core values had to come first.

Consider this wonderful sentence from a sermon of that great poet and religious philosopher of the seventeenth century, John Donne: "Never start with tomorrow to reach eternity. Eternity is not being reached by small steps." We start with the long range and then feed back and say, "What do we do *today?*" The ultimate test is not the beauty of the mission statement. The ultimate test is your performance.

o   o   o

Peter F. Drucker is professor of social science and management at Claremont Graduate University and has consulted with many of the world's leading corporations and nonprofit organizations.

Chapter Twenty-Three

Clock Building, Not Time Telling

James C. Collins
Jerry I. Porras

Imagine you met a remarkable person who could look at the sun or stars at any time of day or night and state the exact time and date: "It's April, 1401, 2:36 A.M., and 12 seconds." This person would be an amazing time teller, and we'd probably revere that person for the ability to tell time. But wouldn't that person be even more amazing if, instead of telling the time, he or she *built a clock* that could tell the time forever, even after he or she was dead and gone?[1]

Having a great idea or being a charismatic visionary leader is "time telling"; building a company that can prosper far beyond the presence of any single leader and through multiple product life cycles is "clock building." In the first pillar of our findings, we demonstrate how the builders of visionary companies tend to be clock builders, not time tellers. They concentrate primarily on building an organization—building a ticking clock—rather than on hitting a market just right with a visionary product idea and riding the growth curve of an attractive product life cycle. And instead of concentrating on acquiring the individual personality traits of visionary leadership, they take an architectural approach and concentrate on building the organizational traits of visionary companies. The primary output of their efforts is not the tangible implementation of a great idea, the expression of a charismatic personality, the gratification of their ego, or the accumulation of personal wealth. Their greatest creation is *the company itself* and what it stands for.

We came upon this finding when the evidence from our research punched holes in two widely held and deeply cherished myths that have dominated popular thinking and business school education for years: the myth of the great idea and the myth of the great and charismatic leader. In one of the most fascinating and important conclusions from our research, we found that creating and building a visionary company absolutely does not require *either* a great idea or a great and charismatic leader. In fact, we found evidence that great ideas brought forth by charismatic leaders might be *negatively correlated* with building a visionary company. These surprising findings forced us to look at corporate success from an entirely new angle and through a different lens than we had used before. They also have implications that are profoundly liberating for corporate managers and entrepreneurs alike.

THE MYTH OF THE "GREAT IDEA"

On August 23, 1937, two recently graduated engineers in their early twenties with no substantial business experience met to discuss the founding of a new company. However, they had no clear idea of what the company would make. They only knew that they wanted to start a company with each other in the broadly defined field of electronic engineering. They brainstormed a wide range of initial product and market possibilities, but they had no compelling "great idea" that served as the founding inspiration for the fledgling company [established in 1938].

Bill Hewlett and Dave Packard decided to first start a company and *then* figure out what they would make. They just started moving forward, trying anything that might get them out of the garage and pay the light bills. According to Bill Hewlett:

> *When I talk to business schools occasionally, the professor of management is devastated when I say that we didn't have any plans when we started—we were just opportunistic. We did anything that would bring in a nickel. We had a bowling foul-line indicator, a clock drive for a telescope, a thing to make a urinal flush automatically, and a shock machine to make people lose weight. Here we were, with about $500 in capital, trying whatever someone thought we might be able to do.*[2]

The bowling foul-line indicator didn't become a market revolution. The automatic urinal flushers and fat-reduction shock machines didn't go anywhere, either. In fact, the company stumbled along for nearly a year before it got its first big sale—eight audio oscilloscopes to Walt Disney for work on the movie *Fantasia*. Even then, Hewlett-Packard continued its unfocused ways, sputtering and tinkering with a variety of products, until it got a boost from war contracts in the early 1940s.

Texas Instruments, in contrast, traces its roots to a highly successful initial concept. TI began life in 1930 as Geophysical Service, Inc., "the first independent company to make reflection seismograph surveys of potential oil fields, and its Texas labs developed and produced instruments for such work."[3] TI's founders, unlike Hewlett and Packard, formed their company to exploit a *specific* technological and market opportunity.[4] TI started with a "great idea." HP did not.

Neither did Sony. When Masaru Ibuka founded his company in August of 1945, he had no specific product idea. In fact, Ibuka and his seven initial employees had a brainstorming session—*after* starting the company—to decide what products to make. According to Akio Morita, who joined the company shortly after its founding, "The small group sat in conference . . . and for weeks they tried to figure out what kind of business this new company could enter in order to make money to operate."[5] They considered a wide range of possibilities, from sweetened bean-paste soup to miniature golf equipment and slide rules.[6] Not only that, Sony's first product attempt (a simple rice cooker) failed to work properly and its first significant product (a tape recorder) failed in the marketplace. The company kept itself alive in the early days by stitching wires on cloth to make crude, but sellable, heating pads.[7] In comparison, Kenwood's founder, unlike Ibuka at Sony, appeared to have a specific category of products in mind. He christened his company with the name "Kasuga Wireless Electric Firm" in 1946 and "since its foundation," according to the *Japan Electronics Almanac*, "Kenwood has always been a specialist pioneer in audio technology."[8]

Like fellow legendaries Ibuka and Hewlett, Sam Walton also started without a great idea. He went into business with nothing other than the desire to work for himself and a little bit of knowledge (and a lot of passion) about retailing. He didn't wake up one day and say, "I have this great idea around which I'm going to start a company." No. Walton started in 1945 with a single Ben Franklin franchise five-and-dime store in the small town of Newport, Arkansas. "I had no vision of the scope of what I would start," Walton commented in a *New York Times* interview, "but I always had confidence that as long as we did our work well and were good to our customers, there would be no limit to us."[9] Walton built incrementally, step by step, from that single store until the "great idea" of rural discount popped out as a natural evolutionary step almost two decades after he started his company. He wrote in *Made in America:*

> *Somehow over the years folks have gotten the impression that Wal-Mart was something that I dreamed up out of the blue as a middle aged man, and that it was just this great idea that turned into an over-night success. But [our first Wal-Mart store] was totally an outgrowth of every-thing we'd been doing since [1945]—another case of me being unable to leave well enough alone, another experi-ment. And like most over-night successes, it was about twenty years in the making.[10]*

In a twist of corporate irony, Ames Stores (Wal-Mart's com-parison in our study), had a four-year head start over Sam Wal-ton's company in rural discount retailing. In fact, Milton and Irving Gilman founded Ames in 1958 specifically to pursue the "great idea" of rural discount retailing. They "believed that dis-count stores would succeed in small towns" and the company achieved $1 million in sales in its first year of operation.[11] (Sam Walton didn't open his first rural discount retail store until 1962; until then, he had simply operated a collection of small, main-street variety stores.)[12] Nor was Ames the only other company that had a head start over Walton. According to Walton biographer Vance Trimble, "Other retailers were out there [in 1962] trying to do just what he was doing. Only he did it better than nearly anyone."[13]

HP, Sony, and Wal-Mart put a large dent in the widely held mythology of corporate origins—a mythology that paints a picture of a far-seeing entrepreneur founding his or her company to capitalize on a visionary product idea or visionary market insight. This mythology holds that those who launch highly successful companies usually begin first and foremost with a brilliant idea (technology, product, market potential) and then ride the growth curve of an attractive product life cycle. Yet this mythology—as compelling and pervasive as it is—does not show up as a general pattern in the founding of the visionary companies.

Indeed, few of the visionary companies in our study can trace their roots to a great idea or a fabulous initial product. J. Willard Marriott had the desire to be in business for himself, but no clear idea of what business to be in. He finally decided to start his company with the only viable idea he could think of: take out a franchise license and open an A&W root beer stand in Washington, D.C.[14] Nordstrom started as a small, single-outlet shoe store in downtown Seattle (when John Nordstrom, just returned from the Alaska Gold Rush, didn't know what else to do with himself).[15] Merck started merely as an importer of chemicals from Germany.[16] Procter & Gamble started as a simple soap and candle maker—one of eighteen such companies in Cincinnati in 1837.[17] Motorola began as a struggling battery eliminator repair business for Sears radios.[18] Philip Morris began as a small tobacco retail shop on Bond Street in London.[19]

Furthermore, some of our visionary companies began life like Sony—with outright failures. 3M started as a failed corundum mine, leaving 3M investors holding stock that fell to the barroom exchange value of "two shares for one shot of cheap whiskey."[20] Not knowing what else to do, the company began making sandpaper. 3M had such a poor start in life that its second president did not draw a salary for the first eleven years of his tenure. In contrast, Norton Corporation, 3M's comparison in the study, began life with innovative products in a rapidly growing market, paid steady annual dividends in all but one of its first fifteen years of operations, and multiplied its capital fifteenfold during the same time.[21]

Bill Boeing's first airplane failed ("a handmade, clumsy seaplane copied from a Martin seaplane" which flunked its Navy trials), and his company faced such difficulty during its first few years of operations that it entered the furniture business to keep itself aloft![22] Douglas Aircraft, in contrast, had superb initial success with its first airplane. Designed to be the first plane in history to make a coast-to-coast nonstop trip and to lift more load than its own weight, Douglas turned the design into a torpedo bomber which he sold in quantity to the Navy.[23] Unlike Boeing, Douglas never needed to enter the furniture business to keep the company alive.[24]

Walt Disney's first cartoon series *Alice in Cartoon Land* (ever heard of it?) languished in the theaters. Disney biographer Richard Schickel wrote that it was "by and large a limp, dull and cliché ridden enterprise. All you could really say for it was that it was a fairly ordinary comic strip set in motion and enlivened by a photographic trick."[25] Columbia Pictures, unlike Disney, attained substantial success with its first theater release. The film, *More to Be Pitied Than Scorned* (1922), cost only $20,000 and realized income of $130,000, thus launching Columbia forward with a sizable cash cushion that funded the making of ten additional profitable movies in less than two years.[26]

WAITING FOR "THE GREAT IDEA" MIGHT BE A BAD IDEA

In all, *only three* of the visionary companies began life with the benefit of a specific, innovative, and highly successful initial product or service—a "great idea": Johnson & Johnson, General Electric, and Ford. And even in the GE and Ford cases, we found some slight dents in the great idea theory. At GE, Edison's great idea turned out to be inferior to Westinghouse's great idea. Edison pursued direct current (DC) system, whereas Westinghouse promoted the vastly superior alternating current (AC) system, which eventually prevailed in the U.S. market.[27] In Ford's case, contrary to popular mythology, Henry Ford didn't come up with the idea of the Model T and *then* decide to start a company around that idea. Just the opposite. Ford was able to take full advantage of the Model T concept because he already had a *company* in place as a launching pad. He founded the Ford Motor Company in 1903 to capitalize on his automotive engineering talent—his third company in as many years— and introduced five models (Models A, B, C, F, and K) before he launched the famous Model T in October of 1908.[28] In fact, Ford was one of 502 firms founded in the United States between 1900 and 1908 to make automobiles—hardly a novel concept at the time. In contrast to the visionary companies, we traced the founding roots of eleven comparison companies much closer to the great-idea model: Ames, Burroughs, Colgate, Kenwood, McDonnell Douglas, Norton, Pfizer, R.J. Reynolds, Texas Instruments, Westinghouse, and Zenith.

In other words, we found that the visionary companies were much less likely to begin life with a "great idea" than the comparison companies in our study. Furthermore, whatever the initial founding concept, we found that the visionary companies were less likely to have early entrepreneurial success than the comparison companies. In only three of eighteen pairs did the visionary company have greater initial success than the comparison company, whereas in ten cases, the comparison company had greater initial success than the visionary company. Five cases were indistinguishable. *In short, we found a negative correlation between early entrepreneurial success and becoming a highly visionary company.* The long race goes to the tortoise, not the hare.

If you are a prospective entrepreneur with the desire to start and build a visionary company but have not yet taken the plunge because you don't have a "great idea," we encourage you to lift from your shoulders the burden of the great-idea myth. Indeed, the evidence suggests that it might be better to *not* obsess on finding a great idea before launching a company. Why? Because the great-idea approach shifts your attention away from seeing the company as your ultimate creation.

The Company Itself Is the Ultimate Creation

In courses on strategic management and entrepreneurship, business schools teach the importance of starting first and foremost with a good idea and well-developed product/market strategy, and *then* jumping through the "window of opportunity" before it closes. But the people who built the visionary companies often didn't behave or think that way. In case after case, their actions flew in the face of the theories being taught at the business schools.

Thus, early in our project, we had to reject the great idea or brilliant strategy explanation of corporate success and consider a new idea. We had to put on a different lens and look at the world backward. We had to *shift from seeing the company as a vehicle for the products to seeing the products as a vehicle for the company*. We had to embrace the crucial difference between time telling and clock building.

To quickly grasp the difference between clock building and time telling, compare GE and Westinghouse in their early days. George Westinghouse was a brilliant product visionary and prolific inventor who founded fifty-nine other companies besides Westinghouse.[29] Additionally, he had the insight that the world should favor the superior AC electrical system over Edison's DC system, which it eventually did.[30] But compare George Westinghouse to Charles Coffin, GE's first president. Coffin invented not a single product. But he sponsored an innovation of great significance: the establishment of the General Electric Research Lab, billed as "America's first industrial research laboratory."[31] George Westinghouse told the time; Charles Coffin built a clock. Westinghouse's greatest creation was the AC power system; Coffin's greatest creation was the General Electric Company.

Luck favors the persistent. This simple truth is a fundamental cornerstone of successful company builders. The builders of visionary companies were highly persistent, living to the motto: Never, never, *never* give up. But what to persist *with*? Their answer: The company. *Be prepared to kill, revise, or evolve an idea* (GE moved away from its original DC system and embraced the AC system), *but never give up on the company*. If you equate the success of your company with success of a specific idea—as many businesspeople do—then you're more likely to give up on the company if that idea fails; and if that idea happens to succeed, you're more likely to have an emotional love affair with that idea and stick with it too long, when the company should be moving vigorously on to other things. But if you see the ultimate creation as the company, not the execution of a specific idea or capitalizing on a timely market opportunity, then you can persist beyond any specific idea—good or bad—and move toward becoming an enduring great institution.

For example, HP learned humility early in its life, due to a string of failed and only moderately successful products. Yet Bill Hewlett and Dave Packard kept tinkering, persisting, trying, and experimenting until they figured out how to build an innovative company that would express their core values and earn a sustained reputation for great products. Trained as engineers, they could have pursued their goal by *being* engineers. But they didn't. Instead, they quickly made the transition from designing products to designing an organization—creating an environment—conducive to the creation of great products. As early as the mid-1950s, Bill Hewlett displayed a lock-building perspective in an internal speech:

> *Our engineering staff [has] remained fairly stable. This was by design rather than by accident. Engineers are creative people, so before we hired an engineer we made sure he would be operating in a stable and secure climate. We also made sure that each of our engineers had a long range opportunity with the company and suitable projects on which to work. Another thing, we made certain that we had adequate supervision so that our engineers would be happy and would be productive to the maximum extent. . . . [The process of] engineering is one of our most important products [emphasis added]. . . . We are going to put on the best engineering program you have ever seen. If you think*

we have done well so far, just wait until two or three years from now when we get all of our new lab people producing and all of the supervisors rolling. You'll see some real progress then![32]

Dave Packard echoed the clock-building orientation in a 1964 speech: "The problem is, how do you develop an environment in which individuals can be creative? . . . I believe that you have to put a good deal of thought to your organizational structure in order to provide this environment."[33] In 1973, an interviewer asked Packard what specific *product* decisions he considered the most important in the company's growth. Packard's response didn't include one single product decision. He answered entirely in terms of organizational decisions: developing an engineering team, a pay-as-you-go policy to impose fiscal discipline, a profit-sharing program, personnel and management policies, the "HP Way" philosophy of management, and so on. In a fitting twist, the interviewer titled the article, "Hewlett Packard Chairman Built Company by Design, Calculator by Chance."[34]

Similarly, Masaru Ibuka's greatest "product" was not the Walkman or the Trinitron; it was Sony the company and what it stands for. Walt Disney's greatest creation was not *Fantasia*, or *Snow White*, or even Disneyland; it was the Walt Disney Company and its uncanny ability to make people happy. Sam Walton's greatest creation wasn't the Wal-Mart concept; it was the Wal-Mart Corporation—an organization that could implement retailing concepts on a large scale better than any company in the world. Paul Galvin's genius lay not in being an engineer or inventor (he was actually a self-educated but twice-failed businessman with no formal technology training),[35] but in his crafting and shaping of an innovative engineering organization that we've come to call the Motorola Company. William Procter and James Gamble's most significant contribution was not hog fat soap, lamp oils, or candles, for these would eventually become obsolete; their primary contribution was something that can never become obsolete: a highly adaptable organization with a "spiritual inheritance"[36] of deeply ingrained core values transferred to generation after generation of P&G people.

We ask you to consider this crucial shift in thinking—the shift to seeing the company itself as the ultimate creation. If you're involved in building and managing a company, this shift has significant implications for how you spend your time. It means spending less of your time thinking about specific product lines and market strategies, and spending more of your time thinking about organization design. It means spending less of your time thinking like George Westinghouse, and spending more of your time thinking like Charles Coffin, David Packard, and Paul Galvin. It means spending less of your time being a time teller, and spending more of your time being a clock builder.

We don't mean to imply that the visionary companies never had superb products or good ideas. They certainly did. And, as we'll discuss later in the book, most of them view their products and services as making useful and important contributions to customers' lives. Indeed, these companies don't exist just to "be a company"; they exist to do something useful. But we suggest that *the continual stream of great products and services from highly visionary companies stems from them being outstanding organizations, not the other way around*. Keep in mind that all products, services, and great ideas, no matter how visionary, eventually become obsolete. But a visionary company does not necessarily become obsolete, not if it has the organizational ability to continually change and evolve beyond existing product life cycles.

Similarly, all leaders, no matter how charismatic or visionary, eventually die. But a visionary company does not necessarily die, not if it has the organizational strength to transcend any individual leader and remain visionary and vibrant decade after decade and through multiple generations.

This brings us to a second great myth.

THE MYTH OF THE GREAT AND CHARISMATIC LEADER

When we ask executives and business students to speculate about the distinguishing variables—the root causes—in the success of the visionary companies, many mention "great leadership." They point to George W. Merck, Sam Walton, William Procter, James Gamble, William E. Boeing, R. W. Johnson, Paul Galvin, Bill Hewlett, Dave Packard, Charles Coffin, Walt Disney, J. Willard Marriott, Thomas J. Watson, and John Nordstrom. They argue that these chief executives displayed high levels of persistence, overcame significant obstacles, attracted dedicated people to the organization, influenced groups of people toward the achievement of goals, and played key roles in guiding their companies through crucial episodes in their history.

But—and this is the crucial point—so did their counterparts at the comparison companies! Charles Pfizer, the Gilman brothers (Ames), William Colgate, Donald Douglas, William Bristol, John Myers, Commander Eugene F. McDonald (Zenith), Pat Haggarty (TI), George Westinghouse, Harry Cohn, Howard Johnson, Frank Melville—these people *also* displayed high levels of persistence. They *also* overcame significant obstacles. They *also* attracted dedicated people to the organization. They *also* influenced groups of people toward the achievement of goals. They *also* played key roles in guiding their companies through crucial episodes in their history. A systematic analysis revealed that the comparison companies were just as likely to have solid "leadership" during the formative years as the visionary companies.

In short, we found no evidence to support the hypothesis that great leadership is the distinguishing variable during the critical, formative stages of the visionary companies. Thus, as our study progressed, we had to reject the great-leader theory; it simply did not adequately explain the *differences* between the visionary and comparison companies.

Charisma Not Required

Before we describe what we see as the crucial difference between the early shapers of visionary companies versus the comparison companies (for we do think there is a crucial difference), we'd like to share an interesting corollary: *A high-profile, charismatic style is absolutely not required to successfully shape a visionary company.* Indeed, we found that some of the most significant chief executives in the history of the visionary companies did not have the personality traits of the archetypal high-profile, charismatic visionary leader.

Consider William McKnight. Do you know who he is? Does he stand out in you mind as one of the great business leaders of the twentieth century? Can you describe his leadership style? Have you read his biography? If you're like most people, you know little or nothing about William McKnight.

As of 1993, he had not made it onto *Fortune* magazine's "National Business Hall of Fame."[37] Few articles have ever been written about him. His name doesn't appear in the *Hoover's Handbook* sketch of the company's history.[38] When we started our research, we're embarrassed to say, we didn't even recognize his name. Yet the company McKnight guided *for fifty-two years* (as general manager from 1914 to 1929, chief executive from 1929 to 1949, and chairman from 1949 to 1966) earned fame and admiration with businesspeople around the world; it carries the revered name Minnesota, Mining, and Manufacturing Company (or 3M for short). 3M is famous; McKnight is not. We suspect he would have wanted it exactly that way.

McKnight began work in 1907 as a simple assistant bookkeeper and rose to cost accountant and sales manager before becoming general manager. We could find no evidence that he had a highly charismatic leadership style. Of the nearly fifty references to McKnight in the company's self-published history, only one refers to his personality, and that described him as "a soft-spoken, gentle man."[39] His biographer described him as "a good listener," "humble," "modest," "slightly stooped," "unobtrusive and soft-spoken," "quiet, thoughtful, and serious."[40]

McKnight is not the only significant chief executive in the history of the visionary companies who breaks the archetypal model of the charismatic visionary leader. Masaru Ibuka of Sony had a reputation as being reserved, thoughtful, and introspective.[41] Bill Hewlett reminded us of a friendly, no-nonsense, matter-of-fact, down-to-earth farmer from Iowa. Messrs. Procter and Gamble were stiff, prim, proper, and reserved—even deadpan.[42] Bill Allen—the most significant CEO in Boeing's history—was a pragmatic lawyer, "rather benign in appearance with a rather shy and infrequent smile."[43] George W. Merck was "the embodiment of 'Merck restraint.' "[44]

We've worked with quite a few managers who have felt frustrated by all the books and articles on charismatic business leadership and who ask the sensible question, "What if high-profile charismatic leadership is just not my style?" Our response: Trying to develop such a style might be wasted energy. For one thing, psychological evidence indicates that personality traits get set relatively early in life through a combination of genetics and experience, and there is little evidence to suggest that by the time you're in a managerial role you can do much to change your basic personality style.[45] For another—and even more important—our research indicates that you don't need such a style anyway.

Please don't misunderstand our point here. We're not claiming that the architects of these visionary companies were poor leaders. We're simply pointing out that a high-profile, charismatic style is clearly not required for building a visionary company. (In fact, we speculate that a highly charismatic style might show a slight negative correlation with building a visionary company, but the data on style are too spotty and soft to make a firm statement.) We're also pointing out—and this is the essential point of this section—that *both* sets of companies have had strong enough leaders at normative stages that great leadership, be it charismatic or otherwise, cannot explain the superior trajectories of the visionary companies over the comparison companies.

We do not deny that the visionary companies have had superb individuals atop the organization at critical stages of their history. They often did. Furthermore, we think it unlikely that a company can remain highly visionary with a continuous string of mediocre people at the top. In fact, we found that the visionary companies did a better job than the comparison companies at developing and promoting highly competent managerial talent from inside the company, and they thereby attained greater *continuity* of excellence at the top through multiple generations. But, as with great products, perhaps *the continuity of superb individuals atop visionary companies stems from the companies' being outstanding organizations, not the other way around.*

Consider Jack Welch, the high-profile CEO at General Electric in the 1980s and early 1990s. We cannot deny that Welch played a huge role in revitalizing GE or that he brought immense energy, drive, and a magnetic personality with him to the CEO's office. But obsessing on Welch's leadership style diverts us from a central point: Welch grew up in GE; he was a product of GE as much as the other way around. Somehow GE *the organization* had the ability to attract, retain, develop, groom, and select Welch the leader. GE prospered long before Welch and will probably prosper long after Welch. After all, Welch was not the first excellent CEO in GE's history, and he probably will not be the last. Welch's role was not insignificant, but it was only a small slice of the entire historical story of the General Electric Company. The selection of Welch stemmed from a good corporate architecture—an architecture that traces its roots to people like Charles Coffin, who, in contrast to George Westinghouse, took an architectural approach to building the company.

AN ARCHITECTURAL APPROACH: CLOCK BUILDERS AT WORK

As in the case of Charles Coffin versus George Westinghouse, we did see in our study differences between the two groups of early shapers, but the differences were more subtle than "great leader" versus "not great leader." The key difference, we believe, is one of orientation—the evidence suggests to us that the key people at formative stages of the visionary companies had a stronger organizational orientation than in the comparison companies, regardless of their personal leadership style. As the study progressed, in fact, we became increasingly uncomfortable with the term "leader" and began to embrace the term "architect" or "clock builder." The following contrasts further illustrate what we mean by an architectural, or clock-building, approach.

Citicorp Versus Chase

James Stillman, Citicorp's president from 1891 to 1909 and chairman to 1918, concentrated on organizational development in pursuit of his goal to build a great national bank.[46] He transformed the bank from a narrow parochial firm into "a fully modern corporation."[47] He oversaw the bank as it opened new offices, instituted a decentralized multidivisional structure, constructed a powerful board of directors composed of leading CEOs, and established management training and recruiting programs (instituted three decades earlier than at Chase).[48] *Citibank, 1812–1970* describes how Stillman sought to architect an institution that would thrive far beyond his own lifetime:

> *Stillman intended National City [precursor to Citicorp] to retain its position [as the largest and strongest bank in the United States] even after his death, and to ensure this he filled the new building with people who shared his own vision and entrepreneurial spirit, people who would build an organization. He would step aside himself and let them run the bank.*[49]

Stillman wrote in a letter to his mother about his decision to step aside, to the role of chairman, so that the company could more easily grow beyond him:

> *I have been preparing for the past two years to assume an advisory position at the Bank and to decline re-election as its official head. I know this is wise and it not only relieves me of the responsibility of details, but gives my associates an opportunity to make names for themselves [and lays] the foundation for limitless possibilities, greater even for the future than what has been accomplished in the past.*[50]

Albert Wiggin, Stillman's counterpart at Chase (president from 1911 to 1929), did not delegate at all. Decisive, humorless, and ambitious, Wiggin's primary concern appeared to be with his own aggrandizement. He sat on the boards of fifty other companies and ran Chase with such a strong, centralized controlling hand that *Business Week* wrote, "The Chase Bank is Wiggin and Wiggin is the Chase Bank."[51]

Wal-Mart Versus Ames

No doubt Sam Walton had the personality characteristics of a flamboyant, charismatic leader. We cannot help but think of his shimmy-shaking down Wall Street in a grass skirt and flower leis backed by a band of hula dancers (to fulfill a promise to employees for breaking 8 percent profit), or his leaping up on store counters and leading hundreds of screaming employees through a rousing rendition of the Wal-Mart Cheer. Yes, Walton had a unique and powerful personality. *But so did thousands of other people who didn't build a Wal-Mart.*

Indeed, the key difference between Sam Walton and the leaders at Ames is not that he was a more charismatic leader, but that he was much more of a clock builder—an architect. By his early twenties, Walton had pretty much settled upon his personality style; he spent the bulk of his life in a never-ending quest to build and develop the capabilities of the Wal-Mart organization, not in a quest to develop his leadership personality.[52] This was true even in Walton's own eyes, as he wrote in *Made in America*:

> *What nobody realized, including a few of my own managers at the time, was that we were really trying from the beginning to become the very best operators—the most professional managers—that we could. There's no question that I have the personality of a promoter. . . . But underneath that personality, I have always had the soul of an operator, somebody who wants to make things work well, then better, then the best they possibly can. . . . I was never in anything for the short haul; I always wanted to build as fine a retailing organization as I could.*[53]

For example, Walton valued change, experimentation, and constant improvement. But he didn't just preach these values, he instituted concrete *organizational* mechanisms to stimulate change and improvement. Using a concept called "A Store Within a Store," Walton gave department managers the authority and freedom to run each department as if it were their own business.[54] He created cash awards and public recognition for associates who contribute cost saving and/or service enhancements ideas that could be reproduced at other stores. He created "VPI (Volume Producing Item) Contests" to encourage associates to attempt creative experiments.[55] He instituted merchandise meetings, to discuss experiments that should be selected for use throughout the entire chain, and Saturday morning meetings, which often featured an individual employee who tried something novel that worked really well.

Profit sharing and employee stock ownership produced a direct incentive for employees to come up with new ideas, so that the whole company might benefit. Tips and ideas generated by associates got published in the Wal-Mart internal magazine.[56] Wal-Mart even invested in a satellite communications system "to spread all the little details around the company as soon as possible."[57] In 1985, stock analyst A. G. Edwards described the ticking Wal-Mart clock:

> *Personnel operate in an environment where change is encouraged. For example, if a . . . store associate makes suggestions regarding [merchandising or cost savings ideas], these ideas are quickly disseminated. Multiply each suggestion by over 750 stores and by over 80,000 employees (who can potentially make suggestions) and this leads to substantial sales gains, cost reductions and improved productivity.[58]*

Whereas Walton concentrated on creating an organization that would evolve and change on its own, Ames leaders dictated all changes from above and detailed in a book the precise steps a store manager should take, leaving no room for initiative.[59] Whereas Walton groomed a capable successor to take over the company after his death (David Glass), the Gilmans had no such person in place, thus leaving the company to outsiders who did not share their philosophy.[60] Whereas Walton passed along his clock-building orientation to his successor, postfounder CEOs at Ames recklessly pursued disastrous acquisitions in a blind, obsessive pursuit of raw growth for growth's sake, gulping down 388 Zayre stores in one bite. In describing Wal-Mart's key ingredient for future success, David Glass said "Wal-Mart associates will find a way" and "Our people are relentless."[61] Ames CEO of the same era said, "The real answer and the only issue is market share."[62]

In a sad note, a 1990 *Forbes* article on Ames noted, "Co-founder Herbert Gilman has seen his creation destroyed."[63] On a happier note, Sam Walton died with his creation intact and the belief that it could prosper long beyond him, stronger than ever. He knew that he would probably not live to the year 2000, yet shortly before he died in 1992, he set audacious goals for the company out to the year 2000, displaying a deep confidence in what the company could achieve independent of his presence.[64]

Motorola Versus Zenith

Motorola's founder, Paul Galvin, dreamed first and foremost about building a great and lasting company.[65] Galvin, architect of one of the most successful technology companies in history, did not have an engineering background, but he hired excellent engineers. He encouraged dissent, discussion, and disagreement, and gave individuals "the latitude to show what they could do largely on their own."[66] He set challenges and gave people immense responsibility so as to stimulate the organization and its people to grow and learn, often by failures and mistakes.[67] Galvin's biographer summarized, "He was not an inventor, but a builder whose blueprints were people."[68] According to his son, Robert W. Galvin, "My father urged us to reach out . . . to people—to all the people—for their leadership contribution, yes their creative leadership contribution. . . . Early on, [he] was obsessed with management succession. *Ironically, he did not fear his own demise. His concern was for the company* [emphasis added]."[69]

In contrast, Zenith's founder, Commander Eugene F. McDonald, Jr., had no succession plan, thus leaving a void

of talent at the top after his unexpected death in 1958.[70]
McDonald was a tremendously charismatic leader who moved
the company forward primarily through the sheer force of his
gigantic personality. Described as "the volatile, opinionated
mastermind of Zenith," McDonald had "colossal self-assur-
ance . . . based on a very high opinion of his own judgment."[71]
He expected all except his closest friends to address him as
"Commander." A brilliant tinkerer and experimenter who
pushed many of his own inventions and ideas, he had a rigid
attitude that almost caused Zenith to miss out on television.[72]
A history of Zenith states:

> *McDonald's flamboyant style was echoed in the company's
> dramatic advertising methods and this style, coupled with
> innovative genius and an ability to sense changes in public
> tastes, meant that for more than three decades, in the pub-
> lic perception McDonald was Zenith.*[73]

Two and a half years after McDonald's death, *Fortune* magazine commented: "[Zenith] is still growing and reaping profits from the drive and imagination of its late founder.
McDonald's powerful personality remains a palpable influence
in the company. But Zenith's future now depends on its ability
and new drive to meet conditions McDonald never anticipated."[74] A competitor commented, "As time goes on, Zenith
will miss McDonald more and more."[75]

Galvin and McDonald died within eighteen months of each
other.[76] Motorola sailed successfully into new arenas never
dreamed of by Galvin; Zenith languished and, as of 1993, it
never regained the energy and innovative spark that it had during McDonald's lifetime.

Walt Disney Versus Columbia Pictures

Quick, stop and think: Disney. What comes to mind? Can you create a clear image or set of images that you associate with Disney? Now do the same thing for Columbia Pictures. What comes to mind? Can you put your finger on distinct and clear images? If you're like most people, you can conjure up images of what Disney means, but you probably had trouble with Columbia Pictures.

In the case of Walt Disney, it is clear that Walt brought immense personal imagination and talent to building Disney. He personally originated many of Disney's best creations, including *Snow White* (the world's first-ever full-length animated film), the character of Mickey Mouse, the Mickey Mouse Club, Disneyland, and EPCOT Center. By any measure, he was a superb time teller. But, even so, in comparison to Harry Cohn—Disney's counterpart at Columbia Pictures—Walt was much more of a clock builder.

Cohn "cultivated his image as a tyrant, keeping a riding whip near his desk and occasionally cracking it for emphasis, and Columbia had the greatest creative turnover of any major studio due largely to Cohn's methods."[77] An observer of his funeral in 1958 commented that the thirteen hundred attendees "had not come to bid farewell, but to make sure he was actually dead."[78] We could find no evidence of any concern for employees by Cohn. Nor could we find any evidence that he took steps to develop the long-term capabilities or distinct self-identity of Columbia Pictures as an institution.

The evidence suggests that Cohn cared first and foremost about becoming a movie mogul and wielding immense personal power in Hollywood (he became the first person in Hollywood to assume the titles of president *and* producer) and cared little or not at all about the qualities and identity of the Columbia Pictures Company that might endure beyond his lifetime.[79] Cohn's personal purpose propelled Columbia Pictures forward for years, but such personal and egocentric ideology could not possibly guide and inspire a company after the founder's death. Upon Cohn's death, the company fell into listless disarray, had to be rescued in 1973, and was eventually sold to Coca-Cola.

Walt Elias Disney, on the other hand, spent the day before he died in a hospital bed thinking out loud about how to best develop Disney World in Florida.[80] Walt would die, but Disney's ability to make people happy, to bring joy to children, to create laughter and tears would not die. Throughout his life, Walt Disney paid greater attention to developing his company and its capabilities than did Cohn at Columbia. In the late 1920s, he paid his creative staff more than he paid himself.[81] In the early 1930s, he established art classes for all animators, installed a small zoo on location to provide live creatures to help improve their ability to draw animals, invented new animation team processes (such as storyboards), and continually invested in the most advanced animation technologies.[82] In the late 1930s, he installed the first generous bonus system in the cartoon industry to attract and reward good talent.[83] In the 1950s, he instituted employee "You Create Happiness" training programs and, in the 1960s, he established Disney University to orient, train, and indoctrinate Disney employees.[84] Harry Cohn took none of these steps.

Granted, Walt did not clock build as well as some of the other architects in our study, and the Disney film studio languished for nearly fifteen years after his death as Disneyites ran around asking themselves, "What would Walt do?"[85] But the fact remains that Walt, unlike Cohn, created an institution much bigger than himself, an institution that could still deliver the "Disney Magic" to kids at Disneyland decades after his death. During the same time period that Columbia ceased to exist as an independent entity, the Walt Disney Company mounted an epic (and ultimately successful) fight to prevent a hostile takeover. To the Disney executives and family, who could have made a tidy multimillion-dollar profit on their stock had the raiders been successful, Disney had to be preserved as an independent entity *because it was Disney*. In the preface to his book *Storming the Magic Kingdom*, a superb account of the Disney takeover attempt, John Taylor wrote:

> *To accept [the takeover offer] was unthinkable. Walt Disney Productions was not just another corporate entity . . . that needed to be rationalized by liquidation of its assets to achieve maximum value for its shareholders. Nor was Disney just another brand name. . . . The company's executives saw Disney as a force shaping the imaginative life of children around the world. It was woven into the very fabric of American culture. Indeed, its mission—and it did, they believed, have a mission as important as making money for its stockholders—was to celebrate American values.*[86]

Disney went on in the 1980s and 1990s to rekindle the heritage installed by Walt decades earlier. In contrast, Cohn's company had little to save or rekindle. No one felt Columbia had to be preserved as an independent entity; if the shareholders could get more money by selling out, then so be it.

The Message for CEOs,
Managers, and Entrepreneurs

One of the most important steps you can take in building a visionary company is not an action, but a shift in perspective. We're doing nothing less than asking you to make a shift in thinking as fundamental as those that preceded the Newtonian revolution, the Darwinian revolution, and the founding of the United States.

Prior to the Newtonian revolution, people explained the world around them primarily in terms of a God that made specific decisions. A child would fall and break his arm, and it was an act of God. Crops failed; it was an act of God. People thought of an omnipotent God who made each and every specific event happen. Then in the 1600s people said, "No, that's not it! What God did was to put in place a universe with certain principles, and what we need to do is figure out how those principles work. God doesn't make all the decisions. He set in place processes and principles that would carry on."[87] From that point on, people began to look for basic underlying dynamics and principles of the entire system. That's what the Newtonian revolution was all about.

Similarly, the Darwinian revolution gave us a dramatic shift in thinking about biological species and natural history—a shift in thinking that provides fruitful analogies to what we've seen in the visionary companies. Prior to the Darwinian revolution, people primarily presumed that God created each and every species intact and for a specific role in the natural world: Polar bears are white because God created them that way; cats purr because God created them that way; robins have red breasts because God created them that way. We humans have a great need to explain the world around us by presuming that someone or something must have had it all figured out—something must have said, "We need robins with red breasts to fit here in the ecosystem." But if the biologists are right, it doesn't work that way. Instead of jumping directly to robins with red breasts (time telling), we have instead an *underlying process* of evolution (the genetic code, DNA, genetic variation and mutation, natural selection) which eventually produces robins with red breasts that appear to fit perfectly in the ecosystem.[88] The beauty and functionality of the natural world springs from the success of its underlying processes and intricate mechanisms in a marvelous "ticking clock."

Likewise, we're asking you to see the success of visionary companies—at least in part—as coming from underlying processes and fundamental dynamics embedded in the organization and not primarily the result of a single great idea or some great, all-knowing, godlike visionary who made great decisions, had great charisma, and led with great authority. If you're involved in building and managing a company, we're asking you to think less in terms of being a brilliant product visionary or seeking the personality characteristics of charismatic leadership, and to think more in terms of being an *organizational* visionary and building the characteristics of a visionary company.

Indeed, we're asking you to consider a shift in thinking analogous to the shift required to found the United States in the 1700s. Prior to the dramatic revolutions in political thought of the seventeenth and eighteenth centuries, the prosperity of a European kingdom or country depended in large part on the quality of the king (or, in the case of England, perhaps the queen). If you had a good king, then you had a good kingdom. If the king was a great and wise leader, then the kingdom might prosper as a result.

Now compare the good-king frame of reference with the approach taken at the founding of the United States. The critical question at the Constitutional Convention in 1787 was not "Who should be president? Who should lead us? Who is the wisest among us? Who would be the best king?" No, the founders of the country concentrated on such questions as "What *processes* can we create that will give us good presidents long after we're dead and gone? What type of enduring country do we want to build? On what principles? How should it operate? What guidelines and mechanisms should we construct that will give us the kind of country we envision?"

Thomas Jefferson, James Madison, and John Adams were not charismatic visionary leaders in the "it all depends on me" mode.[89] No, they were organizational visionaries. They created a constitution to which they and all future leaders would be subservient. They focused on building a country. They rejected the good-king model. They took an architectural approach. They were clock builders!

But notice: In the case of the United States, it's not a cold, mechanistic Newtonian or Darwinian clock. It's a clock based on human ideals and values. It's a clock built on human needs and aspirations. It's a clock with a *spirit*.

The important thing to keep in mind is that once you make the shift from time telling to clock building, most of what's required to build a visionary company *can be learned*. You don't have to sit around waiting until you're lucky enough to have a great idea. You don't have to accept the false view that until your company has a charismatic visionary leader, it cannot become a visionary company. There is no mysterious quality or elusive magic. Indeed, once you learn the essentials, you—and all those around you—can just get down to the hard work of making your company a visionary company.

o   o   o

James C. Collins is a management consultant. Previously he was on the faculty at the Stanford University Graduate School of Business.

Jerry I. Porras is a consultant and professor emeritus of organizational behavior and change at the Stanford University Graduate School of Business.

Chapter Twenty-Four

Be Your Own Seer

Gary Hamel

Look around you. Look at the individuals and companies that have been champions of business concept innovation. Do this, and you will see that rule-busting, wealth-creating innovation doesn't come out of corporate planning. It doesn't usually come from some corporate "incubator" division. It doesn't come out of product development. And it doesn't often come from blue-sky R&D. More and more, innovation comes not from the triumph of big science (important as it is in removing *physical* constraints to innovation), but from the triumph of contrarianism (which leaps over the *mental* constraints). It is the idiot savant, who asks a fresh question and then answers it using parts that already exist, who is so often the author of the new. That's because industry revolution is *conceptual* innovation. It comes from the mind and soul of a malcontent, a dreamer, a smart-ass, and not from some bespectacled boffin or besuited planner.

FORGET THE FUTURE

From Nostradamus to Alvin Toffler, individuals and organizations have long been obsessed with trying to see the future. The goal is to somehow get advance warning of "what will be." Yet in my experience, industry revolutionaries spend little time gazing deeply into the future. While there are some aspects of the future that are highly probable—the cost of bandwidth will go down, our ability to manipulate genes will go up—most of what will constitute the future simply can't be known.

Forecasting attempts to predict what *will* happen. This is largely futile. As Samuel Goldwyn once said, "Only a fool would make predictions—especially about the future." Recognizing this, companies have sought ways of coping with the future's inherent unpredictability. One response is to rehearse a range of futures via scenarios. Scenario planning speculates on what *might* happen. The goal is to develop a number of alternate scenarios as a way of sensitizing oneself to the possibility that the future may be quite unlike the present. By focusing in on a few big uncertainties—what might happen to the price of oil, how the Green movement might develop, what could happen to global security—scenario planning lets a company rehearse a range of possible futures.

Scenario planning has many strengths, but it is not, by nature, proactive. Its implicit focus is on how the future may undermine the *existing* business model. In that sense it tends to be defensive—what might that big, bad future do to us—rather than offensive—how can we write our will on the future. There is little in scenario planning that suggests a firm can proactively shape its environment, that it can take advantage of changing circumstances *right now*. At least in practice, it is more often threat-focused than opportunity-focused. It is more about stewardship than entrepreneurship. Companies must do more than rehearse potential futures. After all, the goal is not to speculate on what *might* happen, but to imagine what you can *make* happen.

Another response to the future's inherent unpredictability is to become more "agile." Strategic flexibility is certainly a virtue in uncertain times. The ability to quickly reconfigure products, channels, and skills is essential to maintaining one's relevance in a world that is shaken, not stirred. But agility is no substitute for a vision of a radically new business model. Agility is great, but if a company is no more than agile, it will be a perpetual follower—and in the age of revolution even fast followers find few spoils.

Companies fail to create the future not because they fail to predict it but because they fail to *imagine* it. It is curiosity and creativity they lack, not perspicuity. So it is vitally important that you understand the distinction between "the future" and "the unimagined," between *knowing* what's next and *imagining* what's next.

SEE DIFFERENT, BE DIFFERENT

You can't be a revolutionary without a revolutionary point of view. And you can't buy your point of view from some boring consulting company. Nor can you borrow it from some rent-a-guru. You have to become your own seer, your own guru, and your own futurist.

Seeing over the horizon, finding the unconventional, imagining the unimagined—innovation comes from a new way of seeing and a new way of being. Learn to see different, learn to be different, and you will discover the different. Not only that, you will *believe* it, deeply. And maybe, just maybe, you will *build* it. How to see. How to be. Two more critical steps in your training as an industry revolutionary.

Listen to Bill Gross, founder of idealab!, a factory for new Internet businesses that spawned CarsDirect.com, NetZero, and GoTo.com, among others.

> *It's almost better to look for where there's no market segment. Then companies that have that inertia, that have a cannibalization problem, stay off you for a while and give you a chance to get big enough to build a brand and get a network effect going. Then they'll have a hard time catching up.*

Gross is not interested in bumping some other sumo wrestler out of the ring. He's interested in inventing games entirely outside the ring. This is the essence of industry revolution. Without a widespread capacity to imagine and design radical new business concepts, a company will be unable to escape decaying strategies. You know that tired old saw, "You have to be willing to cannibalize your own business"? Well, how likely is it that a company will cannibalize an existing business unless it has some incredibly compelling alternatives in view? I don't think the problem is that companies are unwilling to cannibalize themselves. I think the problem is that they don't have enough good *reasons* to cannibalize themselves. When was the last time you hung on to a good option when you had a much better option in view? It's simple. You have to have some fairly attractive birds in the bush to loosen your grip on the bird in the fist. But it's not always easy to spot the birds in the bush. That's why you must learn to see different and be different.

Alan Kay, who fathered the personal computer while at Xerox's Palo Alto Research Center and is now an "imagineer" at Disney, is a font of zippy aphorisms. One of my favorites: "Perspective is worth 80 IQ points." Alan knows that a fresh way of seeing is often more valuable than sheer brainpower. Impressionism. Cubism. Surrealism. Postmodernism. Each revolution in art was based on a reconception of reality. It wasn't the canvas, the pigments, or the brushes that changed, but how the artist perceived the world. In the same sense, it's not the tools that distinguish industry revolutionaries from humdrum incumbents—not the information technology they harness, not the processes they use, not their facilities. Instead, it is their ability to escape the stranglehold of the familiar.

The essence of strategy is variety. But there is no variety in strategy without variety in how individuals view the world. Do you see differently? Do you have a point of view that is at odds with industry norms? The point is simple: you're going to have to learn how to unlock your own imagination before you can unlock your company's imagination. You must become the merchant of new perspective within your organization.

So what are ways we can school ourselves in the art of seeing past the familiar to the truly novel? The rest of this chapter describes a variety of disciplines that will help you imagine what *could* be. They fall into two broad categories: be a novelty addict, and be a heretic.

BE A NOVELTY ADDICT

A whole lot of what's changing simply can't be seen from where you're sitting. You have an obstructed view. You have to get off your butt and search for new experiences, go to new places, learn new things, reach out to new people. In the age of revolution, the most dangerous words are "need to know." How the hell do you know what you need to know? You MUST find a way of continually surprising yourself. What you don't know but *could* know is much more important than what you don't know and *can't* know. You MUST become a novelty addict.

Find the Discontinuities

Would-be revolutionaries, intent on discovering uncontested competitive space, think about the future very differently than prognosticators and scenario planners. They know you can't see the future. Their goal is less to understand the future than to understand the revolutionary portent in what is *already* changing. More specifically, they are looking for things where the *rate of change* is changing—for inflection points that foreshadow significant discontinuities. Those who fail to notice these nascent discontinuities will be rudely awakened by those who were paying attention.

They are also looking for things that are changing at *different rates*. Sooner or later, the thing that is changing more quickly will impact the thing that is changing more slowly—in other words, rates of change between different phenomena ultimately converge. For years the cosmetics industry assumed that women were interested only in glamour, that their sense of self-worth was directed proportional to the sparkle in a man's eye. As Charlie Revson, the founder of Revlon, once put it, "We sell hope in a bottle." As women gained their economic independence, the image of women as "eye candy" lagged further and further behind the reality of their changing self-perception. This lag was exploited by The Body Shop with its message that glamour is fine, but sometimes you just want to pamper yourself a bit and take good care of your skin. *Change differentials* often point to revolutionary opportunities.

Here's a visual illustration. Imagine that you attach one end of a piece of elastic to a hardback book. You begin pulling the other end. Slowly the elastic stretches. The book doesn't move. But when you reach the limit of the elastic, the book starts moving with a jerk. The "slack" disappears when some revolutionary says, "Wait a minute. Why is this thing just sitting there when everything around it is moving?" For years the car selling paradigm in the United States has been stuck in neutral. While "category killers" consolidated distribution in other industries, car retailing remained a patchwork of mostly local dealerships. While you could get 24/7 technology support for your home computer, you could get your car serviced only between the hours of 8 A.M. and 5 P.M., and only Monday through Friday. While you could comparison shop a dozen different TV brands at Circuit City, no equivalent auto superstore carried the full range of leading brands. But recently a slew of outsiders, mostly Internet start-ups, has been working overtime to "snap" car retailing into the twenty-first century.

It's not enough to know what's changing. You also have to be aware of things that are changing at different rates, for it is the juxtaposition of the two that points to opportunities for industry revolution. Discontinuities and change differentials—that is where you look for inspiration.

Try to find the pattern in these three revolutions in sports equipment:

- A couple of decades back Prince pioneered oversized tennis rackets, and it is still the number-one brand in the industry.

The frying-pan size rackets have a giant sweet spot that helps to propel off-center shots across the net.

o Calloway invented the "Big Bertha" line of golf clubs, and Eli Calloway has become the patron saint of hackers everywhere. With an enlarged hitting area and perimeter weighting, the clubs dramatically increased the odds that high-handicap golfers could get the ball airborne and flying straight.

o Elan was the first to introduce super-sidecut, or "parabolic," skis, an innovation that has given the ski equipment industry a much-needed boost. With a broad tip and tail and narrow waist, the new skis help even the most nonathletic skiers lay down curvaceous tracks.

What discontinuities were these three innovations exploiting? Beyond materials technology, they were exploiting the fact that baby boomers are the first generation in history that refuse to grow old. They may not have the eye-hand coordination they used to have, but they still love the sound of a tennis ball hitting the sweet spot. They don't have quite the rotation they used, but they still want to hit the living daylights out of a golf ball. Their knees are a bit dodgy, but they still want to make turns like Hermann Maier. Come to think of it, Viagra's been exploiting the same discontinuity: seniors who refuse to grow old gracefully and want great sex right up to the end.

Here are some essential questions for every wannabe revolutionary:

o Where and in what ways is change creating the potential for new rules and new space?

o What is the potential for revolution inherent in the things that are changing *right now,* or have *already* changed?

○ What are the discontinuities we could exploit?

○ What aspect of what's changing can we come to under-stand better than anyone else in our industry?

○ What's the deep dynamic that will make our new business concept oh-so-relevant right now?

If you don't have an answer to these questions, there is virtu-ally no chance you or your company is going to be an industry revolutionary.

In 1984 John Naisbitt wrote in his book *Megatrends* that information would become a critical source of competitive advantage and that the "information float" would disappear as a way to make money. He argued that customers would demand a combination of "high tech" and "high touch." Instead of forc-ing technology on consumers, companies would learn how to use technology to improve service. He described a world in which hierarchies would give way to networks, and companies would become more virtual. He also hypothesized a shift from reliance on institutional help to more self-reliance in everything from health care to pensions. He foresaw a world in which con-sumers would use their wallets to enforce their values. Data mining, call centers, 24/7 customer support, outsourcing, sup-ply chain integration, "green" energy, companies against ani-mal testing—all these things are logical outgrowths of the forces Naisbitt described in 1984. How effective was your com-pany in harnessing these discontinuities to create new business models and new sources of competitive advantage? If your com-pany got caught behind the curve, it wasn't because these trends were invisible; it's because they were ignored.

If you're paying attention to discontinuities, there's little that will surprise you. It's pretty simple. Individuals who get startled by the future weren't paying attention. One person's inevitability is another person's rude awakening. The question is, ARE YOU PAYING ATTENTION?

A novelty addict is always on the hunt for what's changing. Every discontinuity prompts a "where does this lead" question. Let's practice. We'll start with a particularly noisome discontinuity. A recent study suggested that the average middle manager gets 190 messages a day: 52 phone messages, 30 e-mail messages, 22 voice mails, 18 letters, 15 faxes, and so on. I don't have to tell you, this is a discontinuity. In the old days, when someone sent you a letter, they didn't expect to receive a response for at least a week. When they sent a fax, they expected a next-day response. Now, when they send an e-mail, they expect a reply within an hour or so. But it gets worse. With instant messaging, people *know* when you're online, and when they send you a message, they expect you to interrupt what you're doing and answer them *immediately*. It used to be that secretaries kept the world at bay—until downsizing turned middle managers into receptionists and filing clerks. It may be that we've taken accessibility to the point where meaningful work will simply grind to a halt. How ironic that in a world populated by "knowledge workers," there is virtually no time left to think. You may be able to manage the present in tiny splinters of time, but you certainly can't invent radical new business models if your attention has been smashed into minute-sized shards. This is a discontinuity. Can you see an opportunity in this? Let's take it a step further.

In a recent cartoon, a dad and his young daughter are walking along a beach. The dad is dressed in suit and tie and has a briefcase in one hand. His daughter is wearing her bathing suit. As she vainly tugs at her father's sleeve, he says, "Not now, dear,

Daddy's working." Where *don't* you work these days? We are tethered to our jobs to an extent that is almost feudal. But there are opportunities lurking inside the insidious discontinuity of 24/7 accessibility. What about an electronic gatekeeper that could scan phone calls, e-mails, voice mails, and even faxes? Caller ID? Hah! I want automatic message screening. Every couple of hours a little menu would pop up on my computer screen telling me who was queuing for my attention. I could tell my digital gatekeeper who I was willing to communicate with in a given day or week and how important it was that I make contact with any given individual. I could also tell it when I was willing to be interrupted and when I was not. (Imagine never, ever having a telemarketer interrupt dinner again!) I could assign a different level of "interruptability" to different times of the day or week. People and issues that exceeded some urgency threshold would get to break through into my consciousness. People below the threshold wouldn't get through. I could also give a few people (family) an "attention override" privilege that would let them intrude anytime. Trust me, some revolutionary is going to help us regain control of our fragmented lives. There's a billion-dollar opportunity inside this discontinuity. You get the point? Keep asking yourself, What's changing? What's the opportunity this presents? Do this at least a dozen times a week. Get addicted to change.

Search Out Underappreciated Trends

There is no proprietary data about the future. Whatever *you* can know about what's changing in the world, so can everyone else. So you've got to look where others are not looking. The good news is that most people in an industry are blind in the same way—they're all paying attention to the same things, and *not* paying attention to the same things. For example, if you work at Shell or Schlumberger, you know a lot about the three-dimensional representation of complex information. Complicated computer models portray seismographic data in a rich graphical format. This is how petroleum engineers "see" underground. Likewise, the folks at Pixar the computer animation company, are experts at visualization. Now talk to a senior partner in a big accounting company. How much does this person know about complex graphical modeling? Not enough. If you want to understand the financial performance of a large global company, you have to comb through columns of black and white data, searching for variances and calculating financial ratios. Ugh! Why isn't this information presented in three dimensions, dynamically? Why can't you "fly" over the globe, and "drop into" your German subsidiary? See that red mountain over there? That's inventory, and it's growing. See that lake over there? That's one of those famous "profit pools," and it's shrinking by the hour. See all those people massed at the border? Those are your employees leaving for better opportunities. You get the idea. But you can't get the picture—yet. Odds are it won't be an accounting company that reinvents the display of accounting data—unless the senior partners start hanging around Silicon Graphics or Pixar. But there's little doubt that Excel will one day look as antiquated as green ledger paper.

Next time you go to an industry conference or pick up a trade magazine, ask yourself, What is *no one* talking about? Search for what's not there. There's a reason that outsiders typically reinvent industries. The outsiders come from a different context—one that allows them to see new possibilities. William Gibson puts it beautifully: "The future has already happened, it's just unequally distributed." The future may not have happened yet in your industry, or your company, or your country, but it has happened somewhere. Revolutionaries are experts at *knowledge arbitrage*—moving insights between the hip and the un-hip, the knowing and the unknowing, the leading edge and the trailing edge. So get a bigger keyhole!

Find the Big Story

Next, search for transcendent themes. One of the reasons many people fail to fully appreciate what's changing is because they're down at ground level, lost in a thicket of confusing, conflicting data. You have to make time to step back and ask yourself, What's the big story that cuts across all these little facts? For example, consider five seemingly unrelated trends:

- In most developed countries, people are getting married later in life. No longer do people expect to find a mate while still at school.
- More people are telecommuting or working from home. Home-based businesses are one of the fastest-growing parts of the economy.
- The number of single-parent families has been steadily increasing. Single parents are run ragged trying to balance work and family—personal time is a rare luxury.
- New social standards governing the behavior of people at work make it ever more difficult to form romantic relationships with co-workers.
- E-mail and the Internet absorb more and more of people's time. All the hours in front of the PC are hours of aloneness—unless virtual communities fill all your social needs.

Can you see an overarching theme here? It's individual isolation. We're living in a world where it is more and more difficult for people to find time to connect. No wonder online dating sites like Matchmaker.com and eCRUSH are booming. But did *you* see it coming?

Recognizing patterns in complex data is a bit of an art. Some of it is just raw, conceptual ability. But if you've ever won a game of Scrabble or solved a challenging puzzle, you'll do fine. Keep a list of things that strike you as new or different. Every once in a while, scan that list and search for broad themes. If you can get above the trees, you'll have a view that few others can match.

Follow the Chain of Consequences

The world is a system. Something changes here, and it will affect something over there. Yet most people stop with first-order effects—they don't have the discipline to think through the knock-on effects. Jim Taylor, coauthor of *The 500-Year Delta*, Iomega's executive vice president, and dedicated trend-watcher, predicted a 10,000 Dow Jones Industrial Average in 1992. Here's how he did it:

> *I saw a number that estimated how much people were going to save as they got older. About 15 million people a year would become 50 years old, and they would throw a lot of liquidity into the market. So I made a prediction that the Dow would pass through 10,000. When you see a trend, it's a matter of asking, "What would this mean?"*

Paul Saffo, director and Roy Amara Fellow at the Institute for the Future, makes the point this way:

I think about it as "orders of impact." First order, second order, etc. When an earthquake happens you have a whole series of waves that follow. The first order of the auto was the horseless carriage. The second order was the traffic jam. The third-order impact was the move toward the suburbs. This led in turn to the creation of huge metropolitan areas.

No executive or manager should be surprised by the recent spate of books on corporate values and "loyalty." This concern around how to build organizational cohesion is the second-order effect of a first-order change: the steadily declining ratio of supervisors to operators or managers to staff in corporations. To cope, companies need a solid value system because more and more they must rely on people's judgment. Whenever you see something changing, begin to work through the chain of consequences. Get in the practice of asking a series of "and then what" questions. As you learn to do this, the future will become less and less of a surprise to you.

Dig Deeper

Sometimes creating proprietary foresight is just a matter of slogging through more data. You can't create economic value out of a superficial understanding of what's changing. For example, a short news item noting that some teenagers are spending more time online than in front of the TV is of almost no value. The real question is, Which kids are going online? Where are they going online? What, exactly, is it about the online experience that is more compelling to them than television? How much time do they spend online in a given day or week? What do they find cool or geeky online? And so on.

Know What's Not Changing

The deep needs of human beings change almost not at all. Go back to Aristotle and the wants of man—little has changed. What changes is how we address our wants. Change gives us better tools. Opportunities come when we can imagine how to use our new tools to address our deepest desires. As Jim Taylor puts it, "The nature of human beings is the eye in the middle of the hurricane." We want to be loved, we want to be known, we want to communicate, we want to celebrate, we want to explore, we want to laugh, we want to know, we want to see new vistas, we want to leave some footprints in the sands of history. Any discontinuity that allows you to slake one of these thirsts more fully is an opportunity in the making.

If you think about human beings for a minute, you shouldn't be surprised that the Web was a chat room before it was a department store, or that Internet porn generates substantially more than 70 percent of all the revenue earned by online content providers (dwarfing games, sports, and music).[1] To be an industry revolutionary, you must be as perfectly attuned to the timeless as to the ever-changing. You must also let yourself be informed by the recurring themes of history. History has much to teach you about how discontinuities will play themselves out. For example, advances in genetics are slowly turning humans into creators. History suggests that the battle between the spiritual and the scientific over the proper use of genetic knowledge may be as heated as Galileo's clash with the Catholic church over humankind's place in the cosmos and Darwin's run-in with creationists.

The speed of the Internet's takeoff surprised most people, but that it happened should have been no surprise—because the interstate highway system provided an almost perfect historical analogy. The automobile had existed for around 50 years before the interstate highway system began to connect communities across America. Within a decade of the interstate's introduction suburbs were springing up, city centers were withering, corporations were building office towers in what had been cornfields, and commuters were commuting. It wasn't the car per se, but the ability to connect communities that changed the distribution of work and commerce. Likewise, computers had existed for about 50 years before the Internet took off. Before the Net, computers had been islands of computational power. Once connected, they began to transform society in ways even more dramatic than the interstate highway but also in ways that are entirely consistent with timeless aspects of human nature.

See It, Feel It

You don't fall in love with a photograph or a resume, you fall in love with the experience of *being* with someone. In a similar way, you can't understand a discontinuity merely by reading about it, you can understand it only by living it. To be fully grounded in what is changing, you must move from the analytical to the experiential. Let me share a couple of examples. A few years back I was working with a large Nordic firm, perched on the edge of the Arctic Circle. This company was filled with brilliant engineers who designed technologically brilliant products that were boring to look at and sometimes difficult to use. I broke the bad news—if they wanted their products to be highly desirable and highly relevant, they were going to have to learn something about global lifestyles. Off the engineers trooped—to Venice Beach in California, to Greenwich Village in New York, and down The Kings Road in London. They saw trendy style-setters wearing the latest fashion accessories. They came across people who had pierced every possible protuberance. They saw how designers in other fields were using colors and shapes in new ways. And they didn't see any of their competitors. How do you explain lifestyles with an overhead projector? Face to face with the edge, the engineers "got it." They went back and designed products in crazy hues with edgy designs and easy-to-use customer features.

People don't embrace an opportunity because they see it, they embrace it because they *feel* it. And to feel it, they have to experience it. If you want to teach someone in your organization about a discontinuity or give them a glimpse of a bold, new opportunity, you're going to have to design an experience.

To create a demo, or a prototype, or even tell a compelling story, you have to do some mental prototyping. You need more than a fragment of an idea. You have to build a story around it: why this is important, what difference it will make, who will care, how people will use this, what it will look like, taste like, and more. Radical alternatives are hard for people to imagine. You have to build a bridge between the world you're living in and the world everyone else is living in.

It's not always easy to make something new and ethereal, real and tangible. But think of this: Ask just about any kid to draw a picture of heaven, and you'll get back an imaginative illustration. If an eight-year-old can draw a picture of Paradise, *you* have no excuse.

Get a Routine

Swim in the new. Sounds easy, but the ocean is a big place. How do you avoid drowning in data? You need some kind of routine. I can't tell you what your routine should be, but I can say what works for some folks.

John Naisbitt's routine for finding the edge is simple: he reads newspapers from around the world for several hours each day, hunting for patterns in things that get reported but don't yet generate a lot of ink. Marc Andreessen, the inventor of the Internet browser, has a different routine:

> *Pay attention to things that are taking off, even if they're only taking off at a small scale. One of the things that surprised me about the Internet is the number of things that I was aware of when they were small-scale things, not commercial, that are now picking up users and attention. Even if I was skeptical at the time, in most cases these are now billion-dollar companies. So you want to pay attention to small-scale successes because they're probably going to become large-scale successes.*

What are your routines? How often do you pick up a magazine you've never read before? How often do you go to an industry convention for an industry you know little about? How often do you hang out with people who are very different from you? Are you on the edge or in the hinterlands? Do you have any friends in venture capital who can tell you what's happening out on the fringe? Do you know what kind of start-ups are calling on the VP for business development in your company? Have you been tracking all the IPOs across your broad competitive domain? If not, get plugged in. Find the small things, play an imaginary game of "scale up," and then ask, If this thing became really big, what kind of a difference would it make? Who would be affected?

Insights come out of new conversations. All too often, strategy conversations in large companies have the same 10 people talking to the same 10 people for the fifth year in a row. They can finish each other's sentences. You're not going to learn anything new in this setting. Travel is still the fastest way to start a bunch of new conversations. It has the added benefit of turning the background into the foreground. When you travel to an exotic destination you're suddenly reminded of how much you take for granted and how there are alternatives to the familiar habits of your life. It was his experience with the casual warmth of Italian coffee bars that gave Howard Schultz the idea for Starbucks. Familiarity is the enemy. It slowly turns everything into wallpaper. Travel makes you a stranger. It puts you at odds. It robs you of your prejudices. If you can't travel, find a good bookstore and pick up the *Globe & Mail* (Toronto), *The Daily Telegraph* (London), *The South China Morning Post* (Hong Kong), *The New Straits Times* (Singapore), or some other foreign newspaper, or find them online. If your understanding of what's changing in the world comes from network television news, the *Wall Street Journal*, and *Time* magazine, you're going to miss the future.

Be a Heretic

It is not enough to be a novelty addict. You must be a heretic as well. Heretics, not prophets, create revolutions. You can immerse yourself in what's changing, but you'll only see the opportunities to leverage change in novel ways if you can escape the shackles of tradition. There is much that individuals cannot imagine simply because they are prisoners of their own dogma. In this sense, the challenge is not "long-term" thinking but "unconventional" thinking. The real issue is not the present versus the future but the orthodox versus the heterodox.

There is an enormous danger in viewing what's changing through the lens of what already is. People saw plastic, when it was first invented, as a substitute for existing materials—steel, wood, and leather. (Remember Corfam shoes?) Eventually, plastic got the chance to be plastic. Can you imagine a hula hoop, compact disc, or videotape made out of anything else? In the age of revolution the future is not just more of the past—it is profoundly different than the past. Whether or not *you* succeed in escaping the past is, in a way, quite irrelevant. The future's going to get invented, with you or without you. But if you want to build the new, you must first dismantle your existing belief system and burn for scrap anything that is not endlessly and universally true.

Ask yourself this question: What are the industry dogmas my company has knowingly chosen to violate? Can't think of any? Then don't expect to outperform industry averages. Industry revolutionaries create strategies that are subversive, not submissive. To do this, you must "deconstruct" the belief system that prevents individuals in your organization from imagining unorthodox strategies.

In most companies it is virtually impossible to redesign business models without first challenging the dominant mental models. Mental models spring out of and reinforce the current business model.

A business model is a "thing." The mental model is a set of beliefs about the "thing." The mental model reflects the "central tendency" of beliefs around the key business concept design variables:

- What is our business mission?
- What is our product/market scope?
- What is the basis for differentiation?
- What core competencies are important?

- What strategic assets do we need to own?
- What core processes are critical?
- How can we best configure our resources?
- How do we go to market?
- What kind of information do we need to serve customers?
- What is the kind of relationship we want with customers?
- How do we price our products and services?
- What is the particular benefit bundle we deliver?
- How do we integrate with suppliers and partners?
- What profit boosters can we exploit?

The more successful a company has been, the more deeply etched are its mental models. In even moderately successful companies, most people take 90 percent of the existing mental model as a given. Design choices made years earlier are seldom revisited. It's difficult to imagine revolutionary strategies when you start with nine-tenths of your brain tied behind your back. Design choices of long ago are seldom challenged in the absence of a crisis. Even then, it often takes a new management team to pull out the old beliefs by their roots. You and your colleagues must learn how to systematically deconstruct the existing set of beliefs around "what business we're in," "how we make money," "who our customers are," and so on.

The first step in your training as a heretic is to admit that you are living inside a mental model—a construct that may not even be of your own making.

You have to know that things are not as they seem—and you must know this at such a deep level that you can challenge the very foundations of what others regard as axiomatic. We are all caught inside theories, inside constructs. Most of us spend our lives elaborating someone else's theory—about how to run an airline or publish a magazine or sell insurance. New facts are either absorbed into the construct or rejected. Seldom do the constructs themselves get altered. The challenge is to break the construct—or at least bend it a bit. To do so, you must first acknowledge that you are inside the construct. Jim Taylor puts it like this: "The more you pay attention to information that supports your worldview, the less you learn. There tends to be a convergence in what any group of people believe is important, despite what might really be important out there."

The problem with the future is not that it is unknowable. The problem with the future is that it is different. If you are unable to think differently, the future will always arrive as a surprise. You know that old bumper sticker, "Question Authority"? Well the authority you most need to question is the authority of your *own* long-held beliefs. This isn't about pricking someone else's conventions. We are all reassured when the world conforms to our prejudices. But confirmation of what you already believe is a complete waste of time. You must look for *disconfirming* evidence for things that don't fit, for things that are ajar. This is hard, because it forces you to write off your depreciating intellectual capital—you must admit not only that you do "not know" many things but that you "wrongly know" many things.

Surface the Dogmas

So how do you cultivate contrarian tendencies and surface the dogmas in your company? One simple device is to ask yourself and your colleagues, What are 10 things you would never hear a customer say about our company or our industry? For example, no customer is ever going to say, "The airline treats its customers with dignity and respect." Few customers would ever say, "It's easy to shop for a better rate on electricity." Fewer still would say, "Banking is fun," or "Hotels always have great food." Once you've identified what customers wouldn't say, ask yourself why they wouldn't say those things. What orthodoxies do they reveal? What opportunities do these orthodoxies create for some unorthodox newcomer? And finally, what would happen if we turned this orthodoxy on its head?

Another way is to ask, What are the 10 things that all the major competitors in this industry believe in common? Then ask, What would happen if each of these assumptions were inverted? What new opportunities would present themselves? How would customers benefit? Clearly, not all industry beliefs are stupid. There's a difference between dogma (the earth is flat) and physics (things fall downward rather than upward). It is seldom a good idea to defy physics. Nevertheless, much of what people in an industry will tell you is God-given is merely human-made. It is your job to turn certainties back into choices.

Never Stop Asking Why

Like children, heretics play an endless game of "why" and "what if." If you've been paying attention to what's changing, you can play a very intelligent game of "what if." For example, What if everything in the world were able to communicate with everything else? What would a vending machine want to talk about? "Hey, it's hot, and at this rate I'm going to be out of orange sodas in a couple of hours." What would a fuel pump say? "Oh, hi there, Jaguar XK8. I know you need premium fuel.

That's what I'll pump." What would a refrigerator say? "My sensors tell me there's something rotten down in the crisper drawer."

Wayne Huizenga asked "why." Before AutoNation, no major car dealer had ever gone public. Says Huizenga:

> Every one of the dealers told me that Ford and General Motors and all the manufacturers would never let a publicly held company own a new-car leadership. And I'd always ask, "Why?" I never got a good answer. So we put some gentle pressure on the manufacturers and made it happen.

Revolutionaries simply ask "why" more than the rest of us.

Celebrate the Stupid

We've all been taught that good answers are more important than good questions. What was true in first grade is infinitely more true when you're in front of the board or your boss. But new questions are at the heart of business concept innovation—and if you're going to ask "why," you've got to be prepared to look foolish once in a while. Listen once more to Marc Andreessen:

> If your goal is to create something new and big, you're going to have to do something that everybody else will laugh at—so that becomes the test. If they're not laughing at it, and you don't get turned down a few times, it's probably not a great idea. In other words, if it's something that makes everybody nod their heads and say, "Yeah, that makes sense," there are probably already a dozen people doing it.

Only stupid questions create new wealth. Of course, there are stupid stupid questions, and there are smart stupid questions. I remember asking a senior executive in one of America's leading hotel chains, "Why is it that someone who checks in at two in the morning has to check out at the same time as the guy who checks in at two in the afternoon?" When I got a blank stare I barged ahead. "Why can't you just have everyone check out 20 hours after they checked in? If I arrive at three in the afternoon, I'll have to check out at eleven the next morning. But if I arrive at ten in the evening, I can keep the room until six P.M. on the day of departure." The hotelier looked at me with a face full of condescension. "Gary," he said, "you don't understand the hotel industry." "*That*," I replied, "is my comparative advantage." You don't ask stupid questions when you're an industry expert. I suggested he go study Hertz. When you rent a car at Hertz, they don't ask you to bring it back at noon. You have it for 24 hours. And the hotel operator has an advantage Hertz doesn't have—the rooms never move. No one promises to leave the room in Chicago and ends up leaving it in Milwaukee instead!

In many companies the premium placed on being "right" is so high that there is virtually no room for speculation and imagination. If you insist on being incontrovertibly right, you will never be new. It's that simple. The fear of being wrong is so strong in many organizations that any idea not backed by a dumpster of data is automatically suspect. The training given M.B.A. students and managers reinforces this tendency. In course after course the message is driven home: the quality of your analysis counts for more than the quality of your imagination.

Go to Extremes

Pick a performance parameter that's important in your business—time, cost, efficiency, quality, speed, whatever. Push this to extremes and ask, Why not? Pushing boundary conditions to the limit is one of John Seely Brown's favorite tricks for blowing up orthodoxies.

> My heuristic is, "Take it to the limit and see what happens." Xerox wants to make copiers that make less noise. I told our people that this wasn't an interesting problem. If you ask us to make a machine that makes no noise, that gets interesting. They said, "That's impossible." I said, "Not if the copier has no moving parts." The question led to a radical shift in architectures in terms of how to think about copiers, printers, and mechanical systems. You'll see some radical products from Xerox that came from exploring impossible questions.

Think of every strategy conversation as your own personal version of the X Games. Get radical.

Find the "And"

Revolutionaries find a way to transcend trade-offs. They just hate it when someone says you can have A or you can have B. Screw it. I want 'em both! Toyota's "and" was a car that was economical to buy *and* of high quality. Where Mercedes-Benz and Chevrolet gave customers an either/or, Toyota offered an *and*. Look around. Where have people accepted "ors" when they would have rather had "ands"? Take one example., There are many who believe we have an educational crisis in America.

Our kids live in a culture literally saturated with entertainment. The number of alternatives to homework grows each year. Hmmm, *South Park* or algebra—that's a tough one. Unless teachers can find a way to make learning educational *and* fun, media moguls will be the real teachers in America. *Edutainment* was the original idea behind *Sesame Street*—no wonder it became one of the most popular kids shows in history—it offered an "and" instead of an "or."

This is how John Naisbitt puts it:

> *You just have to hang out with the paradoxes, hang out with the contradictions until you understand them. When there is a perceived contradiction, I like to look for something that helps to resolve the contradiction. A lot of people have an either/or mentality. We get the Internet and everyone says, "Well newspapers are going to go away." It's not either/or. There will be a change in the mix, that's all.*

Bridle whenever you hear an "or." Search for novel solutions that make trade-offs unnecessary.

Distinguish Form from Function

Why did people think the Internet would kill newspapers? Because they saw newspapers as a *form* (ink smeared on dead trees) rather than as a *function* (sifting through all that happens in a day and selecting out what's really important). While the form of a newspaper may disappear, its function certainly won't. If a newspaper company sees itself in the business of running giant printing presses and distributing newsprint, it may one day be rendered irrelevant. If it sees itself as a current events editor, it will learn to live as happily online as off.

One way of distinguishing function from form is to substitute a verb for a noun. Richard Kovacevich, chief executive of Wells Fargo bank, provides an example: "Banking is essential, banks are not." Banks are things—bricks and mortar. Banking is a function. If I can divorce the function from the thing, I can think about how to deliver the function in radically different ways.

There are some IT executives and technologists who argue that computing is about to enter the "post-PC era." High-capacity networks, linked by powerful hub computers, will feed data to millions of information appliances. International Data Corporation has estimated that by 2005 more information appliances—including set-top boxes, screen phones, and hand-held computers—will be sold than PCs. Couple this with online application service providers that remove the need for you to load up any software other than a browser, and you have a major threat to the existing PC business model. Yet many at Microsoft find this hard to swallow. Their loyalty is to the *form* of the PC, rather than the *function* of network computing. One senior vice president at Microsoft has termed the next wave of computing as the "PC-plus era." At best this is wishful thinking, at worst it is denial. There is little doubt that the form of computing will change dramatically over the next decade or so. Any company that can't distinguish between form and function will get caught inside an obsolete form factor.

Start a New Conversation

The disciplines I've described here are reliable ways to help you discover opportunities for business concept innovation. Yet there's no surefire, mechanical process for creating a bold new "aha." Instead, you must marry a thorough understanding of business concept innovation with the wide-eyed curiosity of a precocious five-year-old. Phrases such as "disciplined imagination," "routine creativity," and "informed intuition" capture the challenge. You already understand the part about being disciplined, well-informed, and following a routine, but what about imagination, creativity, and intuition? These qualities have been bred out of you—first by school, then by work. Yet you can, and must regain your lost curiosity. You must learn to see again with eyes undimmed by precedent. What is familiar and drab must become wondrous and new. The goal of this chapter has been to help you regain your innocence.

Profound insights come out of a cocktail of unexpected problems, novel experiences, random conversations, and newly discovered facts. The goal is to mix this cocktail again and again. Indeed the goal is to *be* the mixer—to encompass within yourself and your team all the elements that combine to produce bursts of deeply creative insight. Not only is this an individual imperative, it is an organizational imperative. No single individual can encompass all that is changing the world. Your cocktail shaker is just so big.

o   o   o

Gary Hamel consults and speaks on strategy and innovation and is a visiting professor at the London Business School.

Part Five

Making It Happen

While leaders are expected to inspire and guide organizations, their ultimate responsibility is to performance and the bottom line. The best-intentioned organization will fail if it can't execute what it plans. Many leaders don't have time to attend to the details of execution, but they must ensure that their organizations do. At the most basic level, leaders need to develop and maintain organizational culture, as explained by Edgar H. Schein, and adapt it as the business environment changes. Gretchen M. Spreitzer and Robert E. Quinn address specifically the creation of a culture that motivates employees to commit to company performance. Larry Bossidy and Ram Charan discuss in greater detail the problem of execution, and what leaders must do to solve it.

The final four chapters focus on a major element of making it happen, leading in times of change. More than ever, a leader needs to stay ahead of the curve and build an organization that can take the next business revolution in stride. In separate chapters, Margaret J. Wheatley and Robert E. Quinn seek to take the fear out of change and view it as a necessity to be met head-on. William Bridges and Susan Mitchell Bridges describe the stages of transition, and Ronald A. Heifetz and Donald L. Laurie present the idea of adaptive change and the benefits of being honest with one's followers about the challenges of change.

Chapter Twenty-Five

The Learning Leader as Culture Manager

Edgar H. Schein

Leaders create, embed, develop, and sometimes deliberately attempt to change cultural assumptions.

Though typically exemplified by the founder, owner, or professional manager who has been promoted to be CEO, leadership can occur anywhere in the organization. Leadership is the attitude and motivation to examine and manage culture. Accomplishing this goal is more difficult lower down in the organization but by no means impossible in that subcultures can be managed just as can overall organizational cultures.

The issues that make the most difference to the kind of leadership required are twofold. First, different stages of organizational development require different kinds of culture management. Second, different strategic issues require a focus on different kinds of cultural dimensions. Each of these points is briefly examined here.

LEADERSHIP IN CULTURE CREATION

In a growing organization leaders externalize their own assumptions and embed them gradually and consistently in the mission, goals, structures, and working procedures of the group. Whether we call these basic assumptions the guiding beliefs, the theories-in-use, the mental models, the basic principles, or the guiding visions on which founders operate, there is little question that they become major elements of the organization's emerging culture (for example, Argyris, 1976; Bennis, 1989; Davis, 1984; Donaldson and Lorsch, 1983; Dyer, 1986; Kotter and Heskett, 1992; Pettigrew, 1979; Schein, 1983).

In a rapidly changing world, the learning leader/founder must not only have vision but must be able to impose it and to develop it further as external circumstances change. Inasmuch as the new members of an organization arrive with prior organizational and cultural experiences, a common set of assumptions can only be forged by clear and consistent messages as the group encounters and survives its own crises. The culture creation leader therefore needs persistence and patience, yet as a learner must be flexible and ready to change.

As groups and organizations develop, certain key emotional issues arise. These have to do with dependence on the leader, with peer relationships, and with how to work effectively. Leadership is needed to help the group identify the issues and deal with them. During this process leaders must often absorb and contain the anxiety that is unleashed when things do not work as they should (Hirschhorn, 1988; Schein, 1983). Leaders may not have the answer, but they must provide temporary stability and emotional reassurance while the answer is being worked out. This anxiety-containing function is especially relevant during periods of learning, when old habits must be given up before new ones are learned. Moreover, if the world is increasingly changing, such anxiety may be perpetual, requiring learning leaders to assume a perpetual supportive role. The traumas of growth appear to be so constant and so powerful that unless a strong leader takes the role of anxiety and risk absorber, the group cannot get through its early stages of growth and fails. Being in an ownership position helps because everyone then realizes that the founder is in fact taking a greater personal financial risk; however, ownership does not automatically create the ability to absorb anxiety. For many leaders this is one of the most important things they have to learn.

When leaders launch new enterprises, they must be mindful of the power they have to impose on those enterprises their own assumptions about what is right and proper, how the world works, and how things should be done. Leaders should not apologize for or be cautious about their assumptions. Rather, it is intrinsic to the leadership role to create order out of chaos, and leaders are expected to provide their own assumptions as an initial road map into the uncertain future. The more aware leaders are of this process, the more consistent and effective they can be in implementing it.

The process of culture creation, embedding, and reinforcement brings with it problems as well as solutions. Many organizations survive and grow but at the same time operate inconsistently or do things that seem contradictory. One explanation of this phenomenon that has been pointed out repeatedly is that leaders not only embed in their organizations what they intend consciously to get across, but they also convey their own inner conflicts and the inconsistencies in their own personal makeup (Schein, 1983; Kets de Vries and Miller, 1984; Miller, 1990). The most powerful signal to which subordinates respond is what catches leaders' attention consistently, particularly what arouses them emotionally. But many of the things to which leaders respond emotionally reflect not so much their conscious intentions as their unconscious conflicts. The organization then either develops assumptions around these inconsistencies and conflicts and they become part of the culture, or the leader gradually loses a position of influence if the behavior begins to be seen as too disruptive or actually destructive. In extreme cases the organization isolates or ejects the founder. In doing so, however, it is not rejecting all of the founder's assumptions but only those that are inconsistent with the core assumptions on which the organization was built.

The period of culture creation, therefore, puts an additional burden on founders—to obtain enough self-insight to avoid unwittingly undermining their own creations. Founding leaders often find it difficult to recognize that the very qualities that made them successful initially, their strong convictions, can become sources of difficulty later on and that they also must learn and grow as their organizations grow. Such insights become especially important when organizations face issues of leadership succession because succession discussions force into the open aspects of the culture that may not have been previously recognized.

What all of this means for leaders of developing organizations is that they must have tremendous self-insight and recognize their own role not only in creating the culture but also their responsibility in embedding and developing culture. Inasmuch as the culture is the primary source of identity for young organizations, the culture creation and development process must be handled sensitively with full understanding of the anxieties that are unleashed when identity is challenged.

LEADERSHIP AT ORGANIZATIONAL MIDLIFE

As the organization develops a substantial history of its own, its culture becomes more of a cause than an effect. As subgroups develop their own subcultures, the opportunities for constructive use of cultural diversity and the problems of integration both become greater. The leader must be able to pay attention to diversity and assess clearly how much of it is useful for further organizational development and how much of it is potentially dysfunctional. The culture is now much less tied to the leader's own personality, which makes it easier to assess objectively, though there are likely to be sacred cows, holdovers from the founding period, that have to be delicately handled.

The leader at this stage must be able to detect how the culture influences the strategy, structure, procedures, and ways in which the group members relate to one another. Culture is a powerful influence on members' perceptions, thinking, and feeling, and these predispositions, along with situational factors, influence members' behavior. Because culture serves an important anxiety-reducing function, members cling to it even if it becomes dysfunctional in relationship to environmental opportunities and constraints.

Leaders at this stage need diagnostic skill to figure out not only what the cultural influences are, but also what their impact is on the organization's ability to change and learn. Whereas founding leaders most need self-insight, midlife leaders most need the ability to decipher the surrounding culture and sub-cultures. To help the organization evolve into whatever will make it most effective in the future, leaders must also have culture management skills. In some instances this may mean increasing cultural diversity, allowing some of the uniformity that may have been built up in the growth stage to erode. In other instances it may mean pulling together a culturally diverse set of organizational units and attempting to impose new common assumptions on them. In either case the leader needs (1) to be able to analyze the culture in sufficient detail to know which cultural assumptions can aid and which ones will hinder the fulfillment of the organizational mission and (2) to possess the intervention skills to make desired changes happen.

Most of the prescriptive analyses of how to maintain the organization's effectiveness through this period emphasize that the leader must have certain insights, clear vision, and the skills to articulate, communicate, and implement the vision, but these analyses say nothing about how a given organization can find and install such a leader. In U.S. organizations in particular, the outside board members probably play a critical role in this process. If the organization has had a strong founding culture, however, its board may be composed exclusively of people who share the founder's vision. Consequently, real changes in direction may not become possible until the organization experiences serious survival difficulties and begins to search for a person with different assumptions to lead it.

One area to explore further here is the CEO's own role in succession. Can the leader of a midlife organization perceive the potential dysfunctions of some aspects of the culture to a sufficient extent to ensure that his or her successor will be able to move the culture in an appropriate new direction? CEOs have a great deal of power to influence the choice of their successor. Do they use that power wisely in terms of cultural issues? For example, it is alleged that one of the main reasons why Reginald Jones as CEO of General Electric "chose" Jack Welch to be his successor was because he recognized in Welch a person who would create the kinds of changes that were necessary for GE to remain viable. Similarly, Steve Jobs "chose" John Sculley to head Apple even though at some level he must have sensed that this choice might eventually lead to the kind of conflict that in the end forced Jobs to leave. The ultimate paradox here is that truly learning leaders may have to face the conclusion that they must replace themselves, that they do not have the vision needed to bring the midlife organization into alignment with a rapidly changing world.

LEADERSHIP IN MATURE AND POTENTIALLY DECLINING ORGANIZATIONS

In the mature stage if the organization has developed a strong unifying culture, that culture now defines even what is to be thought of as leadership, what is heroic or sinful behavior, and how authority and power are to be allocated and managed. Thus, what leadership has created now either blindly perpetuates itself or creates new definitions of leadership, which may not even include the kinds of entrepreneurial assumptions that launched the organization in the first place. The first problem of the mature and possibly declining organization, then, is to find a process to empower a potential leader who may have enough insight to overcome some of the constraining cultural assumptions.

What the leader must do at this point in the organization's history depends on the degree to which the culture of the organization has, in fact, enabled the group to adapt to its environmental realities. If the culture has not facilitated adaptation, the organization either will not survive or will find a way to change its culture. If it is to change its culture, it must be led by someone who can, in effect, break the tyranny of the old culture. This requires not only the insight and diagnostic skill to determine what the old culture is, but to realize what alternative assumptions are available and how to start a change process toward their acceptance.

Leaders of mature organizations must, as has been argued repeatedly, make themselves sufficiently marginal in their own organization to be able to perceive its assumptions objectively and nondefensively. They must, therefore, find many ways to be exposed to their external environment and, thereby facilitate their own learning. If they cannot learn new assumptions themselves, they will not be able to perceive what is possible in their organizations. Even worse, they may destroy innovative efforts that arise within their organizations if those innovative efforts involve countercultural assumptions.

Leaders capable of such managed culture change can come from inside the organization if they have acquired objectivity and insight into elements of the culture. Such cultural objectivity appears to be related to having had a non-conventional career or exposure to many subcultures within the organization (Kotter and Heskett, 1992). However, the formally designated senior managers of a given organization may not be willing or able to provide such culture change leadership. Leadership then may have to come from other boundary spanners in the organization or from outsiders. It may even come from a number of people in the organization, in which case it makes sense to talk of turnaround teams or multiple leadership.

If a leader is imposed from the outside, she or he must have the skill to diagnose accurately what the culture of the organization is, what elements are well adapted and what elements are problematic for future adaptation, and how to change that which needs changing. In other words the leader must be a skilled change manager who first learns what the present state of the culture is, unfreezes it, redefines and changes it, and then refreezes the new assumptions. Talented turnaround managers seem to be able to manage all phases of such changes, but sometimes different leaders will be involved in the different steps over a considerable period of time. They will use all the mechanisms previously discussed in the appropriate combinations to get the job done provided that they have the authority and power to use extreme measures, such as replacing the people who perpetuate the old cultural assumptions.

In summary, leaders play a critical role at each developmental stage of an organization, but that role differs as a function of the stage. Much of what leaders do is to perpetually diagnose the particular assumptions of the culture and figure out how to use those assumptions constructively or to change them if they are constraints.

LEADERSHIP AND CULTURE IN STRATEGY FORMULATION

Many companies have found that they or their consultants can think of new strategies that make sense from a financial, product, or marketing point of view, yet they cannot implement those strategies because such implementation requires assumptions, values, and ways of working that are too far out of line with the organization's existing assumptions. In some cases, the organization cannot even conceive of certain strategic options because they are too out of line with shared assumptions about the mission of the organization and its way of working, what Lorsch (1985) has aptly called "strategic myopia."

The Multi Company built its businesses by capitalizing on the intensive efforts of its research labs to develop "important" products that were "useful to society." Members viewed themselves as a company that produced life-saving drugs, pesticides that enabled countries to improve their food crops, sophisticated chemicals that made other industries possible, and so on. The company's success was based on brilliant research work and the protection from competition that patents allowed.

When the company began to compete in more diversified and mature markets, where patent protection had run out and product utility was not nearly as important as product marketability, some senior managers argued for a more pragmatic marketing strategy. Those managers wanted to decrease the research and development budget, increase marketing expenditures, and teach their colleagues how to think like marketers. But they were unable to convince senior management as a whole, leaving parts of the company in a financially vulnerable position. Clearly, the traditions, values, self-concepts, and assumptions about the nature of Multi made some aspects of the proposed new marketing strategy unthinkable or unacceptable to senior management.

Another example is provided by the Action Company, which became successful by developing a very complex product marketed to very sophisticated customers. The company later developed some smaller, simpler, less expensive versions of this product, which could have been further developed and marketed to less sophisticated customers. Even senior management argued that such low-end products had to be developed, but the product designers and marketers could not deal with the new customer type. The sales and marketing people could not imagine what the concerns of the new, less knowledgeable customer might be, and the product designers continued to be convinced that they could judge product attractiveness themselves. Neither group was motivated to understand the new customer because, unconsciously, they tended to look down on such a customer. The assumption that "dumb users" were not worth designing for was, in fact, held throughout the company, even by senior managers who were advocating low-end products.

To put this in the proper perspective, we must remember that cultural assumptions are the product of past successes. As a result they are increasingly taken for granted and operate as silent filters on what is perceived and thought about. If the organization's environment changes and new responses are required, the danger is that the changes will not be noticed or, even if noticed, that the organization will not be able to adapt because of embedded routines based on past success. Culture constrains strategy by limiting what the CEO and other senior managers are able to think about and what they perceive in the first place.

One of the critical roles of learning leadership, then, is first of all to notice changes in the environment and then to figure out what needs to be done to remain adaptive. I am defining leadership; in this context in terms of the role, not the position. The CEO or other senior managers may or may not be able to fulfill the leadership role, and leadership in the sense that I am defining it can occur anywhere in the organization. However, if real change and learning are to take place, it is probably necessary that the CEO or other very senior managers be able to be leaders in this sense.

Leaders must be somewhat marginal and must be somewhat embedded in the organization's eternal environment to fulfill this role adequately. At the same time, leaders must be well connected to those parts of the organization that are themselves well connected to the environment—sales, purchasing, marketing, public relations and legal, finance, and R&D. Leaders must be able to listen to disconfirming information coming from these sources and to assess the implications for the future or the organization. Only when they truly understand what is happening and what will be required in the way of organizational change can they begin to take action in initiating a learning process.

Much has been said about the need for vision in leaders, but too little has been said about their need to listen, to absorb, to search the environment for trends, and to build the organization's capacity to learn. Especially at the strategic level, the ability to see and acknowledge the full complexity of problems becomes critical. The ability to acknowledge complexity may also imply the willingness and emotional strength to admit uncertainty and to embrace experimentation and possible errors as the only way to learn. In our obsession with leadership vision, we may have made it possible for learning leaders to admit that their vision is not clear and that the whole organization will have to learn together. Moreover, as I have repeatedly argued, vision in a mature organization helps when the organization has already been disconfirmed and members feel anxious and in need of a solution. Much of what learning leaders must do occurs before vision even becomes relevant.

To summarize, the critical roles of leadership in strategy formulation and implementation are (1) to perceive accurately and in depth what is happening in the environment, (2) to create enough disconfirming information to motivate the organization to change without creating too much anxiety, (3) to provide psychological safety by either providing a vision of how to change and in what direction or by creating a process of visioning that allows the organization itself to find a path, (4) to acknowledge uncertainty, (5) to embrace errors in the learning process as inevitable and desirable, and (6) to manage all phases of the change process, including especially the management of anxiety as some cultural assumptions are given up and new learning begins.

LEADERSHIP AND CULTURE IN MERGERS AND ACQUISITIONS

Mergers and acquisitions are usually initiated by the leaders of organizations as ways of growing or becoming more competitive. There is a natural tendency to analyze the merger decision to consider only the primary issues of finance, product, and market mix. Culture may be loosely thought about, but it is only after the merger that it is taken seriously, suggesting that most leaders make the assumption that they can fix cultural problems after the fact. I would argue that leaders must make cultural analysis as central to the initial merger/acquisition decision as is the financial, product, or market analysis.

Mistakes in this area can be costly. A U.S. company realized that it was about to be acquired by a larger British firm. The company conducted an internal audit of its own culture and concluded that being taken over by the British company would be highly unpalatable. It therefore instituted a set of procedures that made the company unattractive (such as "poison pills") and waited for a situation that looked more promising. A French company became a potential buyer and was perceived to be a much better cultural match, so the U.S. company allowed itself to be bought. Six months later the French parent sent over a management team that decimated the U.S. company and imposed processes that were much less compatible than anything the U.S. company had imagined. But it was too late.

What, then, is the role of leadership in these situations? Several critical tasks can be identified. First, leaders must understand their own culture well enough to be able to detect where there are potential incompatibilities with the culture of the other organization. Second, leaders must be able to decipher the other culture, to engage in the kinds of activities that will reveal to them and to the other organization what some of its assumptions are. Third, leaders must be able to articulate the potential synergies or incompatibilities in such a way that others involved in the decision process can understand and deal with the cultural realities. Fourth, if the leader is not the CEO, he or she must be able to convince the CEO or the executive team to take the cultural issues seriously.

Members of planning groups or acquisition teams often develop the cross-cultural insights necessary to make good decisions about mergers and acquisitions but lack the skills to convince their own senior managers to take the cultural issues seriously. Or, alternatively, they get caught up in political processes that prevent the cultural realities from being addressed until after the key decisions have been made. In either case, cultural diagnosis based on marginality and the ability to surmount one's own culture is again revealed as the critical characteristic of leaders. The learning leader in these instances is the one who is able to learn from people in her or his own organization as well as from outsiders or consultants.

Leadership and Culture in
Joint Ventures and Strategic Alliances

Joint ventures and strategic alliances require cultural analysis even more than mergers and acquisitions because cross-national boundaries are more often involved in today's rapidly globalizing world. Deciphering differences between two companies in the same national culture is not as difficult as deciphering both national and company differences when one engages in a joint venture across national boundaries, as research by Salk (1992) shows. One special difficulty is to determine whether the differences that we perceive are attributable to national or organizational cultures. Yet it is important to make this determination because one would have to assume that the likelihood of changing national characteristics is very low.

The role of leadership in these situations is much the same as in the foregoing scenarios, except here leaders must even surmount their national identities. The European subsidiary of a U.S. company that could never find local managers to put on its board because they were all "too emotional" never came to terms with its own stereotype of managers as intrinsically nonemotional people and never realized or accepted that this was based on their U.S. assumptions. Many organizations make international assignments a requirement for a developing general manager. The explicit notion here is that such experience is essential if potential leaders with broader outlooks are to emerge. In other words, the learning leader must become marginal not only with respect to the organizational culture, but even with respect to national and ethnic culture.

IMPLICATIONS FOR THE SELECTION AND DEVELOPMENT OF LEADERS

A dynamic analysis of organizational culture makes it clear that leadership is intertwined with culture formation, evolution, transformation, and destruction. Culture is created in the first instance by the actions of leaders; culture is embedded and strengthened by leaders. When culture becomes dysfunctional, leadership is needed to help the group unlearn some of its cultural assumptions and learn new assumptions. Such transformations sometimes require what amounts to conscious and deliberate destruction of cultural elements. This in turn requires the ability to surmount one's own taken-for-granted assumptions, seeing what is needed to ensure the health and survival of the group, and orchestrating events and processes that enable the group to evolve toward new cultural assumptions. Without leadership in this sense, groups will not be able to adapt to changing environmental conditions. Let us summarize what is really needed to be a leader in this sense.

Perception and Insight

First, the leader must be able to perceive the problem, to have insight into himself or herself and into the culture and its dysfunctional elements. Such boundary-spanning perception can be difficult because it requires one to see one's own weaknesses, to perceive that one's own defenses not only help in managing anxiety but can also hinder one's efforts to be effective. Successful architects of change must have a high degree of objectivity about themselves and their own organizations, and such objectivity results from spending portions of their careers in diverse settings that permit them to compare and contrast different cultures. International experience is therefore one of the most powerful ways of learning.

Individuals often are aided in becoming objective about themselves through counseling and psychotherapy. One might conjecture that leaders can benefit from comparable processes such as training and development programs that emphasize experiential learning and self-assessment. From this perspective one of the most important functions of outside consultants or board members is to provide the kind of counseling that produces cultural insight. It is therefore far more important for the consultant to help the leader figure out for himself or herself what is going on and what to do than to provide recommendations on what the organization should do. The consultant also can serve as a "cultural therapist," helping the leader figure out what the culture is and what parts of it are more or less adaptive.

Motivation

Leadership requires not only insight into the dynamics of the culture but the motivation and skill to intervene in one's own cultural process. To change any elements of the culture, leaders must be willing to unfreeze their own organization. Unfreezing requires disconfirmation, a process that is inevitably painful for many. The leader must find a way to say to his or her own organization that things are not all right and, if necessary, must enlist the aid of outsiders in getting this message across. Such willingness requires a great ability to be concerned for the organization above and beyond the self, to communicate dedication or commitment to the group above and beyond self-interest.

If the boundaries of organization become looser, a further motivational issue arises in that it is less and less clear where a leader's ultimate loyalty should lie—with the organization, with industry, with country, or with some broader professional community whose ultimate responsibility is to the globe and to all of humanity.

Emotional Strength

Unfreezing an organization requires the creation of psychological safety, which means that the leader must have the emotional strength to absorb much of the anxiety that change brings with it and the ability to remain supportive to the organization through the transition phase even if group members become angry and obstructive. The leader is likely to be the target of anger and criticism because, by definition, he or she must challenge some of what the group has taken for granted. This may involve closing down the company division that was the original source of the company's growth and the basis of many employees' sense of pride and identity. It may involve laying off or retiring loyal, dedicated employees and old friends. Worst of all, it may involve the message that some of the founder's most cherished assumptions are wrong in the contemporary context. It is here that dedication and commitment are especially needed to demonstrate to the organization that the leader genuinely cares about the welfare of the total organization even as parts of it come under challenge. The leader must remember that giving up a cultural element requires one to take some risk, the risk that one will be very anxious and in the end worse off, and yet the leader must have the strength to forge the way into this unknown territory.

Ability to Change the Cultural Assumptions

If an assumption is to be given up, it must be replaced or redefined in another form, and it is the burden of leadership to make that happen. In other words, the leader must have the ability to induce cognitive redefinition by articulating and selling new visions and concepts. The leader must be able to bring to the surface, review, and change some of the group's basic assumptions.

At Multi this process had just begun. Many managers were beginning to doubt that the organization's commitment to science-based technical products could sustain the company in the long run. However, to that point no strong leader had emerged to convince the organization that consumer goods marketing through strong customer-oriented organizations could be a source of pride for the company.

The situation in the Action Company is highly ambiguous and difficult at the present time because it is neither clear whether Murphy will be able to sustain some of the original assumptions that he still believes in as the company faces economic downturns and a mature market requiring much tighter cost controls, or whether Murphy's assumptions about what the company needs today are correct, given the rapidly changing environment. Many of the basic assumptions on which Action was built are less and less sustainable as the company finds itself leveling off in sales and shrinking in terms of people, which poses the serious question of whether or not the basic cultural paradigm must be deliberately changed. If Murphy's belief in internal entrepreneurship and empowerment of his organization is to be sustained, he has to find a leadership succession process that will ensure that his successor has assumptions similar to his own.

Ability to Create Involvement and Participation

A paradox of culture change leadership is that the leader must be able not only to lead but also to listen, to emotionally involve the group in achieving its own insights into its cultural dilemmas, and to be genuinely participative in his or her approach to learning and change. The leaders of social, religious, or political movements can rely on personal charisma and let the followers do what they will. In an organization, however, the leader has to work with the group that exists at the moment, because he or she is dependent on the group members to carry out the organization's mission. The leader must recognize that, in the end, cognitive redefinition must occur inside the heads of many members and that will happen only if they are actively involved in the process. The whole organization must achieve some degree of insight and develop motivation to change before any real change will occur, and the leader must create this involvement.

The ability to involve others and to listen to them also protects leaders from attempting to change things that should not be changed. When leaders are brought in from the outside this becomes especially important because some of the assumptions operating in the organization may not fit the leader's own assumptions yet be critical to the organization's success. To illustrate the kinds of mistakes that are possible, we need remember only the period in the Atari Company's history when Warner Communications, the parent company, decided to improve Atari's marketing by bringing in as president an experienced marketing executive from the food industry. This executive brought with him the assumption that the key to success is high motivation and high rewards based on individual performance. He created and imposed an incentive system designed to select the engineers who were doing the best job in inventing and designing new computer games and gave them large monetary rewards. Soon some of the best engineers were leaving, and the company was getting into technical difficulty. What was wrong?

The new executive had created and articulated clear symbols, and everyone had rallied around them. Apparently, what was wrong was the assumption that the incentives and rewards should be based on individual effort. What the president failed to understand, coming from the food industry with its individualistic product management orientation, was that the computer games were designed by groups and teams and that the engineers considered the assignment of individual responsibility to be neither possible nor necessary. They were happy being group members and would have responded to group incentives, but unfortunately, the symbol chosen was the wrong symbol from this point of view. The engineers also noted that the president, with his nontechnical background, was not adept at choosing the best engineers, because their key assumption was that "best" was the product of group effort, not individual brilliance. Given the incompatible assumptions, it is no surprise that the president did not last long. Unfortunately, damage in terms of the loss of employees and in esprit had been done.

Ability to Learn a New Culture

Culture change leaders often have to take over a company in which they did not previously have any experience. If they are to diagnose and possibly change the culture they have entered, it is, of course, mandatory that they first learn what the essence of that culture is. This point raises the question of how much an individual can learn that is totally new. My hypothesis, based on various streams of research on leadership and management, is that leaders can cross boundaries and enter new organizational cultures fairly easily if they stay within a given industry, as defined by a core technology. A manager growing up in one chemical company can probably become the successful CEO of another chemical company and can learn the culture of that company. What appears to be much more difficult is to cross industry or national boundaries, because cognitive frames that are built up early in the manager's career are fundamentally more embedded. The ability of a John Sculley to become a successful leader of Apple is unusual. More typical is the Atari Company story mentioned above. The Action Company has had a series of senior financial officers drawn from the auto industry, and, though they were effective in bringing some new financial methods to the company, one always heard many stories concerning their inability to understand the Action culture and, consequently, to be ultimately ineffective.

In any case, the leader coming into a new organization must be very sensitive to his or her own need to truly understand the culture before assessing it and possibly changing it. A period of learning lasting a year or more, if the situation allows that much time, is probably necessary. If the situation is more critical, the leader could speed up his or her own learning by systematically involving the layers of the organization below him or her in culture deciphering exercises.

Summary and Conclusions

It seems clear that the leaders of the future will have to be perpetual learners. This will require (1) new levels of perception and insight into the realities of the world and also into themselves; (2) extraordinary levels of motivation to go through the inevitable pain of learning and change, especially in a world with looser boundaries in which one's own loyalties become more and more difficult to define; (3) the emotional strength to manage their own and others' anxiety as learning and change become more and more a way of life; (4) new skills in analyzing and changing cultural assumptions; (5) the willingness and ability to involve others and elicit their participation; and (6) the ability to learn the assumptions of a whole new organizational culture.

Learning and change cannot be imposed on people. Their involvement and participation are needed diagnosing what is going on, figuring out what to do, and actually doing it. The more turbulent, ambiguous, and out of control the world becomes, the more the learning process will have to be shared by all the members of the social unit doing the learning. If the leaders of today want to create organizational cultures that will themselves be more amenable to learning they will have to set the example by becoming learners themselves and involving others in the learning process.

The essence of that learning process will be to give organizational culture its due. Can we as individual members of organizations and occupations, as managers, teachers, researchers, and, sometimes, leaders recognize how deeply our own perceptions, thoughts, and feelings are culturally determined? Ultimately, we cannot achieve the cultural humility required to live in a turbulent culturally diverse world unless we can see cultural assumptions within ourselves. In the end, cultural understanding and cultural learning start with self-insight.

o   o   o

Edgar H. Schein is a professor at the Sloan School of Management, Massachusetts Institute of Technology, and a consultant.

Chapter Twenty-Six

Five Disciplines for Unleashing the Power in Your Workforce

Gretchen M. Spreitzer
Robert E. Quinn

Creating real competitive advantage is never easy. That is one of the lessons of failed empowerment efforts. Empowerment is not just another program to be implemented by the human resources or quality departments. It cannot be achieved by crossing off items on a checklist. It does not happen by telling people that they are empowered. It comes from creating a culture in which people develop a mindset characterized by a sense of self-determination, meaning, competence, and impact. And that does not happen overnight.

Experience shows that managers and executives often find it difficult to complete the journey to genuine empowerment. Some don't have the courage to begin. Some get lost along the way. Some stumble and decide to turn around when they are only part of the way there. Many confuse empowerment with a quick fix and give up on it before it has really been tried.

Part of the problem is an insufficient understanding of what genuine empowerment requires of leaders, managers, and organizations. The aim of this chapter is to continue our controlled burn on empowerment notions by introducing what we call the five disciplines of empowerment. These are the disciplines that our research shows are essential to creating a company of leaders. They are not magic bullets; they take dedication, hard work, and persistence. To better understand what implementing these disciplines involves, let's begin by exploring the parallels between undertaking a true empowerment effort and the preparations a novice runner makes for competing in a marathon.

LIKE TRAINING FOR A MARATHON: COMMITMENT, CONSISTENCY, AND INVESTMENT

Have you ever subjected your body and spirit to a grueling physical challenge such as climbing a mountain or running a marathon—one in which you aren't sure you can actually complete the challenge, in which you feel fully extended? This kind of intense experience has many parallels to the empowerment process. Like preparing for a marathon, the journey to empowerment requires sustained discipline, hard work, courage, and mental stamina.

Personal Commitment

Several years ago, a good friend who was a novice runner decided that she wanted to run in a marathon. The problem was that there were unending distractions, including a new project at work and a child to take care of. One particularly cold winter morning Pam woke and made a decision. She would begin that very day to train. If she kept letting the other commitments in her life interfere with her goal, she would never realize her dream.

What was most important is that Pam herself made the decision. Imagine if her husband or her boss told her she *had* to run a marathon. She probably would have found a variety of "good" excuses for why this wasn't the right time and would have blamed her husband or her boss when she suffered her first bout of blisters, aches, and pains. When the first opportunity came along to bow out of the marathon, she probably would have seized it.

The same is true of empowerment. Real empowerment is something that individuals must *choose* to have because they want to be empowered. Recall that one part of an empowered mindset is self-determination. This choice element is critical for building an empowered workforce. Empowerment cannot be mandated, and it cannot be forced. Telling someone to be empowered is like telling someone to be spontaneous. People must want to be empowered, and they must make a personal commitment for it to happen.

Similarly, as we will demonstrate, managers must make a personal commitment to modify their behavior in a way that promotes this kind of mindset. That is one of the crucial messages of this book: To create a climate of empowerment, we must first change ourselves. We cannot have an empowered organization if we behave as we have always behaved. We have to make the commitment to clarify our own values and be willing to act in ways that are consistent with expecting leadership from others.

Part of this commitment is choosing to see the process through, to commit to the long haul. When Pam made her decision to run in the marathon, it was not something that she could go out and do the next day. When she began her training, she could barely run a mile. She had to start with short runs interspersed with walking and had to build up to long-distance running. Had she treated her commitment like most of us treat our New Year's resolutions, she would have tried it for a week, burned out, and gone back to life as usual.

Like training for a marathon, building a climate of empowerment takes time and a sustained, disciplined approach. For example, at Delphi's Oak Creek assembly plant in Michigan, workers were frightened, angry, and resistant to changes aimed at creating more employee involvement. Employees were being asked to work as part of quality circles. The company's managers knew that the company could not survive without the commitment of the workforce. For six months there was little progress; workers simply did not believe that the company was committed to the change. Yet management persisted in the face of the discouraging resistance. This behavior eventually became a signal that management's commitment to employee involvement was real. Slowly, workers began to respond by taking initiative, offering suggestions, and making improvements. With small successes, trust began to grow. Gradually a flood of ideas and initiatives came forth.

Today, those same people work in self-managing teams or "cells" where they determine their own schedules, inspect products for quality and productivity, and communicate directly with customers. The empowerment effort is considered a dramatic success. Costs are down and productivity is way up. But most important, employees act as leaders.

In most companies, that success would never have been achieved. Too often the concept of empowerment sounds nice until people realize that they must commit time and energy to a difficult and long-term process of behavioral change. Without an adequate understanding of the kind of commitment involved, they are like people who give up on the idea of competing in a marathon when their first efforts leave them breathless and aching after they have run only a mile.

Consistency, Consistency, Consistency

Having made her personal commitment, Pam needed to develop a consistent training schedule. To avoid injury, she needed a routine that included beginning and ending her runs with stretching exercises. She had to maintain consistent discipline. She couldn't save her training for the weekends when she had more free time. She had to say no to distracting activities. When her boss needed her to travel, she took along her running gear and declined early morning meetings so she could maintain her schedule. She entered her training time on her Palm Pilot just as she did any other meeting. She negotiated with her husband to take care of some of her home responsibilities.

This kind of consistency is also necessary when we set out to change cultures and behaviors. We have to focus our energies and carve out time for creating a system that fosters empowerment. There will always be pressures to preserve the status quo: to stick with tried-and-true behaviors and avoid taking on new challenges. Resisting those pressures is a key to making the process of empowerment work. If managers are wishy-washy, if their efforts are not focused, their initiative will lack impact. They need to forego activities and behaviors that are contrary to creating a mindset of empowerment. They need to take care not to send mixed messages about what is desired and proclaim a clear message that leadership behavior is a priority. And they need to make sure that their actions are consistent with their rhetoric.

Making the Investment

As Pam soon discovered, preparing to run in a marathon requires making investments: a good pair of running shoes, the right support garments, and nonbinding clothing. It would have been easy for her to say that she could save money by getting by with what she had. But the wrong equipment, such as shoes that were worn out or designed for tennis as opposed to running, could have impaired her training and even caused injury.

Empowerment, too, requires investments. We may need to invest money in training and new technology to equip people to take needed initiatives. We may need to invest in a significant cultural change effort. It is futile to speak of being committed to the empowerment process without also being willing to invest in the resources that make genuine empowerment possible.

A PREVIEW OF THE DISCIPLINES

Our analogy of the marathon runner has emphasized the need for personal commitment, consistency, and the willingness to make appropriate investments. But even the strongest-willed marathon runner needs something more: she needs to know *how* to train, how to pace herself, even how to breathe. In a similar way, many empowerment efforts have failed for lack of specific know-how, a clear-eyed understanding of exactly what to *do* to create and foster a climate of leadership.

That is what our five disciplines of empowerment aim to provide. We choose the word *disciplines* very deliberately to suggest the kind of self-control, regular attention, practice, sacrifice, and practical know-how that genuine empowerment requires. Together the five disciplines stimulate the creative tension that is needed to maintain a climate that fosters leadership at all levels of the organization.

Here we provide an overview of the five disciplines and consider the underlying tensions among them—something that often has not been appreciated in empowerment efforts. The chapters that follow lay out the logic of each of these disciplines and provide specific examples, tools, techniques, and strategies for implementing them.

The First Discipline: Empowering Yourself

The first discipline—*empowering yourself*—sets the stage for the others. If we want others to act like leaders, we must first model the kind of behavior that we expect. To do so, we need to ensure that we ourselves have a sense of self-determination, meaning, competence, and impact in our own work. If we do not, how can we ask our employees to have this mindset?

Our first step, then, must be to assess the level of our own empowerment. This means asking, Who am I? What do I want to be? What is my current level of personal empowerment? Empowerment isn't about preaching, and it isn't about learning ways to get others to be something that we ourselves are not. The empowered leader is a role model who knows that actions speak louder than words.

The Second Discipline:
Continuous Vision and Challenge

The second discipline consists of creating *a clear vision and challenge* to "hook" people to the organization and its mission. As Dennis Bakke, CEO of AES, the global electricity company, has articulated:

> *Our main goal at the beginning was to build a company that we ourselves would want to work in. The actual type of business wasn't really important, to tell you the truth. It could have been an energy conservation company; it could have been steel. The struggle before the deal, for instance, the challenge and creativity required to make it work, taking risks, and even sleepless nights—believe it or not, those things are really fun because they engage people—heart, mind, and soul. And that was the kind of company we set out to create, one in which people could have engaging experiences on a daily basis.[1]*

Our research confirms the wisdom of Bakke's observations. Highly empowered people feel that they understand top management's vision and the strategic direction of the organization. This understanding depends on employees' having access to strategic information about the organization's future direction. Only if they have such information can they take initiative or introduce innovations to advance the organization's goals. Together with a shared vision, this kind of knowledge provides a clear direction so that employees feel they can act autonomously rather than waiting for permission and direction from those in authority. Further, to enlist everyone's best efforts, the vision must provide challenge to employees, thus stretching their capability to improve themselves and the organization.

The Third Discipline:
Continuous Security and Support

The third discipline consists of providing adequate *security and support*. For employees to feel that the system really wants them to act like leaders, they need a sense of social support from their bosses, peers, and subordinates. Accordingly, their efforts to take initiative and risk must be reinforced rather than punished. They must believe that the company will support them as they learn and grow. If this support is weak or missing—if, for example, risk taking is punished when it doesn't turn out well, or if successes are not praised and publicized—employees will worry about seeking permission before acting rather than asking for forgiveness if they make mistakes. This point is exemplified in an often-told story at UPS. Some years ago, an employee went beyond the bounds of his authority to order an extra 737 to ensure timely delivery of a trainload of packages left behind in the Christmas rush. Rather than punish the employee, UPS praised his initiative, and the story survives as proof that the company stands behind such empowered action.

The Fourth Discipline:
Continuous Openness and Trust

The fourth discipline involves creating a climate of *openness and trust*. Part of feeling empowered is knowing that the corporate culture emphasizes the value of the human assets in the organization. As difficult as it is to build such a culture in an environment of downsizing and rapid change, it is essential for employees to feel a sense of participation, openness, concern, and trust. Empowered employees feel that the people in their unit work together to solve problems and that employees' ideas are taken seriously in decision making.

Creating an environment that trusts people to think for themselves and take chances means loosening controls rather than tightening them. It means organizing not more, but less. Roger Sant, the chairman of AES, expresses the point well: "Never tell people how to do their jobs. Instead, present them with a challenge, and then let them choose the best way to attack it. Even when I have an idea or plan, I try to invite people to be part of the problem solving. That way they feel part of the team—and they usually come up with an idea that is better than mine."[2]

The Fifth Discipline: Continuous Guidance and Control

The fifth and final discipline involves providing adequate *guidance and control.* Genuine empowerment doesn't mean that people are turned loose to do whatever they want. In fact, highly empowered people report that they work in units with clear goals, clear lines of authority, and clear task responsibilities. Though they have autonomy, they are aware of the boundaries of their decision-making discretion. They know what they are responsible for achieving and what others have responsibility for. They have clear goals and objectives that are aligned with the vision of the organization.

The key focus of this lever is to reduce the disabling uncertainty and ambiguity that so often accompany empowerment efforts. For example, Marriott has developed "safe zones" so that employees understand which kind of situations allow for empowerment and which do not. These safe zones set boundaries for empowered behavior; they let people know how far they can go with their empowerment. Calling in maintenance to fix a light without approval may be OK, but purchasing a new light may be beyond their safe zone. Without a basic level of structure and control, employees experience chaos rather than empowerment.

UNDERLYING TENSIONS IN THE DISCIPLINES OF EMPOWERMENT

You may have already noticed a key point about the five disciplines that we have described: Some seem almost in conflict with others. On one hand, empowerment involves a sense of personal autonomy that requires trust and an openness to risk. On the other hand, empowerment requires security, support, control, and guidance. You might well ask, Well, then, which is it? Autonomy or direction? Self-confidence or security and support?

Balancing Opposing Forces

Our answer is all of the above. Our research has revealed that genuine empowerment involves implicit tensions. The challenge for managers is not to choose one aspect of empowerment over another, but rather to balance a set of opposing forces that must coexist.

These creative tensions are illustrated in Figure 26.1. The first discipline, *empowering yourself*, which undergirds all the others, contrasts with the other disciplines in that it is focused on the self whereas the other four are focused on the system and context. So the first tension of empowerment involves the need to focus simultaneously on the self and the system. Managers who focus on the self without recognizing and working to change the system they are part of will be too inner-oriented and are likely to be ineffectual in eliciting leadership behaviors from others. By the same token, managers who focus on the system but not the self are likely to behave hypocritically, expecting things of others that they do not model themselves.

The second tension involves the inherent contrast between the disciplines of openness/trust and guidance/control. On one hand, the system must liberate and give power to individuals to act as they see appropriate. On the other hand, the system must maintain control, providing guidance when necessary and setting boundaries. Focusing on freedom without setting appropriate boundaries is likely to produce the "loose cannons" that many organizations fear. But focusing too much on boundaries and guidance will discourage the initiative that empowerment is meant to foster. Both disciplines need to coexist in creative harmony to make empowerment work.

The third tension is between the disciplines of vision/challenge and security/support. On one hand, the system must be future looking, focused on stretching people in new ways to reach their full potential. On the other hand, the system must provide a sense of security and support so that people develop confidence and competence. If we stretch people too much without requisite support systems, they will feel overwhelmed. If we emphasize security without sufficient stretch, the system will become stagnant and people will not be prepared to respond dynamically to changes in the larger environment.

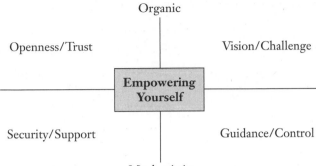

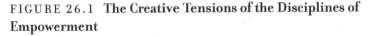

FIGURE 26.1 **The Creative Tensions of the Disciplines of Empowerment**

These observations bring us to the last of the mistaken ideas about empowerment that we need to burn away: that empowerment must come at the expense of values such as control and security, or that adequate control can only be maintained if people do not exercise real power and autonomy. Rather, genuine empowerment requires a willingness to deal with its inherent tensions and maintain a delicate balance of the five disciplines. A company of leaders is not anarchy—but neither is it the traditional command-and-control structure in which only those in authority act with autonomy and initiative. Empowerment, then, involves an apparent paradox—but it is precisely this paradoxical quality that we find in truly empowered organizations.

o   o   o

Gretchen M. Spreitzer is a professor at the University of Michigan Business School and a faculty affiliate at the University of Southern California's Center for Effective Organizations.

Robert E. Quinn is a professor at the University of Michigan Business School and a consultant and speaker.

Chapter Twenty-Seven

The Gap Nobody Knows

Larry Bossidy
Ram Charan
with Charles Burck

The CEO was sitting in his office late one evening, looking tired and drained. He was trying to explain to a visitor why his great strategic initiative had failed, but he couldn't figure out what had gone wrong.

"I'm so frustrated," he said. "I got the group together a year ago, people from all the divisions. We had two off-site meetings, did benchmarking, got the metrics. McKinsey helped us. Everybody agreed with the plan. It was a good one, and the market was good.

"This was the brightest team in the industry, no question about it. I assigned stretch goals. I empowered them—gave them the freedom to do what they needed to do. Everybody knew what had to be done. Our incentive system is clear, so they knew what the rewards and penalties would be. We worked together with high energy. How could we fail?

"Yet the year has come to an end, and we missed the goals. They let me down; they didn't deliver the results. I have lowered earnings estimates four times in the past nine months. We've lost our credibility with the Street. I have probably lost my credibility with the board. I don't know what to do, and I don't know where the bottom is. Frankly, I think the board may fire me."

Several weeks later the board did indeed fire him.

This story—it's a true one—is the archetypal story of the gap that nobody knows. It's symptomatic of the biggest problem facing corporations today. We hear lots of similar stories when we talk to business leaders. They're played out almost daily in the press, when it reports on companies that should be succeeding but aren't: Aetna, AT&T, British Airways, Campbell Soup, Compaq, Gillette, Hewlett-Packard, Kodak, Lucent Technologies, Motorola, Xerox, and many others.

These are good companies. They have smart CEOs and talented people, they have inspiring visions, and they bring in the best consultants. Yet they, and many other companies as well, regularly fail to produce promised results. Then when they announce the shortfall, investors dump their stocks and enormous market value is obliterated. Managers and employees are demoralized. And increasingly, boards are forced to dump the CEOs.

The leaders of all the companies listed above were highly regarded when they were appointed—they seemed to have all of the right qualifications. But they all lost their jobs because they didn't deliver what they said they would. In the year 2000 alone, forty CEOs of the top two hundred companies on *Fortune*'s 500 list were removed—not retired but fired or made to resign. When 20 percent of the most powerful business leaders in America lose their jobs, something is clearly wrong.

In such cases it's not just the CEO who suffers—so do the employees, alliance partners, shareholders, and even customers. And it's not just the CEO whose shortcomings create the problem, though of course he or she is ultimately responsible.

What is the problem? Is it a rough business environment? Yes. Whether the economy is strong or weak, competition is fiercer than ever. Change comes faster than ever. Investors—who were passive when today's senior leaders started their careers—have turned unforgiving. But this factor by itself doesn't explain the near-epidemic of shortfalls and failures. Despite this, there are companies that deliver on their commitments year in and year out—companies such as GE, Wal-Mart, Emerson, Southwest Airlines, and Colgate-Palmolive.

When companies fail to deliver on their promises, the most frequent explanation is that the CEO's strategy was wrong. But the strategy by itself is not often the cause. Strategies most often fail because they aren't executed well. Things that are supposed to happen don't happen. Either the organizations aren't capable of making them happen, or the leaders of the business misjudge the challenges their companies face in the business environment, or both.

Former Compaq CEO Eckhard Pfeiffer had an ambitious strategy, and he almost pulled it off. Before any of his competitors, he saw that the so-called Wintel architecture—the combination of the Windows operating system and Intel's constant innovation—would serve for everything from a palm-held to a linked network of servers capable of competing with mainframes.

Mirroring IBM, Pfeiffer broadened his base to serve all the computing needs of enterprise customers. He bought Tandem, the high-speed, failsafe mainframe manufacturer, and Digital Equipment Company (DEC) to give Compaq serious entry into the services segment. Pfeiffer moved at breakneck speed on his bold strategic vision, transforming Compaq from a failing niche builder of high-priced office PCs to the second-biggest computer company (after IBM) in just six years. By 1998 it was poised to dominate the industry.

But the strategy looks like a pipe dream today. Integrating the acquisitions and delivering on the promises required better execution than Compaq was able to achieve. More fundamentally, neither Pfeiffer nor his successor, Michael Capellas, pursued the kind of execution necessary to make money as PCs became more and more of a commodity business.

Michael Dell understood that kind of execution. His direct-sales and build-to-order approach was not just a marketing tactic to bypass retailers; it was the core of his business strategy. Execution is the reason Dell passed Compaq in market value years ago, despite Compaq's vastly greater size and scope, and it's the reason Dell passed Compaq in 2001 as the world's biggest maker of PCs. As of November 2001, Dell was shooting to double its market share, from approximately 20 to 40 percent.

Any company that sells direct has certain advantages: control over pricing, no retail markups, and a sales force dedicated to its own products. But that wasn't Dell's secret. After all, Gateway sells direct too, but lately it has fared no better than Dell's other rivals. Dell's insight was that building to order, executing superbly, and keeping a sharp eye on costs would give him an unbeatable advantage.

In conventional batch production manufacturing, a business sets its production volume based on the demand that is forecast for the coming months. If it has outsourced component manufacturing and just does the assembling, like a computer maker, it tells the component suppliers what volumes to expect and negotiates the prices. If sales fall short of projections, everybody gets stuck with unsold inventory. If sales are higher, they scramble inefficiently to meet demand.

Building to order, by contrast, means producing a unit after the customer's order is transmitted to the factory. Component suppliers, who also build to order, get the information when Dell's customers place their orders. They deliver the parts to Dell, which immediately places them into production, and shippers cart away the machines within hours after they're boxed. The system squeezes time out of the entire cycle from order to delivery—Dell can deliver a computer within a week or less of the time a order is placed. This system minimizes inventories at both ends of the pipeline, incoming and outgoing. It also allows Dell customers to get the latest technological improvements more often than rivals' customers.

Build-to-order improves inventory turnover, which increases asset velocity, one of the most underappreciated components of making money. Velocity is the ratio of sales dollars to net assets deployed in the business, which in the most common definition includes plant and equipment, inventories, and accounts receivable minus accounts payable. Higher velocity improves productivity and reduces working capital. It also improves cash flow, the life blood of any business, and can help improve margins as well as revenue and market share.

Inventory turns are especially important for makers of PCs, since inventories account for the largest portion of their net assets. When sales fall below forecast, companies with traditional batch manufacturing, like Compaq, are stuck with unsold inventory. What's more, computer components such as microprocessors are particularly prone to obsolescence because performance advances so rapidly, often accompanied by falling prices. When these PC makers have to write off the excess or obsolete inventory, their profit margins can shrink to the vanishing point.

Dell turns its inventory over eighty times a year, compared with about ten to twenty times for its rivals, and its working capital is negative. As a result, it generates an enormous amount of cash. In the fourth quarter of fiscal 2002, with revenues of $8.1 billion and an operating margin of 7.4 percent, Dell had cash flow of $1 billion from operations. Its return on invested capital for fiscal 2001 was 355 percent—an incredible rate for a company with its sales volume. Its high velocity also allows it to give customers the latest technological improvements ahead of other makers, and to take advantage of falling component costs—either to improve margins or to cut prices.

These are the reasons Dell's strategy became deadly for its competitors once PC growth slowed. Dell capitalized on their misery and cut prices in a bid for market share, increasing the distance between it and the rest of the industry. Because of its high velocity, Dell could show high return on capital and positive cash flow, even with margins depressed. Its competition couldn't.

The system works only because Dell executes meticulously at every stage. The electronic linkages among suppliers and manufacturing create a seamless extended enterprise. A manufacturing executive we know who worked at Dell for a time calls its system "the best manufacturing operation I've ever seen."

The chronic underperformers we've mentioned so far have lots of company. Countless others are less than they could be because of poor execution. The gap between promises and results is widespread and clear. The gap nobody knows is the gap between what a company's leaders want to achieve and the ability of their organization to achieve it.

Everybody talks about change. In recent years, a small industry of changemeisters has preached revolution, reinvention, quantum change, breakthrough thinking, audacious goals, learning organizations, and the like. We're not necessarily debunking this stuff. But unless you translate big thoughts into concrete steps for action, they're pointless. Without execution, the breakthrough thinking breaks down, learning adds no value, people don't meet their stretch goals, and the revolution stops dead in its tracks. What you get is change for the worse, because failure drains the energy from your organization. Repeated failure destroys it.

These days we're hearing a more practical phrase on the lips of business leaders. They're talking about taking their organizations to the "next level," which brings the rhetoric down to earth. GE CEO Jeff Immelt, for example, is asking his people how they can use technology to differentiate their way to the next level and command better prices, margins, and revenue growth.

This is an execution approach to change. It's reality-based—people can envision and discuss specific things they need to do. It recognizes that meaningful change comes only with execution.

No company can deliver on its commitments or adapt well to change unless all leaders practice the discipline of execution at all levels. Execution has to be a part of a company's strategy and its goals. It is the missing link between aspirations and results. As such, it is a major—indeed, *the* major—job of a business leader. If you don't know how to execute, the whole of your effort as a leader will always be less than the sum of its parts.

EXECUTION COMES OF AGE

Business leaders are beginning to make the connection between execution and results. After Compaq's board fired Pfeiffer, chairman and founder Ben Rosen took pains to say that the company's strategy was fine. The change, he said, would be "in execution. . . . Our plans are to speed up decision-making and make the company more efficient." When Lucent's board dismissed CEO Richard McGinn in October 2000, his replacement, Henry Schacht, explained: "Our issues are ones of execution and focus."

Clients of high-level headhunters are calling and saying, "Find me a guy who can execute." Writing in IBM's 2000 annual report, Louis V. Gerstner said of Samuel Palmisano, the man who would succeed him, "His real expertise is making sure we execute well." Early in 2001 the National Association of Corporate Directors added "execution" to the list of items that directors need to focus on in evaluating their own performance. Directors, the group says, have to ask themselves how well the company is executing and what accounts for any gap between expectations and management's performance. Very few boards now ask these questions, the group noted.

But for all the talk about execution, hardly anybody knows what it is. When we're teaching about execution, we first ask people to define it. They think they know how, and they usually start out well enough. "It's about getting things done," they'll say. "It's about running the company, versus conceiving and planning. It's making our goals." Then we ask them *how* to get things done, and the dialogue goes rapidly downhill. Whether they're students or senior executives, it is soon clear—to them as well as to us—that they don't have the foggiest idea of what it means to execute.

It's no different when execution is mentioned in books, newspapers, or magazines. You get the impression (implicitly), that it's about doing things more effectively, more carefully, with more attention to the details. But nobody really spells out what they mean.

Even people who pinpoint execution as the cause of failure tend to think of it in terms of attention to detail. Ben Rosen used the right word in his remarks, for example, but if he understood what execution actually requires, Compaq's leadership never got the message.

To understand execution, you have to keep three key points in mind:

○ Execution is a discipline, and integral to strategy.

○ Execution is the major job of the business leader.

○ Execution must be a core element of an organization's culture.

Execution Is a Discipline

People think of execution as the tactical side of business. That's the first big mistake. Tactics are central to execution, but execution is not tactics. Execution is fundamental to strategy and has to shape it. No worthwhile strategy can be planned without taking into account the organization's ability to execute it. If you're talking about the smaller specifics of getting things done, call the process implementation, or sweating the details, or whatever you want to. But don't confuse execution with tactics.

Execution is a systematic process of rigorously discussing hows and whats, questioning, tenaciously following through, and ensuring accountability. It includes making assumptions about the business environment, assessing the organization's capabilities, linking strategy to operations and the people who are going to implement the strategy, synchronizing those people and their various disciplines, and linking rewards to outcomes. It also includes mechanisms for changing assumptions as the environment changes and upgrading the company's capabilities to meet the challenges of an ambitious strategy.

In its most fundamental sense, execution is a systematic way of exposing reality and acting on it. Most companies don't face reality very well. As we shall see, that's the basic reason they can't execute. Much has been written about Jack Welch's style of management—especially his toughness and bluntness, which some people call ruthlessness. We would argue that the core of his management legacy is that he forced realism into all of GE's management processes, making it a model of an execution culture.

The heart of execution lies in the three core processes: the people process, the strategy process, and the operations process. Every business and company uses these processes in one form or the other. But more often than not they stand apart from one another like silos. People perform them by rote and as quickly as possible, so they can get back to their perceived work. Typically the CEO and his senior leadership team allot less than half a day each year to review the plans—people, strategy, and operations. Typically too the reviews are not particularly interactive.

People sit passively watching PowerPoint presentations. They don't ask questions.

They don't debate, and as a result they don't get much useful outcome. People leave with no commitments to the action plans they've helped create. This is a formula for failure. You need robust dialogue to surface the realities of the business. You need accountability for results—discussed openly and agreed to by those responsible—to get things done and reward the best performers. You need follow-through to ensure the plans are on track.

These processes are where the things that matter about execution need to be decided. Businesses that execute, as we shall see, prosecute them with rigor, intensity, and depth. Which people will do the job, and how will they be judged and held accountable? What human, technical, production, and financial resources are needed to execute the strategy? Will the organization have the ones it needs two years out, when the strategy goes to the next level? Does the strategy deliver the earnings required for success? Can it be broken down into doable initiatives? People engaged in the processes argue these questions, search out reality, and reach specific and practical conclusions. Everybody agrees about their responsibilities for getting things done, and everybody commits to those responsibilities.

The processes are also tightly linked with one another, not compartmentalized among staffs. Strategy takes account of people and operational realities. People are chosen and promoted in light of strategic and operational plans. Operations are linked to strategic goals and human capacities.

Most important, the leader of the business and his or her leadership team are deeply engaged in all three. *They* are the owners of the processes—not the strategic planners or the human resources (HR) or finance staffs.

Execution Is the Job of the Business Leader

Lots of business leaders like to think that the top dog is exempt from the details of actually running things. It's a pleasant way to view leadership: you stand on the mountaintop, thinking strategically and attempting to inspire your people with visions, while managers do the grunt work. This idea creates a lot of aspirations for leadership, naturally. Who wouldn't want to have all the fun and glory while keeping their hands clean? Conversely, who wants to tell people at a cocktail party, "My goal is to be a manager," in an era when the term has become almost pejorative?

This way of thinking is a fallacy, one that creates immense damage.

An organization can execute only if the leader's heart and soul are immersed in the company. Leading is more than thinking big, or schmoozing with investors and lawmakers, although those are part of the job. The leader has to be engaged personally and deeply in the business. Execution requires a comprehensive understanding of a business, its people, and its environment. The leader is the only person in a position to achieve that understanding. And only the leader can make execution happen, through his or her deep personal involvement in the substance and even the details of execution.

The leader must be in charge of getting things done by running the three core processes—picking other leaders, setting the strategic direction, and conducting operations. These actions are the substance of execution, and leaders cannot delegate them regardless of the size of the organization.

How good would a sports team be if the coach spent all his time in his office making deals for new players, while delegating actual coaching to an assistant? A coach is effective because he's constantly observing players individually and collectively on the field and in the locker room. That's how he gets to know his players and their capabilities, and how they get firsthand the benefit of his experience, wisdom, and expert feedback.

It's no different for a business leader. Only a leader can ask the tough questions that everyone needs to answer, then manage the process of debating the information and making the right trade-offs. And only the leader who's intimately engaged in the business can know enough to have the comprehensive view and ask the tough incisive questions.

Only the leader can set the tone of the dialogue in the organization. Dialogue is the core of culture and the basic unit of work. How people talk to each other absolutely determines how well the organization will function. Is the dialogue stilted, politicized, fragmented, and butt-covering? Or is it candid and reality-based, raising the right questions, debating them, and finding realistic solutions? If it's the former—as it is in all too many companies—reality will never come to the surface. If it is to be the latter, the leader has to be on the playing field with his management team, practicing it consistently and forcefully.

Specifically, the leader has to run the three core processes and has to run them with intensity and rigor.

Larry: When I appoint a new business manager, I call her into the office to discuss three issues. First, she is to behave with the highest integrity. This is an issue where there are no second chances—breach the rule, and you're out. Second, she must know that the customer comes first. And finally I say, "You've got to understand the three processes, for people, strategy, and operations, and you've got to manage these three processes. The more intensity and focus you put on them, the better you make this place. If you don't understand that, you've got no chance of succeeding here."

Companies that do these processes in depth fare dramatically better than those that just *think* they do. If your company doesn't do them in depth, you aren't getting what you deserve out of them. You put in a lot of time and effort and don't get useful output.

For example, everyone likes to say that people are the most important ingredient in their success. But they often hand off the job of assessing people and rewarding them to the HR staff, then rubber-stamp the recommendations at their reviews. Far too many leaders avoid debating about people openly in group settings. That's no way to lead. Only line leaders who know the people can make the right judgments. Good judgments come from practice and experience.

When things are running well, I spend 20 percent of my time on the people process. When I'm rebuilding an organization, it's 40 percent. I'm not talking about doing formal interviews or selecting staff; I mean really getting to know people. When I go out to visit a plant, I'll sit down for the first half hour with the manager. We'll have a discussion about the capability of his people, looking at who is performing well and who needs help. I'll go to a meeting of the whole staff and listen to what they have to say. Then I'll sit down after the meeting and talk about my impressions of the people and write a letter confirming the agreements made at the meeting. And I'll assess people's performance not just at our formal reviews but two or three times a year.

When we were putting these processes into place at AlliedSignal, one guy—a pretty good guy—said to me at a meeting, "You know, I've got to go through this people ritual again this year." I said, "That's the dumbest comment I've ever heard, because you tell the world how little you know about your job. If you really feel that way, you've got to do something else, because if you're not going to get good at this, you can't be successful." I didn't say it in front of everybody, but I thought to myself, *That just tells me maybe I've got the wrong guy.*

But he didn't do that again. I don't think he ever came to love the people process, but he did it, and he got something out of it. He got to know his staff and made it better.

Leaders often bristle when we say they have to run the three core processes themselves. "You're telling me to micromanage my people, and I don't do that," is a common response. Or, "It's not my style. I'm a hands-off leader. I delegate, I empower."

We agree completely that micromanaging is a big mistake. It diminishes people's self-confidence, saps their initiative, and stifles their ability to think for themselves. It's also a recipe for screwing things up—micromanagers rarely know as much about what needs to be done as the people they're harassing, the ones who actually do it.

But there's an enormous difference between leading an organization and presiding over it. The leader who boasts of her hands-off style or puts her faith in empowerment is not dealing with the issues of the day. She is not confronting the people responsible for poor performance, or searching for problems to solve and then making sure they get solved. She is presiding, and she's only doing half her job.

Leading for execution is not about micromanaging, or being "hands-on," or disempowering people. Rather, it's about active involvement—doing the things leaders should be doing in the first place. As you read on, you'll see how leaders who excel at execution immerse themselves in the substance of execution and even some of the key details. They use their knowledge of the business to constantly probe and question. They bring weaknesses to light and rally their people to correct them.

The leader who executes assembles an architecture of execution. He puts in place a culture and processes for executing, promoting people who get things done more quickly and giving them greater rewards. His personal involvement in that architecture is to assign the tasks and then follow up. This means making sure that people understand the priorities, which are based on his comprehensive understanding of the business, and asking incisive questions. The leader who executes often does not even have to tell people what to do; she asks questions so they can figure out what they need to do. In this way she coaches them, passing on her experience as a leader and educating them to think in ways they never thought before. Far from stifling people, this kind of leadership helps them expand their own capabilities for leading.

Jack Welch, Sam Walton, and Herb Kelleher of Southwest Airlines were powerful presences in their organizations. Just about everybody knew them, knew what they stood for, and knew what they expected of their people. Was it because of their forceful personalities? Yes, but a forceful personality doesn't mean anything by itself. "Chainsaw Al" Dunlap, the celebrated and outspoken champion of savage cost-cutting, had a forceful personality—and he wrecked the companies he was supposedly turning around.

Are leaders like Jack, Sam, and Herb good communicators? Again, yes, but. Communication can be mere boilerplate, or it can mean something. What counts is the substance of the communication and the nature of the person doing the communicating—including his or her ability to listen as well as to talk.

Maybe such people are good leaders because they practice "management by walking around." We've all read the stories about Herb or Sam popping up on the front lines to chat with baggage handlers or stockroom clerks. Sure, walking around is useful and important—but only if the leader doing the walking knows what to say and what to listen for.

Leaders of this ilk are powerful and influential presences because they *are* their businesses. They are intimately and intensely involved with their people and operations. They connect because they know the realities and talk about them. They're knowledgeable about the details. They're excited about what they're doing. They're passionate about getting results. This is not "inspiration" through exhortation or speechmaking. These leaders energize everyone by the example they set.

In his last year as GE's CEO, Jack Welch—as he had done for twenty years in the job—spent a week of ten-hour days reviewing the operating plans of the company's various units. He was intimately involved in the back-and-forth dialogue. Even at the end of his career, Jack wasn't presiding. He was leading by being actively involved.

Execution Has to Be in the Culture

It should be clear by now that execution isn't a program you graft onto your organization. A leader who says, "Okay, now we're going to execute for a change" is merely launching another fad of the month, with no staying power. Just as the leader has to be personally involved in execution, so must everyone else in the organization understand and practice the discipline.

Execution has to be embedded in the reward systems and in the norms of behavior that everyone practices. Indeed, as we will show in chapter 4, focusing on execution is not only an essential part of a business's culture, it is the one sure way to create meaningful cultural change.

One way to get a handle on execution is to think of it as akin to the Six Sigma processes for continual improvement. People practicing this methodology look for deviations from desired tolerances. When they find them, they move quickly to correct the problem. They use the processes to constantly raise the bar, improving quality and throughput. They use them collaboratively across units to improve how processes work across the organization. It's a relentless pursuit of reality, coupled with processes for constant improvement. And it's a huge change in behavior—a change, really, in culture.

Leaders who execute look for deviations from desired managerial tolerances—the gap between the desired and actual outcome in everything from profit margins to the selection of people for promotion. Then they move to close the gap and raise the bar still higher across the whole organization. Like Six Sigma, the discipline of execution doesn't work unless people are schooled in it and practice it constantly; it doesn't work if only a few people in the system practice it. Execution has to be part of an organization's culture, driving the behavior of all leaders at all levels.

Execution should begin with the senior leaders, but if you are not a senior leader, you can still practice it in your own organization. You build and demonstrate your own skills. The results will advance your career—and they may just persuade others in the business to do the same.

WHY PEOPLE DON'T GET IT

If execution is so important, why is it so neglected? To be sure, people in business aren't totally oblivious to it. But what they're mostly aware of is its absence. They know, deep down, that something is missing when decisions don't get made or followed through and when commitments don't get met. They search and struggle for answers, benchmarking companies that are known to deliver on their commitments, looking for the answers in the organizational structure or processes or culture. But they rarely apprehend the underlying lesson, because execution hasn't yet been recognized or taught as a discipline. They literally don't know what they're looking for.

The real problem is that *execution* just doesn't sound very sexy. It's the stuff a leader delegates. Do great CEOs and Nobel Prize winners achieve their glory through execution? Well, yes, in fact, and therein lies the grand fallacy.

The common view of intellectual challenge is only half true. What most people miss today is that intellectual challenge also includes the rigorous and tenacious work of developing and proving the ideas. Perhaps it's the result of the TV generation's upbringing, believing a mythology in which ideas develop instantly into full-blown outcomes.

There are different kinds of intellectual challenges. Conceiving a grand idea or broad picture is usually intuitive. Shaping the broad picture into a set of executable actions is analytical, and it's a huge intellectual, emotional, and creative challenge.

Nobel Prize winners succeed because they execute the details of a proof that other people can replicate, verify, or do something with. They test and discover patterns, connections, and linkages that nobody saw before. It took Albert Einstein more than a decade to develop the detailed proof explaining the theory of relativity. That was the execution—the details of proof in mathematical calculations. The theorem would not have been valid without the proof. Einstein could not have delegated this execution. It was an intellectual challenge that nobody else could meet.

The intellectual challenge of execution is in getting to the heart of an issue through persistent and constructive probing. Let's say a manager in the X division plans an 8 percent sales increase in the coming year, even though the market is flat. In their budget reviews, most leaders would accept the number without debate or discussion. But in an execution company's operating review, the leader will want to know if the goal is realistic. "Fine," she'll ask the manager, "but where will the increase come from? What products will generate the growth? Who will buy them, and what pitch are we going to develop for those customers? What will our competitor's reaction be? What will our milestones be?" If a milestone hasn't been reached at the end of the first quarter, it's a yellow light: something's not going as planned, and something will need to be changed.

If the leader has doubts about the organization's capacity to execute, she may drill down even further. "Are the right people in charge of getting it done," she may ask, "and is their accountability clear? Whose collaboration will be required, and how will they be motivated to collaborate? Will the reward system motivate them to a common objective?" In other words, the leader doesn't just sign off on a plan. She wants an explanation, and she will drill down until the answers are clear. Her leadership skills are such that everyone present is engaged in the dialogue, bringing everyone's viewpoint out into the open and assessing the degree and nature of buy-in. It's not simply an opportunity for her managers to learn from her and she from them; it's a way to diffuse the knowledge to everyone in the plan.

Suppose the issue is how to increase productivity. Other questions will be asked: "We have five programs in the budget, and you say we're going to save at least a couple million dollars on each one. What are the programs? Where is the money going to be saved? What's the timeline? How much is it going to cost us to achieve it? And who is responsible for it all?"

Organizations don't execute unless the right people, individually and collectively, focus on the right details at the right time. For you as a leader, moving from the concept to the critical details is a long journey. You have to review a wide array of facts and ideas, the permutations and combinations of which can approach infinity. You have to discuss what risks to take, and where. You have to thread through these details, selecting those that count. You have to assign them to the people who matter, and make sure which key ones must synchronize their work.

Such decision making requires knowledge of the business and the external environment. It requires the ability to make fine judgments about people—their capabilities, their reliability, their strengths, and their weaknesses. It requires intense focus and incisive thinking. It requires superb skills in conducting candid, realistic dialogue. This work is as intellectually challenging as any we know of.

Leadership without the discipline of execution is incomplete and ineffective. Without the ability to execute, all other attributes of leadership become hollow.

o   o   o

Larry Bossidy is chairman and former CEO of Honeywell International. Previously he was chairman and CEO of AlliedSignal and COO of General Electric Credit.

Ram Charan is an adviser to CEOs and senior executives in companies ranging from start-ups to the *Fortune* 500.

Charles Burck is a writer and editor; previously he was an editor for *Fortune* magazine.

Chapter Twenty-Eight

Change:
The Capacity of Life

Margaret J. Wheatley

We live in a time of great stirring storms, both natural and human-made. Disruptive elements seem to be afoot, gathering strength in air masses that spiral over oceans or in decisions that swirl through the halls of power. The daily news is filled with powerful changes, and many of us feel buffeted by forces we cannot control. It was from this place of feeling battered and bruised that I listened one night to a radio interview with a geologist whose specialty was beaches and shorelines. The interview was being conducted as a huge hurricane was pounding the Outer Banks of the eastern United States. The geologist had studied the Outer Banks for many years and was speaking fondly about their unique geological features. He was waiting for the storm to abate so he could get out and take a look at the hurricane's impact. The interviewer asked: "What do you expect to find when you go out there?" Like the interviewer, I assumed he would present a litany of disasters—demolished homes, felled trees, eroded shoreline. But he surprised me. "I expect," he said calmly, "to find a new beach."

Since that night, I have pondered what it would take for me and my colleagues to bring his clarity to our own work, to understand that this world changes, to be curious about newness. We live in the same world as this geologist, but in the organizations that I work in, change is a feared enemy. Hurricanes, organizational crises, sudden accidents—these are terrible forces that can destroy the deliberate, incremental progress we're all working hard to achieve. We haven't thought that we might *work with the forces of change*. We act quite the opposite; we need to manage change and keep it under control every cautious step of the way. And we think we're being helpful to others when we manage change so carefully, because we believe that people don't like change. Strangely, we assert that it's a particular characteristic of the human species to resist change, even though we're surrounded by tens of millions of other species that demonstrate wonderful capacities to grow, adapt, and change.

Our ideas and sensibilities about change come from the world of Newton. We treat a problematic organization as if it was a machine that had broken down. We use reductionism to diagnose the problem; we expect to find a simple, singular cause for our woes. We sift through all the possible causes of failure, searching for that one broken part—a bad manager, a dysfunctional team, a poor business unit. To repair the organization, all we need to do is replace the faulty part and gear back up to operate at predetermined performance levels.

This is the standard approach to organizational change. It is derived from the best engineering thinking. I believe this approach explains why the majority of organizational change efforts fail. Senior corporate leaders report that up to 75% of their change projects do not yield the promised results. This is a shocking failure rate, but how can we expect anything better until we stop treating organizations as machines?

We also display the influence of Newton when we define the size and scope of our change projects. We think we need to develop sufficient mass to counteract the organization's material weight. In classical physics, mass is important. An object's force is equal to two factors, its mass and its acceleration. We act on this law; if we are trying to change a large organization, we either need large change projects, where the force of our efforts equals the organization's mass, or smaller projects that have a lot of speed. Whichever strategy we choose, we worry about how to influence the organization's *physical size*.

But when we encounter life's processes for change, we enter a new world. We move from billiard balls banging into one another to effect change, to networks that change because of information they find meaningful. We stop dealing with mass and work with energy. We discard mechanistic practices, and learn from the behavior of living systems. New change dynamics become evident.

The new sciences are filled with tantalizing and hopeful processes that foster change. But to learn these lessons, we need to shift what we look for. Many of the reformulations of new science came from just such a shift: Scientists learned to look past an object or thing to the invisible level of dynamic processes. Laying aside the machine metaphor, with its static mechanisms and separated parts, scientists saw something new. They saw the underlying processes that give rise to innumerable and different life forms. They developed answers to explain how life is capable of so much change, so much newness. Some expressed awe and humility as they encountered the unstoppable resiliency of life. Some became poets, reaching for new language to describe their encounters with life's boundless creativity.

I am hopeful that we non-scientists can now make a similar shift. Surrounded by creativity expressed as unending diversity, living in a world proficient at change, which maintains its resiliency through change, I hope we can begin to work with these powers rather than seeking to control or deny them. But the shifts required of us are enormous; they lead us into lands that are foreign and uncharted in Western thought.

The first great shift is this. A system is composed of parts, but we cannot understand a system by looking only at its parts. We need to *work with the whole of a system*, even as we work with individual parts or isolated problems. From a systems consciousness, we understand that no problem or behavior can be understood in isolation. We must account for dynamics operating in the whole system that are displaying themselves in these individual moments. In earlier chapters, I described what this new orientation revealed in both quantum physics and chaos theory. When scientists shifted their vision from the parts to the whole, what looked like chaos revealed inherent order; a chaotic system displayed itself in a strange attractor. What seemed like an aberration of Newtonian laws became lawful; paired electrons refused to act individually and exhibited their inseparable wholeness across vast distances. A systems world cannot be understood by looking only at discrete events or individuals.

But learning to observe the whole of a system is difficult. Our traditional analytic skills can't help us. Analysis narrows our field of awareness and actually prevents us from seeing the total system. We move deeper into the details and farther away from learning how to comprehend the system in its wholeness. Hans-Peter Dürr, former director of the Max Planck Institute, once remarked to me, "There is no analytic language to describe what we are seeing at the quantum level. I can only say that it does not help to analyze things in more detail. The more specific the information, the less relevant it is."

If we can't analyze wholeness, how then do we learn to know it? This is a question that has occupied philosophers and some scientists for many centuries. They each describe new ways of understanding, but their answers feel insufficient. They fail to provide the precise, analytic techniques we think we need to understand anything. I frequently get frustrated by the realization that to perceive the world differently requires new perceptual techniques. We can't move past analysis by being analytic. But if I can't use my traditional ways of knowing, how can I even know enough about a new phenomenon to acknowledge that I need new ways of knowing? (So if you feel frustrated by the following descriptions, I believe this indicates you're making progress.)

As I have struggled to understand a system as a system, I have been drawn to move past cognition into the realm of sensation. The German philosopher Martin Heidegger describes this as a "dwelling consciousness." When we dwell with a group or a problem, we move quietly into our senses, away from our sharpened analytic skills. Now I allow myself to pick up impressions, to notice how something feels, to sit with a group or with a report and call upon my intuition. I try to encourage myself and others to look for images, words, patterns that surface as we focus on an issue. (The Army has been aware that intuition plays a role in their effectiveness; a few years ago, they began studying "commander intuition.")

The great scientist, philosopher, and poet of the early nineteenth century, Johann von Goethe, applied his genius to the problem of seeing the wholeness of nature. He was intrigued to understand any phenomenon not as an isolated event, but as a consequence of its *relationship* to other phenomena. In traditional science, the scientist invents the questions and then interrogates the object of study. But Goethe describes how we can move from interrogation to receptivity, being open to what is occurring, allowing ourselves to be influenced by a whole that we cannot see. We can dwell with the phenomenon and feel how it makes itself known to us.

Goethe describes several ways to sense the whole, and I am particularly challenged by one of his processes—that we can discover the whole by going further into its parts. While this sounds like good old-fashioned reductionism, it is quite different. We inquire into the part as we hold the recognition that it is participating in a whole system. We hold our attention at two levels simultaneously. We recognize that this one thing we are studying is only there because of the rest of the universe.[1] We can understand the whole by noting how it is influencing things at this local level. This manner of thinking, while difficult to grasp for a Western mind, is familiar in Buddhist belief, as illustrated in this brief teaching story:

> All things depend on all other things for their existence. Take, for example, this leaf. . . . Earth, water, heat, sea, tree, clouds, sun, time, space—all these elements have enabled this leaf to come into existence. If just one of these elements was missing, the leaf could not exist. All beings rely on the law of dependent co-arising. The source of one thing is all things.[2]

To study a problem from this sensibility requires us to explore the relationship between the part and the whole, but not to confuse them as identical or interchangeable. This is a different exploration than looking at a system for its fractal patterns or holographic images; in that search, we would look at the part as a miniature version of the whole. Instead, here we look intently at the part in order to see the dynamics operating in the whole system. The part is not the whole, but it can lead us there.

Mostly we don't take time to notice the dynamics that are moving in the whole system, creating effects everywhere. As good engineers, we've been trained to identify the problem part and replace it. But a systems sensibility quickly explains why this repair approach most often fails. Individual behaviors co-evolve as individuals interact with system dynamics. If we want to change individual or local behaviors, we have to tune into these system-side influences. We have to use what is going on in the whole system to understand individual behavior, and we have to inquire into individual behavior to learn about the whole.

Although we've all been trained in reductionist modes of analysis, many people in organizations know firsthand that studying problems in detailed isolation doesn't yield the promised improvements and changes. When I've asked "If we were to solve all the individual problems, every one of them, would this fix the organization?" most people reply "No." Clearly, they understand that there are other forces at work, holding the organization in its troubled state. They may not be able to name them, but they know that they're there.

Seeing the interplay between system dynamics and individuals is a dance of discovery that requires several iterations between the whole and its parts. We expand our vision to see the whole, then narrow our gaze to peer intently into individual moments. With each iteration, we see more of the whole, and gain new understandings about individual elements. We paint a portrait of the whole, surfacing as much detail as possible. Then we inquire into a few pivotal events or decisions, and search for great detail there also. We keep dancing between the two levels, bringing the sensitivities and information gleaned from one level to help us understand the other. If we hold awareness of the whole as we study the part, and understand the part in its relationship to the whole, profound new insights become available.

There are many processes for developing awareness of a whole system—a time line of some slice of the system's history, a mind-map, a collage of images, a dramatization. Any process works that encourages nonlinear thinking and intuition, and uses alternative forms of expression such as drama, art, stories, and pictures. The critical task is to evoke our senses, not just our gray matter. We learn to dwell in multilevel phenomena simultaneously and let our senses lead us to new ways of comprehending.

In one corporation, a business unit wanted to know why they failed to secure a major contract. First, they developed a time line of all the events and decisions they could recall. Everybody had to participate; no one person knew the whole story. (The time line ended up being more than thirty feet long.) Everyone reviewed it, developing a rudimentary sense of the whole system that had resulted in this business failure. Next, the whole group defined which decisions, among the many displayed, felt most critical. They then went into small groups, each group exploring in depth one of those decisions. But because they had started with the whole, their search to understand the parts was already different. Each group then brought its analysis of single decisions back to the whole time line. It became instantly clear that similar patterns of behavior characterized each of these decisions. The whole was revealing its dynamics in each event, but no one would have seen these patterns had they not been aware of the whole. After another iteration of going deeply into different parts of the experience and bringing these back to the whole, a few dynamics stood out clearly. The real work of change came into focus: how to shift those dynamics.

This kind of work must involve the whole group. The whole must go in pursuit of itself; there is no other way to learn who they are. But as people engage together to learn more about their collective identity, it affects them as individuals in a surprising way. They are able to see how their personal patterns and behaviors contribute to the whole. The surprise is that they then take responsibility for changing themselves.

It's important to note that the motivation for individual change is not in response to a boss's demand or a personal need for self-improvement. A larger context has emerged because of this collaborative process, and it is this context that motivates people to change. They have developed a deeper awareness of the work, not of personalities or particular parts of the organization. They want *the work* to be more effective, and they now see how they individually can better contribute to that outcome.

If the first shift challenges us to think differently about parts and wholes, the second shift focuses us on the organizing dynamics of a living system. The organization of a living system bears no resemblance to organization charts. Life uses networks; we still rely on boxes. But even as we draw our boxes, people are ignoring them and organizing as life does, through networks of relationships. To become effective at change, we must leave behind the *imaginary organization* we design and learn to work with the *real organization*, which will always be a dense network of interdependent relationships.

The new science keeps reminding us that in this participative universe, nothing living lives alone. Everything comes into form because of relationship. We are constantly called to be in relationship—to information, people, events, ideas, life. Even reality is created through our participation in relationships. We choose what to notice; we relate to certain things and ignore others. Through these chosen relationships, we co-create our world.

If we are interested in effecting change, it is crucial to remember that we are working with these webs of relations, not with machines. Once we recognize that organizations are webs, there is much we can learn about organizational change just from contemplating spider webs. Most of us have had the experience of touching a spider web, feeling its resiliency, noticing how slight pressure in one area jiggles the entire web. If a web breaks and needs repair, the spider doesn't cut out a piece, terminate it, or tear the entire web apart and reorganize it. *She reweaves it*, using the silken relationships that are already there, creating stronger connections across the weakened spaces.

The most profound strategy for changing a living network comes from biology, although we could learn it directly from a spider. If a system is in trouble, it can be restored to health by connecting it to more of itself. To make a system stronger, we need to create stronger relationships. This principle has taught me that I can have faith in the system. The system is capable of solving its own problems. The solutions the system needs are usually already present in it. If a system is suffering, this indicates that it lacks sufficient access to itself. It might be lacking information, it might have lost clarity about who it is, it might have troubled relationships, it might be ignoring those who have valuable insights.

To bring health to a system, connect it to more of itself. The primary change strategy becomes quite straightforward. In order to change, *the system needs to learn more about itself from itself.* The system needs processes to bring it together. Many different processes will work, whatever facilitates self-discovery and creates new relationships simultaneously. The whole system eventually must be involved in doing this work; it can't be done by outside experts or small teams.

My colleagues and I focus on helping a system develop greater self-knowledge in three critical areas. People need to be connected to the fundamental *identity* of the organization or community. Who are we? Who do we aspire to become? How shall we be together? And people need to be connected to *new information.* What else do we need to know? Where is this new information to be found? And people need to be able to reach past traditional boundaries and develop *relationships* with people anywhere in the system. Who else needs to be here to do this work with us?

As a system inquires into these three domains of identity, information, and relationships, it becomes more self-aware. It has become more connected to the truth of who it is, more connected to its environment and customers, more connected to people everywhere in the system. These new connections develop greater capacity; the system becomes healthier.

There are many stories of increased organizational effectiveness gained from creating new connections in these three domains, although frequently even the implementers seem not to understand the source of their success. For example, in the very best quality programs, employees were first connected to a new identity or meaning for their work, such as exceptional customer service or the design of highly productive work processes. New statistical tools gave these employees new information about their work. They could use this to achieve and often surpass the new standards they had set for themselves. Participative problem-solving processes and self-managed teams facilitated workers' connecting with one another and sharing expertise. Just as important were the new connections with customers and suppliers—those formerly estranged from the system were invited inside to contribute.

The novelist E. M. Forster said "Just connect." But of course, it's not quite that simple. We have all been to many events and meetings that offered great opportunity for people to connect with each other, yet nothing happened. People didn't step forward to find one another, nothing significant was discussed, everyone hid in their own boxes waiting to be coaxed out.

These bad parties and boring meetings illustrate the next shift to consider as we learn to work with life's capacity for change. Any living thing will change only if it *sees change as the means of preserving itself.*

All life lives in the midst of an unending stream of data. How do we select what to pay attention to from so much noise? We use the lens of self. We, like all life, choose what to notice because of who we are. We use the process of *self-reference.* We are free to choose, but we choose on the basis of self. This process is essential for all life and, if repressed or denied, the organism dies. Self-reference explains *why* any living system is motivated to change. It will change to stay the same.

In humans, self-reference becomes more complex because of capacities that differentiate us from most other species. We possess consciousness and are capable of reflection. We are able to think about a past and a future. No longer anchored to just the present moment, we can dream about what we want, and imbue events with meaning. We still see the world through a self, but to this self has been added the dimensions of time and meaning.

It's hard to look at modern life and see our capacities for reflection or meaning-making. We don't use our gifts to be more aware or thoughtful. We're driven in the opposite direction. Things move too fast for us to reflect, demanding tasks give us no time to think, and we barely notice the lack of meaning until forced to stand still by illness, tragedy, or job loss. But in spite of our hurry, we cannot stop life's dynamic of self-reference or the human need for meaning. If we want to influence any change, anywhere, we need to work with this powerful process rather than deny its existence. We need to understand that all change results from a change in meaning. Meaning is created by the process of self-reference. We change only if we decide that the change is meaningful to who we are. Will it help us become who we want to be? Or gain us more of what we think we need to preserve ourselves?

From becoming attuned to this dynamic, I've come to believe that both individual and organizational change start from the same place. People need to explore an issue sufficiently to *decide whether new meaning is available and desirable.* They will change only if they believe that a new insight, a new idea, or a new form helps them become more of who they are. If the work of change is at the level of an entire organization or community, then the search for new meaning must be done as a collective inquiry.

To put this realization into practice has required significant changes on my part. Now my first desire with a group is to learn who they are, what self they are referencing. I can never learn this by listening to some self-reports, or taking the word of a few people. I discover who they are by noticing what's meaningful to them as they are engaged in their work. What issues and behaviors get their attention? What topics generate the most energy, positive and negative? I have to be curious to discover these answers. And I have to be *working with them*, not sitting on the side observing behavior or interviewing individuals. In the process of doing actual work, the real identity of the group, not some fantasy image, always becomes visible.

There's another aspect to this work that is important to me. I assume that even in the presence of a group or collective identity, there are as many different interpretations as there are people in the group. I assume I will discover multiple and divergent interpretations for everything that occurs. So I try to put ideas and issues on the table as experiments to discover these different meanings, not as my recommendations for what *should* be meaningful. I try to stay open to the different reactions I get, rather than instantly categorizing people as resistors or allies (although this is not always easy). I expect diverse responses; gradually, I'm even learning to welcome them. It has been fascinating to notice how many interpretations the different members of a group can give to the same event. I am both astonished and confident that, as quantum theory and biology teach, no two people see the world exactly the same.

However you do it, discovering what is meaningful to a person, group, or organization is the first essential task. We discover this by looking into our actual, day-to-day work. It doesn't help to go off and talk about meaning or behaviors in the abstract. We need to be able to see what we are doing as we are doing it; this is where the true learning is. To develop this "observer self" requires practice, curiosity, and patience.

But as we engage in this process of exploring diverse interpretations and learning to observe our patterns, oftentimes we discover a unifying energy that makes the work of change possible. If we discover an issue whose significance we share with others, those others are transformed into colleagues. If we recognize a shared sense of injustice or a common dream, magical things happen to people. Past hurts and negative histories get left behind. People step forward to work together. We don't hang back, we don't withdraw, we don't wait to be enticed. We seek each other out, eager to discover who else might help. The call of the problem sounds louder than past grievances or our fears of failure. We have found something important to work on, and, because we want to make a difference, we figure out how to do the work, together.

I've come to appreciate that real change happens in personal behaviors, or at larger scale in entire organizations, only when we take time to discover this sense of what's worthy of our shared attention. We don't accept an organizational redesign because a leader tells us it is necessary. We choose to accept it if, and only if, we see how this new design enables us to contribute more to what we've defined as meaningful. And we don't accept diversity because we've been told it's the right thing to do. Only as we're engaged together in work that is meaningful do we learn to work through the differences and value them. Change becomes much easier when we focus first on creating a meaning for the work that can embrace us all. Held by this rich center of meaning, we let go of many other grievances and work around traditional hindrances.

I've worked with some college faculties torn apart by the availability of technology. The more technologically eager faculty accuse the reticent ones of being out-of-date and resistant to change—they berate their colleagues for not climbing on the technology bandwagon. I always suggest that a different conversation is needed. What if we stop assuming that technology's value to a teacher is self-evident? What if we stop assuming that anybody who doesn't adopt new technology is an antiquated Luddite whose only interest is to stop the march of progress? If we give up those assumptions, we can begin a different conversation, one that helps us connect to one another and learn more about how we each see the world. We can step back from the technology issue and ask one another what called us into teaching. We can listen to the aspirations that are voiced. What we will hear is that most of us went into teaching for noble purposes—we wanted to make a difference in the lives of students and to advance human wisdom.

If we have this conversation *first*, we can discover one another as colleagues. *Then* we are ready to talk about technology. How might computers assist a professor to become more effective at his or her craft? How might technology make it easier to do the work they have defined as meaningful? If those links are made between professional purpose and technical tools, more colleagues will log on to e-mail, and use the computers sitting on their desks.

This process of inquiring into the meaning of our work helps us move past the labeling behavior so common these days. We are quick to assign people to a typology and then dismiss them, as if we really knew who they were. And our frantic need to implement changes we know are crucial to our organization's survival leads us to grasp for scapegoats. We know we'd be successful if it weren't for all those "resistors," those stubborn and scared colleagues who reject anything new. (We label ourselves also, but more generously, as "early adopters" or "cultural creatives.")

In our crazed haste, we don't have time to be curious about who a person is, or why they're behaving as they do. But when we dwell in the meaning we each ascribe to our work, we might discover common issues and problems that we both deem significant. Then change becomes possible. We move past the labels and notice another human being wants to make some small contribution to something we care about. We discard the divisive categories and want to work together. How else but through our joining can we create the change we both want to see in the world?

Meaningful information lights up a network and moves through it like a windswept brushfire. Meaningless information, in contrast, smolders at the gates until somebody dumps cold water on it. The capacity of a network to communicate with itself is truly awe inspiring; its transmission capability far surpasses any other mode of communication. But a living network will transmit only *what it decides is meaningful.* I have watched information move instantaneously across great distances in a global company; I have watched information in four-color graphics die before it ever came off the printer. To use a network's communication capacity, we must notice that its transmission power is directly linked to the meaningfulness of the information.

From witnessing how networks can communicate around the world with information they deem essential, I've come to believe that "preaching to the choir" is exactly the right thing to do. If I can help those who already share certain beliefs and dreams sing their song a little clearer, a little more confidently, I know they will take that song back to their networks. I don't have to touch everybody; I just have to support those first courageous voices and encourage them to put it out on their own airwaves. Soon large populations in diverse places will have heard the song because someone in their network had their voice amplified by meeting the choir. We gain courage from learning we're part of a choir. We sing better when we know we're not alone.

Nothing described by Newtonian physics has prepared us to work with the behavior of living networks. We were taught that change occurs in increments, one person at a time. We not only had to design the steps; we also had to take into account the size of the change object. The force of our efforts had to equal the weight of what we were attempting to change. But now we know something different. We're working with networks, not billiard balls. We don't have to push and pull a system, or bully it to change; we have to participate with colleagues in discovering what's important to us. Then we feed that into our different networks to see if our networks agree.

In working with networks, size is not the issue. The same fundamental dynamics are always at work in any living system, no matter how small or large. Self-reference and meaning-making never cease; therefore, change is always possible through those processes. Of course, people in different locations or levels of an organization will have interpretations and dynamics specific to them. But the work of change is always the same. We need to find ways to get their attention; we need to discover what's meaningful to them. Size doesn't matter, but meaning does.

As we contemplate how networks change themselves, it helps to remember that we are working with energy, not matter. Energy behaves differently than matter. It fills the universe, possibly traveling many times faster than the speed of light. It moves through invisible media and connections. Meaning has many of the qualities of energy. It doesn't exist in physical form anywhere. We make it up as we self-reference our way through life. Since it doesn't exist in material form, it too is not subject to the laws that govern matter. Its behavior can't be explained by Newtonian physics.

The energetic nature of meaning is another reason to give up organizational change strategies that are based on Newtonianism and the manipulation of discrete pieces. Matter doesn't matter. We can stop striving to achieve critical mass, we can let go of the need for programs that roll out (or over) the entire organization, we can abandon the need to train every individual, we can stop feeling thwarted if we don't get the support of the top of the organization. Instead, we can work locally, finding the meaning-rich ideas and processes that create energy in one area of the system. If we succeed in generating energy in one area, then we can watch what our networks do with our work. Who lit up and took notice? Where have our ideas traveled to? If we answer these questions, we learn who might be ready to take up this work next. My partner, Myron Kellner-Rogers, describes his approach to organizational change as "I start anywhere and follow it everywhere."

In this chapter, I've described what I believe to be the primary processes of life that facilitate change. If we are to ally ourselves with these processes and life's extraordinary capacity for change, there is one last essential shift in our thinking. Although we see change at the material level, it is caused by processes that are immaterial. We must look for these *invisible processes rather than the things that they engender.* From the early Greek Heraclitus to the most recent thinking in science, life is described as a process, a process of becoming.[3] When scientists look behind the physical manifestations, or peer into the emptiness of space or cells, they see what had gone unnoticed—the processes that give rise to forms. Similar work is now required of us in organizations. We must look behind the things of organizations to work with the processes that gave them birth.

This shift in orientation requires many new practices, some of which I've indicated or described. But the greatest challenge for me lies not in adopting any one new method, but in learning generally to live in a process world. It's a completely new way to be. Life demands that I participate with things as they unfold, to expect to be surprised, to honor the mystery of it, and to see what emerges. These were difficult lessons to learn. I was well-trained to create things—plans, events, measures, programs. I invested more than half my life in trying to make the world conform to what I thought was best for it. It's not easy to give up the role of master creator and move into the dance of life.

But what is the alternative, for me or you? Our dance partner insists that we put ourselves in motion, that we learn to live with instability, chaos, change, and surprise. We can continue to stand immobilized on the shoreline, trying to protect ourselves from life's insistent gales, or we can begin moving. We can mourn the erosion of our plans, or we can set out to discover something new.

Morihei Ueshiba, the founder of the martial art of Aikido, was a small man who could turn back the onslaughts of opponents many times his weight and size with movements that were imperceptible. He appeared to be perfectly centered, anchored to the ground in an extraordinary way. But this was not the case. His ability came not from superior balance, but from superb levels of self-awareness. As he described it, he was quicker to notice when he was off-balance, and faster at returning to center.

He perfectly describes how to move in harmony with life rather than to resist it. First, we must know what "center" feels like. We must know who we are, our patterns of behavior, our values, our intentions. The ground of our identity and experience must feel familiar to us; we must know what it feels like to be standing in it. But we don't expect that we will be perfectly balanced in that center all the time. We know that we will drift into the wrong activities or be thrown off-balance by life's chaos. But we also will recognize when we've moved off too far, and will be able to recall ourselves more quickly to who we want to be.

Ueshiba Sensei also highlights a quality of attention—we must keep participating in the moment. The changing nature of life insists that we stop hiding behind our plans or measures and give more attention to what is occurring right in front of us, right now. We need to become curious about what's going on, what just happened. The present moment overflows with information about ourselves and our environment. But most of those learnings fly by unobserved because we're preoccupied with our images of how we want the world to be.

Being present in the moment doesn't mean that we act without intention or flow directionless through life without any plans. But we would do better to attend more carefully to *the process* by which we create our plans and intentions. We need to see these plans, standards, organization charts not as objects that we complete, but as processes that enable a group to keep clarifying its intent and strengthening its connections to new people and new information. We need less reverence for the objects we create, and much more attention to the processes we use to create them. Healthy processes create better relationships among us, more clarity about who we are, and more information about what's going on around us. With these new connections, we grow healthier. We develop greater capacity to know what to do. We weave together an organization as resilient and flexible as a spider's web.

As we learn to live and work in this process world, we are rewarded with other changes in our behavior. I believe we become gentler people. We become more curious about differences, more respectful of one another, more open to life's surprises. It's not that we become either more hopeful or pessimistic, but we do become more patient and accepting. I like to believe we change in this way because we are willing to move into the dance. Although it looked frantic from the outside, difficult to learn and impossible to master, our newfound gentleness speaks to a different learning. Life is a good partner. Its demands are not unreasonable. A great capacity for change lives in every one of us.

o   o   o

Margaret J. Wheatley is a consultant and speaker, professor at Cambridge College and Brigham Young University's Marriott School of Management, and president of the Berkana Institute, a global charitable foundation.

Chapter Twenty-Nine

The Fear of Change and Why Risk Is Necessary

Robert E. Quinn

I once worked with a top management team of a very large company. I came to know the individuals very well. They were bright, honest, sincere, and hardworking. In an effort to improve their organization, they had decided to send all the senior people to a well-known seminar on quality. These executives, upon returning from the enlightening seminar, decided to implement the ideas in their organization. Together they developed a reasonable plan and initiated the change effort.

A short time later, while we were doing some strategic planning, the team made numerous references to the new quality philosophy. They were making assumptions that quality, morale, productivity, and profit would all improve because of the new philosophy. They listed the alterations in behavior and productivity they expected to see in each area of the company.

They were planning the future of their company around the premise that these significant changes would happen.

Upon hearing their comments, I shared with them a story that was told to me by a vice-president at another company. Three years before, that company had sent all its senior executives to the same seminar. They also anticipated that their new plan would yield dramatic improvements in quality, morale, productivity, and profit. However, three years later, they found that their immense effort had little, if any, impact.

Given the sizable investment they had already made, the executives were transfixed by my story. They waited anxiously for an explanation of the failure. Almost in unison they asked, "Why did it fail?" Instead of explaining, I asked them to tell me why it failed.

A long, heavy silence fell in the room. Finally, one of the most influential members of the group said, "The leaders of the company didn't change their behavior." I nodded and pointed out that they themselves had made a lot of assumptions about the behavior that was going to change in others. Now I challenged them: "Identify one time when one of you said that you were going to change your behavior."

Again there was a long pause. Something important and unusual was happening. The members of this group were suddenly seeing something that few people ever clearly see—the incongruity of asking for change in others while failing to exhibit the same level of commitment in themselves.

Since they expressed a sincere desire to change their organization, they asked me for advice. I described some simple practices that had succeeded for others. These practices would give them the tools they needed to change their stagnant patterns and systems. They were quiet for a time—a time of quiet terror and inner reflection. It was as if they were standing at the edge of a very dangerous cliff and peeking over. They decided to adjourn and think about the issues.

It is tempting to belittle these people. How dare they exhibit such arrogance? Though we may be tempted to condemn these managers, we should first reflect on what we would do in similar situations. We regularly exhibit the same behavior. In confronting life's problems, we readily see the shortcomings of others and how these shortcomings contribute to the problem at hand. The problem is always caused by the boss, peer, subordinate, spouse, child, schoolteacher, or some other person.

We cannot easily recognize that the problem is part of the system in which we play an active role. Our first inclination is always from a perspective that externalizes the problem, keeps it somewhere "out there." Because the problem is out there, it is always others who need to change. Our first thought is to tell them to change. Our second is to force them. Painful experience tells us that this route is usually less than successful and often disastrous, producing undesirable and unproductive results.

TELLING, COERCING, AND THE CHECKLIST MENTALITY

Years ago, I developed a simple role play. In this role play, two volunteers are asked to come forward. They are given a brief description of their roles. They are spouses who experienced a whirlwind courtship and have just returned from their honeymoon. After a wonderful breakfast, the wife leans back and lights up a cigarette. Since meeting his wife, the man has had but one reservation, her smoking. He decides that he can no longer suppress his concern.

At this point, I ask the husband to begin a conversation with his beloved. The dynamics are very predictable. The husband tells the wife that her smoking is a problem. She grows defensive and angry. He resorts to factual information and reports that there is a scientific link between smoking and cancer. She rebuffs this argument. Then he brings up the issue of commitment and intimate relationships, in some way suggesting that their marriage may not survive. She usually agrees.

Life is full of situations in which we would very much like another person to change behavior. We want our neighbors to not impinge on our rights. We want our child to not leave the bike in the middle of the driveway. We want our mother to stop interfering. We want people who work for us to have more of a sense of urgency.

In our attempts to address such problem situations, we usually begin by simply telling these persons what the problem is and how they might change. When the change is small or clearly to their liking, this strategy tends to work. In most cases, however, it fails. The other persons have little interest in responding to our need. If the issue at hand really matters, we then turn to coercion, often suggesting or making some kind of threat. Like a criminal with a pointed gun, we can get, for a short while, the behavior change we desire, but it is unlikely to last, and the long-term relationship tends to be damaged.

In organizations, I watch managers engage in the strategy of change by telling. The manager knows that the people in the organization should make some important change, so this item goes on their "to do" list. At the appropriate time, the manager gives a speech or writes a memo instructing people to change.

The manager then places a check next to the item on the "to do" list. The change has been implemented. What more can be expected?

Weeks or months later, signals begin to emerge suggesting that the requested change has not taken place. Usually the manager chooses to ignore these signals. Sometimes, however, the pressure for the change is too high and the problem cannot be neglected. Next the manager will usually resort to coercion. This results in short-term compliance and long-term resistance. The common result is for the change effort to fail.

It is striking to me that so many new programs that initiate change in organizations fail. It is also striking that once a change effort fails, the effort tends to be ignored. These failures are seldom analyzed. Such analysis would be too painful. As a result, little learning takes place.

When we experience failure, it is natural to externalize the problem—to blame some factor that was outside our control. Once in a while this actually does happen. But I have seldom heard anyone say, "The change didn't happen because I failed to model the change process for everyone. I failed to reinvent myself. It was a failure of courage on my part."

One key to successful leadership is continuous personal change. Personal change is a reflection of our inner growth and empowerment. Empowered leaders are the only ones who can induce real change. They can forcefully communicate at a level beyond telling. By having the courage to change themselves, they model the behavior they are asking of others. Clearly understood by almost everyone, this message, based in integrity, is incredibly powerful. It builds trust and credibility and helps others confront the risk of empowering themselves.

At the personal level, the key to successful living is continuous personal change. Personal change is the way to avoid slow death. When we are continually growing, we have an internal sense of meaning and impact. We are full of energy and radiate a successful demeanor. To have such feelings in a continually changing environment, we must continually realign ourselves with our environment. This requires that we do an unnatural thing—that we exercise the discipline to take an unusual perspective.

Taking the Third Perspective First

A friend of mine, Michael Jibson, tells a story about taking his family to the San Francisco Zoo. Soon after arriving at the zoo, the family walked into a playground area. Michael's smallest son dearly loved playgrounds, particularly the swings. The boy quickly raced over, jumped into a swing, and began pumping himself skyward.

After a short time, the other children were ready to move on. The youngest, however, was still happily swinging. The siblings tried to persuade him to leave but were unsuccessful. The boy's mother tried a more caring approach, but she, too, failed miserably. The other children then began to complain loudly. A drama was emerging, and strangers were stopping to watch. Michael's wife looked at him, her unspoken message clear: "You are the father of this child. Do something!"

Michael, having been to the zoo before, knew that around the corner was a carousel. He also knew that the boy loved carousals even more than he loved the swings. So Michael explained that there was a carousel around the corner and that the youngster would be even happier there.

Nearly any experienced parent can predict what happened next. The boy was unmoved by the fatherly logic. Michael's frustration peaked, and persuasion turned to threat. Finally, the boy was dragged, kicking and squealing, from the swing and continued to protest until the family arrived at the carousel. Suddenly his eyes grew large with excitement. His tears disappeared as he mounted a wooden horse and smiled and waved to his parents.

We can reflect on this story from at least three perspectives. First, we can take the uninvolved perspective of the passing stranger. We can shake our heads in judgment of the parents who failed to perform their roles without resorting to force. The perspective is that of the distant, analytical observer, of the uninvolved judge, of the Monday morning quarterback. In our own lives, we slip into this perspective easily and often.

Second, we could take the perspective of the two loving but frustrated parents who were struggling to make an intervention in a real situation. The perspective of the responsible actor, trying to make change in the world, is a challenge for the ages. At the conceptual and emotional levels, we often aspire to it. From the perspective of observed actor, we often consciously or unconsciously flee from it. Here we often, like the parents in the story, experience frustration and failure.

Finally, there is the perspective of the self-centered little boy holding tightly to his swing. Our first temptation is to argue that for mature adults such as ourselves, that is too big a stretch and hardly worth consideration. This is, of course, a rationalization to protect us from considering the most painful perspective of all: one of the last things we want to consider is our own selfishness and immaturity. We resist reflecting on our own fear of change. Yet the truth is that we are exactly like the immature and selfish boy who refuses to leave the swing.

The problem is that to grow, to take the journeys on which our growth is predicated, we must confront our own immaturity, selfishness, and lack of courage. In a sense, life is all about our forceful, often overpowering need to take journeys, yet our tendency is to grip the swings ever more tightly. The decisions we make about our journeys determine how our self is aligned with our surrounding environment.

Why Risk Is Necessary

There was a company that gave a critical product introduction assignment to a plant manager. The new product was a key element in the company's overall corporate strategy. It was imperative that the product be launched successfully.

The plant management team made an overall assessment of the project and discovered a problem. In exchange for cooperation, the local union demanded lifelong employment, a concept that was radical at the time. The local managers knew that if they called the corporate human resources division for permission, they would be turned down or extensively delayed by bureaucratic process. They also knew that if they proceeded without permission, they could be fired. After a painful review, they decided to meet the request of the local union and proceeded to do so.

The product launch was highly successful. Afterward, there was a follow-up meeting with a group of people from corporate headquarters. Initially, the meeting went very well. Then the proceedings turned to the role of the union. The senior executives were elated with the story that unfolded and discussed how the concept might be implemented elsewhere. Some of the second-level people were far less pleased.

This story illustrates an important dilemma. If the members of the plant management team had failed, they would very likely have lost their jobs for undermining the labor relations policy of the company. Yet if the launch had not taken place, the corporation would have suffered a significant strategic and financial setback.

Organizations need people to conform. Traditionally, rules and procedures have been established to ensure stability and predictability in the organization. These rules and procedures are important, and a lot of time and effort is invested in ensuring their implementation. The rules bind the organization together and make coordination possible. Nevertheless, today's rules and procedures often represent solutions to yesterday's problems. The old rules often encumber an organization that tries to resolve new challenges from the external environment. To remain vital, an organization must adapt to its changing external demands. But this will happen only if a few people are willing to take a few serious risks. Organizational change always begins with a personal change.

To survive, organizations need leaders who take risks and who care enough to die for the organization—which would kill them for caring. Most organizations have few such people. When these leaders emerge, they usually have a vision, and their behavior reflects a transformational paradigm. They are self-authorizing and often follow unconventional methods that are based on moral principles rather than organizational pressures.

IF YOU ARE NOT RISKING YOUR JOB, YOU ARE NOT DOING YOUR JOB

Neil Sendelbach is a gifted designer of executive education at Ford. For several years, he and I were jointly responsible for the creation and administration of the Ford–University of Michigan Leadership, Education, and Development Program (LEAD). This program was designed to transform the mind-sets of three thousand middle managers at Ford. We set out to help them initiate change in their organization and to empower them so that they would more effectively take leadership roles. Initially, most of the participants were cynical about the objectives of the program. Many of their early comments were statements of skepticism and powerlessness like "Does my boss know what is being taught here? I can't do anything in this organization. It is my boss who should be in this program, not me." The feelings of helplessness were gradually displaced as we explored an array of possibilities. As their attitudes gradually changed, they proposed a new theme: "Just do it," or JDI. This statement was posted on a sign for other groups who would go through the program.

During the early hours of each succeeding program, participants asked about the JDI sign. They often had a cynical response. A senior executive visited one such session. During the discussion with this executive, the newly arrived and still uncertain participants, seeking "permission" to be empowered, shared their cynicism about the JDI theme. They suggested that such an approach at Ford could be dangerous. The executive pondered this for a moment and then told a personal story.

As a young middle manager, he was notified by his boss that Henry Ford II wanted to expand a particular area of the business and that he was to complete the analytical work. He performed the analyses and came to a troublesome conclusion. His data suggested that the endeavor should be dropped altogether. He confided the details to his immediate boss and was told to "redo" the analyses. He repeated his work but arrived at the same conclusion. He returned to his boss and reiterated that if Mr. Ford proceeded with his plan, he would be making a mistake. At this point, a very unusual thing happened. Five layers of hierarchy cleared out of the way, and he was given the opportunity to make his presentation directly to Mr. Ford.

Ford was less than happy with the conclusions and asked the young man some very difficult questions. The young man was able to answer each one. Eventually, Mr. Ford announced that he was convinced, and the proposed expansion was canceled.

It is interesting to note that the man left the presentation without receiving any feedback. He had no idea if he had just destroyed his career. A few months later, he was transferred to Brazil. He spent the next several years wondering if he had been exiled. Many years later, he ran into someone at Ford headquarters who had been present at his presentation. The person told him, "You might be interested to know that after your presentation, Henry said, 'We need more young men like that one.'"

The executive reflected on his story for a moment and then said, "Every couple of years, you need to bet your job, or else you are not doing your job." His statement had a strong impact on the audience. He continued, "Yes, 'JDI' is correct. But you also have to remember something else." He walked to the sign that read "JDI" and wrote four more letters, "BDBS." He turned to the group and said, *"But don't be stupid.* You can't be wild, flying off on every issue. You have to pick the issues that really matter. When the good of the company is being sacrificed, then you have to take a stand."

Making a difference is important for both the individual and the organization. Though we often prefer to believe that nothing can be done about the awful problems we face, there comes a time when we have to take on the system because the system needs to change. There comes a time when we need to "just do it."

When we do decide to initiate action, there are no written guarantees, no insurance policies that will save us if we fail. The possibility of failure is a constant companion who walks beside every real leader. Leaders cope with this presence because they understand that whenever they sacrifice their principles for pressure, both they and the system take another step toward slow death. They are willing to accept the necessary risk because it is the right thing to do. They care enough to risk dying for the organization, which would kill them for caring.

○   ○   ○

Robert E. Quinn is a professor at the University of Michigan Business School and a consultant and speaker.

Chapter Thirty

Leading Transition

William Bridges
Susan Mitchell Bridges

Change is nothing new to leaders, or their constituents. We understand by now that organizations cannot be just endlessly "managed," replicating yesterday's practices to achieve success. Business conditions change and yesterday's assumptions and practices no longer work. There must be innovation, and innovation means change.

Yet the thousands of books, seminars, and consulting engagements purporting to help "manage change" often fall short. These tools tend to neglect the dynamics of personal and organizational transition that can determine the outcome of any change effort. As a result, they fail to address the leader's need to coach others through the transition process. And they fail to acknowledge the fact that leaders themselves usually need coaching before they can effectively coach others.

In years past, perhaps, leaders could simply order changes. Even today, many view it as a straightforward process: establish a task force to lay out what needs to be done, when, and by whom. Then all that seems left for the organization is (what an innocent-sounding euphemism!) to implement the plan. Many leaders imagine that to make a change work, people need only follow the plan's implicit map, which shows how to get from here (where things stand now) to there (where they'll stand after the plan is implemented). "There" is also where the organization needs to be if it is to survive, so anyone who has looked at the situation with a reasonably open mind can see that the change isn't optional. It is essential.

Fine. But then, why don't people "Just Do It"? And what is the leader supposed to do when they Just Don't Do It—when people do not make the changes that need to be made, when deadlines are missed, costs run over budget, and valuable workers get so frustrated that when a headhunter calls, they jump ship?

Leaders who try to analyze this question after the fact are likely to review the change effort and how it was implemented. But the details of the intended change are often not the issue. The planned outcome may have been the restructuring of a group around products instead of geography, or speeding up product time-to-market by 50 percent. Whatever it was, the change that seemed so obviously necessary has languished like last week's flowers.

That happens because transition occurs in the course of every attempt at change. Transition is the state that change puts people into. The change is external (the different policy, practice, or structure that the leader is trying to bring about), while transition is internal (a psychological reorientation that people have to go through before the change can work).

The trouble is, most leaders imagine that transition is automatic—that it occurs simply because the change is happening. But it doesn't. Just because the computers are on everyone's desk doesn't mean that the new individually accessed customer database is transforming operations the way the consultants promised it would. And just because two companies (or hospitals or law firms) are now fully "merged" doesn't mean that they operate as one or that the envisioned cost savings will be realized.

Even when a change is showing signs that it may work, there is the issue of timing, for transition happens much more slowly than change. That is why the ambitious timetable that the leader laid out to the board turns out to have been wildly optimistic: it was based on getting the change accomplished, not on getting the people through the transition.

Transition takes longer because it requires that people undergo three separate processes, and all of them are upsetting.

Saying goodbye. The first requirement is that people have to let go of the way that things—and, worse, the way that they themselves—used to be. As the folk wisdom puts it, "You can't steal second base with your foot on first." You have to leave where you are, and many people have spent their whole lives standing on first base. It isn't just a personal preference you are asking them to give up. You are asking them to let go of the way of engaging or accomplishing tasks that made them successful in the past. You are asking them to let go of what feels to them like their whole world of experience, their sense of identity, even "reality" itself.

On paper it may have been a logical shift to self-managed teams, but it turned out to require that people no longer rely on a supervisor to make all decisions (and to be blamed when things go wrong). Or it looked like a simple effort to merge two work groups, but in practice it meant that people no longer worked with their friends or reported to people whose priorities they understood.

Shifting into neutral. Even after people have let go of their old ways, they find themselves unable to start anew. They are entering the second difficult phase of transition. We call it the neutral zone, and that in-between state is so full of uncertainty and confusion that simply coping with it takes most of people's energy. The neutral zone is particularly difficult during mergers or acquisitions, when careers and policy decisions and the very "rules of the game" are left in limbo while the two leadership groups work out questions of power and decision making.

The neutral zone is uncomfortable, so people are driven to get out of it. Some people try to rush ahead into some (often any) new situation, while others try to backpedal and retreat into the past. Successful transition, however, requires that an organization and its people spend some time in the neutral zone. This time in the neutral zone is not wasted, for that is where the creativity and energy of transition are found and the real transformation takes place. It's like Moses in the wilderness: it was there, not in the Promised Land, that Moses was given the Ten Commandments; and it was there, and not in the Promised Land, that his people were transformed from slaves to a strong and free people (see Exhibit 30.1, "Lessons from the Wilderness").

EXHIBIT 30.1 **Lessons from the Wilderness**

Even a great leader like Moses faced a trying test of his leadership in the neutral zone. But he was up to the task, so take note of some of his methods:

Magnify the plagues. To make the old system (Pharaoh) "let go" of his people, Moses called down plagues—and didn't stop until the old system gave way. At this stage, problems are your friend. Don't solve them; they convince people that they need to let go of the old way.

Mark the ending. What a symbolic "boundary event" Moses had! After his people crossed the Red Sea, there was no turning back!

Deal with the "murmuring." Don't be surprised when people lose confidence in your leadership in the neutral zone: Where are we going? Does he know the way? What was ever wrong with Egypt anyway? In periods of transition, look for opportunities to have contact with the individuals in transition; distance will be interpreted as abandonment. And show your concern for them by engaging them in conversation about the issues that are most on their minds; you may think there are more important things to talk about, but *they* don't think so.

Give people access to the decision makers. Moses (aided by his OD specialist, Jethro) appointed a new cadre of judges in the

Today it won't take 40 years, but a shift to self-managed teams, for instance, is likely to leave people in the neutral zone for six months, and a major merger may take two years to find its way out of the neutral zone. The change can continue forward on something close to its own schedule while the transition is being attended to, but if the transition is not dealt with, the change may collapse. People cannot do the new things that the new situation requires until they come to grips with what is being asked.

Moving forward. Some people fail to get through transition because they do not let go of the old ways and make

EXHIBIT 30.1 *(continued)*

wilderness to narrow the gap between the people and the decision makers.

Capitalize on the creative opportunity provided by the neutral zone. It was in the wilderness, not in the Promised Land, that the big innovation took place: the Ten Commandments were handed down. It will be in the neutral zone that many of your biggest breakthroughs occur.

Resist the urge to rush ahead. It seems as though little is happening in the neutral zone, but this is where the transformation is taking place. Don't jeopardize it by hurrying.

Understand that neutral-zone leadership is special. Moses did not enter the Promised Land. His kind of leadership fit the neutral zone, where things are confusing and fluid. But it was Joshua who could lead in the more settled state of the Promised Land. A literal new leader isn't needed, though, just a new style of leadership. Establishing a new beginning requires a much more logical approach, with an appeal to the followers' understanding, while the fluidity and ambiguity of the neutral zone makes an emotional connection between the leader and the followers more critical.

---

an ending; others fail because they become frightened and confused by the neutral zone and don't stay in it long enough for it to do its work on them. Some, however, do get through these first two phases of transition, but then freeze when they face the third phase, the new beginning. For that third phase requires people to begin behaving in a new way, and that can be disconcerting—it puts one's sense of competence and value at risk. Especially in organizations that have a history of punishing mistakes, people hang back during the final phase of transition, waiting to see how others are going to handle the new beginning.

Helping Leaders Lead Change

Understanding the transition process is a requirement for almost any senior executive. However, it is when the organization is in transition that leaders themselves often need help. They are so close to the changes that have been launched that they may fail to

- Remember that they themselves took some time to come to terms with the necessary change—and that their followers will need at least as long to do so (see Figure 30.1)

- Understand why anyone would not embrace change, and so believe that their followers are ignorant, rigid, or outright hostile to the new direction

- See that it is the transitions, not necessarily the changes themselves, that are holding people back and thereby threatening to make their change unworkable

Most leaders come from backgrounds where technical, financial, or operational skills were paramount, and those skills provide little help when it comes to leading people through transition. Such leaders may be pushing the limits of their understanding of the future, and they need perspective and advice. That is where a trusted colleague, confidant, coach, or consultant can offer valuable counsel to the leader. This person's background or professional affiliation can vary widely; what matters is that she or he understands how to help people through transition. It is a role that is far more interpersonal and collaborative than is played by most consultants or trainers accustomed to teaching a skill or prescribing a solution.

No training program can prepare a leader for managing a transition. Yet no leader can effectively lead change—which is

The higher leaders sit in an organization, the more quickly they tend to move through the change process. Because they can see the intended destination before others even know the race has begun, senior managers often forget that others will take longer to make the transition: letting go of old ways, moving through the neutral zone, and finally, making a new beginning.

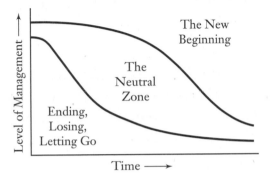

FIGURE 30.1 **The Marathon Effect**

what leadership is all about—without understanding and, ultimately, experiencing—the transition process. What leaders need, instead, is individualized assistance whereby they learn to

- Create plans to bring their followers through the particular transition they face—not through generic "change." A trainer can teach leaders a generalized approach ("The Ten Steps . . ."), but a good coach can help leaders discover their own best approaches.

- Work with their own goals, limitations, and concerns to create a development plan that prepares them for the future.

Times of transition are becoming the rule rather than the exception. Yet few leaders know how to prepare for the challenges that lie ahead. Transition leadership skills must be congruent with, must capitalize and build on, the leader's own strengths and talents. They cannot be found in a set of theoretical leadership skills.

The transition adviser works collaboratively with each leader to assess the leader's place in the three-part transition, the strengths the leader brings and how to leverage them, and what the current situation demands. It is a personal and completely customized process.

A Method for Managing Transition

Although the details of a transition management plan are unique to each situation, the adviser must help a leader with the following essential steps:

1. Learn to describe the change and why it must happen, and do so succinctly—in one minute or less. It is amazing how many leaders cannot do that.

2. Make sure that the details of the change are planned carefully and that someone is responsible for each detail, that time lines for all the changes are established, and that a communications plan explaining the change is in place.

3. Understand (with the assistance of others closer to the change) just who is going to have to let go of what—what is ending (and what is not) in people's work lives and careers—and what people (including the leader) should let go of.

4. Make sure that steps are taken to help people respectfully let go of the past. These may include "boundary" actions (events that demonstrate that change has come), a constant stream of information, and understanding and acceptance of the symptoms of grieving, as well as efforts to protect people's interests while they are giving up the status quo.

5. Help people through the neutral zone with communication (rather than simple information) that emphasizes con-

nections with and concern for the followers. To keep reiterating the "4 P's" of transition communications:

The *purpose:* Why we have to do this

The *picture:* What it will look and feel like when we reach our goal

The *plan:* Step by step, how we will get there

The *part:* What you can (and need to) do to help us move forward

6. Create temporary solutions to the temporary problems and the high levels of uncertainty found in the neutral zone. For example, one high-tech manufacturer, when announcing a plant closing, made interim changes in its reassignment procedures, bonus compensation plans, and employee communications processes to make sure that displaced employees suffered as little as possible, both financially and psychologically. Such efforts should include transition monitoring teams that can alert the leader to unforeseen problems—and disband when the process is done.

7. Help people launch the new beginning by articulating the new attitudes and behaviors needed to make the change work—and then modeling, providing practice in, and rewarding those behaviors and attitudes. For example, rather than announcing the grandiose goal of building a "world-class workforce," leaders of transition must define the skills and attitudes that such a workforce must have, and provide the necessary training and resources to develop them.

Coaching for Change

Since the ability to manage transition is tied to the realities of an actual leader in an actual situation, mutual trust between adviser and leader is essential. Only that way can leaders be honest enough to bring their fears and concerns to the surface quickly, hear what the situation is really "saying" rather than focusing on a program that a consultant is trying to sell, and gain the personal insight and awareness of the transition process that can be carried into the future.

Because this transition management relationship is a close and ongoing one, the adviser gets to know the leader's situation well and follows it as it changes. Understanding the dynamics of transition is far removed from the kind of leadership training most organizations provide. Traditional trainers and consultants seldom possess such intimate knowledge of their client. Whatever personal coaching they provide is usually subsumed in the teaching of a generic skill or body of knowledge. And because the relationship is time-limited, there is a natural pressure to produce quick, clear results.

However, because transition advisers work within the context of the situation at hand, their focus is not on how to "be a leader" or even how to "change an organization" but on how to provide the particular kind of leadership that an organization in transition demands. For that reason, the results of the relationship are very specific: the development of new skills and behaviors geared to the needs of the unique time and circumstances in which the person leads.

New Models of Leadership

Once you understand transition, you begin to see it everywhere. You realize that many of the issues commonly addressed as leadership, learning, or organizational development challenges are really an inevitable part of transition. Indeed, in today's organizations, without experiencing and successfully managing a difficult transition, no leader can be effective for very long. That suggests reinventing most models of leadership development. The best leadership development programs implicitly address the challenge of understanding change—they are experiential, tailored to the needs of the leader, and based on delivering real-world results. But most could be strengthened by explicit attention to transition management.

The final lesson that the process of transition holds for leadership development is that the relationship between adviser and leader is not much different from that between a leader and the people that she or he "leads." We treat that word ironically because the leadership that is appropriate to a modern, fast-moving organization—where work is based on task and mission rather than job description, and is distributed among contributors inside and outside the organization—takes on a new meaning. It is not the drum-major-at-the-head-of-the-parade leadership appropriate to yesterday's organization; it is the give-and-take, person-centered leadership by which the sports coach gets the best effort out of each member of a team.

The kind of leadership most effective today is similar to the kind of service that the best consultant gives a client: collaborative assistance that is both problem-solving and developmental. Its target is both the situation and the professional capability of the person. Today's leader, in a fundamental sense, is a coach, and the leader can best learn that role by being coached.

o   o   o

William Bridges is a writer and principal of William Bridges & Associates. He helps individuals and organizations deal more effectively with change. He has published nine books, including

Managing Transition, *JobShift*, and *Creating You & Co.* The *Wall Street Journal* has named him one of the top ten executive development presenters in the United States.

Susan Mitchell Bridges is a principal of William Bridges & Associates who specializes in leadership development. She has consulted with executives and teams in leading transition and implementing change for over twenty years.

Chapter Thirty-One

The Work of Leadership

Ronald A. Heifetz
Donald L. Laurie

To stay alive, Jack Pritchard had to change his life. Triple bypass surgery and medication could help, the heart surgeon told him, but no technical fix could release Pritchard from his own responsibility for changing the habits of a lifetime. He had to stop smoking, improve his diet, get some exercise, and take time to relax, remembering to breathe more deeply each day. Pritchard's doctor could provide sustaining technical expertise and take supportive action, but only Pritchard could adapt his ingrained habits to improve his long-term health. The doctor faced the leadership task of mobilizing the patient to make critical behavioral changes; Jack Pritchard faced the adaptive work of figuring out which specific changes to make and how to incorporate them into his daily life.

Companies today face challenges similar to the ones that confronted Pritchard and his doctor. They face adaptive challenges. Changes in societies, markets, customers, competition, and technology around the globe are forcing organizations to clarify their values, develop new strategies, and learn new ways of operating. Often the toughest task for leaders in effecting change is mobilizing people throughout the organization to do adaptive work.

Adaptive work is required when our deeply held beliefs are challenged, when the values that made us successful become less relevant, and when legitimate yet competing perspectives emerge. We see adaptive challenges every day at every level of the workplace—when companies restructure or reengineer, develop or implement strategy, or merge businesses. We see adaptive challenges when marketing has difficulty working with operations, when cross-functional teams don't work well, or when senior executives complain, "We don't seem to be able to execute effectively." Adaptive problems are often systemic problems with no ready answers.

Mobilizing an organization to adapt its behaviors in order to thrive in new business environments is critical. Without such change, any company today would falter. Indeed, getting people to do adaptive work is the mark of leadership in a competitive world. Yet for most senior executives, providing leadership and not just authoritative expertise is extremely difficult. Why? We see two reasons. First, in order to make change happen, executives have to break a long-standing behavior pattern of their own: providing leadership in the form of solutions. This tendency is quite natural because many executives reach their positions of authority by virtue of their competence in taking responsibility and solving problems. But the locus of responsibility for problem solving when a company faces an adaptive challenge must shift to its people. Solutions to adaptive challenges reside not in the executive suite but in the collective intelligence of employees at all levels, who need to use one another as resources, often across boundaries, and learn their way to those solutions.

Second, adaptive change is distressing for the people going through it. They need to take on new roles, new relationships, new values, new behaviors, and new approaches to work. Many employees are ambivalent about the efforts and sacrifices required of them. They often look to the senior executive to take problems off their shoulders. But those expectations have to be unlearned. Rather than fulfilling the expectation that they will provide answers, leaders have to ask tough questions. Rather than protecting people from outside threats, leaders should allow them to feel the pinch of reality in order to stimulate them to adapt. Instead of orienting people to their current roles, leaders must disorient them so that new relationships can develop. Instead of quelling conflict, leaders have to draw the issues out. Instead of maintaining norms, leaders have to challenge "the way we do business" and help others distinguish immutable values from historical practices that must go.

Drawing on our experience with managers from around the world, we offer six principles for leading adaptive work: "getting on the balcony," identifying the adaptive challenge, regulating distress, maintaining disciplined attention, giving the work back to people, and protecting voices of leadership from below. We illustrate those principles with an example of adaptive change at KPMG Netherlands, a professional-services firm.

GET ON THE BALCONY

Earvin "Magic" Johnson's greatness in leading his basketball team came in part from his ability to play hard while keeping the whole game situation in mind, as if he stood in a press box or on a balcony above the field of play. Bobby Orr played hockey in the same way. Other players might fail to recognize the larger patterns of play that performers like Johnson and Orr quickly understand, because they are so engaged in the game that they get carried away by it. Their attention is captured by the rapid motion, the physical contact, the roar of the crowd, and the pressure to execute. In sports, most players simply may not see who is open for a pass, who is missing a block, or how the offense and defense work together. Players like Johnson and Orr watch these things and allow their observations to guide their actions.

Business leaders have to be able to view patterns as if they were on a balcony. It does them no good to be swept up in the field of action. Leaders have to see a context for change or create one. They should give employees a strong sense of the history of the enterprise and what's good about its past, as well as an idea of the market forces at work today and the responsibility people must take in shaping the future. Leaders must be able to identify struggles over values and power, recognize patterns of work avoidance, and watch for the many other functional and dysfunctional reactions to change.

Without the capacity to move back and forth between the field of action and the balcony, to reflect day to day, moment to moment, on the many ways in which an organization's habits can sabotage adaptive work, a leader easily and unwittingly becomes a prisoner of the system. The dynamics of adaptive change are far too complex to keep track of, let alone influence, if leaders stay only on the field of play.

We have encountered several leaders, some of whom we discuss in this article, who manage to spend much of their precious time on the balcony as they guide their organizations through change. Without that perspective, they probably would have been unable to mobilize people to do adaptive work. Getting on the balcony is thus a prerequisite for following the next five principles.

IDENTIFY THE ADAPTIVE CHALLENGE

When a leopard threatens a band of chimpanzees, the leopard rarely succeeds in picking off a stray. Chimps know how to respond to this kind of threat. But when a man with an automatic rifle comes near, the routine responses fail. Chimps risk extinction in a world of poachers unless they figure out how to disarm the new threat. Similarly, when businesses cannot learn quickly to adapt to new challenges, they are likely to face their own form of extinction.

Consider the well-known case of British Airways. Having observed the revolutionary changes in the airline industry during the 1980s, then chief executive Colin Marshall clearly recognized the need to transform an airline nicknamed Bloody Awful by its own passengers into an exemplar of customer service. He also understood that this ambition would require more than anything else changes in values, practices, and relationships throughout the company. An organization whose people clung to functional silos and valued pleasing their bosses more than pleasing customers could not become "the world's favorite airline." Marshall needed an organization dedicated to serving people, acting on trust, respecting the individual, and making teamwork happen across boundaries. Values had to change throughout British Airways. People had to learn to collaborate and to develop a collective sense of responsibility for the direction and performance of the airline. Marshall identified the essential adaptive challenge: creating trust throughout the organization. He is one of the first executives we have known to make "creating trust" a priority.

To lead British Airways, Marshall had to get his executive team to understand the nature of the threat created by dissatisfied customers: Did it represent a technical challenge or an adaptive challenge? Would expert advice and technical adjustments within basic routines suffice, or would people throughout the company have to learn different ways of doing business, develop new competencies, and begin to work collectively?

Marshall and his team set out to diagnose in more detail the organization's challenges. They looked in three places. First, they listened to the ideas and concerns of people inside and outside the organization—meeting with crews on flights, showing up in the 350-person reservations center in New York, wandering around the baggage-handling area in Tokyo, or visiting the passenger lounge in whatever airport they happened to be in. Their primary questions were, Whose values, beliefs, attitudes, or behaviors would have to change in order for progress to take place? What shifts in priorities, resources, and power were necessary? What sacrifices would have to be made and by whom?

Second, Marshall and his team saw conflicts as clues—symptoms of adaptive challenges. The way conflicts across functions were being expressed were mere surface phenomena; the underlying conflicts had to be diagnosed. Disputes over seemingly technical issues such as procedures, schedules, and lines of authority were in fact proxies for underlying conflicts about values and norms.

Third, Marshall and his team held a mirror up to themselves, recognizing that they embodied the adaptive challenges facing the organization. Early in the transformation of British Airways, competing values and norms were played out on the executive team in dysfunctional ways that impaired the capacity of the rest of the company to collaborate across functions and units and make the necessary trade-offs. No executive can hide from the fact that his or her team reflects the best and the worst of the company's values and norms, and therefore provides a case in point for insight into the nature of the adaptive work ahead.

Thus, identifying its adaptive challenge was crucial in British Airways' bid to become the world's favorite airline. For the strategy to succeed, the company's leaders needed to understand themselves, their people, and the potential sources of conflict. Marshall recognized that strategy development itself requires adaptive work.

Regulate Distress

Adaptive work generates distress. Before putting people to work on challenges for which there are no ready solutions, a leader must realize that people can learn only so much so fast. At the same time, they must feel the need to change as reality brings new challenges. They cannot learn new ways when they are overwhelmed, but eliminating stress altogether removes the impetus for doing adaptive work. Because a leader must strike a delicate balance between having people feel the need to change and having them feel overwhelmed by change, leadership is a razor's edge.

A leader must attend to three fundamental tasks in order to help maintain a productive level of tension. Adhering to these tasks will allow him or her to motivate people without disabling them. First, a leader must create what can be called a *holding environment.* To use the analogy of a pressure cooker, a leader needs to regulate the pressure by turning up the heat while also allowing some steam to escape. If the pressure exceeds the cooker's capacity, the cooker can blow up. However, nothing cooks without some heat.

In the early stages of a corporate change, the holding environment can be a temporary "place" in which a leader creates the conditions for diverse groups to talk to one another about the challenges facing them, to frame and debate issues, and to clarify the assumptions behind competing perspectives and values. Over time, more issues can be phased in as they become ripe. At British Airways, for example, the shift from an internal focus to a customer focus took place over four or five years and dealt with important issues in succession: building a credible executive team, communicating with a highly fragmented organization, defining new measures of performance and compensation, and developing sophisticated information systems. During that time, employees at all levels learned to identify what and how they needed to change.

Thus, a leader must sequence and pace the work. Too often, senior managers convey that everything is important. They start new initiatives without stopping other activities, or they start too many initiatives at the same time. They overwhelm and disorient the very people who need to take responsibility for the work.

Second, a leader is responsible for direction, protection, orientation, managing conflict, and shaping norms (see Exhibit 31.1). Fulfilling these responsibilities is also important for a manager in technical or routine situations. But a leader engaged in adaptive work uses his authority to fulfill them differently. A leader provides direction by identifying the organization's adap-

EXHIBIT 31.1 Adaptive Work Calls for Leadership

Leader's Responsibilities	Type of Situation	
	Technical or Routine	*Adaptive*
Direction	Define problems and provide solutions	Identify the adaptive challenge and frame key questions and issues
Protection	Shield the organization from external threats	Let the organization feel external pressures within a range it can stand
Orientation	Clarify roles and responsibilities	Challenge current roles and resist pressure to define new roles quickly
Managing conflict	Restore order	Expose conflict or let it emerge
Shaping norms	Maintain norms	Challenge unproductive norms

tive challenge and framing the key questions and issues. A leader protects people by managing the rate of change. A leader orients people to new roles and responsibilities by clarifying business realities and key values. A leader helps expose conflict, viewing it as the engine of creativity and learning. Finally, a leader helps the organization maintain those norms that must endure and challenge those that need to change.

Third, a leader must have presence and poise; regulating distress is perhaps a leader's most difficult job. The pressures to restore equilibrium are enormous. Just as molecules bang hard against the walls of a pressure cooker, people bang up against leaders who are trying to sustain the pressures of tough, conflict-filled work. Although leadership demands a deep understanding of the pain of change—the fears and sacrifices associated with major readjustment—it also requires the ability to hold steady and maintain the tension. Otherwise, the pressure escapes and the stimulus for learning and change is lost.

A leader has to have the emotional capacity to tolerate uncertainty, frustration, and pain. He has to be able to raise tough questions without getting too anxious himself. Employees as well as colleagues and customers will carefully observe verbal and nonverbal cues to a leader's ability to hold steady. He needs to communicate confidence that he and they can tackle the tasks ahead.

Maintain Disciplined Attention

Different people within the same organization bring different experiences, assumptions, values, beliefs, and habits to their work. This diversity is valuable because innovation and learning are the products of differences. No one learns anything without being open to contrasting points of view. Yet managers at all levels are often unwilling—or unable—to address their competing perspectives collectively. They frequently avoid paying attention to issues that disturb them. They restore equilibrium quickly, often with work avoidance maneuvers. A leader must get employees to confront tough trade-offs in values, procedures, operating styles, and power.

That is as true at the top of the organization as it is in the middle or on the front line. Indeed, if the executive team cannot model adaptive work, the organization will languish. If senior managers can't draw out and deal with divisive issues, how will people elsewhere in the organization change their behaviors and rework their relationships? As Jan Carlzon, the legendary CEO of Scandinavian Airlines System (SAS), told us, "One of the most interesting missions of leadership is getting people on the executive team to listen to and learn from one another. Held in debate, people can learn their way to collective solutions when they understand one another's assumptions. The work of the leader is to get conflict out into the open and use it as a source of creativity."

Because work avoidance is rampant in organizations, a leader has to counteract distractions that prevent people from dealing with adaptive issues. Scapegoating, denial, focusing only on today's technical issues, or attacking individuals rather than the perspectives they represent—all forms of work avoidance— are to be expected when an organization undertakes adaptive work. Distractions have to be identified when they occur so that people will regain focus.

When sterile conflict takes the place of dialogue, a leader has to step in and put the team to work on reframing the issues. She has to deepen the debate with questions, unbundling the issues into their parts rather than letting conflict remain polarized and superficial. When people preoccupy themselves with blaming external forces, higher management, or a heavy workload, a leader has to sharpen the team's sense of responsibility for carving out the time to press forward. When the team fragments and individuals resort to protecting their own turf, leaders have to demonstrate the need for collaboration. People have to discover the value of consulting with one another and using one another as resources in the problem-solving process. For example, one CEO we know uses executive meetings, even those that focus on operational and technical issues, as opportunities to teach the team how to work collectively on adaptive problems.

Of course, only the rare manager intends to avoid adaptive work. In general, people feel ambivalent about it. Although they want to make progress on hard problems or live up to their renewed and clarified values, people also want to avoid the associated distress. Just as millions of U.S. citizens want to reduce the federal budget deficit, but not by giving up their tax dollars or benefits or jobs, so, too, managers may consider adaptive work a priority but have difficulty sacrificing their familiar ways of doing business. People need leadership to help them maintain their focus on the tough questions. Disciplined attention is the currency of leadership.

GIVE THE WORK BACK TO PEOPLE

Everyone in the organization has special access to information that comes from his or her particular vantage point. Everyone may see different needs and opportunities. People who sense early changes in the marketplace are often at the periphery, but the organization will thrive if it can bring that information to bear on tactical and strategic decisions. When people do not act on their special knowledge, businesses fail to adapt.

All too often, people look up the chain of command, expecting senior management to meet market challenges for which they themselves are responsible. Indeed, the greater and more persistent distresses that accompany adaptive work make such dependence worse. People tend to become passive, and senior managers who pride themselves on being problem solvers take decisive action. That behavior restores equilibrium in the short term but ultimately leads to complacency and habits of work avoidance that shield people from responsibility, pain, and the need to change.

Getting people to assume greater responsibility is not easy. Not only are many lower-level employees comfortable being told what to do, but many managers are accustomed to treating subordinates like machinery that requires control. Letting people take the initiative in defining and solving problems means that management needs to learn to support rather than control. Workers, for their part, need to learn to take responsibility.

Jan Carlzon encouraged responsibility taking at SAS by trusting others and decentralizing authority. A leader has to let people bear the weight of responsibility. "The key is to let them discover the problem," he said. "You won't be successful if people aren't carrying the recognition of the problem and the solution within themselves." To that end, Carlzon sought widespread engagement.

For example, in his first two years at SAS, Carlzon spent up to 50% of his time communicating directly in large meetings and indirectly in a host of innovative ways: through workshops, brainstorming sessions, learning exercises, newsletters, brochures, and exposure in the public media. He demonstrated through a variety of symbolic acts—for example, by eliminating the pretentious executive dining room and burning thousands of pages of manuals and handbooks—the extent to which rules had come to dominate the company. He made himself a pervasive presence, meeting with and listening to people both inside and outside the organization. He even wrote a book, *Moments of Truth* (HarperCollins, 1989), to explain his values, philosophy, and strategy. As Carlzon noted, "If no one else read it, at least my people would."

A leader also must develop collective self-confidence. Again, Carlzon said it well: "People aren't born with self-confidence.

Even the most self-confident people can be broken. Self-confidence comes from success, experience, and the organization's environment. The leader's most important role is to instill confidence in people. They must dare to take risks and responsibility. You must back them up if they make mistakes."

PROTECT VOICES OF LEADERSHIP FROM BELOW

Giving a voice to all people is the foundation of an organization that is willing to experiment and learn. But, in fact, whistle-blowers, creative deviants, and other such original voices routinely get smashed and silenced in organizational life. They generate disequilibrium, and the easiest way for an organization to restore equilibrium is to neutralize those voices, sometimes in the name of teamwork and "alignment."

The voices from below are usually not as articulate as one would wish. People speaking beyond their authority usually feel self-conscious and sometimes have to generate "too much" passion to get themselves geared up for speaking out. Of course, that often makes it harder for them to communicate effectively. They pick the wrong time and place, and often bypass proper channels of communication and lines of authority. But buried inside a poorly packaged interjection may lie an important intuition that needs to be teased out and considered. To toss it out for its bad timing, lack of clarity, or seeming unreasonableness is to lose potentially valuable information and discourage a potential leader in the organization.

That is what happened to David, a manager in a large manufacturing company. He had listened when his superiors encouraged people to look for problems, speak openly, and take responsibility. So he raised an issue about one of the CEO's pet projects—an issue that was deemed "too hot to handle" and had been swept under the carpet for years. Everyone understood that it was not open to discussion, but David knew that proceeding with the project could damage or derail key elements of the company's overall strategy. He raised the issue directly in a meeting with his boss and the CEO. He provided a clear description of the problem, a rundown of competing perspectives, and a summary of the consequences of continuing to pursue the project.

The CEO angrily squelched the discussion and reinforced the positive aspects of his pet project. When David and his boss left the room, his boss exploded: "Who do you think you are, with your holier-than-thou attitude?" He insinuated that David had never liked the CEO's pet project because David hadn't come up with the idea himself. The subject was closed.

David had greater expertise in the area of the project than either his boss or the CEO. But his two superiors demonstrated no curiosity, no effort to investigate David's reasoning, no awareness that he was behaving responsibly with the interests of the company at heart. It rapidly became clear to David that it was more important to understand what mattered to the boss than to focus on real issues. The CEO and David's boss together squashed the viewpoint of a leader from below and thereby killed his potential for leadership in the organization. He would either leave the company or never go against the grain again.

Leaders must rely on others within the business to raise questions that may indicate an impending adaptive challenge. They have to provide cover to people who point to the internal contradictions of the enterprise. Those individuals often have the perspective to provoke rethinking that people in authority do not. Thus, as a rule of thumb, when authority figures feel the reflexive urge to glare at or otherwise silence someone, they should resist. The urge to restore social equilibrium is quite powerful, and it comes on fast. One has to get accustomed to getting on the balcony, delaying the impulse, and asking, What is this guy really talking about? Is there something we're missing?

Doing Adaptive Work at KPMG Netherlands

The highly successful KPMG Netherlands provides a good example of how a company can engage in adaptive work. In 1994, Ruud Koedijk, the firm's chairman, recognized a strategic challenge. Although the auditing, consulting, and tax-preparation partnership was the industry leader in the Netherlands and was highly profitable, growth opportunities in the segments it served were limited. Margins in the auditing business were being squeezed as the market became more saturated, and competition in the consulting business was increasing as well. Koedijk knew that the firm needed to move into more profitable growth areas, but he didn't know what they were or how KPMG might identify them.

Koedijk and his board were confident that they had the tools to do the analytical strategy work: analyze trends and discontinuities, understand core competencies, assess their competitive position, and map potential opportunities. They were considerably less certain that they could commit to implementing the strategy that would emerge from their work. Historically, the partnership had resisted attempts to change, basically because the partners were content with the way things were. They had been successful for a long time, so they saw no reason to learn new ways of doing business, either from their fellow partners or from anyone lower down in the organization. Overturning the partners' attitude and its deep impact on the organization's culture posed an enormous adaptive challenge for KPMG.

Koedijk could see from the balcony that the very structure of KPMG inhibited change. In truth, KPMG was less a partnership than a collection of small fiefdoms in which each partner was a lord. The firm's success was the cumulative accomplishment of each of the individual partners, not the unified result of 300 colleagues pulling together toward a shared ambition. Success was measured solely in terms of the profitability of individual units. As one partner described it, "If the bottom line was correct, you were a 'good fellow.' " As a result, one partner would not trespass on another's turf, and learning from others was a rare event. Because independence was so highly valued, confrontations were rare and conflict was camouflaged. If partners wanted to resist firmwide change, they did not kill the issue directly. "Say yes, do no" was the operative phrase.

Koedijk also knew that this sense of autonomy got in the way of developing new talent at KPMG. Directors rewarded their subordinates for two things: not making mistakes and delivering a high number of billable hours per week. The emphasis was not on creativity or innovation. Partners were looking for errors when they reviewed their subordinates' work, not for new understanding or fresh insight. Although Koedijk could see the broad outlines of the adaptive challenges facing his organization, he knew that he could not mandate behavioral change. What he could do was create the conditions for people to discover for themselves how they needed to change. He set a process in motion to make that happen.

To start, Koedijk held a meeting of all 300 partners and focused their attention on the history of KPMG, the current business reality, and the business issues they could expect to face. He then raised the question of how they would go about changing as a firm and asked for their perspectives on the issues. By launching the strategic initiative through dialogue rather than edict, he built trust within the partner ranks. Based on this emerging trust and his own credibility, Koedijk persuaded the partners to release 100 partners and nonpartners from their day-to-day responsibilities to work on the strategic challenges. They would devote 60% of their time for nearly four months to that work.

Koedijk and his colleagues established a strategic integration team of 12 senior partners to work with the 100 professionals (called "the 100") from different levels and disciplines. Engaging people below the rank of partner in a major strategic initiative was unheard of and signaled a new approach from the start: Many of these people's opinions had never before been valued or sought by authority figures in the firm. Divided into 14 task forces, the 100 were to work in three areas: gauging future trends and discontinuities, defining core competencies, and grappling with the adaptive challenges facing the organization. They were housed on a separate floor with their own support staff, and they were unfettered by traditional rules and regulations. Hennie Both, KPMG's director of marketing and communications, signed on as project manager.

As the strategy work got under way, the task forces had to confront the existing KPMG culture. Why? Because they literally could not do their new work within the old rules. They could not work when strong respect for the individual came at the expense of effective teamwork, when deeply held individual beliefs got in the way of genuine discussion, and when unit loyalties formed a barrier to cross-functional problem solving. Worst of all, task force members found themselves avoiding conflict and unable to discuss those problems. A number of the task forces became dysfunctional and unable to do their strategy work.

To focus their attention on what needed to change, Both helped the task forces map the culture they desired against the current culture. They discovered very little overlap. The top descriptors of the current vulture were: develop opposing views, demand perfection, and avoid conflict. The top characteristics of the desired culture were: create the opportunity for self-fulfillment, develop a caring environment, and maintain trusting relations with colleagues. Articulating this gap made tangible for the group the adaptive challenge that Koedijk saw facing KPMG. In other words, the people who needed to do the changing had finally framed the adaptive challenge for themselves: How could KPMG succeed at a competence-based strategy that depended on cooperation across multiple units and layers if its people couldn't succeed in these task forces? Armed with that understanding, the task force members could become emissaries to the rest of the firm.

On a more personal level, each member was asked to identify his or her individual adaptive challenge. What attitudes, behaviors, or habits did each one need to change, and what specific actions would he or she take? Who else needed to be involved for individual change to take root? Acting as coaches and consultants, the task force members gave one another supportive feedback and suggestions. They had learned to confide, to listen, and to advise with genuine care.

Progress on these issues raised the level of trust dramatically, and task force members began to understand what adapting their behavior meant in everyday terms. They understood how to identify an adaptive issue and developed a language with which to discuss what they needed to do to improve their collective ability to solve problems. They talked about dialogue, work avoidance, and using the collective intelligence of the group. They knew how to call one another on dysfunctional behavior. They had begun to develop the culture required to implement the new business strategy.

Despite the critical breakthroughs toward developing a collective understanding of the adaptive challenge, regulating the level of distress was a constant preoccupation for Koedijk, the board, and Both. The nature of the work was distressing. Strategy work means broad assignments with limited instructions; at KPMG, people were accustomed to highly structured assignments. Strategy work also means being creative. At one breakfast meeting, a board member stood on a table to challenge the group to be more creative and toss aside old rules. This radical and unexpected behavior further raised the distress level: No one had ever seen a partner behave this way before. People realized that their work experience had prepared them only for performing routine tasks with people "like them" from their own units.

The process allowed for conflict and focused people's attention on the hot issues in order to help them learn how to work with conflict in a constructive manner. But the heat was kept within a tolerable range in some of the following ways:

º On one occasion when tensions were unusually high, the 100 were brought together to voice their concerns to the board in an Oprah Winfrey–style meeting. The board sat in the center of an auditorium and took pointed questions from the surrounding group.

○ The group devised sanctions to discourage unwanted behavior. In the soccer-crazy Netherlands, all participants in the process were issued the yellow cards that soccer referees use to indicate "foul" to offending players. They used the cards to stop the action when someone started arguing his or her point without listening to or understanding the assumptions and competing perspectives of other participants.

○ The group created symbols. They compared the old KPMG to a hippopotamus that was large and cumbersome, liked to sleep a lot, and became aggressive when its normal habits were disturbed. They aspired to be dolphins, which they characterized as playful, eager to learn, and happily willing to go the extra mile for the team. They even paid attention to the statement that clothes make: It surprised some clients to see managers wandering through the KPMG offices that summer in Bermuda shorts and T-shirts.

○ The group made a deliberate point of having fun. "Play-time" could mean long bicycle rides or laser-gun games at a local amusement center. In one spontaneous moment at the KPMG offices, a discussion of the power of people mobilized toward a common goal led the group to go outside and use their collective leverage to move a seemingly immovable concrete block.

○ The group attended frequent two- and three-day off-site meetings to help bring closure to parts of the work.

These actions, taken as a whole, altered attitudes and behaviors. Curiosity became more valued than obedience to rules. People no longer deferred to the senior authority figure in the room; genuine dialogue neutralized hierarchical power in the battle over ideas. The tendency for each individual to promote his or her pet solution gave way to understanding other perspectives. A confidence in the ability of people in different units to work together and work things out emerged. The people with the most curious minds and interesting questions soon became the most respected.

As a result of confronting strategic and adaptive challenges, KPMG as a whole will move from auditing to assurance, from operations consulting to shaping corporate vision, from business-process reengineering to developing organizational capabilities, and from teaching traditional skills to its own clients to creating learning organizations. The task forces identified $50 million to $60 million worth of new business opportunities.

Many senior partners who had believed that a firm dominated by the auditing mentality could not contain creative people were surprised when the process unlocked creativity, passion, imagination, and a willingness to take risks. Two stories illustrate the fundamental changes that took place in the firm's mind-set.

We saw one middle manager develop the confidence to create a new business. He spotted the opportunity to provide KPMG services to virtual organizations and strategic alliances. He traveled the world, visiting the leaders of 65 virtual organizations. The results of his innovative research served as a resource to KPMG in entering this growing market. Moreover, he represented the new KPMG by giving a keynote address discussing his findings at a world forum. We also saw a 28-year-old female auditor skillfully guide a group of older, male senior partners through a complex day of looking at opportunities associated with implementing the firm's new strategies. That could not have occurred the year before. The senior partners never would have listened to such a voice from below.

LEADERSHIP AS LEARNING

Many efforts to transform organizations through mergers and acquisitions, restructuring, reengineering, and strategy work falter because managers fail to grasp the requirements of adaptive work. They make the classic error of treating adaptive challenges like technical problems that can be solved by tough-minded senior executives.

The implications of that error go to the heart of the work of leaders in organizations today. Leaders crafting strategy have access to the technical expertise and the tools they need to calculate the benefits of a merger or restructuring, understand future trends and discontinuities, identify opportunities, map existing competencies, and identify the steering mechanisms to support their strategic direction. These tools and techniques are readily available both within organizations and from a variety of consulting firms, and they are very useful. In many cases, however, seemingly good strategies fail to be implemented. And often the failure is misdiagnosed: "We had a good strategy, but we couldn't execute it effectively."

In fact, the strategy itself is often deficient because too many perspectives were ignored during its formulation. The failure to do the necessary adaptive work during the strategy development process is a symptom of senior managers' technical orientation. Managers frequently derive their solution to a problem and then try to sell it to some colleagues and bypass or sandbag others in the commitment-building process. Too often, leaders, their team, and consultants fail to identify and tackle the adaptive dimensions of the challenge and to ask themselves, Who needs to learn what in order to develop, understand, commit to, and implement the strategy?

The same technical orientation entraps business-process-reengineering and restructuring initiatives, in which consultants and managers have the know-how to do the technical work of framing the objectives, designing a new work flow, documenting and communicating results, and identifying the activities to be performed by people in the organization. In many instances, reengineering falls short of the mark because it treats process redesign as a technical problem: Managers neglect to identify the adaptive work and involve the people who have to do the changing. Senior executives fail to invest their time and their souls in understanding these issues and guiding people through the transition. Indeed, engineering is itself the wrong metaphor.

In short, the prevailing notion that leadership consists of having a vision and aligning people with that vision is bankrupt because it continues to treat adaptive situations as if they were technical: The authority figure is supposed to divine where the company is going, and people are supposed to follow. Leadership is reduced to a combination of grand knowing and salesmanship. Such a perspective reveals a basic misconception about the way businesses succeed in addressing adaptive challenges. Adaptive situations are hard to define and resolve precisely because they demand the work and responsibility of managers and people throughout the organization. They are not amenable to solutions provided by leaders; adaptive solutions require members of the organization to take responsibility for the problematic situations that face them.

Leadership has to take place every day. It cannot be the responsibility of the few, a rare event, or a once-in-a-lifetime opportunity. In our world, in our businesses, we face adaptive challenges all the time. When an executive is asked to square conflicting aspirations, he and his people face an adaptive challenge. When a manager sees a solution to a problem—technical in many respects except that it requires a change in the attitudes and habits of subordinates—he faces an adaptive challenge. When an employee close to the front line sees a gap between the organization's purpose and the objectives he is asked to achieve, he faces both an adaptive challenge and the risks and opportunity of leading from below.

Leadership, as seen in this light, requires a learning strategy. A leader, from above or below, with or without authority, has to engage people in confronting the challenge, adjusting their values, changing perspectives, and learning new habits. To an authoritative person who prides himself on his ability to tackle hard problems, this shift may come as a rude awakening. But it also should ease the burden of having to know all the answers and bear all the load. To the person who waits to receive either the coach's call or "the vision" to lead, this change may also seem a mixture of good news and bad news. The adaptive demands of our time require leaders who take responsibility without waiting for revelation or request. One can lead with no more than a question in hand.

o   o   o

Ronald A. Heifetz is director of the Leadership Education Project and founding director of the Center for Public Leadership at Harvard University.

Donald L. Laurie is founder and managing director of Oyster International, a consulting firm specializing in strategic management issues.

Notes

CHAPTER ONE

1. The authors of *In Search of Excellence* (New York: HarperCollins, 1982), Tom Peters and Robert Waterman, actually allude to the importance of leadership, despite their best efforts. They write, "We must admit that our bias at the beginning was to discount the role of leadership heavily. . . . Unfortunately, what we found was that associated with almost every excellent company was a strong leader (or two) who seemed to have had a lot to do with making the company excellent in the first place."

James C. Collins and Jerry I. Porras, in writing *Built to Last* (New York: HarperCollins, 1995), take their arguments about the importance of culture to an extreme. Regarding the success of Jack Welch, they argue that he was able to change General Electric because he had grown up in the company and was a product of its robust culture. Unfortunately, this is the wrong read from the Welch experience. As I discuss later in this chapter, Welch was not successful because he was a product of the GE culture. Rather, he had survived in spite of it. The first thing Welch did was dismantle the business portfolio the company had built over 100 years and scrap the internal bureaucracy.

2. Edgar H. Schein, *Organizational Culture and Leadership*, 2nd ed. (San Francisco: Jossey-Bass, 1992).

3. Bob Ortega, "Life Without Sam," *Wall Street Journal*, January 4, 1995, p. A1.

4. Judith Dobrzynski, "Rethinking IBM," *Business Week*, October 4, 1993, p. 86; Amy Cortese and Ira Sager, "Lou Gerstner Unveils His Battle Plan," *Business Week*, April 4, 1994, p. 96.

5. AlliedSignal's productivity grew at an average annual rate of 5.6% from 1991 to 1996; John S. McClenahan, "52 Fiefdoms No More," *Industry Week*, January 20, 1997, p. 58.

6. Richard Notebaert, personal interview, March 1996.

7. "Up with Upsizing," *Pittsburgh Post-Gazette*, March 10, 1996, p. E1.

8. Patrick Spain and James Talbot, *Hoover's Handbook of American Companies, 1996* (Austin, Tex.: Reference Press, 1996).

9. Spain and Talbot, *Hoover's Handbook;* Andrew S. Grove, *Only the Paranoid Survive* (New York: Doubleday, 1996), p. 45.

10. Spain and Talbot, in *Hoover's Handbook of American Companies, 1996,* note that Dell started his business selling computer components after enrolling at the University of Texas in 1983. By 1984, Dell's dorm-room business was bringing in $80,000 per month.

11. Grove, *Only the Paranoid Survive*, p. 49.

12. Grove, *Only the Paranoid Survive*, p. 47.

13. Paul Carroll, *Big Blues* (New York: Random House, 1993), pp. 261–262.

14. David Kirkpatrick, "IBM Is Back with New PCs and a New Attitude," *Fortune*, November 11, 1996, p. 28.

15. Grove, *Only the Paranoid Survive*, p. 64.

16. Carol Loomis, "King John Wears an Uneasy Crown," *Fortune*, January 11, 1993, p. 44.

17. Leslie Cauley, "IBM Plans to Oust John Akers as Chief/Tradition Proves to Be His Undoing," *USA Today*, January 27, 1993, p. 1B.

18. Gary McWilliams, "Can DEC Beat the Big Blue Blues?" *Business Week*, August 13, 1990, p. 114.

19. Gary McWilliams, "Crunch Time at DEC," *Business Week*, May 4, 1992, p. 30.

20. McWilliams, "Can DEC," p. 114.

21. Maria Shao, "Ken Olsen Resurfaces," *Boston Globe*, March 24, 1993, p. 1.

22. Under founder Ken Olsen, DEC did not weather the storm of the PC revolution well. DEC underwent three major reorganizations between 1988 and 1993. It flip-flopped on important strategies. It staked its future on developing a RISC chip in-house in 1987. It killed this program in 1988 and then revived it again later.

Internal competition made managers more concerned with protecting their fiefs than operating the company successfully. In 1989, with cracks in the company clearly visible, DEC announced plans to reduce its workforce. However, after only three years, only 10,000 people had left the 126,000-employee company.

All this resulted in a sliding market value that has gone from $26 billion in 1987 to $4.6 billion in July 1992, when Olsen was forced out; McWilliams, "Crunch Time at DEC," p. 30. On December 31, 1996,

DEC's market value was up to $5.6 billion, a far cry from the value added by other companies in its industry. In April 1997, it was trading at $26 a share, making it worth roughly one-third of its annual revenue. Compare that with Hewlett-Packard, which is worth 1.25 times its revenue; Rita Kosella, "Solving the DEC Puzzle," *Forbes*, May 5, 1997, p. 45.

23. All Richard Notebaert quotes are from a personal interview conducted in March 1996.

24. Grove provides an excellent description of the changes occurring in the computer industry, which I have summarized here, in *Only the Paranoid Survive*.

25. Grove, *Only the Paranoid Survive*, p. 91.

26. Grove, *Only the Paranoid Survive*, p. 87.

27. Spain and Talbot, *Hoover's Handbook*.

28. Grove, *Only the Paranoid Survive*, p. 89.

29. The painful remaking of Intel took nearly two full years. The crisis in memory chips began for the company in the fall of 1984. In 1985 and 1986, the company took some steps to battle the situation. In mid-1985, the infamous discussion between Moore and Grove took place. The transformation of the company to its focus on microprocessors was completed by mid-1986; Grove, *Only the Paranoid Survive*, pp. 88, 95.

30. Grove, *Only the Paranoid Survive*, pp. 142–145.

31. Spain and Talbot, *Hoover's Handbook*. The scraps left over by Intel in the microprocessor market are picked up by AMD and Cyrix, with roughly 5% of the market, who make Intel-compatible chips. The next most formidable competitors are IBM and Motorola, who share the 3.3% of the market belonging to Power PC chips; Paul C. Judge, "Why the Fastest Chip Didn't Win," *Business Week*, April 28, 1997, p. 92.

32. Grove, *Only the Paranoid Survive*, p. 97.

33. Noel M. Tichy and Stratford Sherman, *Control Your Destiny or Someone Else Will* (New York: Doubleday, 1993), pp. 27, 29, 317; General Electric.

34. Tichy and Sherman, *Control Your Destiny*, p. 65.

35. Welch simplified GE's structure by taking out layers between his office and the businesses; Tichy and Sherman, *Control Your Destiny*, pp. 282–283.

36. Letter to Shareholders, *General Electric Annual Report*, 1995.

37. John F. Welch Jr., remarks at the Operating Managers Conference, Boca Raton, Fla., 1994.

38. Welch began the Quality program in 1995. He has stated that it will achieve Six Sigma quality (3.4 defects per million operations in manufacturing or service processes). In his 1996 annual report letter,

Welch reported that GE's quality efforts had already paid for themselves and that the additional investment of $300 million in 1997 would bring in an additional $400 to $500 million in savings. This focus on tangible results is a Welch hallmark from the days of Work-Out. If the Quality program succeeds at GE, it will be the biggest, fastest, most successful application of quality principles ever. The different results from this program versus quality programs that floundered at other companies are the result of the fact that it is being used by leaders at a company with a leadership heritage that can make quality work.

39. Welch, remarks at the Operating Managers Conference, Boca Raton, Fa., 1994.

CHAPTER THREE

1. This incident was recounted by one of the people we interviewed, who was an eyewitness to these events.

2. L. F. Berkman, L. Leo-Summers, and R. I. Horwitz, "Emotional Support and Survival After Myocardial Infarction: A Prospective, Population-Based Study of the Elderly," *Annals of Internal Medicine*, 1992, *117*, 1003–1009.

3. Anika Rosengren and others, "Stressful Life Events, Social Support and Mortality in Men Born in 1933," *British Medical Journal*, 1983, *207*, 1102–1106.

4. Thomas Lewis, Fari Amini, and Richard Lannon, *A General Theory of Love* (New York: Random House, 2000).

5. Robert Levenson, University of California at Berkeley, personal communication.

6. Howard Friedman and Ronald Riggio, "Effect of Individual Differences in Nonverbal Expressiveness on Transmission of Emotion," *Journal of Nonverbal Behavior*, 1981, *6*, 32–58.

7. Janice R. Kelly and Sigal G. Barsade, "Moods and Emotions in Small Groups and Work Teams," working paper, Yale School of Management, New Haven, Conn., 2001.

8. C. Bartel and R. Saavedra, "The Collective Construction of Work Group Moods," *Administrative Science Quarterly*, 2000, *45*, 187–231.

9. Peter Totterdell and others, "Evidence of Mood Linkage in Work Groups," *Journal of Personality and Social Psychology*, 1998, *74*, 1504–1515.

10. Peter Totterdell, "Catching Moods and Hitting Runs: Mood Linkage and Subjective Performance in Professional Sports Teams," *Journal of Applied Psychology*, 2000, *85*, 848–859.

11. See Wallace Bachman, "Nice Guys Finish First: A SYMLOG

Analysis of U.S. Naval Commands," in Richard Brian Polley, A. Paul Hare, and Philip J. Stone (eds.), *The SYMLOG Practitioner: Applications of Small Group Research* (New York: Praeger, 1988).

12. Anthony T. Pescosolido, "Emotional Intensity in Groups," doctoral dissertation, Department of Organizational Behavior, Case Western Reserve University, 2000.

13. Howard Gardner, *Leading Minds: An Anatomy of Leadership* (New York: Basic Books, 1995).

14. V. U. Druskat and A. T. Pascosolido, "Leading Self-Managing Work Teams from the Inside: Informal Leader Behavior and Team Outcomes." Unpublished manuscript, 2001.

15. See, for example, Jennifer M. George and Kenneth Bettenhausen, "Understanding Prosocial Behavior, Sales Performance, and Turnover: A Group-Level Analysis in Service Context," *Journal of Applied Psychology*, 1990, *75*, 698–706.

16. R. C. Sinclair, "Mood, Categorization Breadth, and Performance Appraisal," *Organizational Behavior and Human Decision Processes*, 1988, *42*, 22–46.

17. Jennifer M. George, "Emotions and Leadership: The Role of Emotional Intelligence," *Human Relations*, 2000, *53*, 1027–1055.

18. See, for example, Gordon H. Bower, "Mood Congruity of Social Judgments," in Joseph Forgas (ed.), *Emotion and Social Judgments* (Oxford: Pergamon Press, 1991).

19. See, for example, Jacqueline Wood, Andrew Matthews, and Tim Dalgleish, "Anxiety and Cognitive Inhibition," *Emotion*, 2001, *1*, 166–181.

20. Sigal G. Barsade, "The Ripple Effect: Emotional Contagion in Groups," Working Paper no. 98, Yale School of Management, New Haven, Conn., 2000.

21. John Basch and Cynthia D. Fisher, "Affective Events-Emotions Matrix: A Classification of Work Events and Associated Emotions," in Neal M. Ashkanasy, Charmine E. J. Härtel, and Wilfred J. Zerbe (eds.), *Emotions in the Workplace: Research, Theory, and Practice* (Westport, Conn.: Quorum Books, 2000).

22. Jeffrey B. Henriques and Richard J. Davidson, "Brain Electrical Asymmetries During Cognitive Task Performance in Depressed and Nondepressed Subjects," *Biological Psychiatry*, 1997, *42*, 1039–1050.

23. Cynthia D. Fisher and Christopher S. Noble, "Affect and Performance: A Within-Persons Analysis." Paper presented at the annual meeting of the Academy of Management, Toronto, 2000.

24. Cynthia D. Fisher, "Mood and Emotions While Working: Missing

Pieces of Job Satisfaction?" *Journal of Organizational Behavior,* 2000, *21,* 185–202. See also Howard Weiss, Jeffrey Nicholas, and Catherine Daus, "An Examination of the Joint Effects of Affective Experiences and Job Beliefs on Job Satisfaction and Variations in Affective Experiences over Time," *Organizational Behavior and Human Decision Processes,* 1999, *78,* 1–24.

25. See A. M. Isen, "Positive Affect," in Tim Dalgleish and Mick J. Power (eds.), *Handbook of Cognition and Emotion* (Hoboken, N.J.: Wiley, 1999).

26. See Cynthia D. Fisher and Christopher S. Noble, "Emotion and the Illusory Correlation Between Job Satisfaction and Job Performance." Paper presented at the second Conference on Emotions in Organizational Life, Toronto, August 2000.

27. Martin E. Seligman and Peter Schulman, "The People Make the Place," *Personnel Psychology,* 1987, *40,* 437–453.

28. R. W. Clouse and K. L. Spurgeon, "Corporate Analysis of Humor," *Psychology,*1995, *32,* 1–24.

29. Sigal G. Barsade and others, "To Your Heart's Content: A Mode of Affective Diversity in Top Management Teams," *Administrative Science Quarterly,*2000, *45,* 802–836.

30. Lyle Spencer, paper presented at the meeting of the Consortium for Research on Emotional Intelligence in Organizations, Cambridge, Mass., April 19, 2001.

31. Benjamin Schneider and D. E. Bowen, *Winning the Service Game* (Boston: Harvard Business School Press, 1995).

32. David McClelland, "Identifying Competencies with Behavioral-Event Interviews," *Psychological Science,* 1998, *9,* 331–339; Daniel Williams, *Leadership for the 21st Century: Life Insurance Leadership Study* (Boston: LOMA/Hay Group, 1995).

33. More technically, the styles were found to account for 53 to 72 percent of the variance in organizational climate. See Stephen P. Kelner Jr., Christine A. Rivers, and Kathleen H. O'Connell, *Managerial Style as a Behavioral Predictor of Organizational Climate* (Boston: McBer, 1996).

34. Much the same argument has been made in George and Bettenhausen, "Understanding Prosocial Behavior"; and in Neal M. Ashkanasy and Barry Tse, "Transformational Leadership as Management of Emotion: A Conceptual Review," in Ashkanasy, Härtel, and Zerbe, *Emotions in the Workplace.*

CHAPTER SIX

1. Warren G. Bennis, *On Becoming a Leader* (Boston: Addison-Wesley, 1988), p. 146.

2. Telephone interview, April 1998.

3. "FC Roper Starch Survey: The Web," *Fast Company*, October 1999, p. 302.

4. Public Allies, *New Leadership for a New Century* (Washington, D.C.: Public Allies, 1998).

CHAPTER SEVEN

Argyris, C. *Interpersonal Competence and Organizational Effectiveness.* Homewood, Ill.: Irwin, 1962.

Aubrey, B., and Tilliette, B. *Savoir faire savoir: L'apprentissage de l'action en entreprise* [Knowing and teaching: Action learning in the enterprise]. Paris: InterÉditions, 1990.

Barnes, L. B., and Kriger, M. P. "The Hidden Side of Organizational Leadership." *Sloan Management Review*, Fall 1986, pp. 15–25.

Bass, B. M. *Leadership and Performance Beyond Expectations.* New York: Free Press, 1985.

Bennis, W. G., and Nanus, B. *Leaders: Strategies for Taking Charge.* New York: HarperCollins, 1985.

Blanchard, K., and Johnson, S. *The One-Minute Manager.* New York: Morrow, 1982.

Bradford, D. L., and Cohen, A. R. *Managing for Excellence.* New York: Wiley, 1984.

Briand, M. "People, Lead Thyself." *Kettering Review*, Summer 1993, pp. 38–46.

Burns, J. M. *Leadership.* New York: HarperCollins, 1978.

Carlzon, J. *Moments of Truth.* New York: Ballinger, 1987.

Chandler, A. D., Jr. *The Visible Hand: The Managerial Revolution in American Business.* Cambridge, Mass.: Harvard University Press, 1977.

Cleveland, H. *The Knowledge Executive: Leadership in an Information Society.* New York: Dutton, 1985.

Collins, J. C., and Porras, J. I. *Built to Last: Successful Habits of Visionary Companies.* New York: HarperBusiness, 1994.

Fiedler, F. E. *A Theory of Leadership Effectiveness.* New York: McGraw-Hill, 1967.

Fiedler, F. E., and Chemers, M. *Leadership and Effective Management.* Glenview, Ill.: Scott, Foresman, 1974.

Gardner, J. W. *Handbook of Strategic Planning.* Hoboken, N.J.: Wiley, 1986.

Gardner, J. W. *On Leadership.* New York: Free Press, 1989.

Greenleaf, R. K. "The Servant as Leader." Newton Center, Mass.: Robert K. Greenleaf Center, 1973.

Hall, R. H. *Organizations: Structures, Processes, and Outcomes.* (4th ed.) Upper Saddle River, N.J.: Prentice Hall, 1987.

Hampton, W. J., and Norman, J. R. "General Motors: What Went Wrong—Eight Years and Billions of Dollars Haven't Made Its Strategy Succeed." *Business Week*, March 16, 1987, p. 102.

Heifetz, R. A. *Leadership Without Easy Answers*. Cambridge, Mass.: Belknap Press, 1994.

Hersey, P. *The Situational Leader*. New York: Warner Books, 1984.

Hollander, E. P. *Leadership Dynamics*. New York: Free Press, 1978.

House, R. J. "The Path-Goal Theory of Effectiveness." *Administrative Science Quarterly*, 1971, *16*, 321–338.

Iacocca, L., and Novak, W. *Iacocca*. New York: Bantam Books, 1984.

Kanter, R. M. *The Change Masters: Innovations for Productivity in the American Corporation*. New York: Simon & Schuster, 1983.

Kaufer, N., and Leader, G. C. "Diana Lam (A)." Case. Boston University, 1987a.

Kaufer, N., and Leader, G. C. "Diana Lam (B)." Case. Boston University, 1987b.

Kotter, J. P. *The Leadership Factor*. New York: Free Press, 1988.

Kouzes, J. M., and Posner, B. Z. *The Leadership Challenge: How to Get Extraordinary Things Done in Organizations*. San Francisco: Jossey-Bass, 1987.

Lee, A. *Call Me Roger*. Chicago: Contemporary Books, 1988.

Levinson, H. *The Exceptional Executive*. Cambridge, Mass.: Harvard University Press, 1968.

Likert, R. *New Patterns of Management*. New York: McGraw-Hill, 1961.

Likert, R. *The Human Organization*. New York: McGraw-Hill, 1967.

Murphy, J. T. *Managing Matters: Reflections from Practice*. Monograph. Cambridge, Mass.: Graduate School of Education, Harvard University, 1985.

"On a Clear Day You Can Still See General Motors." *Economist*, December 2, 1989, pp. 77–80.

Oshry, B. *Seeing Systems: Unlocking the Mysteries of Organizational Life*. San Francisco: Berrett-Koehler, 1995.

O'Toole, P. *Corporate Messiah: The Hiring and Firing of Million-Dollar Managers*. New York: Morrow, 1984.

Peters, T. J., and Waterman, R. H., Jr. *In Search of Excellence*. New York: HarperCollins, 1982.

Ridout, C. F., and Fenn, D. H. "Job Corps." Boston: Harvard Business School Case Services, 1974.

Sennett, R. *Authority*. New York: Knopf, 1980.

Simmel, G. *The Sociology of Georg Simmel*. New York: Free Press, 1950.

Sloan, A. P., Jr. *My Years with General Motors*. New York: Macfadden, 1965.

Vroom, V. H., and Yetton, P. W. *Leadership and Decision Making*. Pittsburgh: University of Pittsburgh Press, 1973.

Waterman, R. H., Jr. *What America Does Right: Learning from Companies That Put People First*. New York: Norton, 1994.

Weber, M. *The Theory of Social and Economic Organization*. (T. Parsons, trans.). New York: Free Press, 1947.

CHAPTER EIGHT

1. We now use readiness in place of maturity because it is a more descriptive term of a person's ability and willingness to perform a specific task.

2. Adopted from Paul Hersey, *Situational Selling* (Escondido, Calif.: Center for Leadership Studies, 1985), p. 19.

3. Ibid.

4. Ibid.

5. Adopted from Paul Hersey, *Situational Selling* (Escondido, Calif.: Center for Leadership Studies, 1985), pp. 25–26.

CHAPTER ELEVEN

Campbell, J. *The Hero with a Thousand Faces*. New York: Bollingen Foundation, 1949.

Kofman, F., and Senge, P. M. "The Heart of Learning Organizations." *Organizational Dynamics*, 1993, *20*, 5–21.

CHAPTER THIRTEEN

1. J. Conger, "The Dark Side of Leadership," *Organizational Dynamics*, 1990, *19*, 44–55.

2. J. Martin, "Ignore Your Customer," *Fortune*, May 1, 1995, pp. 121–126.

3. J. Wilke, "At Digital Equipment, a Resignation Reveals Key Problem: Selling," *Wall Street Journal*, April 26, 1994, pp. 1ff; E. Jensen, "NBC News President, Burned by Staged Fire and GM, Will Resign," *Wall Street Journal*, March 2, 1993, pp. 1ff.

4. R. Rose, "After Turning Around Giddings & Lewis, Fife Is Turned Out Himself," *Wall Street Journal*, June 22, 1993, pp. 1ff.

5. M. W. McCall Jr. and M. M. Lombardo, *Off the Track: Why and How Successful Executives Get Derailed* (Greensboro, N.C.: Center for Creative Leadership, 1983).

6. R. Gibson, "Personal 'Chemistry' Abruptly Ends Rise of Kellogg President," *Wall Street Journal*, November 28, 1989, pp. A1, A8.

7. M. Cox and J. Roberts, "How the Despotic Boss of Simon &

Schuster Found Himself Jobless," *Wall Street Journal*, July 6, 1994, pp. 1ff.

8. J. Steinbeck, *The Log from the Sea of Cortez* (New York: Viking, 1962), p. 158.

9. Quoted in W. Safire and L. Safir, *Words of Wisdom* (New York: Simon & Schuster, 1989), p. 32.

10. A. Taylor III, "The Odd Eclipse of a Star CEO," *Fortune*, February 11, 1991, p. 88.

11. B. Saporito, "The Eclipse of Mars," *Fortune*, November 28, 1994, p. 92.

12. J. Byrne, W. Symonds, and J. Siler, "CEO Disease," *Business Week*, April 1, 1991, pp. 52–60.

13. Byrne and others, "CEO Disease."

14. Jensen, "NBC News President."

15. W. Manchester, *American Caesar* (New York: Dell, 1979), pp. 751–769.

16. Manchester, *American Caesar*, quoting Gunther, pp. 566–567.

17. M. W. McCall Jr. and J. Clair, "Why Physician Managers Fail," *Physician Executive*, 1990, *16*(3), 6–9; *16*(4), 8–12.

18. Manchester, *American Caesar*, p. 567.

19. R. Suskind and S. Alexander, "Fired Sunbeam Chief Harangued and Hazed Employees, They Say," *Wall Street Journal*, January 14, 1993, p. A8.

20. Quoted in Byrne and others, "CEO Disease," p. 55.

21. P. Ingrassia and J. White, "Stempel Quits as Head of General Motors; Workers Fear Cost Cutting Will Quicken," *Wall Street Journal*, October 27, 1992, pp. A3, A5.

22. M. W. McCall Jr., M. M. Lombardo, and A. M. Morrison, *The Lessons of Experience: How Successful Executives Develop on the Job* (New York: Free Press, 1989).

23. Cox and Roberts, "Despotic Boss."

24. P. De Llosa, "Famous Failures: Where They Are Now," *Fortune*, May 1, 1995, p. 53.

25. Cox and Roberts, "Despotic Boss."

26. D. Campbell, *If I'm in Charge Here, Why Is Everybody Laughing?* (Niles, Ill: Argus Communications, 1980), p. 62.

27. W. Bennis, *Why Leaders Can't Lead: The Unconscious Conspiracy* (San Francisco: Jossey-Bass, 1990).

CHAPTER FIFTEEN

Argyris, C. "Teaching Smart People How to Learn." *Harvard Business Review*, May-June 1991, pp. 99–109.

Ashford, S. J. "The Role of Feedback Seeking in Individual Adaptation: A Resource Perspective." *Academy of Management Journal*, 1986, *29*, 465–487.

Barrick, M. R., and Mount, M. K. "The Big Five Personality Dimensions and Job Performance: A Meta-Analysis. *Personnel Psychology*, 1991, *44*, 1–26.

Brockner, J. Self-Esteem at Work: Research, Theory, and Practice. San Francisco: New Lexington Press, 1988.

Bunker, K., and Webb, A. *Learning How to Learn from Experience: Impact of Stress and Coping*. Greensboro, N.C.: Center for Creative Leadership, 1992.

Conger, J. A. *Learning to Lead: The Art of Transforming Managers Into Leaders*. San Francisco: Jossey-Bass, 1992.

Gardner, H. *Frames of Mind: The Theory of Multiple Intelligences*. New York: Basic Books, 1993.

Kernis, M. H., and others. "There's More to Self-Esteem Than Whether It's High or Low: The Importance of Stability." *Journal of Personality and Social Psychology*, 1993, *65*, 1190–1204.

Lee, R., Guthrie, V., and Young, D. "The Lessons of Life at Work: Continuous Personal Development." *Career Planning and Adult Development Journal*, 1995, *11*(3), 31–35.

Leslie, J. B., and Fleenor, J. W. *Feedback to Managers*. (3rd ed.) Greensboro, N.C.: Center for Creative Leadership, 1998.

Lombardo, M. M., and Eichinger, R. W. *Eighty-Eight Assignments for Development in Place: Enhancing the Development Challenge of Existing Jobs*. Greensboro, N.C.: Center for Creative Leadership, 1989.

McCall, M. W., Jr., Lombardo, M. M., and Morrison, A. M. *The Lessons of Experience: How Successful Executives Develop on the Job*. New York: Free Press, 1989.

McCrae, R. R., and Costa, P. T., Jr. "Openness to Experience," in R. Hagan and W. H. Jones (eds.), *Perspectives in Personality*, Vol. 1. Greenwich, Conn.: JAI Press, 1985.

McCrae, R. R., and Costa, P. T., Jr. "Validation of the Five-Factor Model Across Instruments and Observers." *Journal of Personality and Social Psychology*, 1987, *52*, 81–90.

Ruderman, M. N., Ohlott, P. J., and McCauley, C. D. (1996). "Developing from Job Experiences: The Role of Self-Esteem and Self-Efficacy." Paper presented at the meeting of the Society for Industrial and Organizational Psychology, San Diego, April 1996.

Tornow, W. W., and London, M. (eds.). *Maximizing the Value of 360-Degree Feedback: A Process for Successful Individual and Organizational Development*. San Francisco: Jossey-Bass, 1998.

Van Velsor, E., and Musselwhite, W. C. "The Timing of Training,

Learning, and Transfer." *Training and Development Journal*, 1986, *40*(8), 58–59.

Van Velsor, E., Ruderman, M. N., and Phillips, D. "The Lessons of Looking Glass: Management Simulations and the Real World of Action." *Leadership and Organization Development Journal*, 1989, *10*(6), 27–31.

Young, D., and Dixon, N. *Helping Leaders Take Effective Action: A Program Evaluation.* Greensboro, N.C.: Center for Creative Leadership, 1996.

CHAPTER SIXTEEN

1. Korn/Ferry International and Columbia University Graduate School of Business, *Reinventing the CEO* (New York: Korn/Ferry International and Columbia University Graduate School of Business, 1989), p. 41.

2. As a few examples of this variation, 93 percent of U.S. executives rated ethical behavior as highly important now, and 96 percent responded that it will be highly important in the year 2000; 79 percent and 76 percent were the ratings from Japanese executives; 78 percent and 81 percent were from those in the Western European community; Korn/Ferry and Columbia University, *Reinventing the CEO*, p. 89.

3. These numbers varied by country. For example, being honest, upright, and ethical were very important to 87 percent of Canadian office workers, to 80 percent of workers in the European Economic Community, and to 72 percent of those in Japan; Steelcase, *Worldwide Office Environment Index Summary Report* (Grand Rapids, Mich.: Steelcase, 1991), p. 7.

4. P. Jordan (prod.), *The Credibility Factor* (Carlsbad, Calif.: CRM Films, 1991) (videotape). This video features coauthors James M. Kouzes and Barry Z. Posner and provides case examples of the principles and practices described herein.

5. Jordan, *The Credibility Factor.*

6. Korn/Ferry and Columbia University, *Reinventing the CEO*, p. 90.

7. Korn/Ferry and Columbia University, *Reinventing the CEO*, p. 89.

8. Jordan, *The Credibility Factor.*

9. J. M Kouzes and B. Z. Posner, *The Leadership Challenge: How to Get Extraordinary Things Done in Organizations* (San Francisco: Jossey-Bass, 1987).

10. W. H. Schmidt and B. Z. Posner, "The Values of American Managers: An Update Updated," *California Management Review*, 1992, *34*(3), 80–94; B. Z. Posner and W. H. Schmidt, "An Updated Look at the Val-

ues and Expectations of Federal Government Executives," *Public Administration Review*, 1993, *54*, 18–26.

11. See, for example, D. K. Berlo, J. B. Lemert, and R. J. Mertz, "Dimensions for Evaluating the Acceptability of Message Sources," *Public Opinion Quarterly*, 1969, *33*, 563–576.

12. M. De Pree, *Leadership Is an Art* (New York: Doubleday, 1989), p. 9.

13. *Business Week*, April 20, 1992.

CHAPTER SEVENTEEN

1. See James K. Galbraith, *Created Unequal: The Crisis in American Pay* (New York: Free Press, 1998).

2. Laura Koss-Feder, "Perks That Work," *Time*, November 9, 1998.

3. Richard Sennett, *The Corrosion of Character: The Personal Consequences of Work in the New Capitalism* (New York: Norton, 1998), p. 31.

4. Immanuel Kant, "On a Supposed Right to Lie from Altruistic Motives," in *Critique of Practical Reason and Other Writings in Moral Philosophy* (Lewis White Beck, trans.) (Chicago: University of Chicago Press, 1949).

5. See Robert J. Samuelson, *The Good Life and Its Discontents: The American Dream in the Age of Entitlements* (New York: Times Books, 1995).

CHAPTER EIGHTEEN

1. O'Toole uses the term *Rushmorean* to describe the values-based leadership of the four presidents who are depicted at Mount Rushmore. They practiced inclusionary leadership based on what was morally right and possessed common values of integrity, trust, listening, and a respect for followers.

2. Mario Bunge, "A Critical Examination of the New Sociology of Science," *Philosophy of the Social Sciences*, 1991, *21*, 524,

3. Gary Wills, *Certain Trumpets* (New York: Simon & Schuster, 1994).

4. The information in the remainder of this chapter is drawn from a variety of sources. All of the positive information about Jack Welch can be found in Noel Tichy and Stratford Sherman, *Control Your Own Destiny or Someone Else Will* (New York: Doubleday, 1993). Sherman's cover story "Inside the Mind of Jack Welch" (*Fortune*, March 27, 1989) and the January 25, 1989, cover "Jack Welch's Lesson for Success" bracket *Fortune*'s one-sided reporting of the rise of Welch. Not until September 5, 1994, did *Fortune* find fault with their unflawed CEO: Terence Paré's "Jack Welch's Nightmare on Wall Street" concluded that it was Welch's leadership that had created the environment in which the

Kidder scandal could occur ("Like it or not, the scandals at Kidder Peabody were brought on by GE's management"; p. 48). We have also studied Warren Bennis's uncut taped interviews with Jack Welch and Max De Pree. (Edited versions are available from Video Publishing House, Schaumburg, Ill.)

5. McCall displayed a transparency with these two quotes at a seminar for the Dwight D. Eisenhower Leadership Development Program at the University of Southern California on December 7, 1993.

6. W. Bynner (trans.), *The Way of Life According to Laotzu* (New York: Berkley, 1986).

CHAPTER NINETEEN

1. The names in the accounts of Steve Lewis and Peter Adario have been changed to protect the privacy of the principals involved.

CHAPTER TWENTY

Bolman, L. G., and Deal, T. E. *Leading with Soul: An Uncommon Journey of Spirit.* San Francisco: Jossey-Bass, 1995.

Campbell, D. "If I'm in Charge, Why Is Everyone Laughing?" Paper presented at the Center for Creative Leadership, Greensboro, N.C., 1983.

Collins, J. C., and Porras, J. I. *Built to Last: Successful Habits of Visionary Companies.* New York: HarperBusiness, 1994.

Cox, T., Jr. *Cultural Diversity in Organizations: Theory, Research, and Practice.* San Francisco: Berrett-Koehler, 1994.

De Geus, A. "Companies: What Are They?" *RSA Journal,* June 1995, pp. 26–35.

De Pree, M. *Leadership Is an Art.* New York: Dell, 1989.

Farkas, C. M., and De Backer, P. *Maximum Leadership: The World's Leading CEOs Share Their Five Strategies for Success.* New York: Henry Holt, 1996.

Gallos, J. V., Ramsey, V. J., and Associates. *Teaching Diversity: Listening to the Soul, Speaking from the Heart.* San Francisco: Jossey-Bass, 1997.

Griffin, E. *The Reflective Executive: A Spirituality of Business and Enterprise.* New York: Crossroad, 1993.

Haas, R., quoted in Waterman (1994), p. 140.

Hamel, G., and Prahalad, C. K. *Competing for the Future: Breakthrough Strategies for Seizing Control of Your Industry and Creating the Markets of Tomorrow.* Boston: Harvard Business School Press, 1994.

Kidder, T. *Among School Children.* Boston: Houghton Mifflin, 1989.

Labich, K. "Is Herb Kelleher America's Best CEO? *Fortune,* May 2, 1994, pp. 44–52.

Levering, R., and Moskowitz, M. *The 100 Best Companies to Work for in America.* New York: Plume, 1993.

Morrison, A. M. *The New Leaders: Guidelines on Leadership Diversity in America.* San Francisco: Jossey-Bass, 1992.

Peters, T. J., and Waterman, R. H., Jr. *In Search of Excellence.* New York: HarperCollins, 1982.

Petzinger, T. *Hard Landing: The Epic Contest for Power and Profits That Plunged the Airlines into Chaos.* New York: Times Business, 1995.

Ryan, M. "They Call Their Boss a Hero." *Parade,* September 8, 1996, pp. 4–5.

Solomon, R. C. *Ethics and Excellence: Cooperation and Integrity in Business.* Oxford: Oxford University Press, 1993.

Treacy, M., and Wiersema, F. *The Discipline of Market Leaders: Choose Your Customers, Narrow Your Focus, Dominate Your Market.* Boston: Addison-Wesley, 1995.

Waterman, R. H., Jr. *What America Does Right: Learning from Companies That Put People First.* New York: Norton, 1994.

Whitmyer, C. *In the Company of Others.* New York: Putnam, 1993.

CHAPTER TWENTY-ONE

Bennis, W. G., and Nanus, B. *Leaders: The Strategies for Taking Charge.* New York: HarperCollins, 1985.

Halberstam, D. *The Powers That Be.* New York: Dell, 1979.

Mead, M. "Towards More Vivid Utopias," in G. Kateb (ed.), *Utopia.* New York: Atherton Press, 1971.

Shekerjian, D. *Uncommon Genius: How Great Ideas Are Born.* New York: Viking, 1990.

Thomas, B. *Walt Disney: An American Tradition.* New York: Simon & Schuster, 1976.

CHAPTER TWENTY-THREE

1. The original inspiration for this analogy came from a lecture series on intellectual history and the Newtonian Revolution titled "The Origin of the Modern Mind," taught by Alan Charles Kors, professor of history, University of Pennsylvania, and captured on audiotape as part of the Superstar Teacher Series from the Teaching Company, Washington, D.C.

2. Hewlett-Packard Company Archives, "An Interview with Bill Hewlett," 1987, p. 4.

3. "Research Packed with Ph.D.s," *Business Week,* December 22, 1956, p. 58.

4. John McDonald, "The Men Who Made T.I.," *Fortune,* November 1961, p. 118.

5. Akio Morita, *Made in Japan* (New York: Dutton, 1986), pp. 44–57.

6. Nick Lyons, *The Sony Vision* (New York: Crown, 1976), pp. 4–5.

7. Morita, *Made in Japan*, pp. 44–57.

8. *Japan Electronics Almanac* (1988), p. 282.

9. Vance H. Trimble, *Sam Walton* (New York: Dutton, 1990), p. 121.

10. Sam Walton with John Huey, *Made in America: My Story* (New York: Doubleday, 1992), p. 35.

11. Patrick Spain and James Talbot, *Hoover's Handbook of American Companies, 1991* (Austin, Tex.: Reference Press, 1991).

12. Trimble, *Sam Walton*, pp. 102–104.

13. Trimble, *Sam Walton*, pp. 121–122.

14. Robert O'Brien, *Marriott: The J. Willard Marriott Story* (Salt Lake City: Deseret, 1987).

15. John W. Nordstrom, *The Immigrant in 1887* (Seattle: Dogwood Press, 1950), pp. 44–50; "Nordstrom History," company publication, November 26, 1990.

16. *Values and Visions: A Merck Century* (Rahway, N.J.: Merck, 1993), pp. 13–15.

17. "Procter & Gamble Chronology," company publication; Oscar Schisgall, *Eyes on Tomorrow: The Evolution of Procter & Gamble* (New York: Doubleday, 1981), pp. 1–14; Alfred Lief, *It Floats: The Story of Procter & Gamble* (New York: Rinehart, 1958), pp. 14–32.

18. Harry Mark Petrakis, *The Founder's Touch* (New York: McGraw-Hill, 1965), pp. 62–63.

19. "The Philip Morris History," company publication, 1988.

20. *Our Story So Far* (St. Paul, Minn.: 3M, 1977), p. 51.

21. Charles W. Cheape, *Norton Company: A New England Enterprise* (Cambridge, Mass.: Harvard University Press, 1985), p. 12.

22. Robert J. Serling, *Legend and Legacy* (New York: St. Martin's Press, 1992), pp. 2–6.

23. "Take Off for the Business Jet," *Business Week*, September 28, 1963.

24. René J. Francillon, *McDonnell Douglas Aircraft Since 1920* (Annapolis, Md.: Naval Institute Press, 1988), pp. 1–12.

25. Richard Schickel, *The Disney Version* (New York: Simon & Schuster, 1968), pp. 106–107.

26. Clive Hirschhorn, *The Columbia Story* (New York: Crown, 1989), pp. 7–16.

27. Grover and Lagai, *Development of American Industries* (4th ed., 1959), p. 491.

28. Robert Lacey, *Ford: The Men and the Machine* (New York: Ballantine Books, 1986), pp. 47–110.

29. "Centennial Review," Westinghouse company document, 1986.

30. "Centennial Review."

31. Leonard S. Reich, *The Making of American Industrial Research: Science and Business at GE and Bell, 1876–1926* (Cambridge: Cambridge University Press, 1985), pp. 69–71. We cannot verify that GE's lab was definitely America's first, but we do know that it preceded Bell Labs, one of the other early labs, by a full twenty-five years.

32. Bill Hewlett, internal speech, 1956. Courtesy Hewlett-Packard Company Archives.

33. Dave Packard, "Industry's New Challenge: The Management of Creativity," speech given to the Western Electronic Manufacturer's Association, San Diego, September 23, 1964. Courtesy Hewlett-Packard Company Archives.

34. "Hewlett-Packard Chairman Built Company by Design, Calculator by Chance," *AMBA Executive*, September 1977, pp. 6–7.

35. Petrakis, *The Founder's Touch*.

36. Schisgall, *Eyes on Tomorrow*, p. xii.

37. "National Business Hall of Fame Roster of Past Laureates," *Fortune*, April 5, 1993, p. 116.

38. *Hoover's Handbook, 1991*, p. 381.

39. *Our Story So Far*, p. 59.

40. Mildred Houghton Comfort, *William L. McKnight, Industrialist* (Minneapolis: Denison, 1962), pp. 35, 45, 182, 194, 201.

41. Morita, *Made in Japan*, p. 147.

42. Schisgall, *Eyes on Tomorrow*, pp. 1–15.

43. Robert J. Serling, *Legend and Legacy: The Story of Boeing and Its People* (New York: St. Martin's Press, 1992), p. 70.

44. *Values and Visions*, p. 12.

45. Camille B. Wortman and Elizabeth F. Loftus, *Psychology* (New York: McGraw-Hill, 1992), pp. 385–418.

46. Harold van B. Cleveland and Thomas F. Huertas, *Citibank, 1812–1970* (Cambridge, Mass.: Harvard University Press, 1985), p. 32.

47. Cleveland and Huertas, *Citibank, 1812–1970*, p. 301.

48. Cleveland and Huertas, *Citibank, 1812–1970*, pp. 41, 301; John Donald Wilson, *The Chase* (Boston: Harvard Business School Press, 1986), p. 25.

49. Cleveland and Huertas, *Citibank, 1812–1970*, p. 54.

50. Anna Robeson Burr, *Portrait of a Banker: James Stillman, 1850–1918* (New York: Duffield, 1927), p. 249.

51. "Wiggin Is the Chase Bank and the Chase Bank Is Wiggin," *Business Week*, April 30, 1930.

52. See Trimble, *Sam Walton,* pp. 1–45, for a good account of Walton's early life.

53. Walton with Huey, *Made in America,* pp. 78–79.

54. "America's Most Successful Merchant," *Fortune,* September 23, 1991.

55. Much of the detail in this section comes from Walton with Huey, *Made in America,* pp. 225–232.

56. Trimble, *Sam Walton,* p. 274.

57. Walton Huey, *Made in America,* p. 225.

58. Trimble, *Sam Walton,* p. 121.

59. "Industry Overview," *Discount Merchandiser,* June 1977.

60. "Gremlins Are Eating Up the Profits at Ames," *Business Week,* October 19, 1987.

61. "David Glass Won't Crack Under Fire," *Fortune,* February 8, 1993, p. 80.

62. "Pistner Discusses Ames Strategy," *Discount Merchandiser,* July 1990.

63. "James Harmon's Two Hats," *Forbes,* May 28, 1990.

64. Goals for the year 2000 are from a letter we received from a Wal-Mart director in 1991.

65. Petrakis, *The Founder's Touch,* pp. 49, 61.

66. Petrakis, *The Founder's Touch,* pp. 69, 88.

67. Petrakis, *The Founder's Touch,* pp. 114–115.

68. Petrakis, *The Founder's Touch,* p. xi.

69. Robert W. Galvin, *The Idea of Ideas* (Schaumburg, Ill.: Motorola University Press, 1991), pp. 45, 65.

70. "Zenith Bucks the Trend," *Fortune,* December 1960.

71. "At the Zenith and on the Spot," *Forbes,* September 1, 1961.

72. "Zenith Bucks the Trend"; "Irrepressible Gene McDonald," *Reader's Digest,* July 1944; "Commander McDonald of Zenith," *Fortune,* June 1945.

73. *International Directory of Company Histories* (Chicago: St. James Press, 1988), vol. 1, p. 123.

74. "Zenith Bucks the Trend."

75. "Zenith Bucks the Trend."

76. Galvin died in November 1959; McDonald died in May 1958.

77. *International Directory of Company Histories,* vol. 2, p. 135.

78. *International Directory of Company Histories,* vol. 2, p. 135.

79. Clive Hirschhorn, *The Columbia Story* (New York: Crown, 1989).

80. Richard Schickel, *The Disney Version* (New York: Simon & Schuster, 1968), p. 362.

81. Walt Disney Company, *The Disney Studio Story* (Hollywood: Walt Disney, 1987), p. 18.

82. Walt Disney Company, *The Disney Studio Story;* Schickel, *The Disney Version,* p. 180.
83. Walt Disney Company, *The Disney Studio Story* p. 42.
84. *Personnel,* December 1989, p. 53.
85. John Taylor, *Storming the Magic Kingdom* (New York: Ballantine Books, 1987), p. 14.
86. Taylor, *Storming the Magic Kingdom,* p. viii.
87. This paragraph was paraphrased from the lecture series "The Origin of the Modern Mind," by Alan Charles Kors, professor of history, University of Pennsylvania.
88. For the best coverage of the theory of evolution, we suggest Norman K. Wessells and Janet L. Hopson, *Biology* (New York: Random House, 1988), chaps. 9–15, 19, 41–43.
89. For an excellent description of the personalities and processes of the constitutional convention, see Catherine Drinker Bowen, *Miracle at Philadelphia: The Story of the Constitutional Convention, May to September 1787* (Boston: Little, Brown, 1966).

CHAPTER TWENTY-FOUR

1. Michael Kavanagh, "Porn Will Continue to Dominate Web Revenue," *Marketing Week,* May 27, 1999, p. 43.

CHAPTER TWENTY-FIVE

Argyris, C. *Increasing Leadership Effectiveness.* New York: Wiley-Interscience, 1976.
Bennis, W. G. *On Becoming a Leader.* Boston: Addison-Wesley, 1989.
Davis, S. M. *Managing Corporate Culture.* New York: Ballinger, 1984.
Donaldson, G., and Lorsch, J. W. *Decision Making at the Top.* New York: Basic Books, 1983.
Dyer, W. D., Jr. *Culture Change in Family Firms.* San Francisco: Jossey-Bass, 1986.
Hirschhorn, L. *The Workplace Within: Psychodynamics of Organizational Life.* Cambridge, Mass.: MIT Press, 1988.
Kets de Vries, M.F.R., and Miller, D. *The Neurotic Organization: Diagnosing and Changing Counterproductive Styles of Management.* San Francisco: Jossey-Bass, 1984.
Kotter, J. P., and Heskett, J. L. *Corporate Culture and Performance.* New York: Free Press, 1992.
Lorsch, J. W. "Strategic Myopia: Culture as an Invisible Barrier to Change," in R. H. Kilmann and others, *Gaining Control of the Corporate Culture.* San Francisco: Jossey-Bass, 1985.
Miller, D. *The Icarus Paradox.* New York: HarperCollins, 1990.

Pettigrew, A. M. "On Studying Organizational Cultures." *Administrative Science Quarterly*, 1979, *24*, 570–581.

Salk, J. E. "International Shared Management Joint Venture Teams: Their Development Patterns, Challenges, and Possibilities." Unpublished Ph.D. dissertation, Sloan School of Management, Massachusetts Institute of Technology, 1992.

Schein, E. H. "The Role of the Founder in Creating Organizational Culture." *Organizational Dynamics*, Summer 1983, pp. 13–28.

CHAPTER TWENTY-SIX

1. Suzy Wetlauer, "Organizing for Empowerment: An Interview with AES's Roger Sant and Dennis Bakke," *Harvard Business Review*, January-February 1999, p. 112.

2. Wetlauer, "Organizing for Empowerment," p. 112.

CHAPTER TWENTY-EIGHT

1. Henri Bortoft, *The Wholeness of Nature: Goethe's Way Toward a Science of Conscious Participation in Nature* (Hudson, N.Y.: Lindisfarne, 1996), p. 6.

2. Thich Nhat Hanh, *Old Path White Clouds: Walking in the Footsteps of the Buddha* (Berkeley, Calif.: Parallax, 1991), p. 169.

3. Ilya Prigogine, *The End of Certainty: Time, Chaos, and the New Laws of Nature* (New York: Free Press, 1998), p. 10.

Name Index

Subject Index

A

Abbott Laboratories, 200

Ability: as component of follower readiness, 115; to learn, 227–234

Abortion drug conflict, 323–328

Abusiveness: arrogance and, 202–203; charismatic leadership and, 397–398; crisis as justification for, 282–283, 292–293, 295–299; demanding leadership *versus*, 299–306; as flaw that leads to derailment, 195–196, 202–203, 208–209; Jack Welch's "Neutron Jack" leadership and, 287–288, 290–292, 295–306; making enemies and, 208–209; Realist-relativist-contingency leadership and, 282–286, 287–288, 290–292, 295–306. *See also* Arrogance; Toughness

Acceptance, in servant leadership, 122–124

Accessibility: of human resource leaders, 99–100; technology and, 413–414

Accessing-others learning tactics, 234

Achievement need, 232

"Acknowledging the burning platform," 10

Action, bias toward: as learning orientation, 234, 236; as poten-

tial weakness, 192; as talent, 216

"Action Company," 446–447, 455, 458

Activator talent, 216

Adaptation: failure of, 547, 565–566; failure of, as cause of derailment, 204–210; leadership and, 543–567; in mature organizations, 443–444; in midlife organizations, 441; in structural leadership, 97

Adaptive challenges, 543–544; identification of, 547–549, 556–558, 561–562; personal, 561–562

Adaptive change, 543–567; collaborative approach to, 544–545, 553–556, 560–563; conflict and, 548, 551–554; difficulty of, 544–545; distress in, 545, 549–552, 562–564; "getting on the balcony" for, 545–547, 559; in KPMG Netherlands case study, 558–564; leader's responsibilities in, 550–551; need for, 543–544; principles for leading, 545–564

Administrators, leaders *versus*, 89

Admired leader characteristics, 251–266; changes in, 257–259; consistency in, 257; credibility and, 261–265; global and local

Chapter 23: Pages 22–42 from *Built to Last: Successful Habits of Visionary Companies* by James C. Collins and Jerry I. Porras. Copyright © 1994 by James C. Collins and Jerry I. Porras. Reprinted by permission of HarperCollins Publishers Inc., and The Random House Group Limited.

Chapter 24: Excerpts from *Leading the Revolution* by Gary Hamel. Copyright © 2000 Gary Hamel. Harvard Business School Publishing. Used with permission.

Chapter 25: From *Organizational Culture and Leadership*, 2nd edition by Edgar H. Schein. Copyright © 1992 by Jossey-Bass Inc., Publishers. This material is used by permission of John Wiley & Sons, Inc.

Chapter 26: From *A Company of Leaders: Five Disciplines for Unleashing the Power of Your Workforce* by Gretchen Spreitzer and Robert Quinn. Copyright © 2001 by John Wiley & Sons, Inc. This material is used by permission of John Wiley & Sons, Inc.

Chapter 27: From *Execution* by Larry Bossidy and Ram Charan. Copyright © 2002 by Larry Bossidy and Ram Charan. Used by permission of Crown Business, a division of Random House, Inc.

Chapter 28: Reprinted with permission of the publisher. From *Leadership and the New Science*. Copyright © 1999 by Margaret Wheatley, Berrett-Koehler Publishers, Inc., San Francisco, CA. All rights reserved. www.bkconnection.com

Chapter 30: From *A Leader to Leader Guide On Leading Change*, edited by Frances Hesselbein and Rob Johnston. Copyright © 2002 by the Peter F. Drucker Foundation for Nonprofit Management, 320 Park Avenue, 3rd Floor, New York, NY 10022–6839, www.drucker.org. Used by permission of William Bridges and Susan Mitchell Bridges.

Chapter 31: "The Work of Leadership," by Ronald Heifetz and Donald Laurie. Copyright © 2001 Harvard Business School Publishing Corporation. From *Harvard Business Review—Breakthrough Leadership*. Used with permission.